The Western Cemetery of Roman Cirencester

Excavations at the former Bridges Garage
Tetbury Road, Cirencester, 2011–2015

This volume is dedicated to Richard Reece, Cirencester archaeologist extra-ordinaire. Born and bred in Cirencester, it was Richard who single-handedly salvaged precious information on the cemetery during development in 1960. Without his efforts, all knowledge would have been lost. It was appropriate that Richard was present on the site again on 25 February 2015 when a Roman lady of quality called Bodicacia re-emerged into the digital age.

Frontispiece: Richard Reece at Withington Roman villa, Gloucestershire, August 2005

The Western Cemetery of Roman Cirencester

Excavations at the former Bridges Garage Tetbury Road, Cirencester, 2011–2015

Neil Holbrook, Jamie Wright, E.R. McSloy and Jonny Geber

with contributions from

Alistair Barber, Cliff Bateman, Emily Carroll, Sarah Cobain, Peter Davenport, K.M.J. Hayward, Martin Henig, Fiona Roe, Dan Simpson, Roger S.O. Tomlin and Tom Weavill

Principal Illustrators

Aleksandra Osinska and Lucy Martin

Cirencester Excavations Vol. VII

Cirencester 2017

Cotswold Archaeology Cirencester Excavations Vol. VII

Published by Cotswold Archaeology
Building 11, Kemble Enterprise Park, Cirencester, Gloucestershire GL7 6BQ

ISBN 978-0-9934545-3-0

British Library Cataloguing in Publication Data

A catalogue record of this book is available from the British Library

Cotswold
Archaeology

Front cover: the tombstone of Bodicacia
Back cover: the enamelled bronze cockerel figurine; excavation of grave goods from burial B1177; excavation in progress in the south-west corner of the site

Cover design by Aleksandra Osinska, Cotswold Archaeology
Produced by Past Historic, Kings Stanley, Gloucestershire
Printed by Henry Ling Limited, Dorchester

CONTENTS

List of Figures

List of Tables

Summary

This volume is concerned with the results of excavations within the Western Cemetery of Roman Cirencester. The work was undertaken between 2011 and 2015 and resulted in the discovery and lifting of 118 inhumation and 8 cremation burials, making this the largest investigation of a Roman cemetery in Cirencester since the work outside the Bath Gate between 1969 and 1976. The excavation area lay immediately to the south-east of Tetbury Road, which is likely to preserve the course of a Roman road or track, some 150m outside the former Roman town wall. The site had been disturbed by the construction of a former garage, which resulted in varying levels of preservation across the site, but nevertheless it is possible to reconstruct the layout and chronology of the cemetery with reasonable confidence.

Burial had commenced on the site by the earlier 2nd century, and the zone immediately adjacent to Tetbury Road was probably intensively utilised for cremation burial. A walled cemetery was built 12m back from the frontage; only part of its perimeter wall survived but it was in the order of 14m square. Nine inhumation burials survived within its postulated bounds. The pottery from these grave backfills had a clear emphasis on wine amphorae, flagons and tazze, and we may reasonably reconstruct funerary ceremonies that involved the consumption of wine, or the pouring of it as libations, and the burning of substances contained in the tazze. The significance of the walled cemetery seems not to have been restricted solely to those interred within it. A burial of a 2 to 3-year-old child just outside the perimeter wall contained a pottery feeding bottle and a magnificent enamelled bronze figurine of a cockerel, both dateable to the 2nd century. Such figurines are rare finds, with only four or five similar examples known from Britain. They were probably made in northern England but were traded over some distance, as finds from the Low Countries and Germany testify. Cockerels had a well-known association with the god Mercury, herdsman of the dead, and it is conceivable that the figurine was placed in the child's grave to ensure a safe passage into the afterlife. A lead cremation urn was also found in the same area just outside the walled cemetery, another manifestation of the high status of the burial population in this part of the cemetery.

Burial activity was seemingly continuous within the cemetery into the 4th century, and the area used for burial expanded to the south-west beyond some ditches which conceivably defined its original boundaries. The cemetery displays elements of regular planning, with a prevailing orientation dictated by the alignment of the Roman precursor to Tetbury Road. Instances of intercutting amongst burials are not common, so most graves must have been marked above ground in some form. A greater quantity of grave goods was recovered from this cemetery compared to that outside the Bath Gate, reinforcing the higher status of those buried here. Six burials were laid in the grave in a prone (face down) position, two were decapitated and a further example was both prone and decapitated. A small number of so-called discrepant burials is now a common finding in many cemeteries, both urban and rural, and their presence here occasions little surprise.

One very unusual grave had a reused sculpted and inscribed tombstone placed face down immediately on top of a wooden coffin containing an adult male. The tombstone was dedicated to 27-year-old woman called Bodicacia, a previously unrecorded variant of the Celtic name Bodica/Boudica. It probably dates to the 2nd century. Only 15 inscribed tombstones have been previously recorded from Cirencester, the last one found in 1973, so this is a noteworthy discovery made all the more important as it has a good archaeological context. The tombstone had a fine sculpted pediment containing a representation of the god Oceanus. Significantly the face and claws of the god had been deliberately mutilated prior to the placement of the tombstone within the grave. This could be an example of Christian iconoclasm (although other explanations are possible); if so it would be a very rare example of this practice from Roman Britain.

The absence of the latest Roman pottery to reach Cirencester and of coins of the second half of the 4th century may indicate that burial ceased in this part of the cemetery at least not long after the middle of the 4th century. A single Anglo-Saxon pit produced the largest group of early to middle Anglo-Saxon pottery recovered to date from Cirencester and its immediate environs.

Acknowledgements

The 2011 excavation and post-excavation programme was generously funded by St James's Place Wealth Management. The 2014/15 excavations were funded by Citygrove Securities PLC on behalf of St James's Place. We are grateful to the Chairman of St James's Place David Bellamy, Operations Director Sonia Gravestock, Head of Property Management Richard King, and all their staff who displayed great interest in our findings and supported our work. From Citygrove we thank Daemon Sheenhan and Oliver De Chalus, and Hugo Dring and Patrick Murphy from their agents Stace. The 2011 excavation was directed in the field by Jamie Wright, and the second phase of work by Alistair Barber and Tom Weavill. Both campaigns were managed by Cliff Bateman. The post-excavation was managed by Martin Watts and the report was edited by Neil Holbrook. We warmly acknowledge the help of Ralph Jackson, Lizet Kruyff, Francis Macintosh, Michael Marshall and Sally Worrell in providing details of other similar bronze cockerel figurines from Britain and the Continent, and also Karen Barker for her work to conserve the metal and other grave goods. The recovery of the inscribed tombstone created much interest, and we thank Martin Henig and Roger Tomlin for volunteering their expertise so readily in the days following its discovery, and BBC Radio Gloucestershire and BBC Points West for working with us to maximise the public interest in the findings.

We are particularly grateful to Dan Simpson for allowing us to reproduce his poem *Corinium Cockerel*, which was inspired by the discovery of the bronze figurine. Kevin Hayward thanks John Jack at the University of Reading for preparing the thin section of the tombstone and the staff at the Museum of London for allowing him access to photograph, describe and sample material. The illustrations, which are such an important part of this volume, were produced by Aleksandra Osinska, Lucy Martin and Sam O'Leary. Copy editing was by Rachel Tyson.

The project was monitored by Charles Parry of Gloucestershire County Council Archaeological Service and we are grateful for his constructive approach and cooperation when the extent of the cemetery first became apparent.

All the finds have been generously donated by St James's Place to the Corinium Museum, Cirencester, and we thank Amanda Hart and Alison Brookes at the museum for their help in the transfer of the material, and for enabling the enamelled bronze figurine of the cockerel and the inscribed tombstone to go on public display in remarkably quick time.

Finally we are grateful to Dr John Pearce of King's College London for reading an earlier version of the text and for providing many useful comments. This report has benefited greatly from John's advice.

Corinium Cockerel

by Dan Simpson

Go, cockerel: I send you away from my household
and into the next world with my child
she, who was so fond of you in life
demanding to hold and play with you
at every moment of the day
from her waking cry at first light
to her softly-breathing sleep at night.

In some ways you are alive
animated by the craft of the bronze-worker
his hands shaping the prideful curve of breast and wing
the definite fix of comb and wattle
the lively detail of eye and beak
but it was my child who – like some infant Pygmalion –
breathed life into you through her love.

And yet more than this – we all gave you spirit:
in the hollow of your back you hold memories
household stories of a mother's love
everyday moments of a father's affection
sounds of siblings' teasing and laughter
the clash and clatter of an entire household
turning our villa inside out, trying to find you when
    lost.

The dark shade of night's sky lightens to deep blue
after this profoundly long and severe night
and I remember that you are Mercury's creature:
heralding the coming of the light with a cry of triumph
a message from the gods that a new day is here
that we mortals are not forgotten by the gods
hope rising as surely – and slowly – as the sun.

Speak for me now, you who may speak freely with
    Mercury
tell him of my child who can no longer see that light
nor feel the first touch of Sol's warmth
put my anguish into your crowing
give voice to my grief where I can not
so that the gods may know
something of mortal suffering.

Tell Apollo that his medicine does not always work
and that Mors has eager teeth to take one so young
crow for her who can no longer cry
and charge Mercury to see her safe
in her passage to the afterlife
where I may see her again one day
holding you, cockerel, as I hold you now.

This poem was inspired by the recovery of an enamelled bronze figurine of a cockerel from the grave of a 2 to 3-year-old child (Burial B1163).

Dan Simpson is a poet, performer, and producer whose subjects include science and technology; history and place; geek culture and videogames; people and poetry. A former Canterbury Laureate, Dan has appeared at Glastonbury and on the BBC. He was Poet-in-Residence at Waterloo Station, Knole House, and Canterbury Roman Museum. Dan creates pioneering work using crowdsourced and outdoor poetry for organisations such as the Royal Academy of Arts, National Museum of Scotland, and the European Commission. He has had work commissioned by Southbank Centre, Free Word, and Corinium Museum, and his first collection is *Applied Mathematics* from Burning Eye Books.

www.dansimpsonpoet.co.uk

Preface

Cemeteries provide a unique insight into the minds of past societies. The rituals detectable in the archaeological record can tell us much about attitudes to death and the afterlife, and how these varied from place to place and over time. The cemeteries of Roman Cirencester have provided a source of fascination and scholarly interest for generations of antiquarians and archaeologists, and luminaries such as William Stukeley have recorded finds from the cemeteries outside the western defences. Indeed inscribed tombstones are our principal source for the names of former inhabitants of the town, and we can deduce much from them. For instance while Julia Castra is a good Roman name that would not have been out of place in the eternal city itself, that of Nemomnius Verecundus would have immediately marked him out as someone from the north-western provinces. Both found their final resting place in Corinium.

The recent history of archaeological work on the site which is the subject of this volume begins, far from auspiciously, in 1960 when the construction of a new garage threatened to destroy a swathe of the cemetery without record. Fortunately Richard Reece managed single-handedly to salvage as much information as he could in desperate circumstances as construction commenced, and equally commendably produced a report within two years. That publication is notable as it contained an analysis of the human remains by Calvin Wells. Wells was a pioneer in the analysis of human skeletal remains recovered from archaeological excavations, and he was able to develop his work on the burial populations of Roman Cirencester much more fully as a result of work in advance of the construction of a new ring road between 1969 and 1976 which recovered the remains of a further 421 individuals. The publication of that work in 1982 was one of a small number of reports that appeared around that time which represent a step change in the study of Romano-British urban cemeteries thanks to the care devoted to their investigation in the field and the telling detail contained in the analysis of the findings.

In 2011 the opportunity arose to investigate the same area as Richard Reece had worked on in 1960, as the by now redundant garage was redeveloped for new offices for St James's Place Wealth Management.

While it was possible that all traces of the cemetery had been destroyed, past experience told us that this should not be assumed automatically and pockets of survival might occur. In the event preservation was much better than we could have realistically anticipated, and over the course of two separate episodes of investigation Cotswold Archaeology was able to record 118 further inhumation and 8 cremation burials. We also succeeded in generating a lot of popular interest at the time of the investigations. The marvellous discovery of a fine enamelled bronze figurine of a cockerel, made all the more pertinent by its placement in the grave of a 2 to 3-year-old child, generated a lot of interest and the story made *National Geographic* and the cover of *Current Archaeology*, Britain's leading archaeology magazine. The find also inspired a poem, and we are grateful to Dan Simpson for allowing us to reproduce his poem *Corinium Cockerel*, commissioned as part of an exhibition at the Corinium Museum. But this level of interest was surpassed by the discovery of an inscribed tombstone in February 2015 dedicated to a 27-year-old lady called Bodicacia. We coordinated the revelation of the inscription live on BBC radio and social media, and captured the moment on television. This generated considerable world-wide interest, much of it through social media outlets. For this reason we thought it useful to make some mention of the public archaeology outcomes in this volume (Section 7.7).

This volume therefore represents the most significant publication of Roman funerary activity in Cirencester since the 1982 Bath Gate Cemetery report, and hopefully it showcases both the benefits that have accrued from embedding archaeology within the planning process, and also how the study of cemetery evidence has advanced over the last 35 years. Our work would not have been possible without the support of St James's Place Wealth Management, and in particular its Chairman David Bellamy and his colleagues Sonia Gravestock and Richard King. Their interest in our work has allowed us to publish the results of our work in this lavishly illustrated format. This report is by no means the final word on this site, however. Scientific applications to archaeology develop at a rapid pace, and techniques are evolving that will enable us to glean more from the excavated evidence in the future. We hope to develop further research strands over the coming years that will more fully investigate the chronology, geographic origins and familial relationships of the burial population of Corinium. Archaeology is an incremental discipline that builds on the achievements of workers that have gone before us, and for this reason we are delighted to dedicate this volume to Richard Reece. His solo efforts in 1960 laid the foundations for the collaborative team project which has resulted in the present report, the seventh monograph in the Cirencester Excavations series.

Neil Holbrook
Chief Executive, Cotswold Archaeology
December 2016

Chapter 1
Introduction and Background

by Jamie Wright, Cliff Bateman and Neil Holbrook

The site of the former Bridges Garage lies in the corner formed by the junction of Tetbury Road and Hammond Way/A429 on the western side of modern Cirencester (NGR SP 01930177; Figs 1.1–1.2). It lies within the known bounds of a Romano-British cemetery that lay outside the walls of Corinium, and burials had been discovered on the site itself in 1933 and 1960. Planning permission to demolish the garage for the creation of a temporary car park was granted by Cotswold District Council in 2010. Given the low level of groundworks anticipated, no condition requiring archaeological work was placed on this consent. However as part of the demolition work a programme of site remediation to remove deposits contaminated by hydrocarbons associated with the former petrol station was required, and it quickly became apparent that these operations would lead to a high degree of ground disturbance. Following discussions with Gloucestershire County Council Archaeological Service, archaeological advisors to Cotswold District Council, the site owners St James's Place Wealth Management generously commissioned Cotswold Archaeology in September 2011 to undertake a watching brief during the de-contamination work. Initially this entailed the monitoring of contractors' groundworks, but the discovery of intact Romano-British burials led to a reconsideration of this approach and it was agreed by all parties that a full excavation to record and remove the surviving archaeological remains over the majority of the site should be undertaken before any further remediation works took place. The excavations continued until Christmas Eve 2011, by when 71 inhumation and 3 cremation burials had been recovered. Planning permission was granted subsequently for a new office development on the site of the temporary car park, and prior to the start of construction a further phase of archaeological excavation took place to examine those areas to be disturbed by the office block which had not been fully examined in 2011. This

second phase of work took place between December 2014 and February 2015, and by its conclusion the total number of burials recovered from the two phases of work had risen to 118 inhumation and 8 cremation burials, making this the largest investigation of a Roman cemetery in Cirencester since the work at the Bath Gate Cemetery between 1969 and 1976 which recorded 450 inhumation and 3 cremation burials (CE II). The two phases of work at the former Bridges Garage site have been reported in a number of interim publications (*Current Archaeology* 281 (August 2013), 28–34; McSloy and Watts 2013; Adcock 2015).

The site covered an area of 2,713m² and lay 130m outside the Roman town wall. It was generally flat, although the natural ground surface fell by around 1m from the Tetbury Road frontage (at *c.* 116m AOD) to the south-eastern limit of the excavation. The land also rose gradually by *c.* 0.8m from the north-east to the south-west limits. The solid geology is mapped as limestone of the Cornbrash Formation in the north half of the site and mudstone of the Forest Marble Formation in the south half of the site (BGS 2011). In the excavation a natural deposit of silty clay of variable thickness was found to overlie the brash in some places, but almost all the excavated graves were rock cut to some degree.

Tetbury Road is often assumed to overlie the original alignment of the Fosse Way as it approached Cirencester, although whether a metalled road was ever actually constructed on this course before a diversion was introduced which took the road on a sinuous course further to the south to enter the town by the Bath Gate is unknown (CE V, 11–16; Reece 2003). There was no internal street within the Roman town which matched this alignment, and it is not known whether there was a gate at the point where Tetbury Road meets the line of the town defences. Conceivably, however, the alignment could have been defined by a track or minor road rather than a more substantial one, with entry into the town

Fig. 1.1   The location of the excavation

afforded by a small postern gate (as with the Queningate at Canterbury which provided access to a cemetery; Frere *et al.* 1982; Weekes 2011, Cemetery 'East A'). Indeed that Tetbury Road preserves the line of a Roman route way is strongly suggested by the numbers of burials that have been found adjacent to the modern road (recent discoveries in this area, with references to earlier work, are reported in CE VI, 109–31). All of the burials have been found in the course of development to the south-east of Tetbury Road. No development has occurred to the north-west of it as this area is occupied by Cirencester Park, and no recent archaeological work has taken place here. Antiquarian accounts testify to the discovery of cremation burials in, and around, Grismond's Tower, an earthen barrow *c.* 30m in diameter and 4m high which was reused for an ice house in the post-medieval period (Darvill 2014). These cremation burials are likely to be of Roman date and it is not beyond the realms of possibility that Grismond's Tower was a Roman rather than prehistoric barrow, as may also be the case with

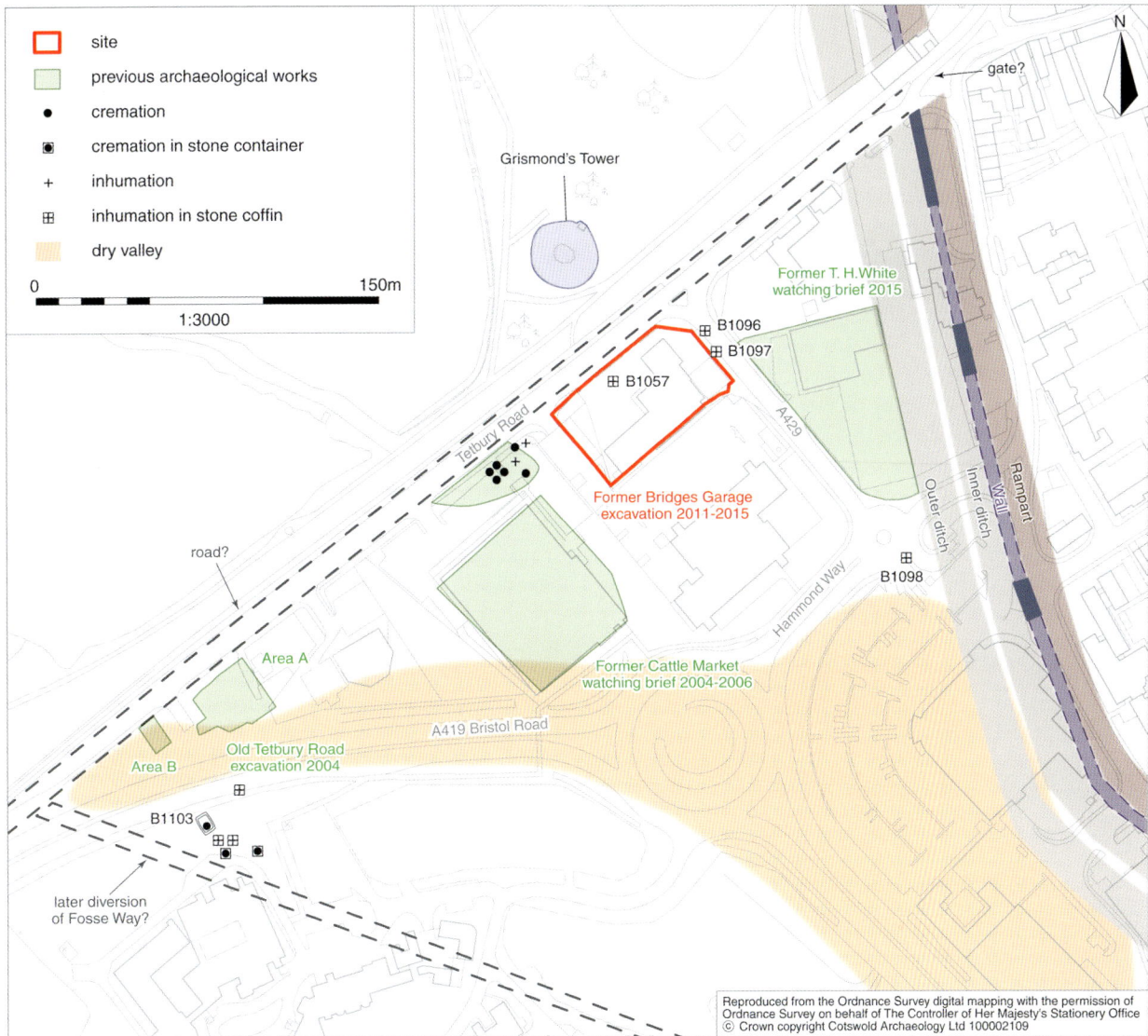

Fig. 1.2   Areas of archaeological investigation in the Western Cemetery

the Tar Barrows on the opposite side of Cirencester (O'Neil and Grinsell 1960, 108, Cirencester no. 6; CE II, MF5, A06–7; Holbrook 2008, 305–10). Whatever its origin, Grismond's Tower would certainly have been a prominent landmark during the Roman period, and thus an obvious focus for burial.

The most important previous archaeological work on the present site was observation by Richard Reece during the construction of the garage in 1960 (Reece 1962). The site is referred to in that report as Oakley Cottage, and it is stressed for clarity that Oakley Cottage/former Bridges Garage occupied exactly the same location and are one and the same. The earliest recorded find from the site was made in 1933 when workmen digging in the garden of Oakley House uncovered a single burial in a stone coffin (CE II, MF5, B1057). From the recorded location this coffin must have lain within the bounds of the current site and its approximate location is marked

on Fig. 2.1. All trace of the hole dug to extract the coffin in 1933 had presumably been removed by an area of general truncation caused by the construction of the garage. Reece's salvage observations were made in September 1960 and he succeeded in recording at least 46 cremation and 9 inhumation burials. Finds recovered comprised the lower part of an inscribed tombstone (RIB III, 3065), 45 cremation vessels and one jet and two bronze bracelets. Given the desperate circumstances of Reece's work no plan could be made of the discoveries, but it is clear that they came from the area of general truncation fronting Tetbury Road revealed in 2011. Only deeply cut archaeological features were found to survive in this area, and so all the cremation burials had evidently been removed in 1960. In March 1975 construction of Hammond Way/A429, which defines the north-east side of the present site, was not accompanied by any systematic archaeological recording. However the Cirencester Excavation Committee (CEC) was able to make salvage records of three badly damaged stone coffins uncovered by ground moving machinery in this area (CE II, MF5, B1096–8). After the opening of Hammond Way to traffic the garage was remodelled by the construction of a new forecourt facing onto this street. This involved the excavation of new petrol storage tanks in the north-east corner of the site, and the removal of topsoil in this area in the summer of 1975 was monitored by the CEC, but revealed no further burials (CE II, MF5, A09). That burials once existed in this area is not in doubt; presumably they had been destroyed by general levelling in 1960. A watching brief during redevelopment on the opposite side of Hammond Way in 2015 (Fig. 1.2, former T.H. White site) recorded no evidence of burials or other Roman features, presumably because the site lay some way back from the frontage of the Roman road or track. The natural ground surface on this site was found to slope down quite steeply as it began to drop away into a former dry valley that lay to the south-east of modern Tetbury Road (CE V, 8–11; Fig. 1.2).

Other work on surrounding sites comprises observations on the site of the Cattle Market, which is now occupied by a leisure centre. The construction of the cattle market just to the west of the site in 1867 revealed numerous burials and a number of cremation vessels, indicating that a cemetery once occupied a large part of that site. Of these, only two stone coffins and three cremation vessels were retained for display in the Corinium Museum (CE II, MF5, B1058–62). Evaluation and watching brief prior to and during the construction of the new leisure centre identified six cremation burials and two extended inhumation burials close to Tetbury Road, but the central area of the site had been heavily disturbed during construction of the cattle market and subsequent car parking facilities (CE VI, 114–17). Observations during the construction (in 1971) and demolition (in 2006) of the former leisure centre, now the site occupied by the offices of St James's Place Wealth Management, produced negative results (CE II, MF5, A09). Further burials were found a short distance further to the south-west of the former Cattle Market in a small excavation known as the Old Tetbury Road site (CE VI, 109–14). Collectively the burials from Oakley Cottage, former Cattle Market, Old Tetbury Road and now the former Bridges Garage site are referred to in this report as the Western Cemetery of Cirencester. The former dry valley to the south-east of modern Tetbury Road serves as a convenient natural feature to differentiate between burials in the Western Cemetery and those on the opposite side of the valley which are referred to as the Bath Gate Cemetery.

Fig. 1.3   Excavation in progress at the north-east end of the site in 2011, with the offices of St James's Place Wealth Management in the background. The level of truncation caused by the former garage led to the natural limestone brash lying just below the modern tarmac

1.1 Investigation Methods

The 2011 watching brief comprised the observation by an archaeologist of all intrusive groundworks. Once burials were discovered, the inhumations were excavated in the field, and soil samples were taken from the graves, predominately from the feet and hand areas. These were sieved for bone and artefact recovery. Cremation burials were block-lifted on site and excavated within a controlled laboratory environment. Features other than graves (ditches, robber trenches) were either fully or sample excavated.

Following the completion of the 2011 fieldwork an assessment was made of the discoveries and recommendations presented for further analysis (CA 2012). That approach was approved by Gloucestershire County Council Archaeological Service, and led to the production of a typescript report concerned with the outcome of those analyses (CA 2014). After the completion of the second phase of fieldwork in 2015 the new findings were integrated with those found in 2011, and this volume presents the consolidated results of both phases of investigation. A detailed osteological catalogue detailing the analysis of each individual human skeleton can be found on line at http://www.cotswoldarchaeology.co.uk/publications-2/monographs/. This provides the supporting data for the analyses and conclusions presented in Chapter 5.

The archive and artefacts from the excavations have been deposited at the Corinium Museum, Cirencester, under accession nos 2014/42 and 2016/55.

1.2 Level of Previous Disturbance

Upon excavation the extent of previous disturbance from the garage, which included a petrol station and forecourt, showrooms, offices and a workshop, became clear. Extending back from the Tetbury Road frontage towards the site of a Roman walled cemetery there was much horizontal truncation in the former position of the garage buildings and the first forecourt. There was a 0.3m drop in the natural ground level after removal of modern overburden, a product of levelling during garage construction to create a level surface around the fuel pumps. Only a scatter of deeply dug inhumation burials (such as B1199) survived here. All other burials had been removed in 1960. To the south-west of the Roman walled cemetery a roughly rectangular area of contaminated ground, *c.* 12m by 9m, had had been removed before the watching brief commenced in September 2011. Adjacent to this was an area of petrol tanks where all deposits had been destroyed when the tanks were installed in 1960. Excavations for the petrol tanks to the north-west of the Roman enclosure had been monitored in 1975 with negative results. Presumably all burials in this area had already been destroyed in 1960. Some indication of the pre-Garage topography of the site is provided by a newspaper report on the discovery of the stone coffin in 1933 when it was recorded that the lid of the coffin lay just over 3 feet (1m) below the surface of the kitchen garden (CE II, MF5, B1057).

Chapter 2
Excavation Results

by Neil Holbrook

There is no certain evidence for any features that pre-date the establishment of the cemetery (Fig. 2.1). It is possible that Ditch B might have been a pre-cemetery land boundary, but this is not certain and it could have been established early in the development of the cemetery and quickly fallen out of use. The cemetery was being used for burial by the middle of the 2nd century at the latest, and conceivably burial could have commenced as early as the later 1st century as cremation burial was taking place at this time at the Old Tetbury Road site to the south-west (CE VI, 109–14).

The principal elements of the cemetery other than the graves were a walled cemetery defined by perimeter Wall C and a small number of ditches (A, B/E, and D/F) which might have marked out burial plots, although burial subsequently spread beyond their limits. A total of 118 inhumation and 8 cremation burials were excavated, to which can be added the 8 inhumation and 46 cremation burials recorded in 1960. The predominant orientation of the graves was fixed with respect to the modern alignment of Tetbury Road, and presumably the road or track which preceded it in the Roman period. Graves were predominantly aligned at right angles to Tetbury Road, with a much smaller number parallel with it (Fig. 2.2). Attempts to phase the graves have been made on the basis of the grave goods which accompanied some burials, and also the pottery contained within the grave backfill. The quantities of pottery in the backfill of the graves which lay outside the walled cemetery were not great and it is likely that much of this was residual material. Notwithstanding these caveats, the burials have been placed into two broad chronological periods (Fig. 2.3). Period 1 comprises graves where the dating evidence is consistent with burial between the late 1st and early 3rd century. These burials tend to concentrate in the area of the walled cemetery. Burials assigned to Period 2 are those which are dated to the late 3rd or 4th century by artefacts, or are stratigraphically late in the

sequence of burial. Many burials, however, could not be closely dated and these are ascribed to Period 1/2. While this phasing is useful as it isolates those graves which were probably dug in the 2nd century from those which are somewhat later, there was almost certainly a continuum of burial activity on the site extending over 200 years, the precise sequence and layout of which is unknowable.

Where reference is made in the sections below to the age at death of individual burials, the following categories are used: neonate (N) = less than 4 weeks; infant (I) = 1–12 months; young child (YC) = 1–5 years; older child (OC) = 6–12 years; adolescent (Adol.) = 13–17 years; young adult (YA) = 18–25 years; early middle adult (EMA) = 26–35 years; late middle adult (LMA) = 36–45 years; older adult (OA) = ≥ 46 years; and adult (Indet. A) = > 18 years.

2.1 Graves Dateable to the Late 1st to Early 3rd Century (Period 1) (Fig. 2.3)

A walled cemetery defined by Wall C survived as an L-shaped robber trench 0.79–0.99m wide and 0.11–0.35m deep with vertical or near vertical sides and a flat base. In places it was cut through clay until it reached the natural limestone which provided a flat base (Fig. 2.4). The variations in the depth of the robber trench were a result of later truncation as the trench gradually petered out to the north-west and south-west. The profile of the feature, along with the presence of sand which may be a remnant of lime mortar, suggests that it was a robber trench for a masonry wall which defined a square or rectangular walled cemetery (it is too large to be a roofed mausoleum; see further below). The south-east wall was in excess of 8.5m long but less than 14.5m as the robber trench was not found on the far side of an area of truncation where grave B1215 would also have been on its projected alignment. The length of the

Fig. 2.1   *Plan of the excavation*

Fig. 2.2   Excavation in progress in the south-west corner of the site. View looking south-east from Tetbury Road. The regularity in burial alignment is apparent. The archaeologists are in the process of excavating graves B1249 and B1259

north-east wall is unknown but was in excess of 8.6m. A timber beamslot 799, 0.2m wide and 0.5m deep with a flat-based profile defined an area *c.* 2.5m wide along the south-east side of the walled cemetery (Fig. 2.1). The purpose of this feature is uncertain. It might have contained a fence which would have provided a screened entranceway into the enclosure (there was no break in the robber trench for the perimeter wall as this point, and so presumably the foundation was continuous, but this does not preclude a doorway at this point). This seems a more likely interpretation of the feature than as a roofed veranda attached to the perimeter wall, as the slot does not appear to have been sufficiently substantial to have supported this. There is no evidence for a continuation of this feature on the north-east side of the enclosure, but given its shallow depth this possibility cannot be entirely excluded. Hard up against the outside face of the perimeter wall of the cemetery, and within the area enclosed by beamslot 799, was an undated large pit 1144. The base of this feature contained a number of large packing stones while the upper fill had frequent inclusions of cremated bone and charcoal.

Within the walled cemetery a single large posthole 791 was found on the same alignment as the north-west–south-east arm of the screen defined by beamslot

799. A gap of *c.* 2m existed between the outside of the perimeter wall and the nearest exterior burials which was maintained throughout the use of the cemetery. Perhaps a path or planting occupied this area?

Some 4m to the south-east of the walled cemetery, and parallel with the alignment of Tetbury Road, was Ditch A which was observed for 35m before it turned through a right angle and headed towards the road frontage. Whether it actually extended as far as the frontage is unknown as it was destroyed by modern truncation after a distance of 4m from the turn. The ditch appeared to terminate at its south-western end, but it was very shallow here, and the apparent terminal could just be a product of truncation. It did not extend to the south-west of ditches B/E, however, as no trace of it was seen of it in an untruncated area that contained just two isolated postholes (605, 607). The ditch appeared to comprise a primary cut and a later recut. The primary ditch was 1.2–1.5m wide and up to 0.7m deep with a slightly rounded V-shaped profile. The primary fill was a brown clay containing many medium to large tabular stones which had probably eroded from the sides of the ditch. The narrower recut was 0.8m wide and up to 0.35m deep. The recut ran directly down the centre of the earlier ditch, and was filled with a brown

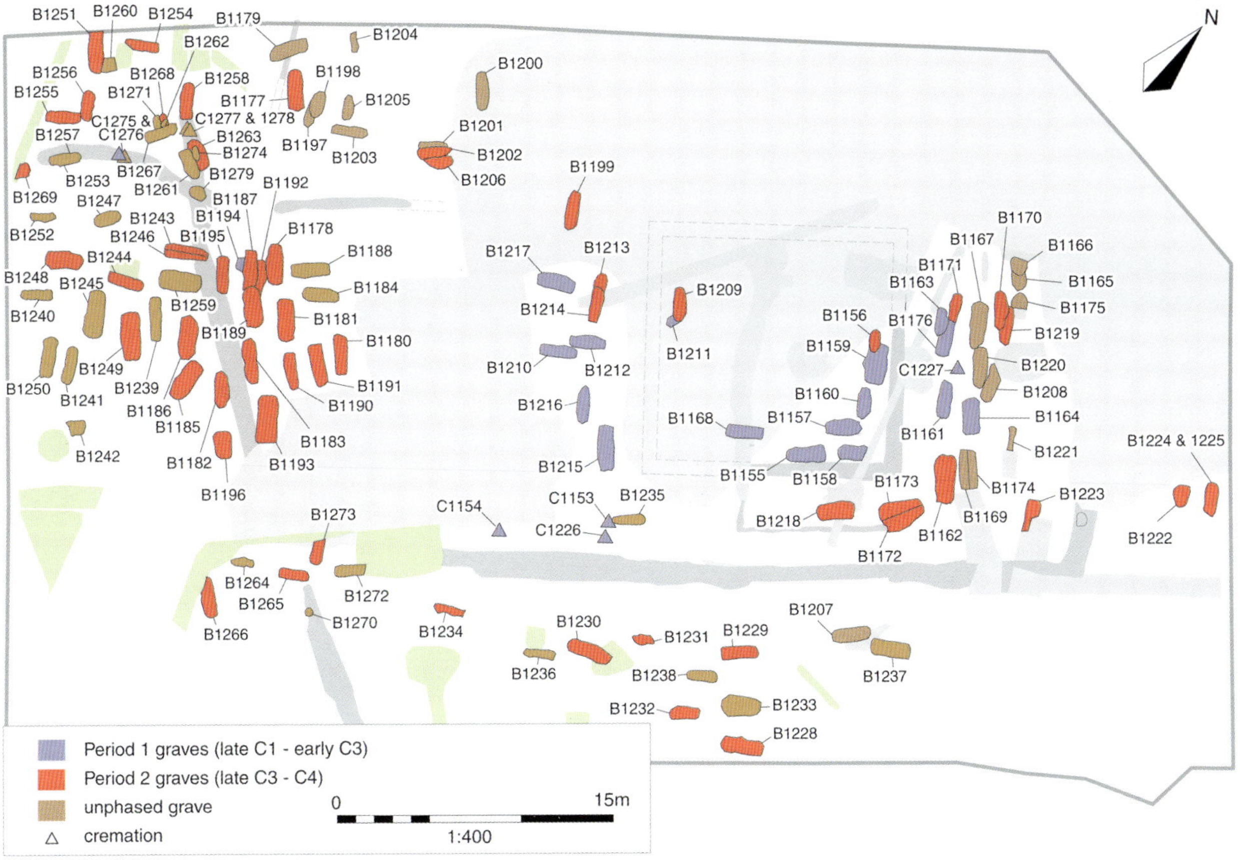

Fig. 2.3   Distribution of dated graves

clay with frequent limestone rubble inclusions, pottery, tile, oyster shells and animal bones. In some excavated sections only a single fill was found, and in one location a tightly grouped cluster of 33 hobnails which may be from discarded footwear. While the recut of Ditch A remained open into the late 3rd or 4th century it may have been dug much earlier. Three inhumation burials (B1222, B1224 and B1225) were found beyond the ditch in the eastern corner of the site which was relatively little disturbed by later truncation, and more were found to the south-east of it (the latter included a number of graves which were certainly late Roman).

Ditch A probably originally terminated close to the line of Ditches B and E which were at an approximate right angle to it. Ditch B was intermittently exposed between later intrusions for a distance of 18m before shallowing out towards a rounded terminal at its north-western end. It was 1.0–1.2m wide and 0.35–0.6m deep with a variable U-shaped or V-shaped profile. The fills comprised a thin primary silty clay with more stony upper fills (the latter particularly pronounced near the north-west terminus). A fragment of a large moulded architectural fragment was recovered from the upper fill (see Architectural Stone, Section 4.3). If this derived from a funerary monument it suggests that the ditch remained open into the late Roman period. This is also

suggested by the alignment of Period 2 inhumation B1258 which lay immediately to the north-west of the terminus and partly cut it. This burial was laid out on the same alignment as the ditch, appearing to form an extension beyond the original terminus, suggesting that the ditch remained, at least in part, a visible earthwork into Period 2. The infilled ditch was also cut by a number of later graves, including cremation burials C1277 and C1278 dug into its top fill. While the cremations may have been deliberately placed into the redundant, yet still visible, ditch, it is also possible that they just survived better in this location as they were dug deeper into the soft ditch fill whereas any surrounding cremation burials that did not penetrate into the hard natural brash have been lost to later truncation.

Ditch B probably continued to the south-east beyond its likely junction with Ditch A: the length of ditch hereabouts is termed Ditch E, but it is quite likely just an extension of Ditch B. The ditch was 1m wide and 0.3m deep, shallowing to an apparent terminus at the north-western end, although this might simply be a product of truncation. B1270 was dug into the top of the ditch and aligned with its presumably still visible course.

Some 14m from the hypothesised position of the western corner of the walled cemetery, and on the same

Fig. 2.4   Robber trench marking the eastern corner of the walled cemetery and graves immediately outside it

alignment as its postulated north-west side, was Ditch D/F which was traced intermittently for a distance of *c.* 20m on a slightly sinuous course before terminating in a rounded terminal. Ditch D/F cut Ditch B and was up to 0.8m wide and had a maximum depth of 0.3m. It had an irregular profile dictated by the bedding of the limestone bedrock. Fill 810, a mottled orange-brown silty clay, contained frequent small to medium stones and produced fragments of animal bone, shell and a human mandible and long bone. The latter finds show that the ditch was still accumulating material during the life of the cemetery. Indeed a cluster of three fragmented skulls, B1279a, b and c, were recovered from the base of Ditch F at the point where it cut through Ditch B. Immediately adjacent to the skulls, and also resting on the base of Ditch F, was a deposit of animal bone. No evidence of a cut through the infilled ditch could be discerned at this point, so it would appear that this material was a deliberate placement at the base of the newly cut ditch, but at the point where it cut the now redundant, yet still visible, Ditch B. The infill of Ditch F was cut by two cremation burials C1275 and C1276, the former probably dating to before the mid 3rd century, which indicates that Ditch D/F was both dug, and largely filled-in, during Period 1.

To the south-west of Ditch B Pit 5136, a small sub-square pit was found just to the south-west of burial B1267. No human remains were found in the pit. Reece (1962, 53) also noted in the area he monitored a 'trench', 2.4m long, 0.3m wide and 0.2m deep packed with charcoal and ash. He wondered whether this might

have been a draught for a large fire, although another interpretation is as a ditch backfilled with fire debris.

Graves within the walled cemetery

Nine inhumation burials lay within the postulated bounds of the walled cemetery and shared a common alignment with it (B1155, B1156, B1157, B1158, B1159, B1160, B1168, B1209 and B1211). B1209 cut B1211 and contained late 3rd-century or later pottery in the grave fill, and B1156 cut B1159 and had pottery of mid 3rd-century or later date in the grave fill, so these two graves could be somewhat later than the others which date to the 2nd century. The quantity of pottery recovered from these nine graves contrasts with the rest of the cemetery, however, and suggests that they form a distinct group (see Roman Pottery, Section 4.3). All the graves were within 2.5m of the enclosure wall which suggests that there was a centrally-placed monument or reserved open space which dictated this arrangement. Graves B1155, B1158 and B1159 were placed hard up against the inside face of the enclosure wall. The graves were of three males, three females, two adults of uncertain sex and one *c.* 8-year-old child (B1160) who was accompanied by a pottery flagon (Table 2.1).

Graves outside the walled cemetery

There was a cluster of Period 1 graves outside, but adjacent to, the walled cemetery. Four inhumation (B1161, B1163, B1164, B1176) and one probable cremation burial (C1227) were buried outside the

Table 2.1 Burials contained within the probable extent of the walled cemetery.
For key to Age group see Table 5.11

Burial	Sex	Age group	Comments
B1155	F	LMA	Much disturbed cremation debris in grave fill.
B1156	?	Adol.	Much disturbed cremation debris in grave fill. Cuts B1159. Mid 3rd to 4th-century pottery in the grave fill.
B1157	M	LMA	Crouched burial.
B1158	F	OA	Some cremation debris in grave fill.
B1159	M	EMA	Stone-lined grave. Cut by B1156.
B1160	?	OC	Stone-lined grave. Pottery flagon placed by upper left leg. Some cremation debris in grave fill. x 1 fowl bone in grave fill.
B1168	M	LMA	Some cremation debris in grave fill.
B1209	F	OA	Much disturbed cremation debris in grave fill. Cuts B1211. Some late 3rd to 4th-century pottery in the grave fill (intrusive?).
B1211	?	EMA	Grave fill heavily truncated. Much disturbed cremation debris in grave fill. Cut by B1209.

north-east perimeter wall. B1161 and B1176 were aligned parallel with the cemetery wall; B1164 was accompanied by an iron key, and B1163 was a 2 to 3-year-old child buried with an enamelled figurine of a cockerel and a pottery tettine. Cremation C1227 was contained in a lead vessel. The wealth of the grave goods in this part of the cemetery is apparent.

To the south-west of the reconstructed extent of the walled cemetery a small cluster of burials was preserved. Three of them (B1210, B1212, B1217) were not aligned parallel with the adjacent wall of the cemetery, like most of the other Period 1 burials, and might be better associated with Period 2 when more graves were dug on a north-east/south-west alignment parallel with Tetbury Road than previously.

Three cremation burials C1153, C1154 and C1226 were found just inside Ditch A to the south of the walled cemetery. Judging from the form of the cremation vessels, C1226 dates to the 2nd century and C1153 to the 3rd century. These are presumably outliers from the main bulk of cremation burials recorded by Reece in 1960 which lay nearer to the Tetbury Road frontage. This is also true of cremation burials C1275 and C1276 placed within the same pit in the south-west part of the site beyond Ditch B, and C1277 and C1278 dug into the infill of that by now redundant ditch.

2.2 Graves Dateable to the Late 3rd to 4th Century (Period 2) (Fig. 2.3)

Burial continued in the area adjacent to the walled cemetery into the late Roman period to judge from the finds recovered from the fills of B1162, B1171, B1173, B1214, B1218, B1219 and B1223 which lay to the north-east, south-east and south-west of it. B1173

and B1218 to the south-west of the walled cemetery demonstrate that the fenced area on this side had ceased to be excluded from burial by this time. B1171 contained a rich array of grave goods, and was dug immediately adjacent to B1163, the cockerel burial, indicating a continued emphasis on rich burial in this particular locality. B1173, B1214 and B1218 also had high-status grave goods.

It is likely that the majority of burials in the western part of the site are late Roman: to the north-east of former Ditch B, which had evidently fallen out of use by this time as its backfill was cut by a number of graves, B1177 contained mid–late 4th-century grave goods, while B1202 had 3rd to 4th-century pottery in the grave fill pottery and cut B1201 and B1206. All the burials aligned north-west/south-east that lay to the south-east of Ditch D are probably late Roman, as are those beyond Ditch B. Eight of the graves in this part of the site had grave goods of this period (B1180, B1185, B1186, B1244, B1248, B1256, B1263, B1269); burials B1196, B1241 and possibly B1269 were decapitated; burials B1241, B1242, B1255 and B1271 were laid prone; B1192 contained late Roman pottery in the grave fill and was cut by B1187 and B1189. Burials to the south-east (beyond) Ditch A also relate to a Period 2 expansion of the cemetery: six burials in this area contained 4th-century grave goods (B1229, B1231, B1234, B1265, B1266, B1273).

2.3 The Layout of the Cemetery

Discussion of the layout of the graves within the cemetery is hampered by the degree of later disturbance. Even the areas outside the deep intrusions have suffered from varying degrees of horizontal truncation and there

Fig. 2.5   The south-west corner of the site looking north-west towards Tetbury Road. To the right the reused tombstone lies face down covering B1267. 1m scales

is a high likelihood that shallow-dug burials, especially cremations, will have been completely removed.

The focal significance of the walled cemetery is apparent from the disposition of Period 1 graves and it must have been built early in the life of the cemetery. The relationship of the enclosure with the cremation burials recovered in 1960 is uncertain, but one possibility is that the walled cemetery was located 12m back from the road frontage as the intervening area was already occupied by cremation burials. B1211/B1209, which may have been just inside or outside the walled cemetery, contained a significant amount of cremated bone, and, in all, 31 graves contained incidental inclusions of cremated bone, the largest quantities of such material deriving from graves in the central and north-eastern part of the site. Much of this debris probably derives from funeral pyres, some perhaps within the walled cemetery, but equally it may derive from earlier cremation burials

disturbed by later grave digging. This is most likely to have been the case with B1177 and B1215 which contained substantial parts of disturbed cremation vessels. The cremation burials must therefore have been concentrated close to the road frontage, although their absence from the area close to the frontage of Tetbury Road at the western corner of the site is notable. Either the focus of cremation burials lay further to the north-east, or they were shallow-dug hereabouts and all trace of them has been lost to truncation except for C1275/C1276 and C1277 and C1278 which had been buried more deeply within the softer backfills of Ditches F and B. The three cremation burials close to the inside lip of Ditch A perhaps belong to a separate episode. The location of burials close to boundary ditches is a common occurrence in rural environments, and these burials might be somewhat later than the main body of cremation burials (C1153 and C1278 are certainly no earlier than the AD 220s and C1226 could be late 2nd century rather than earlier). Two isolated cremation burials were found at the Bath Gate Cemetery, one of which (burial 180) dated to the 3rd or 4th century (CE II, 97–9). A deposit of pyre debris was dumped in Pit 1179 which was cut into the top of infilled Ditch A. This particular section of the ditch (1168) yielded pottery of broadly 2nd to 3rd-century date, although elsewhere the ditch was evidently still accumulating material into the late 3rd century or later. This pit therefore provides further evidence that cremation burial was ongoing at the site into the 3rd century.

The cemetery displays elements of regular planning. The walled cemetery evidently remained a visible feature throughout the Roman period, although the timber screened porch (if that is what it was) fell out of use. A north-west/south-east orientation was that most commonly used for the graves, although a number are at right angles to this, especially in the south-western part of the site (Fig. 2.5). B1194 and B1260, laid out north-east/south-west, were cut by graves on the more usual north-west/south-east alignment, which could suggest that graves orientated north-east/south-west were earlier in the sequence hereabouts. While the opposite situation applies to B1267, that burial looks to be anomalous as it contained a reused tombstone and was dug markedly off alignment compared to the other graves. Beyond Ditch A, where the burials look to represent late expansion of the cemetery, a south-west/north-east alignment parallel with Ditch A predominated. Instances of intercutting are relatively limited (examples include B1165, where only the legs survived after being cut by B1166; B1169 which was 80% lost to B1174 with which it may have formed a pair, and B1267 which contained the reused tombstone and cut three neonate, infant and young child graves B1262, B1268 and B1271). Deviations from the pervasive alignment are few, and the level of organisation apparent stands in marked contrast to the random orientations used for many burials in the Bath Gate Cemetery. It strongly implies that many, if not all of the graves, were marked above ground in some form.

In the area immediately to the north-east of the walled cemetery some possible examples of paired graves can be discerned: B1172 (adult, male) and B1173 (young adult, uncertain sex); B1169 (adult, uncertain sex) and B1174 (late middle adult, male), the latter dug after the former and removing 80% of the earlier skeleton; more questionably B1165 (adult, uncertain sex) and B1166 (adult, uncertain sex) where likewise much of the earlier skeleton was removed by the later one, and B1170 (early middle adult, male) and B1219 (late middle adult, male). The two adjacent richly appointed graves B1163 and B1171 are notable, because to judge from the grave goods B1171 is a good century later than B1163. Indeed it is surely more than coincidence that B1163, a child of *c.* 2–3 years, was the most richly appointed 2nd-century grave in the cemetery, and B1171, a child

of *c.* 6 years, the richest later Roman grave in terms of the number of artefacts. C1227, a probable cremation burial utilising a cylindrical lead vessel, also lay nearby. Presumably B1163 was marked above ground in some fashion, and the significance of this richly appointed child burial was still understood over a century later when another wealthy child burial occurred. Perhaps they were both heirs to an important family, with burial during childhood occasioning the deposition of valuable artefacts?

To the west of the walled cemetery another possible family grouping is represented by B1201 (adult, female), B1206 (older adult, male) and B1202 (late middle adult, female). While the cemetery was perhaps originally bounded by Ditch A, burial subsequently spread beyond it and the feature lost significance. Three burials lay beyond the former ditch to the north-east (B1222, B1224 and B1225) and 17 to the south-east (many, or all, of the latter date to the 4th century to judge from the grave goods recovered from six of the graves). There is some regularity apparent in the layout of B1229, B1233, B1228, B1238 and B1232, perhaps a family grouping (the burials were of three mature males and two children). The layout of the other graves is less regular in the rest of this zone. The dense area of burials near the western corner of the excavation displays some elements of planning, with B1180, B1191, B1190 and B1183 forming a row, as perhaps did B1178, B1192, B1187 and B1195. Some intercutting of burials was apparent in this area. B1274, a mature male, was cut by B1263, a 12 to 14-year-old adolescent who was accompanied by mid to late 4th-century grave goods, and that grave was in turn cut by B1261, a *c.* 2-year-old child. Just to the west of this a sequence of three intercutting, and thus sequential, child graves (B1271, a *c.* 2-year-old child, was cut by B1268 (*c.* 9 months old) and that in turn by B1262 (a neonate)). All three child burials were then cut through by B1267, which was dug noticeably off alignment compared to the prevailing orientation of the cemetery. In B1267 the body of a 45 to 58-year-old male was placed in a timber coffin which then had a reused tombstone of probable 2nd-century date placed above it before the grave was backfilled. The sculptured decoration on the pediment of the tombstone, which depicted the head of the god Oceanus, had been deliberately defaced before the stone was placed in the grave. The positioning of this unusual grave above the three child burials might be more than simple coincidence.

2.4 Anglo-Saxon Pit (Period 3, ?6th to 7th Century)

To the south-east of Ditch A, burials B1207 and B1237 had been cut by a shallow flat-bottomed pit 1004/5066. The cut was 0.3m deep and *c.* 3m long and 1.5m wide. The pit contained a single grey silty clay fill which yielded 61 sherds of Anglo-Saxon pottery, 21 sherds of Roman pottery and a whetstone which can be paralleled in other Saxon deposits. Interpretation of the feature is necessarily difficult but it seems to be too small to be a sunken-featured building, and nor was it accompanied by the usual gable-end postholes.

2.5 Medieval Stone Robbing (Period 4, ?11th to 13th Century)

The only evidence for medieval activity was the robbing of masonry from the perimeter wall of the walled cemetery. The robber trench contained a lower fill of yellowish brown gritty, sandy clay containing small and medium pieces of limestone brash (788). Overlying this was a dark greyish brown gritty silty clay with abundant small and medium stones (787). The presence of two sherds of medieval pottery probably dates this event to the 11th to 13th century and indicates that at least some parts of the enclosure wall survived above ground into this period.

2.6 Dating Evidence from Features other than Graves

The coarseware pottery references derive from the Cirencester fabric series developed by V. Rigby, J. Keely and N. Cooper, which has been described and discussed in CE I–V. References to this series in the text are prefixed by the letters TF (type fabric).

Ditch A
Ditch 1181: Pottery (130 sherds; 437g; 0.33 EVEs). *Coarsewares:* TF 74; 102; 9.
Ditch 618: (46 sherds; 456g; 0.12 EVEs). *Samian:* CG, beaker; EG, Drag. 31, Drag. 31R, Drag. 45, all later Antonine to early 3rd century. *Coarsewares:* TF 74; 102; 17/98; 9; 5; 6; 82.
Ditch 5004/5008/5011/5016/5018: (76 sherds; 976g; 2.50 EVEs): *Samian:* CG, Drag. 31R, Drag. 79; EG, unid. All later Antonine to early 3rd century; *Coarsewares:* TF 74; 102; 95; 5; 17/98; 9/98; 6; 88; 40; 35.

The pottery from this feature was of mixed dating with perhaps the majority, including 15 sherds of samian, probably of the period *c.* AD 150–250. The illustrated flagon (Fig. 4.8; no. 16) is heavily distorted, but presumably a still-functional 'second'. Indicators for deposition of pottery continuing into the later 3rd or 4th centuries are late jar forms in Black-burnished ware (TF 74) and a New Forest beaker sherd (TF 82).

Ditch B
Ditch 863: (2 sherds; 5g; 0.05 EVEs). *Coarsewares:* TF 5.
Ditch recut 869: (6 sherds; 54g). *Coarsewares:* TF 6.
Ditch 5182/5183: (42 sherds; 142g; 0.79 EVEs). *Samian:* SG, Drag. 15/17 pre-Flavian; *Coarsewares:* TF 17.

The dating, albeit limited, suggests that Ditch B was an early feature. The scarcity of pottery from this feature (41 sherds belong to substantially complete, though well-fragmented greyware vessel (Fig. 4.8; no. 12) from the terminal) contrasts with the quantities from Ditches A, and D. Ditch B fell out of use early in the life of the cemetery, and was cut by Ditch F.

Ditch D
Ditch 809: (10 sherds; 60g; 1.09 EVEs). *Samian:* CG, Drag. 37, Hadrianic/Antonine. *Coarsewares:* TF 5; misc wh.

The small quantities of pottery from this feature support 2nd-century dating.

Ditch E
No dateable finds were recorded from this feature.

Ditch F
Ditch 5119/5121/5127/5149: (88 sherds; 1034g; 0.99 EVEs). *Coarsewares:* TF 5; 6; 17/95; 9/95; 10; 35; 40; 95; 11/29.

This short length of ditch produced a moderately large group of pottery which is consistent in its dating in the early or mid 2nd-century range. While samian is absent, this dating is suggested by the abundance of coarseware types TF 5, 6 and 10, and the ring-necked flagons in fabric 9 (Fig. 4.8; no. 13).

Pit 5136
(1 sherd; 3g). Coarseware TF3/24.

The single, small sherd from this feature probably dates to the mid or later 1st century.

Robber trench for Wall C
Robber Trench 789: (34 sherds; 115g; 0.06 EVEs). *Coarsewares:* Medieval oolitic; TF 74; 9; 9/98; 17/98; 6; 35.

This small group includes two small medieval sherds but otherwise it is similar in character to those from the graves within the walled cemetery.

Chapter 3
Grave Catalogue

by Jamie Wright, Tom Weavill, Alistair Barber, E.R. McSloy and Jonny Geber

The catalogue is organised in the following fashion. The numbering of burials commences with C1153 so as to continue the sequence for burials to the west of the town started in CE II, 205, MF5 A03–C01, and continued in CE VI. The catalogue number is prefixed by a letter B for inhumation burials and a letter C for cremation burials. The Cirencester burial number is followed in brackets by the grave and skeleton number ascribed on site. For each entry there is a description of the grave; where an alignment is recorded, the head end is presented first; the posture of the inhumation burials (legs are always extended unless otherwise stated); summary of skeletal preservation and pathology; listing of grave goods; coffin nails; finds from the grave backfill, and finally a suggested date range for the grave. Selected grave goods are discussed in further detail in Chapter 4. The following abbreviations are used: cbm = ceramic building material; Sk = skeleton. For the animal bone: BOS = cattle; O/C = sheep/goat; SUS = pig; EQU =

horse; CAN = dog; ROD = rodent; GAL = fowl; AVE = bird; LM = large-sized mammal; MM = medium-sized mammal. The descriptions of the grave and burial posture are by Jamie Wright and Tom Weavill, artefacts by E.R. McSloy and human and animal bone by Jonny Geber. A full osteological catalogue of all the human remains can be found in the online archive.

3.1 Cremation Burials

C1153 (grave 614) (Figs 3.1–3.2)
Grave: sub-square with steep sides and flat base, 0.4m x 0.38m x 0.17m deep. Grey-brown silty clay fill (615) surrounding a cremation vessel.

Human remains: weight 194.51g (62.46% identified), age 18–44 years, female.

Cremation vessel C1153.1: Dorset Black-burnished ware (TF 74). Neck-less jar; everted, flaring rim and

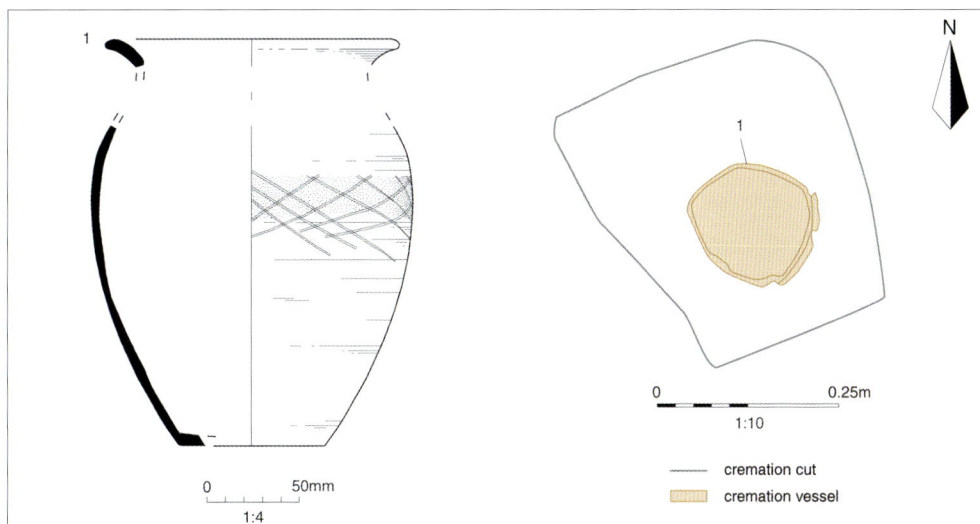

Fig. 3.1 Burial C1153

Fig. 3.2   Burial C1153 during excavation

obtuse-angled burnished lattice. Incomplete but reconstructable to full profile.

Grave fill finds: animal bone 5 x IND.

Date: 3rd century (cremation vessel).

C1154 (grave 617) (Fig. 3.3)

Grave: sub-circular with irregular sides to an irregular
base, 0.3m x 0.25m x 0.15m deep. Orange-brown silty
clay fill (616) surrounding a cremation and an ancillary
vessel.

Human remains: 155.13g (60.61% identified), age 18–
44 years, female.

Cremation vessel C1154.1: Greyware (TF 98) jar or
beaker with zone of vertical ribbing at girth/shoulder.

Ancillary vessel C1154.2: Dorset Black-burnished ware
(TF 74). Lower portion of small jar.

Date: 2nd or 3rd century (cremation vessel/ancillary
vessel).

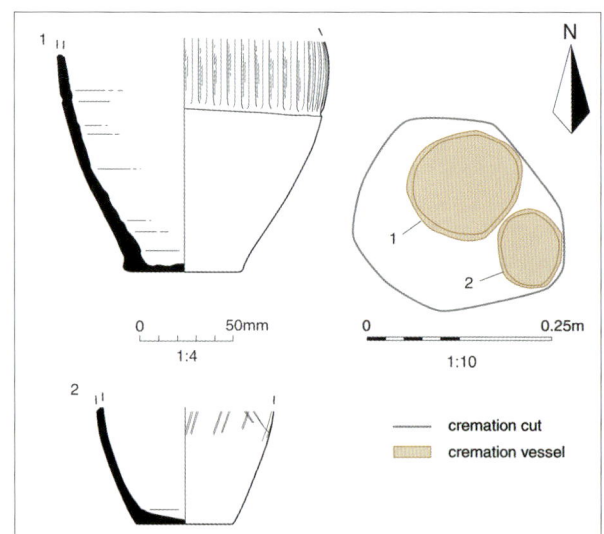

Fig. 3.3   Burial C1154

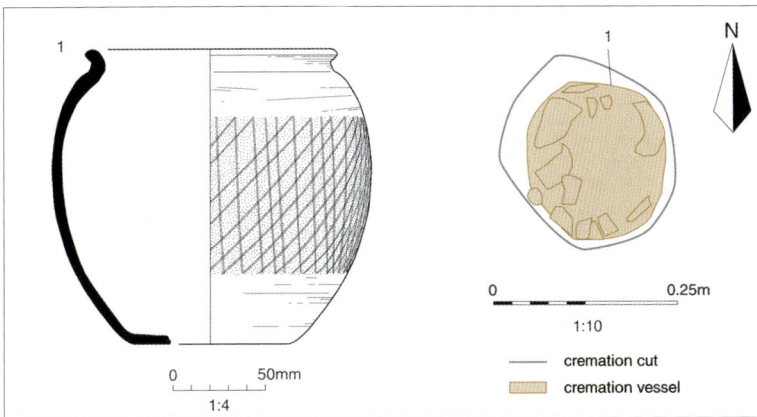

Fig. 3.4   Burial C1226

C1226 (grave 610) (Fig. 3.4)

Grave: sub-circular, with steep sides to sloping base, 0.21m diameter and 0.14m deep. Pale orange-brown silty clay fill (609) surrounding a cremation vessel.

Human remains: weight 199.74g (74.60% identified), age 18–44, sex indeterminable, no pathology noted.

Cremation vessel C1226.1: Dorset Black-burnished ware (TF 74). Neck-less jar with everted rim and acute-angled burnished lattice. Incomplete but reconstructable to full profile.

Date: 2nd century (cremation vessel).

C1227 (grave 773) (Fig. 3.5)

Grave: sub-circular with very steep sides to a flat base, 0.38m x 0.35m x 0.13m deep. Orange-brown sandy clay fill (774) surrounding truncated lead vessel. No cremated bone was present.

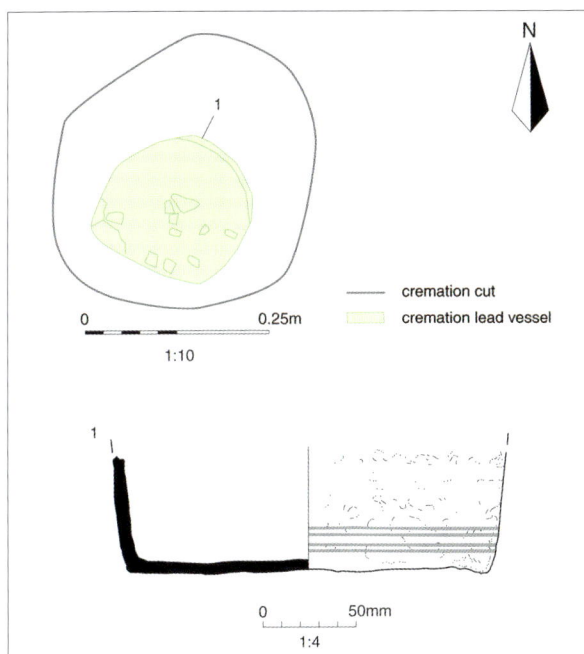

Fig. 3.5   Burial C1227

Cremation vessel C1227.1: Base of lead container. Only the base and lower 30–40mm of the vessel are present. The form of vessel appears to be cylindrical and there is a band of horizontal grooved decoration at the junction of wall and base. Diameter 200mm; thickness 8mm. On excavation it was found to contain no human remains. The extent of truncation makes it possible that the contents were removed as the result of later disturbance. Cylindrical lead containers, some of which were lidded, are known from a number of sites including Caerleon (Wheeler 1929) and London (Brailsford 1958, 65–6; fig. 32.1). An example from Colchester (Crummy 1993, fig. 8.8) dating to the 1st or 2nd centuries featured similar grooved decoration at the base angle.

Date: 1st or 2nd century (cremation vessel).

C1275 (grave 5147, vessel 5145) (Fig. 3.6)

Grave: Sub-oval with vertical? sides and concave? base, 0.5m x 0.2m x 0.15m. Light green-brown clay silt fill around cremation vessel. Within the same cut as C1276 which was dug into the backfill of Ditch F.

Human remains: weight 541.76g (63.68% identified), age 18–44 years, male?

Cremation vessel C1275.1: Dorset Black-burnished ware (TF 74). Lower portion of cooking pot (jar); acute-angled, but close to right-angled, burnished lattice decoration.

Date: late 2nd to early 3rd century (cremation vessel).

C1276 (grave 5147, vessel 5143) (Fig. 3.6)

Grave: same cut as contained C1275.

Human remains: weight 150.98g (74.48% identified), age 18–44 years, sex indeterminate.

Cremation vessel C1276.1: lower portion of jar in coarse reduced fabric (TF 15).

Date: not closely dated.

C1277 (grave 5159, vessel 5151) (Fig. 3.7)

Grave: sub-oval with vertical? sides and concave? base 0.26m x 0.26m x *c.* 0.03m. Vessel flush with cut, no surrounding fill. Heavily disturbed and truncated but

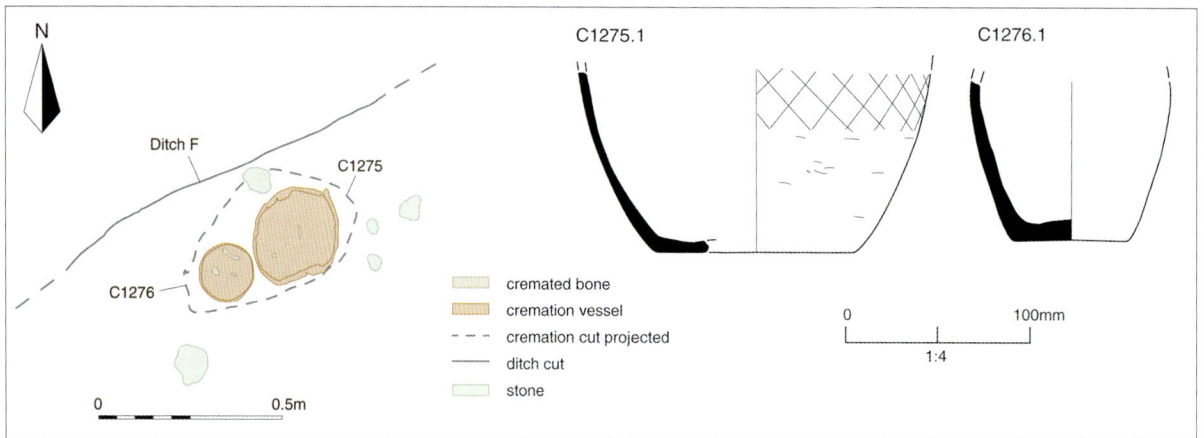

Fig. 3.6   *Burials C1275 and C1276*

line of cut survives. This cremation burial was dug into the backfill of Ditch B.

Human remains: none present, probably due to disturbance and truncation.

Cremation vessel C1277.1: very fragmented greyware (TF 17/98) ?jar. *Not illustrated.*

Date: not closely dated.

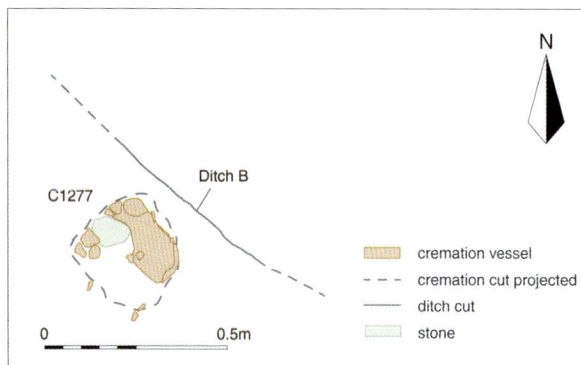

Fig. 3.7   *Burial C1277*

C1278 (vessels 5157, 5153, 5155, within Ditch B) (Fig. 3.8)

Grave: probably three heavily fragmented vessels within upper stony backfill 5184 towards the north-west terminus of Ditch B. No discernible grave cut survived due to heavy disturbance and truncation.

Human remains: none present, probably due to disturbance and truncation.

Cremation vessel C1278.1: Dorset Black-burnished ware (TF 74). Jar/cooking pot. Obtuse-angled lattice below groove. Lead rivet repair.

Cremation vessel C1278.2: Dorset Black-burnished ware (TF 74). Very fragmented, and of indeterminate form. *Not illustrated.*

Cremation vessel C1278.3: Dorset Black-burnished ware (TF 74). Very fragmented, and of indeterminate form. *Not illustrated.*

Date: probably 3rd century.

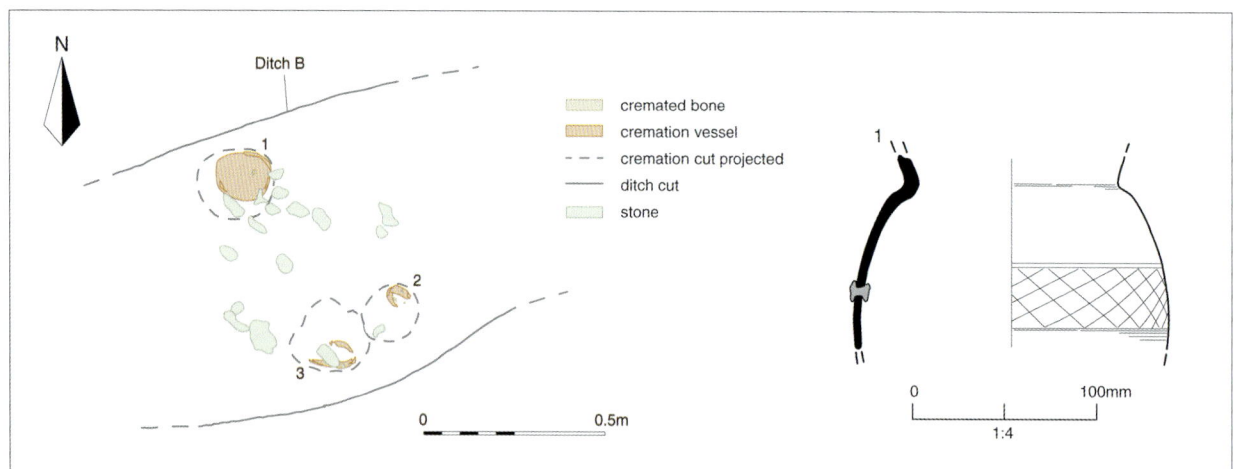

Fig. 3.8   *Burial C1278*

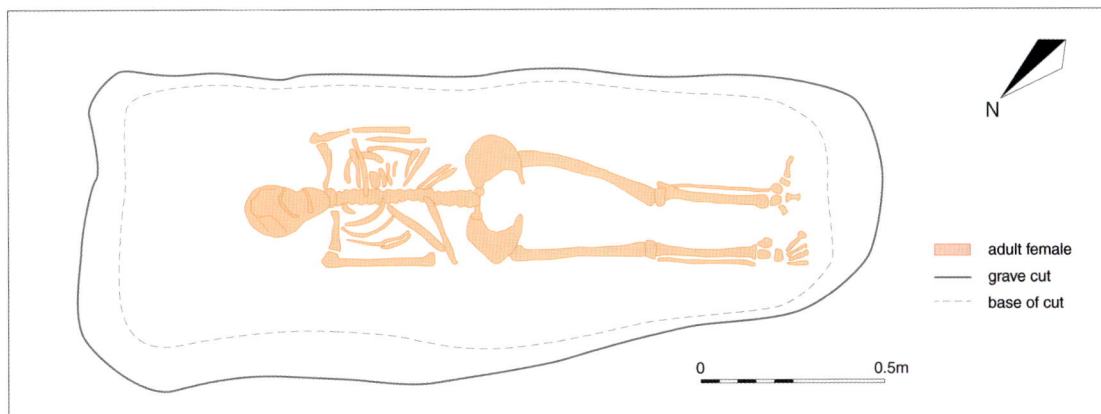

Fig. 3.9 Burial B1155

3.2 Inhumation Burials

B1155 (grave 702; Sk 701) (Fig. 3.9)

Grave: north-east–south-west. Sub-rectangular, wider and deeper to north-east, 45° sides and flat base, 2.12m x 0.82m x 0.31m deep. Two fills: orange-brown silty clay, occasional small stones, in the 0.4m between skull and grave cut (703); mottled orange and dark brown clay silt, frequent small and medium stones and frequent charcoal and ?burnt bone (700) covered 703 and skeleton.

Human remains: supine with arms folded over chest and legs straight, extended, 80% skeletal recovery, age 36–49, female.

Grave goods: B1155.1: iron hobnails x 5. Location: at feet; worn?

Coffin nails: iron x 33 including fragments. Flat headed; none measurable.

Grave fill finds: pottery 118 sherds (TF 35, 9, 9/98, 74, 17/98, 5, 6, 95, 90, 40, 15); cbm x 1; lead strip; worked flint piercer; stone tessera x 1; animal bone: BOS x 1, SUS x 1.

Date: mid 2nd century (grave fill pottery).

B1156 (grave 706; Sk 705) (Fig. 3.10)

Grave: north-west–south-east. Sub-rectangular, shallow sides and flat base >1.3m x 0.64m x 0.1m deep. Brown silty clay fill with frequent fragments of charcoal and burnt bone. Cuts B1159.

Human remains: supine with hands over pelvis, 20% skeletal recovery, age 17–19, indeterminate sex.

Grave goods: B1156.1: iron hobnails x 40. Location: at feet; worn?

Coffin nails: iron x 24, all fragmentary. Flat-headed; 46–71mm.

Grave fill finds: pottery 15 sherds (TF 74, 35, 17, 154b [Drag. 37], 9); glass x 4; cbm x 2; worked flint blade; animal bone: MM x 1.

Date: mid 3rd to 4th century (grave fill pottery).

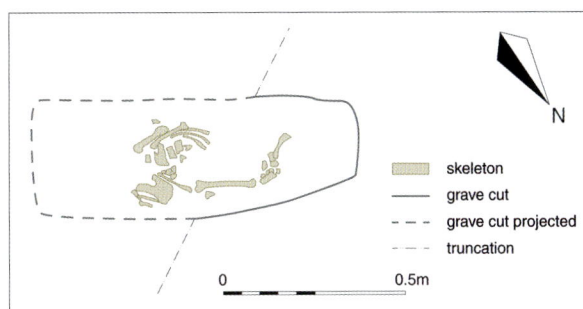

Fig. 3.10 Burial B1156

B1157 (grave 709; Sk 708) (Fig. 3.11)

Grave: south-west–north-east. Rectangular, vertical sides and flat base, 2.07m x 0.88m x 0.9m deep. Single orange-brown silty clay fill with occasional stone and common charcoal, especially to the south-west. Two postholes at the north-east end of the grave.

Human remains: flexed on right side, 85% skeletal recovery, age 39–50, male.

Grave goods: B1157.1: iron hobnails x 15. Location: at feet.

Coffin nails: iron x 14, all fragmentary. Flat-headed.

Grave fill finds: pottery: 104 sherds (TF 35, 74, 5, 9, 9/98, 95, 88, 17/98, 154a [Ritt. 12], 154b [Drag. 37]); glass x 2; cbm x 4; animal bone: BOS x 1, O/C x 3, LM x 3, MM x 1, ROD x 17, IND x 7.

Date: mid 2nd century (grave fill pottery).

B1158 (grave 712; Sk 711) (Fig. 3.12)

Grave: north-east–south-west. Sub-rectangular, sloping sides and flattish base, >1.65m x 0.75m x 0.09m deep. Modern truncation to north-east. Single dark grey-brown silty clay fill with occasional charcoal and burnt bone.

Human remains: supine with one arm over abdomen, 50% skeletal recovery, age 36–60, female.

Possible grave goods: B1158.1: iron hobnails x 2. Location: at feet; worn?

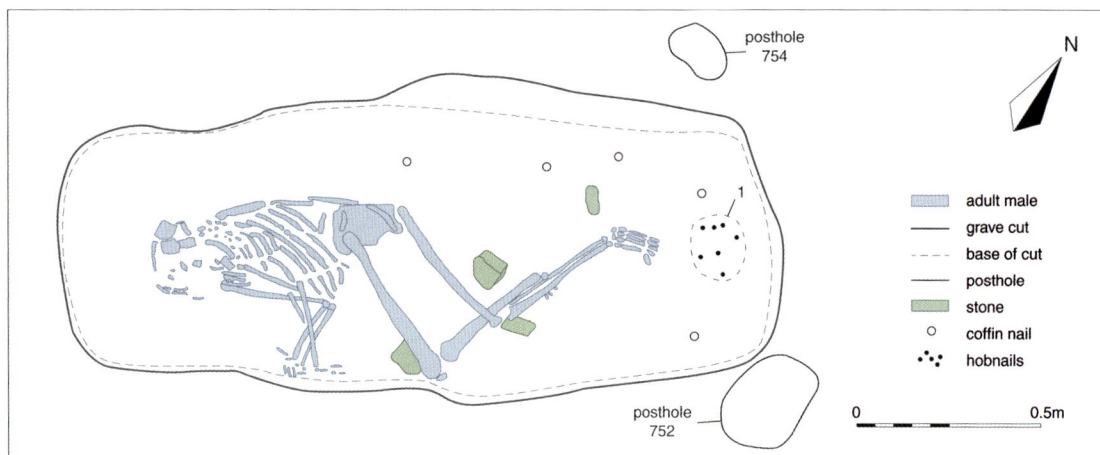

Fig. 3.11   Burial B1157

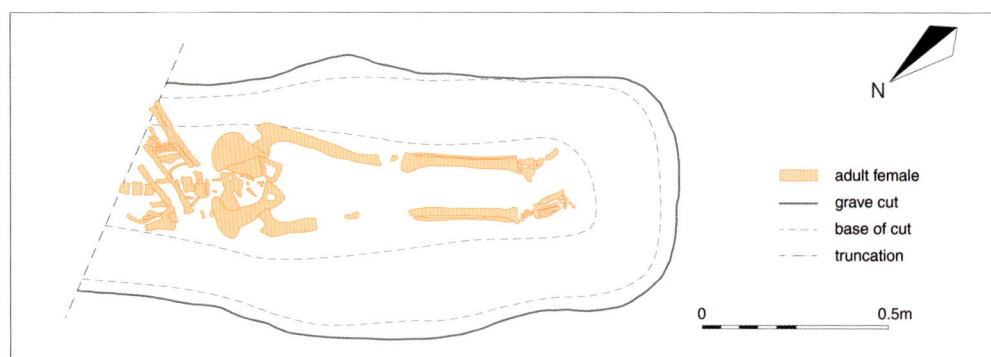

Fig. 3.12   Burial B1158

Coffin nails: iron x 17, all fragmentary. Flat-headed.

Grave fill finds: pottery: 54 sherds (TF 74, 17, 9, 6, 98, 95, 154b, 40, 35); glass x 1; cbm x 6; animal bone: BOS x 1, LM x 1.

Date: late 1st to 2nd century (grave fill pottery).

B1159 (grave 718; Sk 717) (Fig. 3.13)

Grave: north-west–south-east. Rectangular rock cut, vertical sides and flat base 2.18m x 1.05m x 0.3m deep. Two fills: large limestone blocks pitched vertically around the grave edge (727) and a brown sandy clay with occasional stones and charcoal flecks (716). Fill 716 cut by B1156.

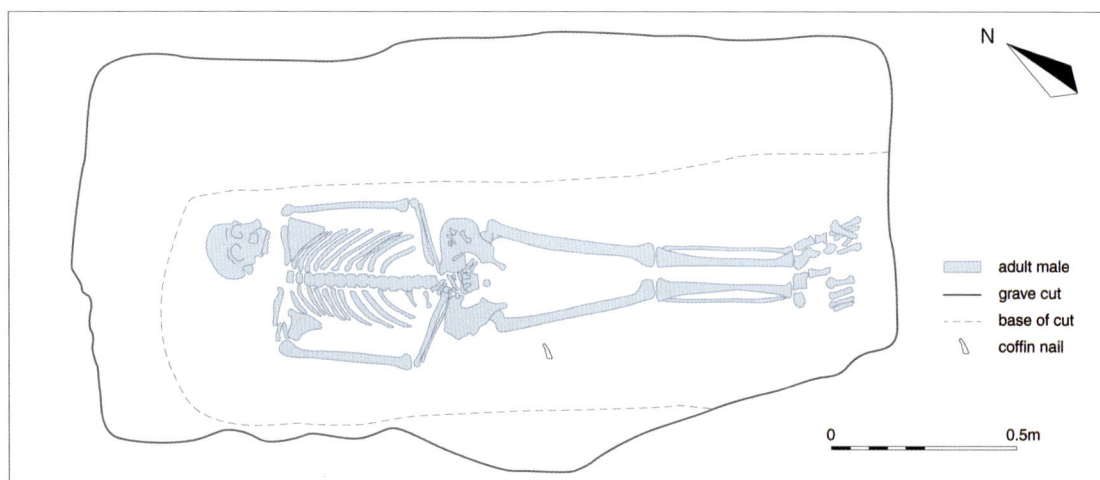

Fig. 3.13   Burial B1159

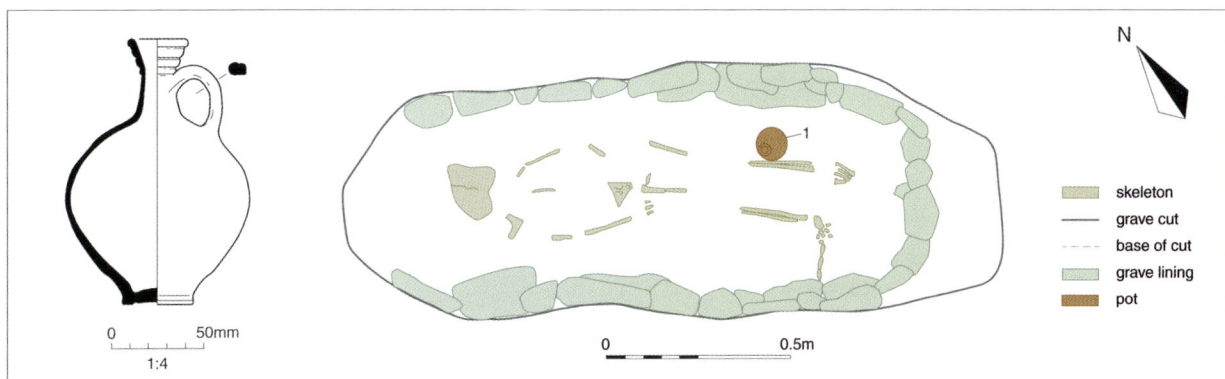

Fig. 3.14   Burial B1160

Human remains: supine with hands over pelvis, 80% skeletal recovery, age 28–42, male.

Grave goods: B1159.1: iron hobnails x 6: Location: at feet; worn?

Coffin nails: iron x 76 including fragments. Flat-headed; 53–97mm.

Grave fill finds: pottery: 63 sherds (TF 9, 35, 74, 98, 5, 81a, 84); cbm x 2; animal bone: CAN x 1, AVE x 1.

Date: mid to late 2nd century (grave fill pottery).

B1160 (grave 715; Sk 719) (Figs 3.14–3.15)
Grave: north-west–south-east. Cut through clay then rock, sub-rectangular, vertical sides and flat base, 1.76m x 0.68m x 0.54m deep. Two fills: limestones pitched vertically around coffin (726) and a dark grey-brown silty clay containing stones and frequent charcoal (714).

Human remains: supine ?with right arm by side and left arm over pelvis, 40% skeletal recovery, age *c.* 8, indeterminate sex.

Grave goods: B1160.1: small ring-necked pottery flagon in North Wiltshire oxidised fabric (TF 9). Height 139mm. Placed upright close to lower left leg.

B1160.2: iron hobnails x 11. Location: at feet; worn?

Coffin nails: iron x 36 including fragments. Flat-headed; 41–90mm.

Grave fill finds: pottery: 67 sherds (TF 95, 35, 9, 5, 6, 90, 98, 154b, 17, 74, 15); glass x 7; cbm x 3; animal bone: BOS x 5, O/C x 2, SUS x 1, EQU x 1, ROD x 2, GAL x 1.

Date: early to mid 2nd century (grave goods and grave fill pottery).

B1161 (grave 720; Sk 721) (Fig. 3.16)
Grave: north-west–south-east. Sub-rectangular with irregularities caused by torn bedrock, vertical sides and flat base 2.1m x 0.65m x 0.68m deep. A brown-orange sandy clay primary fill with frequent stones (722) overlaid by a similar fill 723 which possibly contained cremated bone.

Human remains: supine with right arm by side and left arm over pelvis, 95% skeletal recovery, age 32–45, female.

Fig. 3.15   Burial B1160 during excavation

Grave goods: B1161.1: Copper-alloy small reel-shaped shoe rivets x 27. Length 1–2mm; diameter 1mm. Location: at feet; worn?

B1161.2: iron hobnails x 39: Location: at feet; worn?

Coffin nails: iron x 50 including fragments. Flat-headed; 65–80mm.

Grave fill finds: pottery: 5 sherds (TF 80a, 74); glass x 3; animal bone: O/C x 1.

Date: 2nd to early 3rd century (grave fill pottery).

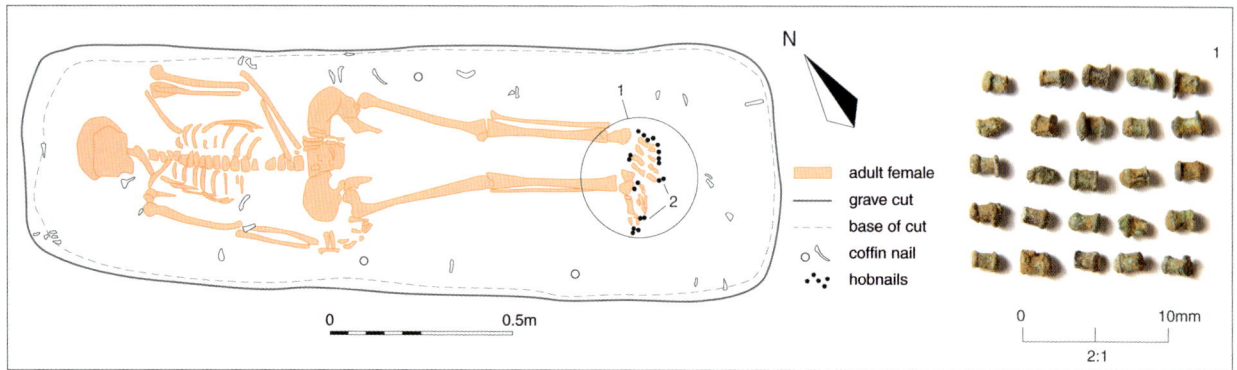

Fig. 3.16   Burial B1161

B1162 (grave 733, Sk 731) (Fig. 3.17)

Grave: north-west–south-east. Rectangular with vertical sides and flat base, 2.57m x 1.18m x 1.1m deep. Coffin clearly defined by nails. A brown silty clay 732 lined the base of the cut to a maximum depth of 0.14m and may represent material not cleaned out before the burial took place. The principal fill (730) was a brown silty clay with many stones, some placed between the coffin and grave cut.

Human remains: supine with arms folded over lower chest, 95% skeletal recovery, age 35–41, female.

Coffin nails: iron x 23 including fragments. Flat-headed; 120–150mm.

Grave fill finds: pottery: 10 sherds (TF 74, 40, 118, 35, 98, 9); animal bone: MM x 1.

Date: late 3rd to 4th century (grave fill pottery).

B1163 (grave 729; Sk 738) (Figs 3.18, 4.5–4.7)

Grave: north-west–south-east. Rectangular with steep sides and base sloping to south-east, 1.5m x 0.65m x 0.1m deep. A single brown silty clay fill with frequent small limestone fragments and occasional charcoal. This grave cut fill 736 of B1176.

Human remains: supine, 90% skeletal recovery, age 2–3, sex indeterminable.

Grave goods: B1163.1: copper-alloy cockerel figurine placed upright beyond the head (Fig. 4.5). Composite construction, comprising three elements, each with enamelled decoration (Figs 4.6–4.7). Broken at a point above the feet and there is a split at the base of the neck and damage also to the enamelling at the breast. The breakage appears to have occurred in antiquity and the feet/base were not deposited. The other damage is probably post-depositional and has resulted in some distortion and the movement forward of the neck/head. The tail plate shows clear traces of solder which matches the opening created by the body and wing cover. This

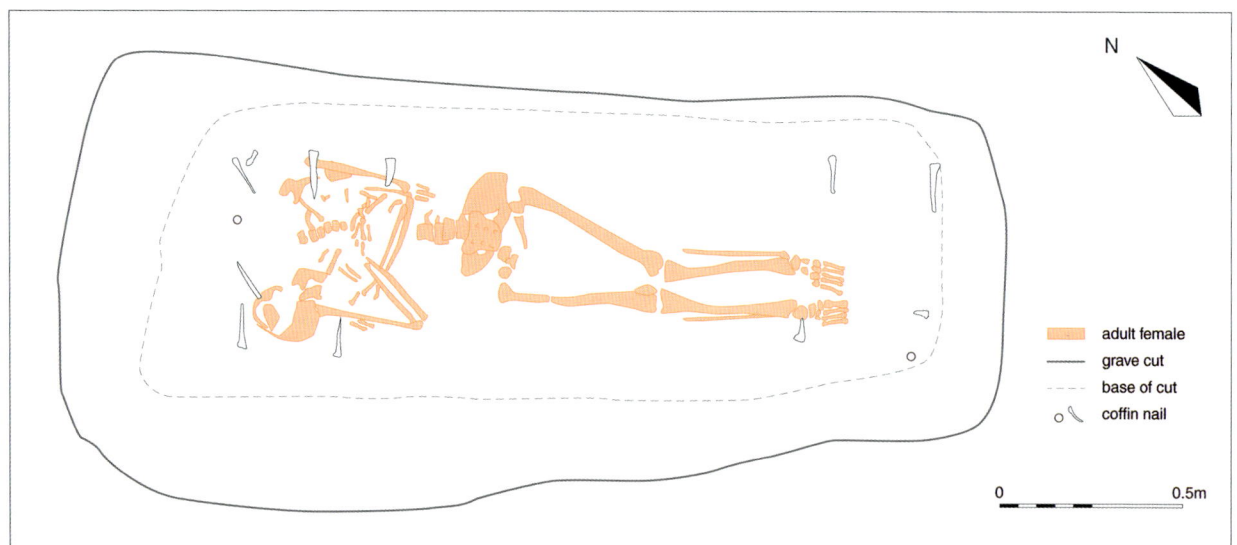

Fig. 3.17   Burial B1162

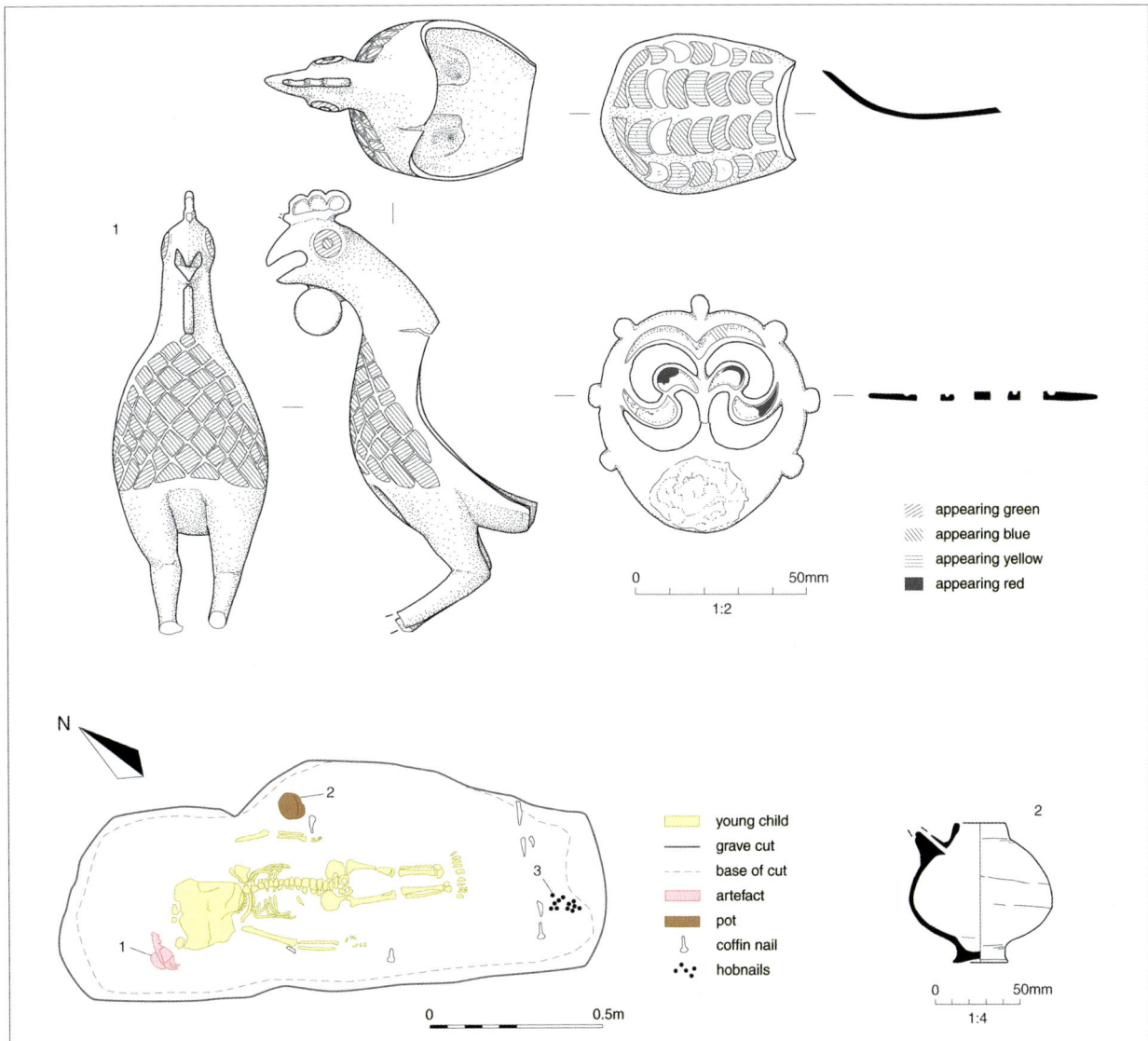

Fig. 3.18   Burial B1163

would appear to be the means by which the figurine was held together. Conservation revealed that traces of the original clay mould core remained within the neck and leg cavities. The interior of the cockerel is 'unfinished', the lozenge-shaped recesses intended for the chest enamelling visible on the inside.

The cockerel is modelled standing, its head thrust forwards and its beak open as if in the act of crowing. The treatment is stylised, in the 'Celtic' mode, the polychrome enamelling suggestive of the plumage of the living animal and the openwork and enamelled tail plate representing the bird's fanned tail. The breast, wings, eyes, comb and tail are inlaid with enamel which largely now appears blue and green. The enamelling to the breast is contained within a lattice of deep lozenge-shaped cells, the lowest being triangular to preserve a straight border. The enamelling to the wing plate occurs as (four) columns of crescent/kidney-shaped cells, the

bordering columns inverted. Only the blue-coloured enamels may be close to their original hue; the present appearance of the other colours is probably the result of decay and the leaching of copper corrosion. Comparison with other examples suggests the use of blue, yellow and red. The tail plate is flat and cordate in form, with seven rounded projections possibly representing the feather tips. The openwork curvilinear/scroll design to the tail is emphasised by enamel, the surviving traces of which appear to be blue and red. Height 125mm; width 49mm.

B1163.2: pottery tettine (feeder bottle). North Wiltshire oxidised fabric (TF 9). Location: close to lower left arm.

B1163.3: iron hobnails x 29. Location: at feet; worn?

Coffin nails: iron x 26, all fragmentary. Flat-headed.

Grave fill finds: pottery: 5 sherds (TF, 98, 17, 6, 154b [Drag. 35]); animal bone: SUS x 1.

Date: early to mid 2nd century (grave goods).

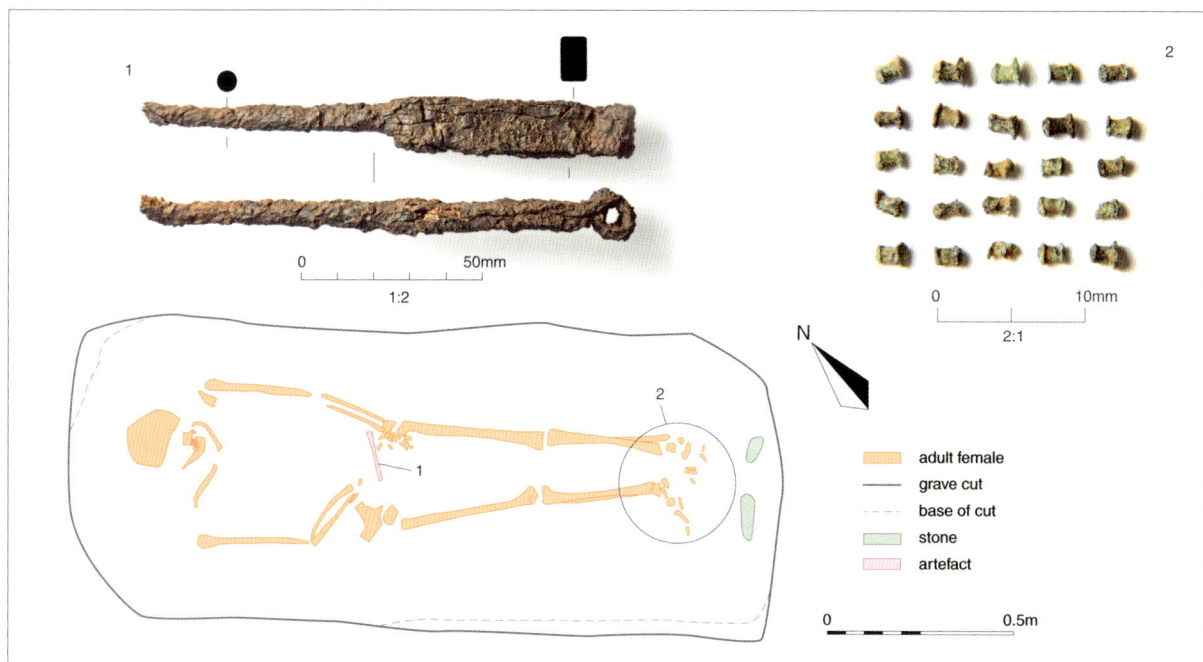

Fig. 3.19   Burial B1164

B1164 (grave 741, Sk 743) (Fig. 3.19)

Grave: north-west–south-east. Rectangular with vertical sides and flat base, 1.9m x 0.8m x 0.73m deep. Single dark brown clay fill with common stones.

Human remains: supine with hands over pelvis and near 1164.1, 65% skeletal recovery, age 25–35, female.

Grave goods: B1164.1: iron key. L-shaped lift key, broken at junction with bit. The handle is strip-like with looped-over terminal, the shaft is square in section. Keys of this form are the most commonly recognised from Roman Britain (Manning 1985, 90). They continue in use throughout the period. Location: lower abdomen, left side. Length: 132mm; section at handle 14.1 x 8.1mm; section at shaft 6.8mm.

B1164.2: Copper-alloy shoe rivets x 29 from foot area. Copper staining to some bones of the feet further suggest that the footwear was worn. Small, reel-shaped. Length 1–2mm; diameter 1mm.

B1164.3: iron hobnails x 38. Location: at feet; worn?

Coffin nails: iron x 73, including fragments. Flat-headed; 65–98mm.

Date: 2nd to 3rd century (grave goods).

B1165 (grave 744, Sk 746) (Fig. 3.20)

Grave: north-west–south-east. Rectangular with vertical sides and horizontal base, >0.7m x 0.8m x 0.4m deep, truncated by B1166. Limestone slabs pitched vertically between coffin and grave cut (745) with a main fill of brown silty clay containing frequent stones (747).

Human remains: supine with only legs surviving, 15% skeletal recovery, age >18, indeterminate sex.

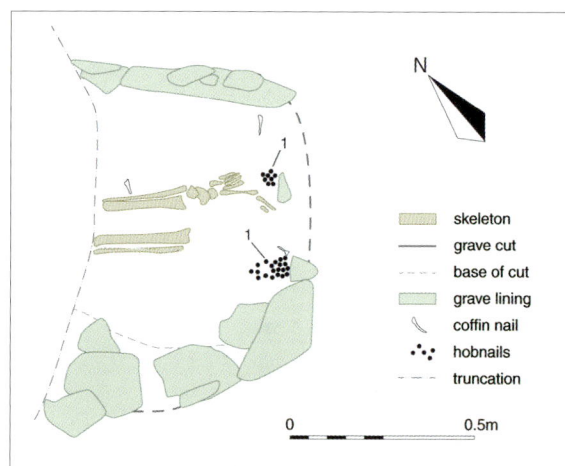

Fig. 3.20   Burial B1165

Grave goods: B1165.1: iron hobnails x 167. Location: at feet; worn?

Coffin nails: iron x 11, fragmentary. Flat-headed.

Grave fill finds: animal bone: LM x 3, GAL x 7, AVE x 4.

Date: 2nd to 4th century (grave goods).

B1166 (grave 748, Sk 750) (Fig. 3.21)

Grave: north-west–south-east. Rectangular with vertical sides and horizontal base, >1m x 0.65m x 0.4m deep. This grave cut grave B1165 and was itself truncated by modern disturbance. Limestone slabs (748) were placed between the coffin and grave cut, including at least

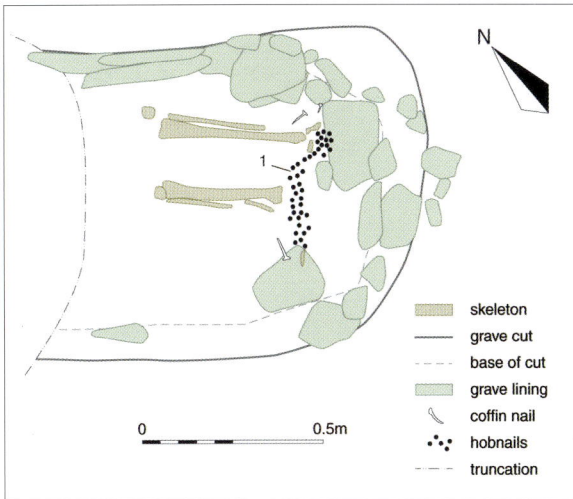

Fig. 3.21   Burial B1166

one sealing disturbed grave B1165. Main fill 751 was a brown silty clay with many large and medium limestone fragments.

Human remains: supine with only legs surviving, 20% skeletal recovery, age >18, indeterminate sex.

Possible grave goods: B1166.1: iron hobnails x 41. Location: at feet.

Coffin nails: iron x 28, fragmentary. Flat-headed.

Grave fill finds: pottery: 2 sherds (TF 9, 6).

Date: 2nd to 4th century (grave goods).

B1167 (grave 756, Sk 758) (Fig. 3.22)

Grave: north-west–south-east. Irregular rectangle wider at the north-west end, sloping sides and flat base, 2.57m x 0.91m–0.81m x 0.2m deep. The grave was cut into clay so the effort to dig it cannot be used to explain its shallowness. Single grey-brown silty clay fill. The grave extended 0.4m beyond the coffin at both the head and feet ends.

Human remains: supine with right arm over pelvis and left arm by side, 75% skeletal recovery, age 20–24, male.

Grave goods: B1167.1: iron hobnails x 244: Location: shin area.

Coffin nails: iron x 74, most fragmentary. Flat-headed. Complete example is 85mm long.

Date: 2nd to 4th century (grave goods).

B1168 (grave 761, Sk 760) (Fig. 3.23)

Grave: south-west–north-east. Rectangular with steep sides and flat base. 2.13m x 0.75m x 0.33m deep. A single yellow-brown silty clay fill contained flecks of charcoal and some burnt bone. Possible posthole 0.2m to the east of the grave.

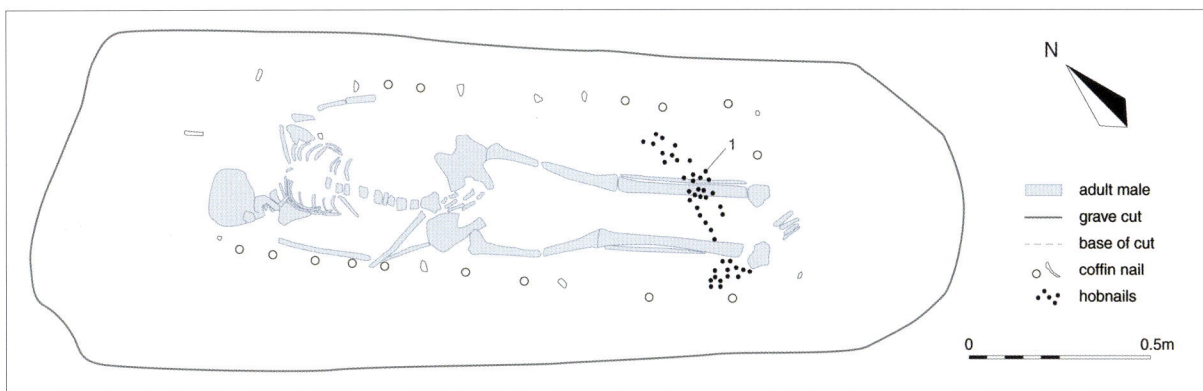

Fig. 3.22   Burial B1167

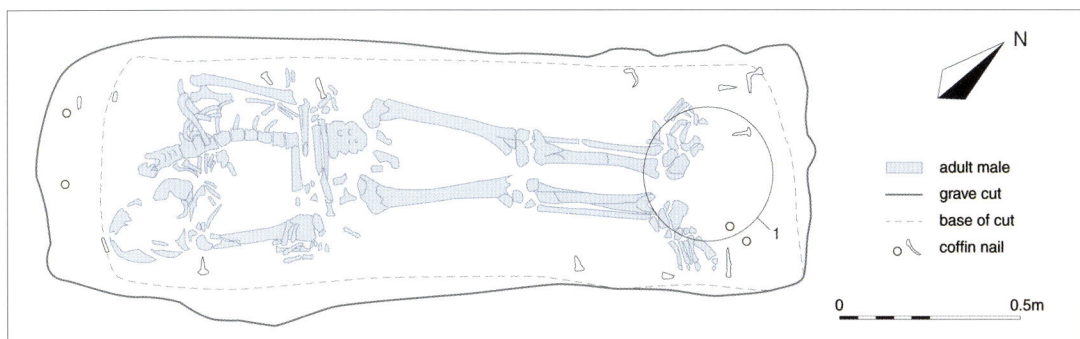

Fig. 3.23   Burial B1168

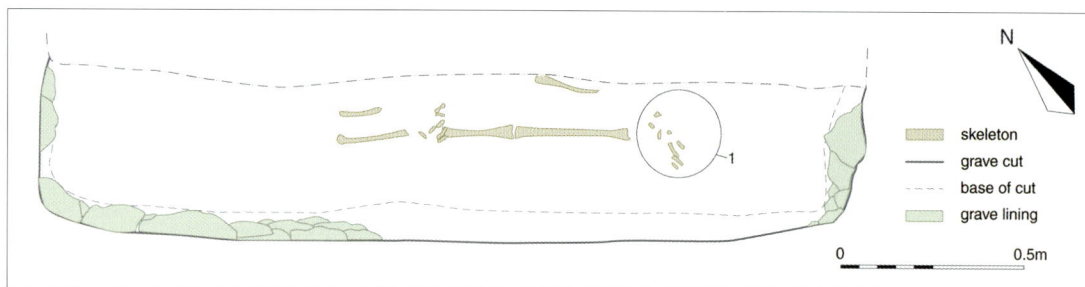

Fig. 3.24   Burial B1169

Human remains: supine with arms next to each other over the abdomen, 90% skeletal recovery, age 26–43, male.

Grave goods: B1168.1: iron hobnails x 10. Location: at feet; worn?

Coffin nails: iron x 30, fragmentary. Flat-headed.

Grave fill finds: pottery: 18 sherds (TF 74, 9, 35, 98); cbm x 2; animal bone: BOS x 1, ROD x 1, AVE x 1.

Date: 2nd century (grave fill pottery).

B1169 (grave 762, Sk 763) (Fig. 3.24)

Grave: north-west–south-east. Rectangular with vertical sides and flat base, 2.2m x >0.46 x 0.55m deep. Suggestion of a stone lining. Single grey-brown silty clay fill contained abundant limestones. A 2mm-wide and 1m-long white line, parallel to the skeleton, seemed to have been a lime coating on the former coffin. Truncated by B1174 with which it forms a probable pair.

Human remains: supine, 20% skeletal recovery, age >18, sex indeterminate.

Possible grave goods: B1169.1: iron hobnail x 1. Location: at feet; worn or stray find.

Coffin nails: iron x 10, most fragmentary. Flat-headed; 50–70mm.

Date: 2nd to 4th century (grave goods).

B1170 (grave 777, Sk 776) (Fig. 3.25)

Grave: north-west–south-east. Sub-rectangular with steep sides to a flat base, 2m x 0.6m x 0.18m deep. Cut the grave fill of B1219. Single brown clay fill with frequent small to medium limestones. Suggestion of a stone lining.

Human remains: supine with right arm by side and left arm over abdomen, 75% skeletal recovery, age 25–35, male.

Grave goods: B1170.1: iron hobnails x 34. Location: at feet; worn?

Coffin nails: iron x 44, most fragmentary. Flat-headed. Complete example is 60mm long.

Grave fill finds: pottery: 2 sherds (TF 74, 35); animal bone: GAL x 1.

Date: 2nd to 4th century (grave goods/grave fill pottery).

B1171 (grave 735, Sk 778) (Figs 3.26–3.27)

Grave: north-west–south-east. Rectangular with apsidal north-west end, vertical sides and flat base, 1.52m x 0.6m x 0.3m deep. The single fill (734) was a mottled orange and yellow-brown sandy clay with abundant brash and occasional charcoal flecks. The grave cut fill 736 of B1176.

Human remains: supine, 75% skeletal recovery, age *c*. 6, sex indeterminable, indications of scurvy and possibly trauma or tuberculosis.

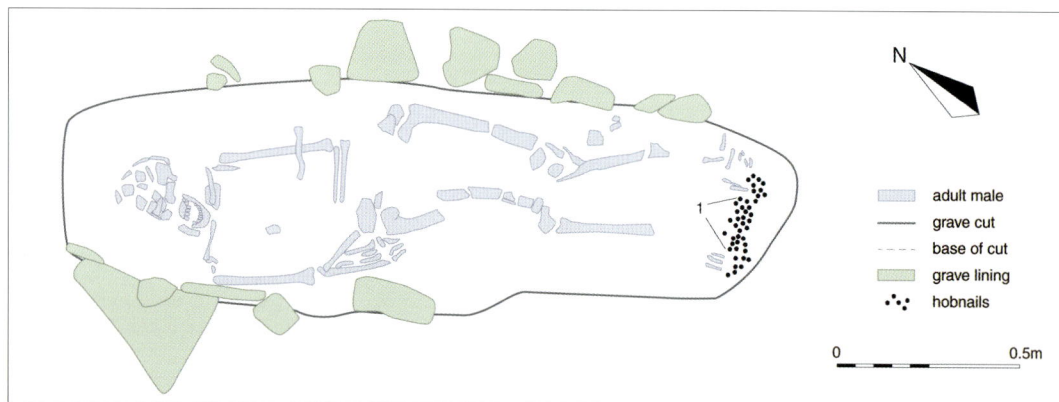

Fig. 3.25   Burial B1170

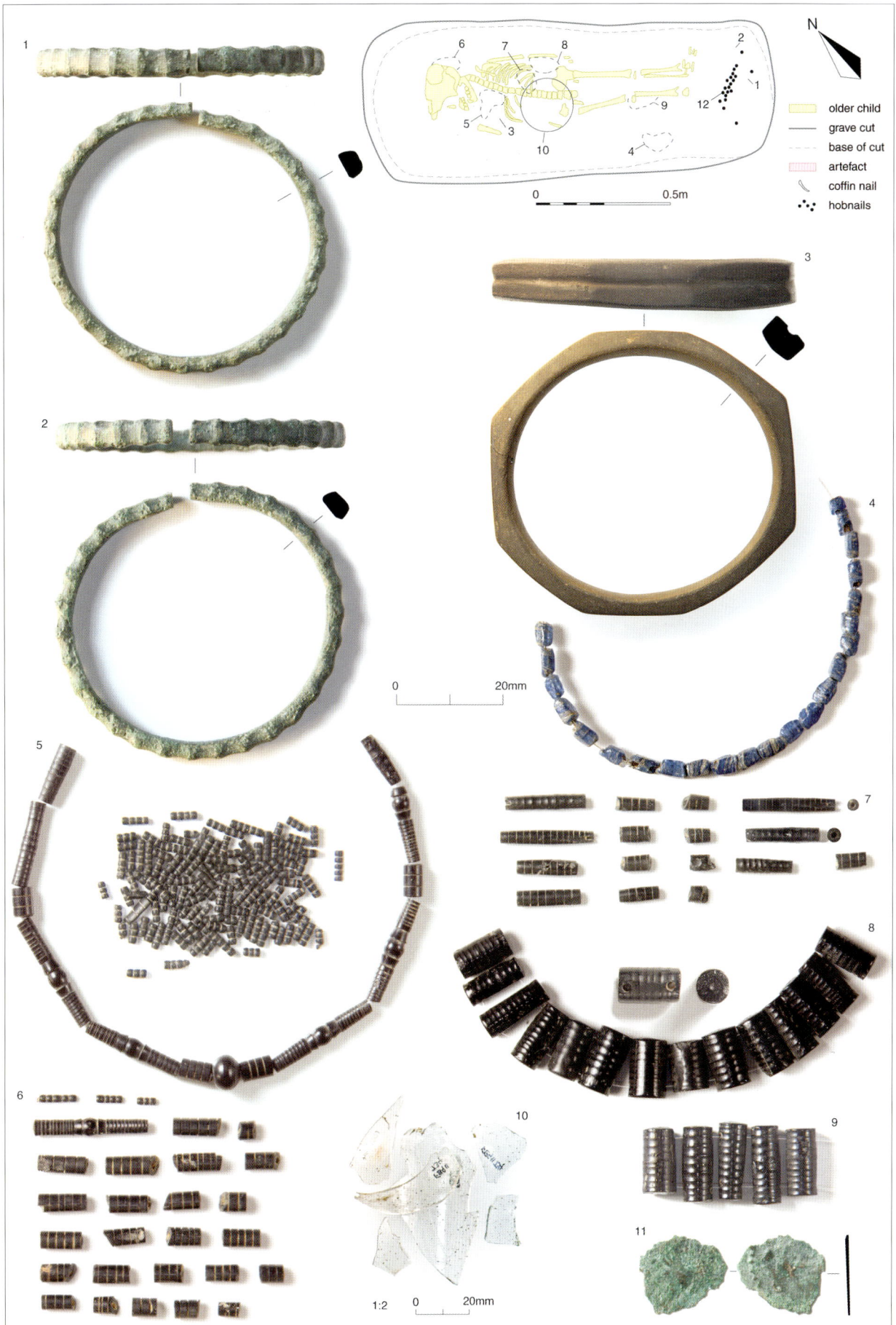

Fig. 3.26   Burial B1171

Fig. 3.27   Detail of the shale bracelet 3 and bead strings 5, 7 and 8 from B1171

Grave goods: B1171.1: copper-alloy bracelet. Penannular, heavy cast type. The inner circumference is plain, the outer face scalloped/beaded. Heavier cast bracelets of late Roman type are discussed by Cool (2010) and there is a close parallel from the Bath Gate Cemetery (CE II, fig. 80, no. 228). Location: at foot of grave, close to B1171.2. Diameter 54.1mm x 50.2mm; section 5mm x 3.5mm.

B1171.2: copper-alloy bracelet. Penannular, heavy cast type. Of identical form to B1171.1 and almost certainly intended as a pair. Location: at foot of grave, close to B1171.1. Diameter 54.2mm x 50mm; section 4.6mm x 3.9mm.

B1171.3: shale bracelet. Octagonal with sub-circular internal circumference. Outer face has single central groove. There is an example in shale, but with double groove, from Silchester (Lawson 1976, 253, no. 44) and other examples are known in jet (Allason-Jones 1996, 31). Location: at right side of chest (not worn). Diameter 54mm x 50mm; section 7.6–9mm x 4.3–4.6mm.

B1171.4: glass beads string. Consists of 29 individual beads and a further 11 fragments. All are of wound, small segmented form (Guido 1978, 91–2) and opaque blue in colour. Similar beads are common components of strung necklaces or armlets of the later 3rd and 4th centuries. Location: in cluster close to the lower right leg. Individual beads are 4–6mm long and 2.7–3mm diameter.

B1171.5: jet beads string. Consists of 153 beads of sub-spherical (1), tubular/ribbed (4), cylinder/segmented (5), 'toggle' (6) and small segmented (137) form. A further 67 beads of small segmented (60) and cylinder/segmented (7) form were recovered from soil samples and could relate to string(s) B1171.5/6. All of the bead forms correspond to known types (Table 4.3), probably produced throughout the later 3rd and 4th centuries (Crummy 1983; Allason-Jones 1996). Located at the right side of the upper chest. The sub-spherical bead is 6.8 x 5.1mm; tubular/ribbed: 11.5–16.2mm long and 4.2–3.2mm diameter; cylinder/segmented: individual segments (3 to 11) are 1.6–1.8mm long and 3.8mm diameter; toggle: 20.4–22.8mm long and 3.5–3.8mm diameter at centre; small segmented: individual segments (2 to 6) are 1mm x 1mm.

B1171.6: jet beads string. Consists of 28 beads of cylinder/segmented (24), toggle (1) and small segmented (3) form. Located at neck, away from the main cluster of B1171.5, but may be part of the same 'string'. Cylinder/segmented: individual segments (2 to 5) are 1.6–1.8mm long and 3.8mm diameter; toggle: 21.8mm long and 3.6mm diameter at centre; small segmented: individual segments (3 to 6) are 1mm x 1mm.

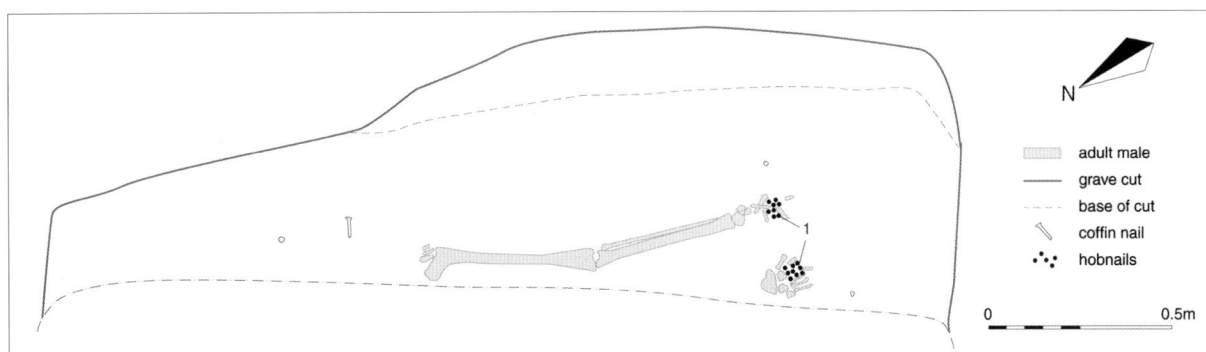

Fig. 3.28 Burial B1172

B1171.7: jet beads string. Consists of 16 beads of tubular/ribbed (3) and cylinder/segmented form (13). Located at lower left side of chest, away from the main cluster B1171.5, but may be part of the same 'string'. Tubular/ribbed: 15.4–11.2mm long x 3–3.2mm diameter; cylinder/segmented: individual segments (3 to 15) are 1.1–1.8mm long and 2.9–3.8mm diameter.

B1171.8: jet beads string/armlet. Consists of 14 beads of ribbed, 'pillar' beads (Allason-Jones 1996, 26, no. 13). Each is double-perforated at right angles to the length of the bead and the ends of each bead with 'chuck point' indentations resulting from lathe manufacture. A stray bead of this form recovered from a soil sample may come either from B1171.8 or B1171.9. Located at lower left abdomen close to left wrist and probably worn as a bracelet. Beads are 9.6–13.6mm long and 4.7–7.4mm in diameter.

B1171.9: jet beads string. Consists of 5 ribbed pillar beads of same form as B1171.8. Located in lower right side of grave, at level of lower knee. Beads are 7.6–12.4mm long and 5.1–6.2mm in diameter.

B1171.10: glass vessel. Comprises 30 fragments of greenish colourless glass of the type characteristic of the 4th century (Cool and Price 1995, 218). Incomplete cylindrical flask with horizontal wheel-cut or abraded lines to the body. The rim does not survive, though the other features suggest this would have been of funnel mouth form (Isings 1957, form 102) common in first half of the 4th century (Cool and Price 1995, 218–19). Located on the right side of the torso/pelvis.

B1171.11: copper-alloy coin. Barbarous radiate *c.* AD 270–90; fragmentary and with details uncertain. From soil sample from torso area. It is uncertain whether this coin was among the grave goods or was a stray find in the grave backfill.

B1171.12: iron hobnails x 36. Location: 17 at feet, worn?; 18 near head.

Coffin nails: iron x 99, most fragmentary. Flat-headed. Complete example is 65mm long.

Grave fill finds: pottery: 9 sherds (TF 95, 6, 17, 9); animal bone: GAL x 22, AVE x 25.

Date: late 3rd to 4th century (grave goods).

B1172 (grave 783, Sk 782) (Fig. 3.28)

Grave: north-east–south-west. Irregular sub-rectangle with steep or vertical sides and a horizontal base, 2.43m x >0.8m x 0.73m deep. Cut by B1173. Single grey-brown silty clay fill with abundant medium to large limestones.

Human remains: supine, 15% skeletal recovery, age >18, male.

Grave goods: B1172.1: iron hobnails x 74. Location: at feet; worn?

Coffin nails?: iron x 9, fragmentary. Flat-headed.

Grave fill finds: animal bone: BOS x 1.

Date: 2nd to 4th century (grave goods).

B1173 (grave 786, Sk 785) (Fig. 3.29)

Grave: south-west–north-east. Sub-rectangular, with steep sides and horizontal base, 2.43m x 0.78m x 0.73m deep. Cuts B1172.

Human remains: supine with right arm by side, 20% skeletal recovery, age 17–25, indeterminable sex.

Grave goods: B1173.1: copper-alloy twisted wire bracelet. Three strand type. Approximately two-thirds complete but missing both terminals. Located above left shoulder (not worn). Diameter 49mm; section 3.5–3.6mm.

B1173.2: glass beads string. Consists of 5 beads of small segmented form (Guido 1978, 91–2), of translucent dark blue (4) and translucent yellow (1). Similar beads are common components of strung necklaces or armlets in the later 3rd and 4th centuries. Location: head area, close to location of B1173.1. Individual beads are 2–4mm long and 2.5–3.5mm diameter.

B1173.3: iron hobnail x 1. Stray find from grave soil?

Coffin nails: iron x 28 including fragments. Flat-headed; 65–83mm.

Grave fill finds: pottery: 3 sherds (TF 74, 98).

Date: late 3rd to 4th century (grave goods).

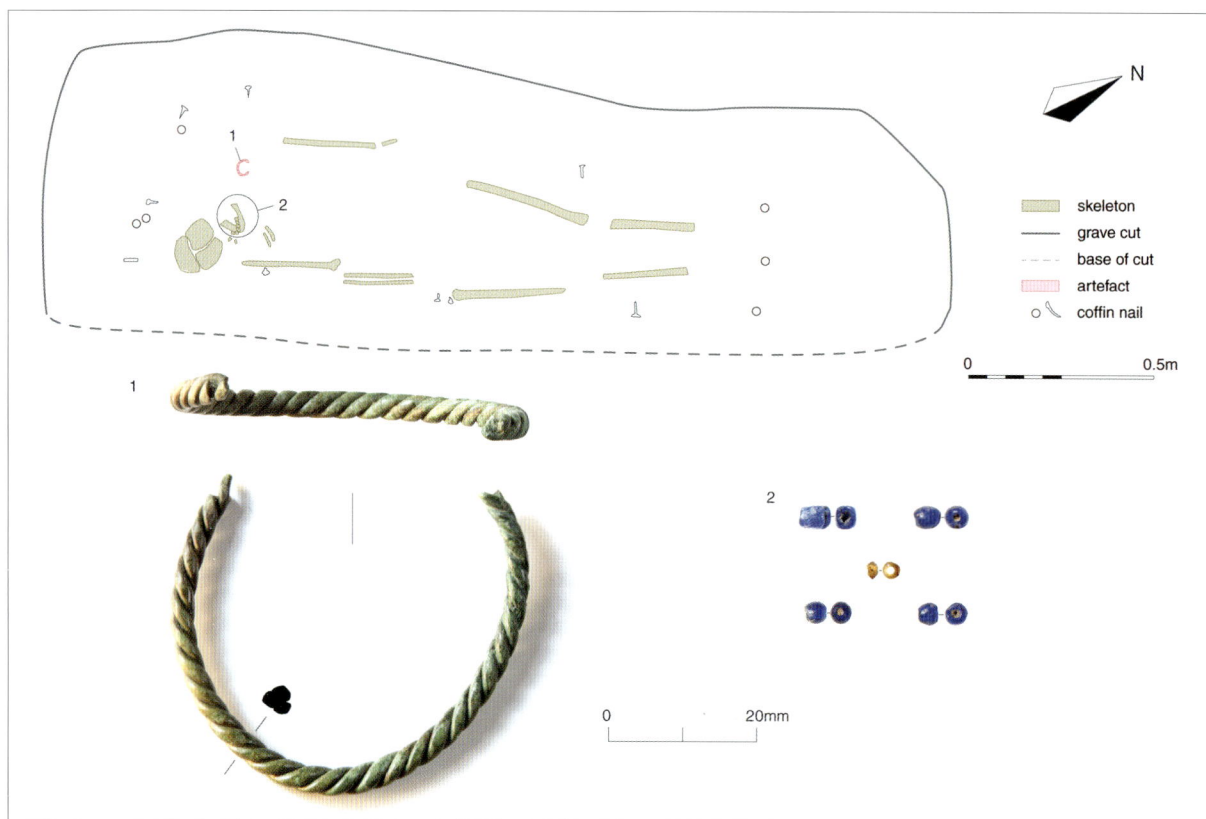

Fig. 3.29   Burial B1173

B1174 (grave 792, Sk 793) (Fig. 3.30)

Grave: north-west–south-east. Rectangular with vertical sides and a flat base, 2.1m x 0.62m x 0.62m deep. Cuts B1169 with which it forms a probable pair.

Human remains: supine with right arm by side and left arm over pelvis, 90% skeletal recovery, age 35–44, male.

Grave goods: B1174.1: iron hobnails x 21. Location: at feet; worn?

Coffin nails: iron x 21 including fragments. Flat-headed; 72–80mm.

Date: 2nd to 4th century (grave goods).

B1175 (grave 795, Sk 796) (Fig. 3.31)

Grave: north-west–south-east. Sub-triangular with gently sloping sides and a flat base, >0.86m x 0.9m x 0.06m deep. A single grey-brown silty clay fill. South-east end truncated by modern garden feature.

Human remains: truncated but the body was probably laid on its right, 35% skeletal recovery, age 25–35, indeterminate sex.

Coffin nails: iron x 2, fragmentary. Shaft fragments.

Grave fill finds: cbm x 3; animal bone: BOS x 1.

Date: not closely dated.

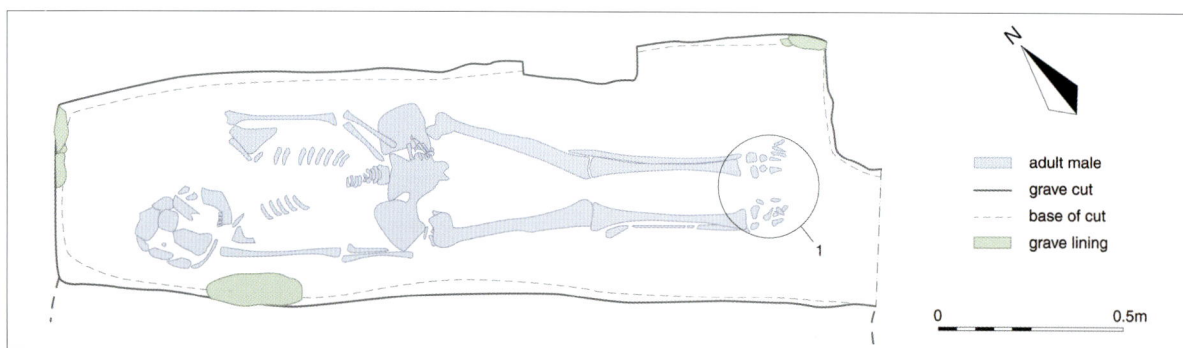

Fig. 3.30   Burial B1174

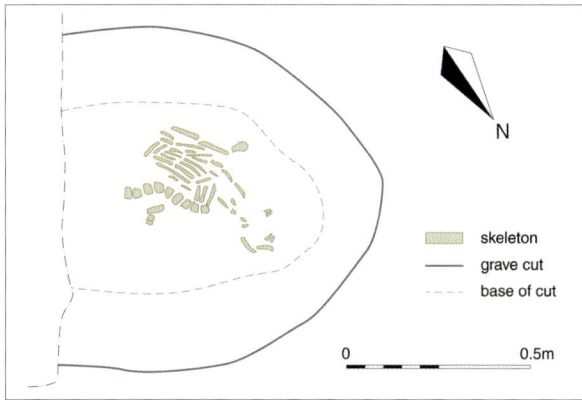

Fig. 3.31 Burial B1175

B1176 (grave 737, Sk 798) (Fig. 3.32)

Grave: north-west–south-east. Sub-rectangular with rounded south-east end, steep/vertical sides to a flat base, >1.9m x 0.77m x 0.22m deep. The single grey-brown clay fill (736) contained abundant charcoal flecks and common stone. The grave fill was cut by B1163 and B1171.

Human remains: supine with both hands over the pelvis, 75% skeletal recovery, age 26–31, sex indeterminate.

Grave goods: B1176.1: iron hobnails x 71. One cluster of 60 by left leg, second cluster of 11 beyond coffin, 0.2m from pelvis.

Coffin nails: iron x 73, most fragmentary. Flat-headed. Complete example is 84mm long.

Grave fill finds: pottery: 32 sherds (TF 35, 9, 6, 74); vessel glass x 1; copper alloy: x 1 stud; animal bone: MM x 2.

Date: 2nd century (grave fill pottery).

B1177 (grave 802, Sk 805) (Figs 3.33–3.34)

Grave: north-west–south-east. Rectangular with slight apsidal north-west end and vertical sides to flat base, 2.21m x 0.64m x 0.44m deep. The grave backfill, 803, was a grey-brown silty clay with frequent small stones.

Human remains: supine with hands over pelvis, 90% skeletal recovery, age 19–24, female.

Grave goods: B1177.1–6 were recovered as part of a soil block which was subsequently micro-excavated (Fig. 3.34). The block contained at least six items, certainly or probably representing armlets/bracelets. The block was located in the area of the right wrist. The items appear not to have been worn but may have been within a bag or similar placed close to the hand.

B1177.1: copper-alloy bracelet. Hollow/tubular form made from thin sheet and very fragmentary. Sub-square in section; the join at the inside edge is possibly soldered. All but the inner face with repoussé decoration; the design is alternating zones of cabled and cross-hatch motifs. Occurrences of hollow form bracelets are rare and Continental origins have been claimed (Swift 2000). Insular origins are thought more likely by Cool (2010, 298), who lists occurrences from five locations in Britain, the majority from graves of 4th-century date. B1177.1 and B1218.1 are similar to an example from Lankhills, Winchester, which is of mid/later 4th-century date (Cool 2010, fig. 3.51). External diameter approximately 70mm; section 6.1mm x 5mm.

B1177.2: shale bracelet. Plain annular form. Sub-circular in section with faceted inner face (as Lawson 1976, fig. 4; no. 26c). Fragmentary and distorted. External diameter 64mm; section 5.7mm x 5.2mm.

B1177.3: bone bracelet. In three fragments, some portions partially decayed. The terminals are squared, each with a small rivet hole. The sheet metal fixing is absent, though the green staining to both terminals indicates that this was of copper alloy. Bracelets of this form were among the most common from the cemeteries at Lankhills (Clarke 1979, 313, type B) and Poundbury, Dorchester (Greep 1993), and are likely to be a 4th-century type. External diameter approximately 70mm; section 6mm x 3.2mm.

B1177.4: bone bracelet. In two fragments, much distorted. The form is as for B1177.3, though with part

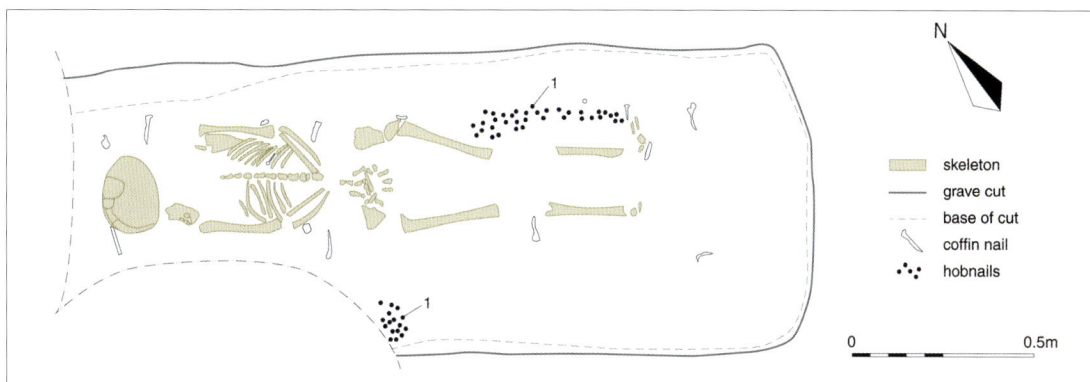

Fig. 3.32 Burial B1176

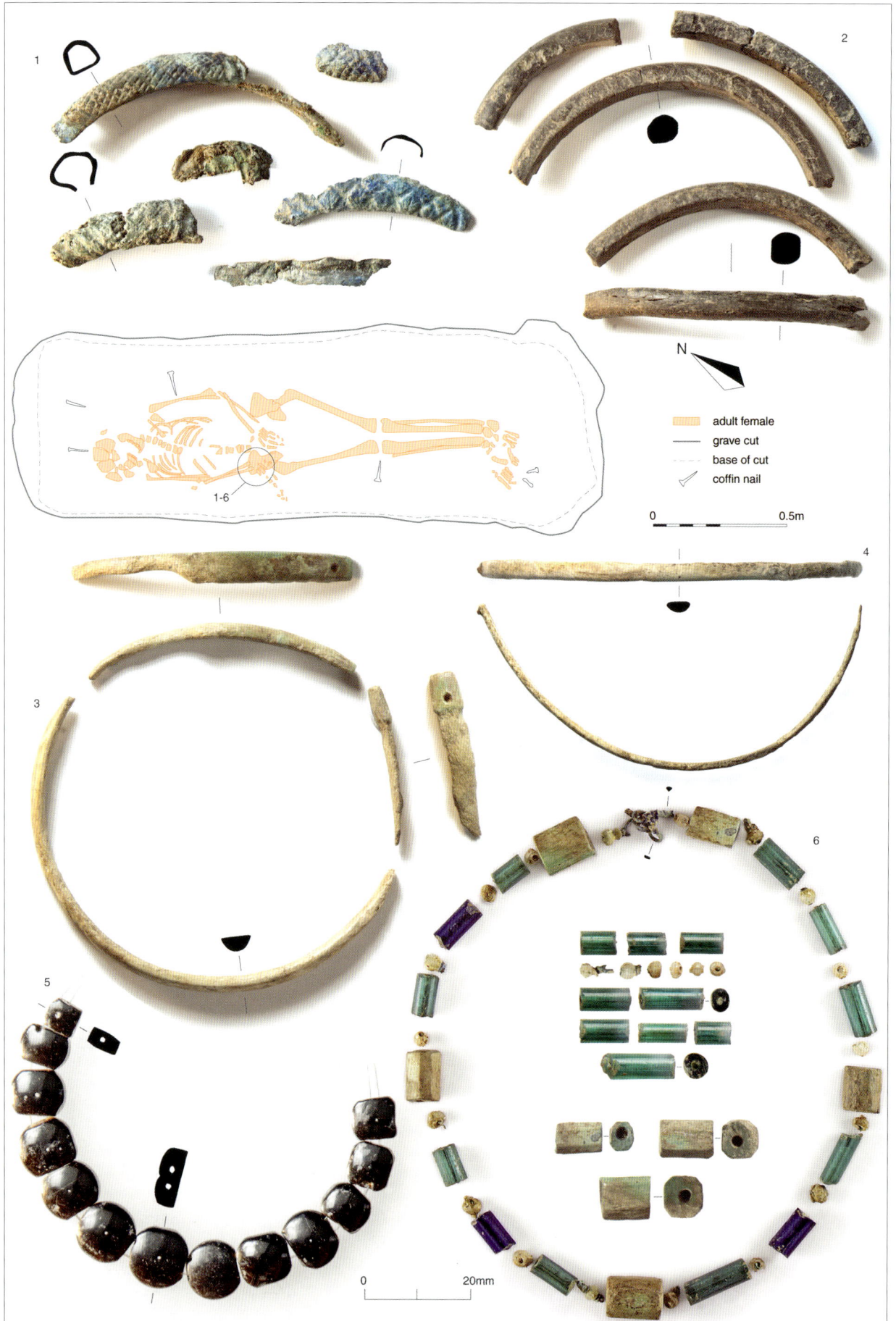

Fig. 3.33 Burial B1177

Fig. 3.34 Burial B1177, artefacts 1–6 during excavation

of the sheet copper-alloy fixing surviving and one iron rivet *in situ*. The bracelet has 'sprung' (straightened) and partially decayed. Section 6.5mm x 2.8mm.

B1177.5: jet arm ornament? Made up of 13 beads (1 is fragmentary), all of similar, sub-circular, plano-convex and double-perforated form. Eight exhibit 'chuck point' indentations to the domed upper surface. Beads of this form are known from 4th-century burials from Colchester (Crummy 1983, 33), Ruxox Farm, Maulden, Bedfordshire (Wells *et al.* 2004, 427, no. 146) and Dunstable, Bedfordshire (Matthews 1981, 62). Diameter 11.4–9.5mm x 10.5–7.3mm; thickness 4.3–3.7mm.

B1177.6: armlet? Comprises 40 beads, of which 5 are of bone, 12 glass and 23 glass/glass paste, fixed to a 'chain' of copper-alloy wire now in approximately 30 small fragments. The original form is uncertain though there are parallels for such articulating neck/arm ornaments, utilising beads of differing materials for example from Dunstable (Matthews 1981, fig. 30, no. 29), Lankhills (Cool 2010, 182, fig. 3.191) and Poundbury (Guido and Mills 1993, fig. 72, no. 5). Bone beads (x 5): faceted, an unequal octagon in section. The use of bone as beads is seemingly rare though the form echoes that of late Roman beads in other materials. Two beads of similar form were recorded from a grave at Lankhills which was dated *c.* AD 350–70 (Clarke 1979, 296). Individual

beads are 9–9.8mm long; 4.8–8mm in section. Glass beads (x 9): cylinder form in translucent green glass (Guido 1978, 94–6). Individual beads are 8.5–10mm long; 3.5mm diameter. Glass beads (x 3): cylinder form in translucent dark blue glass (ibid.). Individual beads are 8–9mm long; 3.5mm diameter. Glass or glass paste beads (x 23): small segmented type (ibid., 91–2), opaque whitish in colour. Individual beads are 2mm long; 2.5mm diameter. The copper-alloy wire chain is much fragmented (approximately 30 fragments) and brittle. The links consist of short straight lengths of wire on to which the beads were secured by knots or twists and with looped over and twisted terminals. There is an elaborately twisted/knotted link which is similar to those in the Poundbury 'necklace' (Guido and Mills 1993, fig. 72, no. 5). The wire is square in section, approximately 0.5mm 'gauge'.

B1177.7: iron hobnails x 7 from the area of the head (2) and feet (5).

Coffin nails: iron x 32, including fragments. Flat-headed; 82–105mm.

Grave fill finds: pottery: 67 sherds (TF 6, 74, 9, 5, 17, 98, 95). Includes a substantial portion of a jar in TF 74, presumably a disturbed cremation vessel; glass x 2; animal bone: O/C x 1, IND x 1.

Date: mid to late 4th century (grave goods).

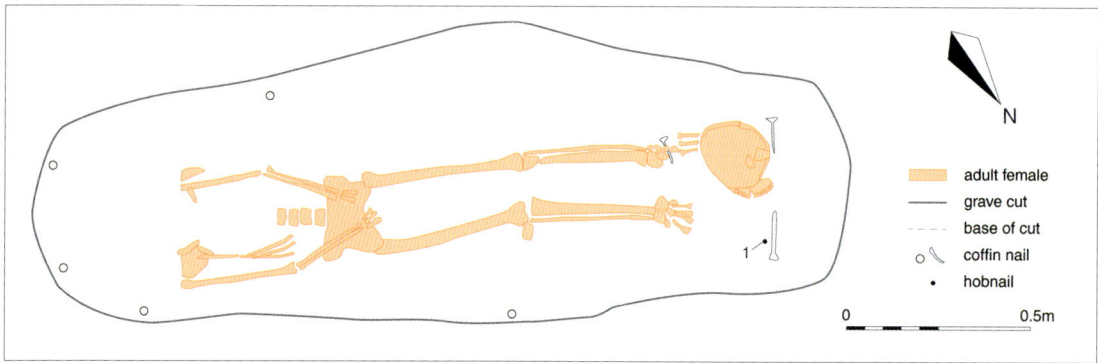

Fig. 3.35   Burial B1178

B1178 (grave 808, Sk 807) (Fig. 3.35)

Grave: south-east–north-west. Rectangular with near vertical sides and a flat base, 2.21m x 0.73m x 0.61m deep. Single fill of grey-brown silty clay containing medium to large limestones, some pitched vertically around grave edge. Cut B1194.

Human remains: supine with hands over pelvis, decapitated with head just below feet, 90% skeletal recovery, age 28–48, female.

Grave goods: B1178.1: iron hobnail x 1. Location: at feet; worn or stray find.

Coffin nails: iron x 23 including fragments. Flat-headed, 75–135mm.

Grave fill finds: pottery: 1 sherd (TF 74).

Date: 2nd to 4th century (grave goods/grave fill pottery).

B1179 (grave 815, Sk 817) (Fig. 3.36)

Grave: north-east–south-west. Sub-rectangular with steep sides to a flat base, 2.1m x 0.76m x 0.21m deep. Single dark brown silty clay fill with some stones. Burial truncated through pelvis by modern pipe trench.

Human remains: supine, 80% skeletal recovery, age 25–35, female.

Grave fill finds: pottery: 11 sherds (TF 6, 74, 5, 9, 17);

glass x 1 (heat-distorted); iron x 3; nail fragments from general grave fill; animal bone: SM x 1, AVE x 1.

Date: 2nd to 4th century (grave fill pottery).

B1180 (grave 820, Sk 821) (Fig. 3.37)

Grave: north-west–south-east. Rectangular with apsidal north-west end, vertical sides to flat base, 2.23m x 0.75m x 0.4m deep. Single fill was a grey-brown silty clay with common small stones. The coffin fitted tightly into the grave.

Human remains: supine or resting on its right side with right arm flexed away from body and left arm over the pelvis, 95% skeletal recovery, age 30–49, female.

Grave goods: B1180.1: jet beads string. Consists of 38 beads, of which 35 are from the head area. All are of cylinder/segmented form. Individual segments (2 to 4) are 2mm long and 3.5mm diameter.

B1180.2: iron hobnail x 1. Location: at feet, worn or stray find.

Coffin nails: iron x 3 including fragments. Flat-headed; measurable example is 82mm.

Grave fill finds: pottery: 3 sherds (TF 98, 74); cbm x 1.

Date: late 3rd to 4th century (grave goods).

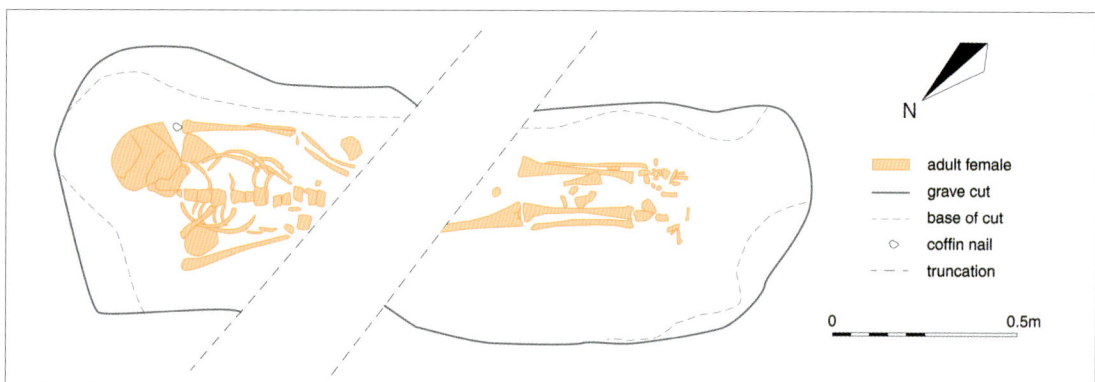

Fig. 3.36   Burial B1179

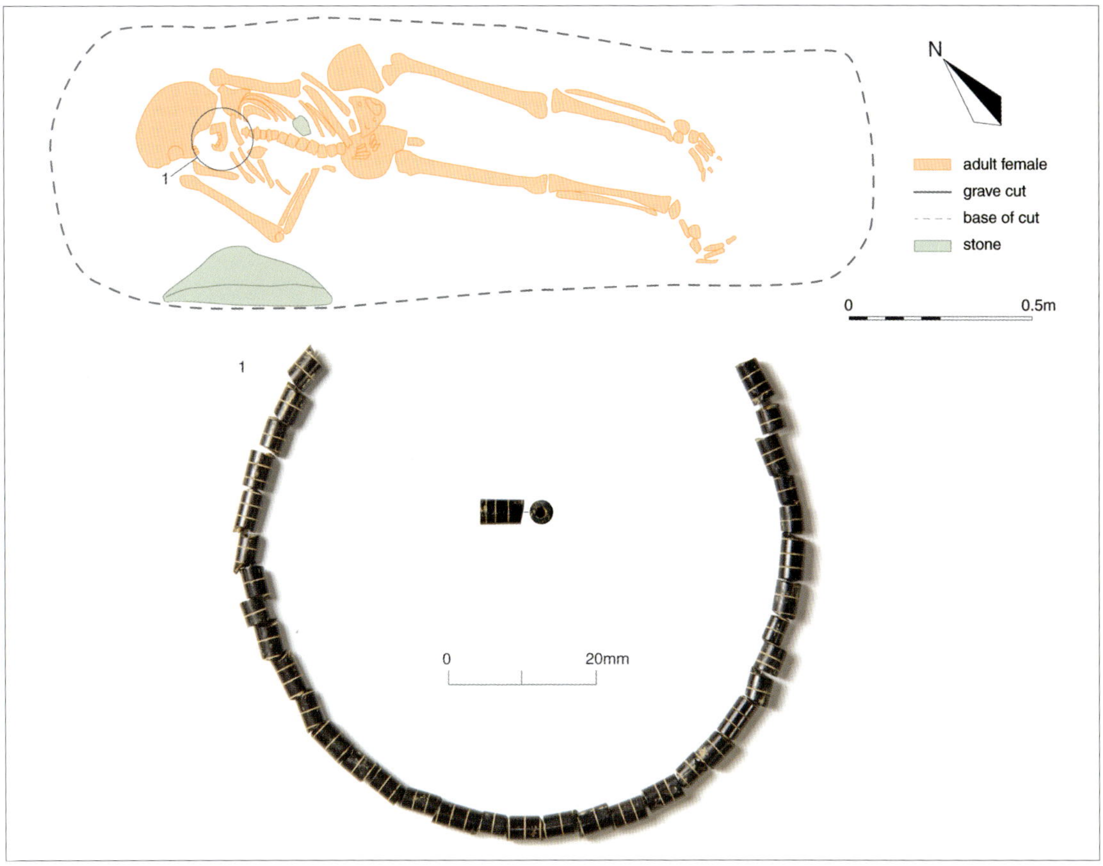

Fig. 3.37   Burial B1180

B1181 (grave 823, Sk 824) (Fig. 3.38)
Grave: north-west–south-east. Rectangular with slightly apsidal south-eastern end, vertical sides to flat base, 2.36m x 0.75m x 0.57m deep. Single grey-brown silty clay fill with very frequent limestone fragments.

Human remains: supine with right arm just over pelvis and left arm by side, 95% skeletal recovery, age 37–44, female.

Coffin nails: iron x 17, most fragmentary. Flat-headed; measurable example is 72mm.

Grave fill finds: animal bone: GAL x 1.

Date: not closely dateable.

B1182 (grave 828, Sk 827) (Fig. 3.39)
Grave: north-west–south-east. Sub-rectangular, steep sides to flat base, 1.98m x 0.74m x 0.12m deep. Single grey-brown silty clay fill contained frequent small and medium stones. Grave cut infilled Ditch B.

Human remains: supine with right hand over pelvis and left lower arm not recovered, 45% skeletal recovery, age 25–35, female.

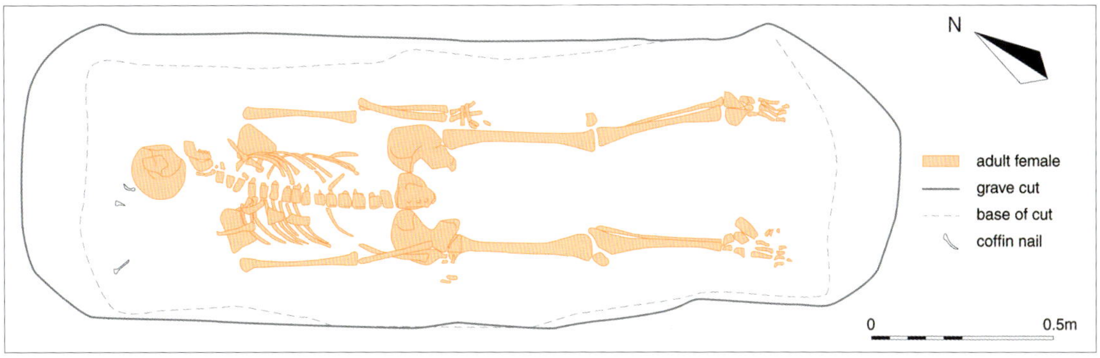

Fig. 3.38   Burial B1181

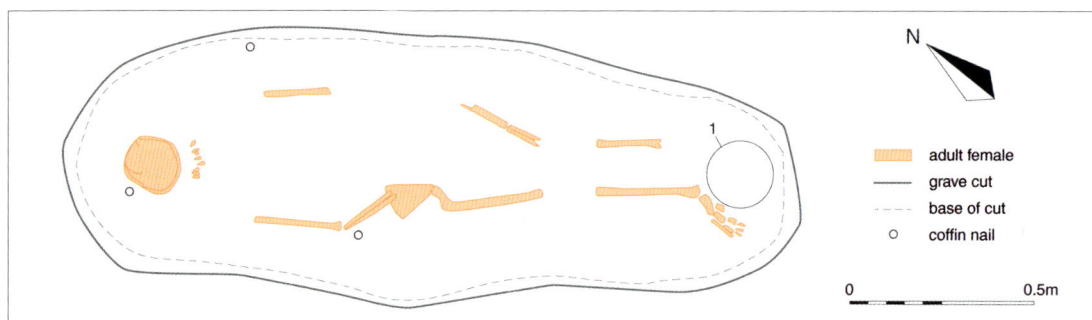

Fig. 3.39   Burial B1182

B1182.1: iron hobnails x 20. Location: at feet; worn?

Coffin nails: iron x 6, all fragmentary. Flat-headed.

Grave fill finds: animal bone: SUS x 1.

Date: 2nd to 4th century (grave goods).

B1183 (grave 829, Sk 830) (Fig. 3.40)

Grave: north-west–south-east. Sub-rectangular, very steep sides to flat base, 2.45m x 0.8m x 0.5m maximum. Single orange-brown silty clay fill with frequent small and medium stones.

Human remains: supine with right arm by side and left arm over pelvis, 95% skeletal recovery, age 37–58, male.

Coffin nails: iron x 26, most fragmentary. Flat-headed; 2 measurable examples are 70mm.

Grave fill finds: pottery: 2 sherds (TF 74).

Date: 2nd to 4th century (grave fill pottery).

B1184 (grave 834, Sk 833) (Fig. 3.41)

Grave: north-east–south-west. Rectangular with rounded ends, vertical sides to a flat base, 2.04m x 0.59m x 0.59m deep. The single grey-brown silty clay fill contained frequent small and medium stones.

Skeletal remains: supine with right arm over pelvis and left arm by side, 85% skeletal recovery, age 36–39, male.

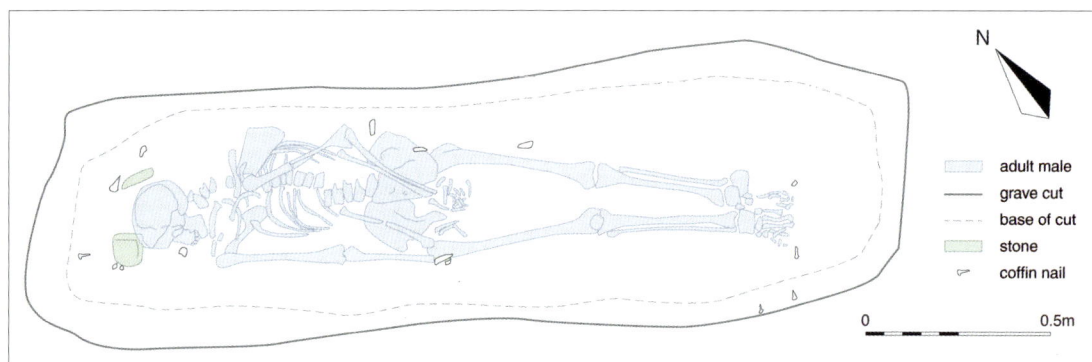

Fig. 3.40   Burial B1183

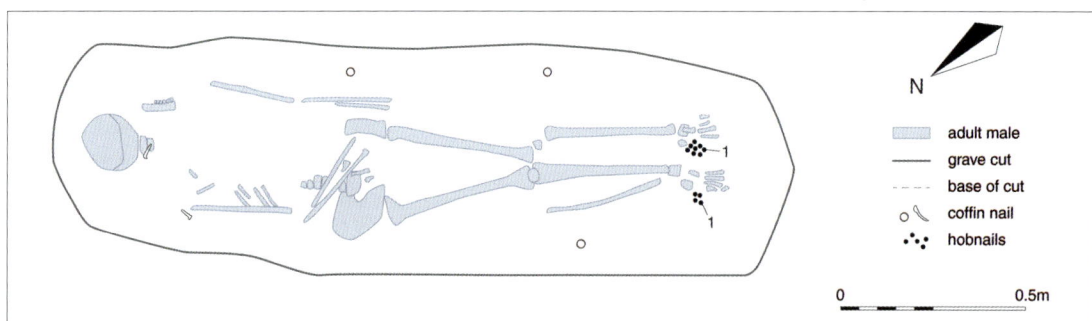

Fig. 3.41   Burial B1184

Grave goods: B1184.1: iron hobnails x 37. Location: at feet; worn?

Coffin nails: iron x 11, all fragmentary. Flat-headed; measurable example 52mm.

Grave fill finds: pottery: 1 sherd (TF 74).

Date: 2nd to 4th century (grave goods/grave fill pottery).

B1185 (grave 835, Sk 836) (Fig. 3.42)
Grave: north–south. Sub-rectangular, vertical sides to flat base, 2.2m x 0.85m x 0.8m deep. A pale yellow-brown silty clay filled the base of the cut to a maximum height of 0.15m (837), and contained small lenses of varying colours (842–4). The principal fill (841) was an orange-brown silty clay with many large limestones (some perhaps a deliberate lining).

Skeletal remains: supine with right arm by side and left hand over pelvis, 90% skeletal recovery, age 20–29, female.

Fig. 3.42   Burial B1185

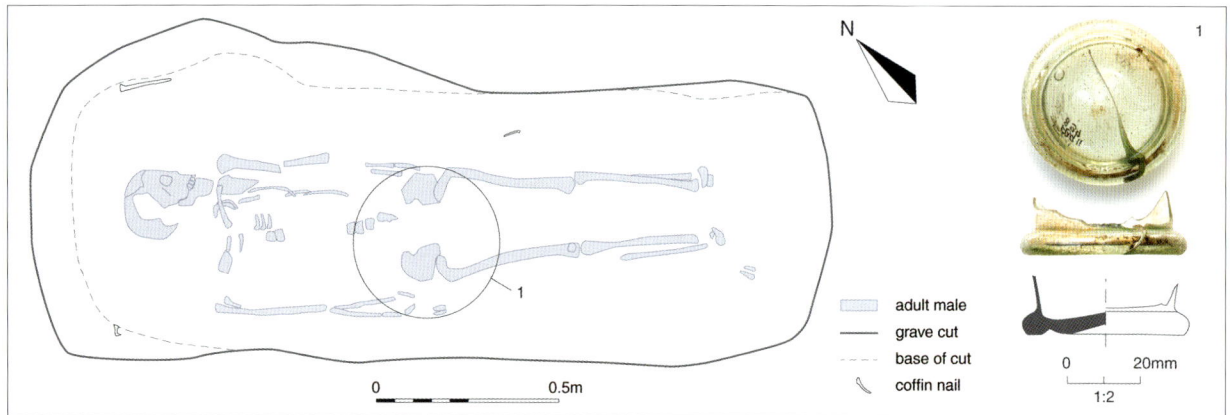

Fig. 3.43   Burial B1186

Grave goods: B1185.1: ten fragments from probably two copper-alloy strip bracelet(s) located at the upper left arm/shoulder. The outer edge is decorated by notches alternately from each face. The end of the largest fragment is bent. It is not clear if this was post-depositional, though other disturbance evident in the grave suggests that this is probable. Strip bracelets were a common form from late Roman Britain and parallels for the decoration include examples from Uley, Gloucestershire (Woodward and Leach 1993, 165, fig. 128. 7). External diameter approximately 70mm; section 2.6mm x 1.2mm.

B1185.2: three fragments from a jet bracelet of plain, annular form with sub-rectangular section (incomplete). Located at upper left arm and probably worn, but fragmentation and disturbance makes this uncertain. Thickness 5.4mm; width 7.4mm; external diameter approximately 66.4mm.

B1185.3: six fragments from a bone or ivory bracelet of 'cable' (s-twist) form. Located at the pelvis close to the right hand and probably worn. Thickness 3.7mm; width 7mm; external diameter uncertain.

B1185.4: iron hobnails x 66. Located (placed?) close to left knee.

Coffin nails: iron x 25 including fragments. Flat-headed; 67–90mm.

Grave fill finds: pottery: 8 sherds (TF 85, 98).

Date: mid to late 4th century (grave goods).

B1186 (grave 838, Sk 840) (Fig. 3.43)
Grave: north-west–south-east. Sub-rectangular with vertical sides to a flat base, 2.2m x 0.81m x 0.59m deep. Single dark brown silty clay fill contained frequent limestone.

Human remains: supine with arms by sides, 40% skeletal recovery, age 23–35, male.

Grave goods: B1186.1: glass vessel in 66 fragments. Location: hands area. The lower portion of a free-blown vessel in greenish colourless glass of the type typical of the 4th century (Cool and Price 1995, 218). Globular lower body with a tubular base ring and a concavity at the base centre. The most likely vessel form it represents is a globular, two-handled jug of a type made throughout the 4th century (Isings 1957, form 129, 220–1).

Coffin nails: iron x 7, all fragmentary. Flat-headed.

Date: 4th century (grave goods).

B1187 (grave 848, Sk 847) (Fig. 3.44)
Grave: north-west–south-east. Sub-rectangular with vertical sides to a flat base, 1.99m x 0.74m x 0.43m deep. Single fill was grey-brown silty clay with frequent

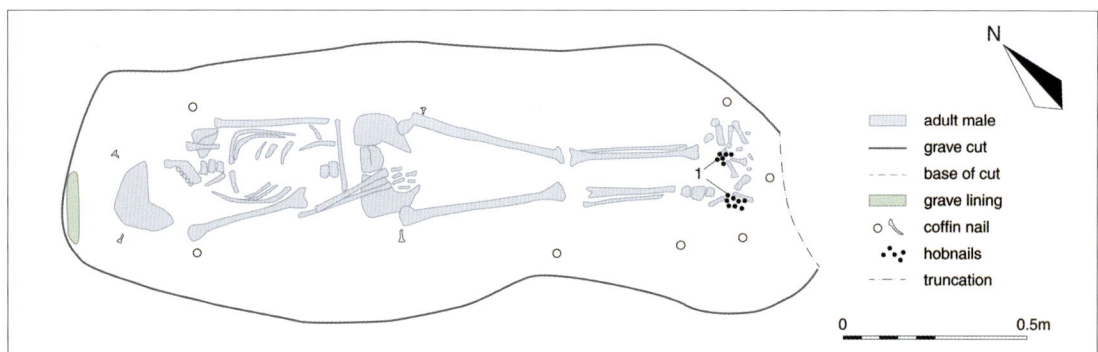

Fig. 3.44   Burial B1187

medium to large stones. This fill was cut by B1189. This grave cut B1192 and B1194.

Human remains: supine with right arm over pelvis and left arm over abdomen, 90% skeletal recovery, age 41–55, male.

Grave goods: B1187.1: iron hobnails x 85. Location: at feet; worn.

Coffin nails: iron x 14, most fragmentary. Flat-headed. Measurable examples 60mm and 110mm.

Grave fill finds: pottery: 10 sherds (TF 74).

Date: mid 3rd to 4th century (grave fill pottery).

B1188 (grave 849, Sk 850) (Fig. 3.45)

Grave: north-east–south-west. Rectangular with vertical sides to a flat base, 2.1m x 0.85m x 0.44m deep. Single pale yellow-brown sandy clay fill with common medium-sized stones. There was a 0.4m-wide gap between the feet and the end of the grave cut.

Human remains: prone with both hands beneath pelvis, 75% skeletal recovery, age 42–68, female.

Grave goods: B1188.1: iron hobnails x 22. Location: at feet; worn.

Coffin nails: iron x 14, all fragmentary. Flat-headed.

Grave fill finds: pottery: 3 sherds (TF 74).

Date: 2nd to 4th century (grave goods/grave fill pottery).

B1189 (grave 854; Sk 853) (Fig. 3.46)

Grave: north-west–south-east. Sub-rectangular with vertical sides to flat base, 2.03m x 0.87m x 0.52m deep. Grey-brown silty clay fill with abundant medium and large limestones. One stone pitched vertically between coffin and grave cut. Grave cut B1187 and B1192.

Human remains: supine with both hands over pelvis, 90% skeletal recovery, age 32–48, male.

Grave goods: B1189.1: iron hobnails x 60. Location: at feet; worn.

Coffin nails: iron x 18, most fragmentary. Flat-headed. Measurable examples are 66mm and 75mm.

Date: 2nd to 4th century (grave goods).

B1190 (grave 855, Sk 856) (Fig. 3.47)

Grave: north-west–south-east. Sub-rectangular with slightly curved south-western side, vertical sides to a flat base, 2.2m x 0.7m x 0.4m deep. The single brown silty clay fill contained frequent medium-sized stones.

Human remains: supine with right arm flexed to left

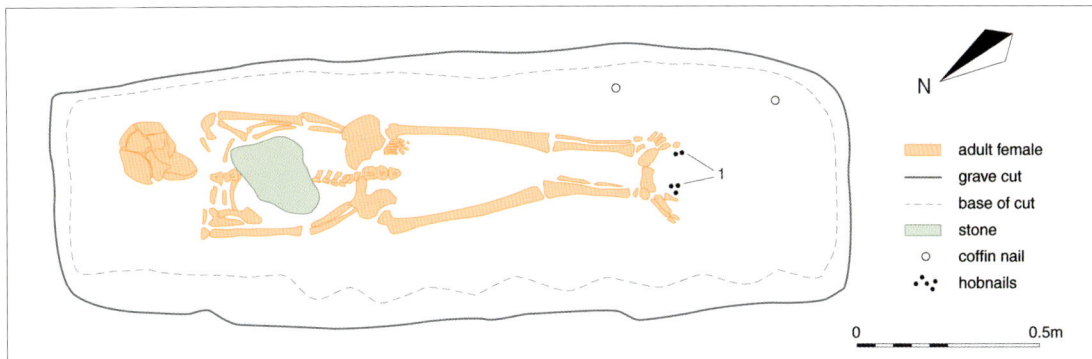

Fig. 3.45   Burial B1188

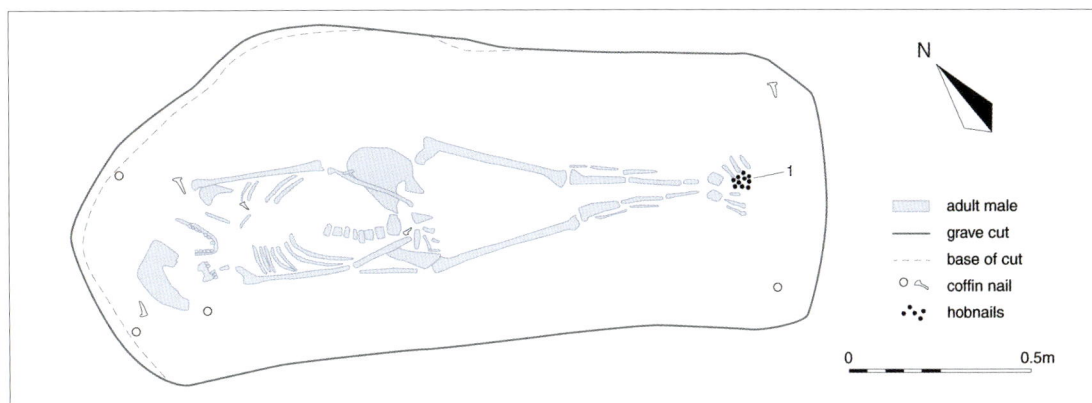

Fig. 3.46   Burial B1189

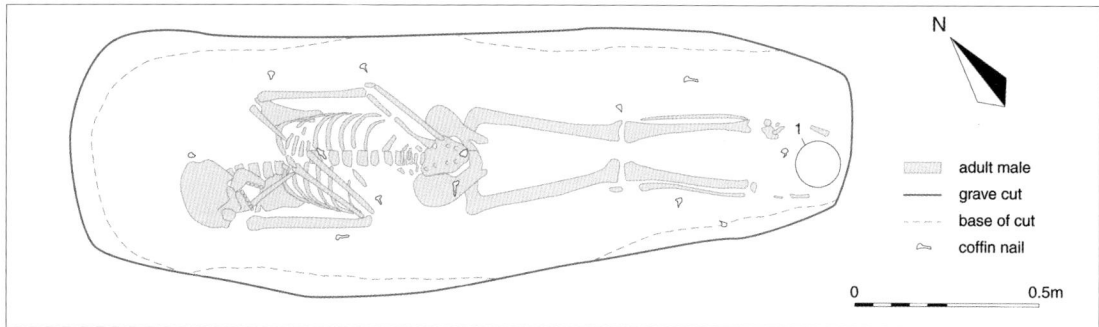

Fig. 3.47   Burial B1190

shoulder and left arm over pelvis, 95% skeletal recovery, age 37–44, male.

Grave goods: B1190.1: iron hobnails x 123. Location: at feet; worn.

Coffin nails: iron x 18, all fragmentary. Flat-headed. None measurable.

Grave fill finds: pottery: 4 sherds (TF 6, 9, 74).

Date: 2nd to 4th century (grave goods/grave fill pottery).

B1191 (grave 860, Sk 859) (Fig. 3.48)
Grave: north-west–south-east. Sub-rectangular with rounded south-eastern end, 2.35m x 0.73m x 0.61m

deep. A single grey-brown silty clay fill contained medium to large limestones.

Human remains: supine with right arm by side and left arm over abdomen, 95% skeletal recovery, age 31–45, male.

Coffin nails: iron x 14, all fragmentary. Flat-headed. None measurable.

Date: not closely dateable.

B1192 (grave 874, Sk 873) (Fig. 3.49)
Grave: north-west–south-east. Sub-rectangular with rounded base, 2.15m x 0.7m x 0.65m deep. A single

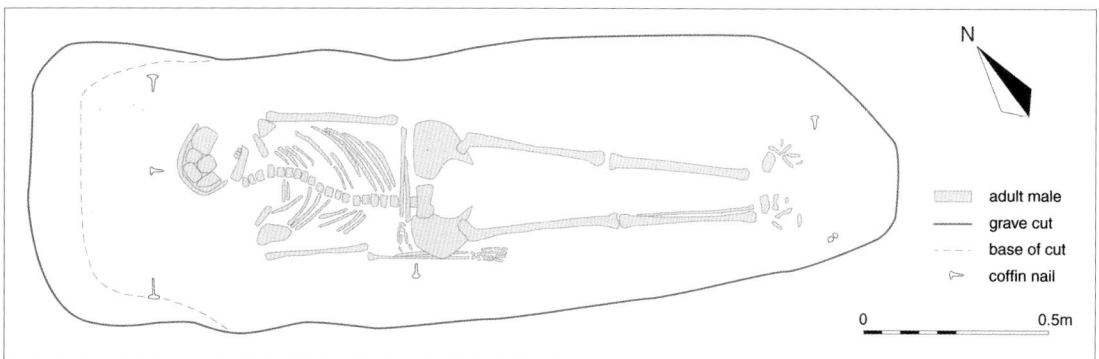

Fig. 3.48   Burial B1191

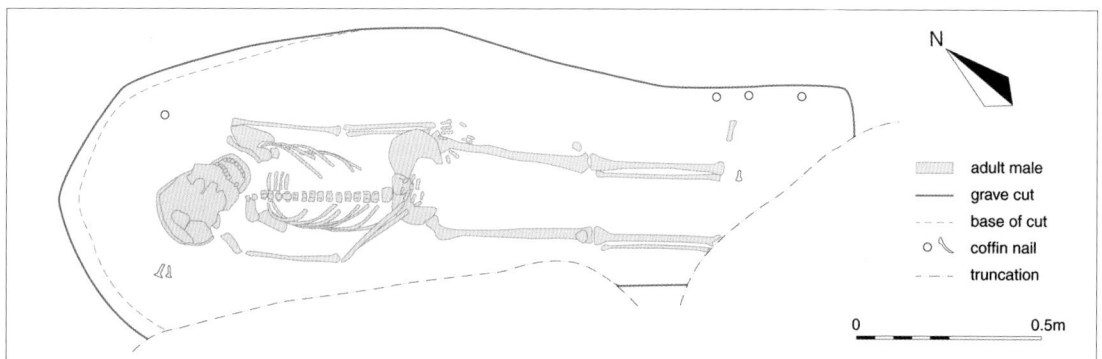

Fig. 3.49   Burial B1192

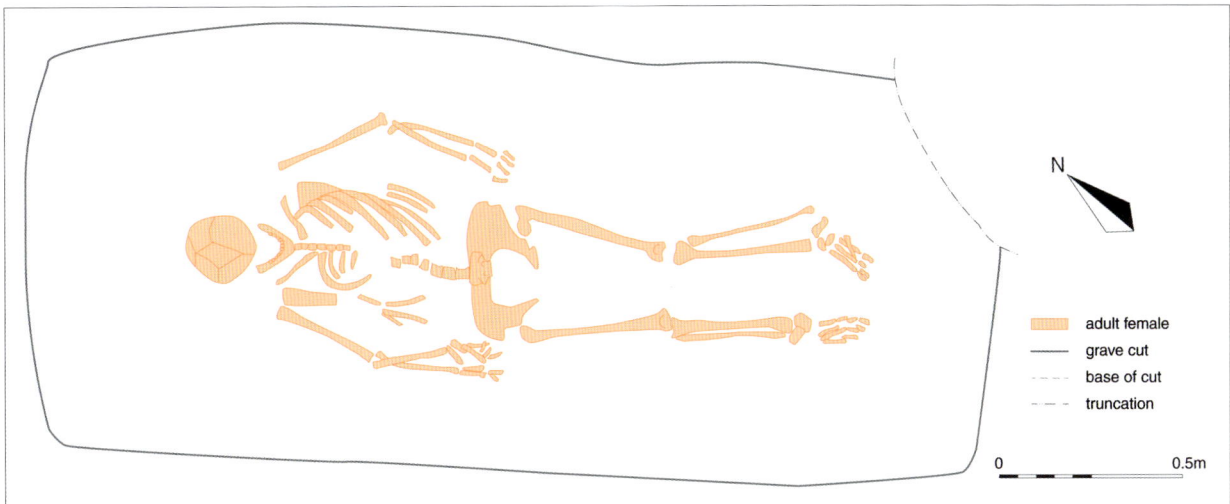

Fig. 3.50   Burial B1193

fill of grey-brown silty clay with abundant medium and large limestone fragments. This grave cut B1194 and was in itself cut by B1187 and B1189.

Human remains: supine with right hand over pelvis and left arm by side, 90% skeletal recovery, age 17–18, male.

Coffin nails: iron x 12, all fragmentary. Flat-headed. None measurable.

Grave fill finds: pottery: 26 sherds (TF 74, 98).

Date: late 3rd to 4th century (grave fill pottery).

B1193 (grave 862, Sk 875) (Fig. 3.50)
Grave: north-west–south-east. Sub-rectangular, with vertical sides and a flat base, 2.74m x 1.16m x 0.48m deep. This is a large grave *c.* 0.5m wider and 0.8m longer than the skeleton. Single grey-brown silty clay fill with frequent large limestones. The south-eastern end of the grave was truncated during decontamination works. The southern corner of the grave cut the fill of Ditch B.

Human remains: supine, with arms were flexed outwards, 95% skeletal recovery, age 27–40, female.

Coffin nails: iron x 17, all fragmentary. Flat-headed. None measurable. The distribution of nails (not marked on the plan) shows that either the coffin was 0.3m longer than the body or there was a box beyond the head.

Grave fill finds: pottery: 34 sherds (TF 74, 9, 98); cbm x 2; lead x 1 fragment; iron hobnail x 1; animal bone: O/C x 1.

Date: 2nd to 4th century (grave fill pottery).

B1194 (grave 878, Sk 877) (Fig. 3.51)
Grave: north-east–south-west. ?Rectangular with very steep sides to a flat base, >0.5m x 0.67m x 0.34m deep. Orange-brown silty clay fill. This grave was cut by B1187, B1192 and B1178.

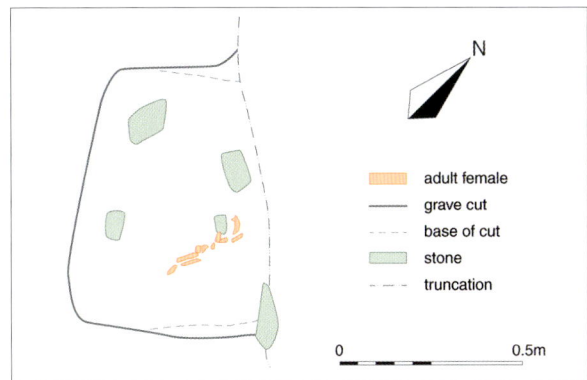

Fig. 3.51   Burial B1194

Human remains: supine, 10% skeletal recovery, age 25–35, female.

Coffin nails: iron x 7, most fragmentary.

Date: not closely dateable.

B1195 (grave 867, Sk 879) (Fig. 3.52)
Grave: north-west–south-east. Sub-rectangular with vertical sides and a flat base, 2.08m x 0.66m x 0.62m deep. The single grey-brown silty clay fill contained abundant limestone fragments in the top 0.3m. The grave cut backfilled Ditch B.

Human remains: supine with arms by sides and ?legs crossed, 90% skeletal recovery, age 25–31, female.

Grave goods: B1195.1: iron hobnails x 32. Location: at feet; ?worn.

Coffin nails: iron x 16, most fragmentary. Flat-headed. 65–90mm.

Grave fill finds: pottery: 9 sherds (TF 5, 74); cbm x 1.

Date: 2nd to 4th century (grave goods/grave fill pottery).

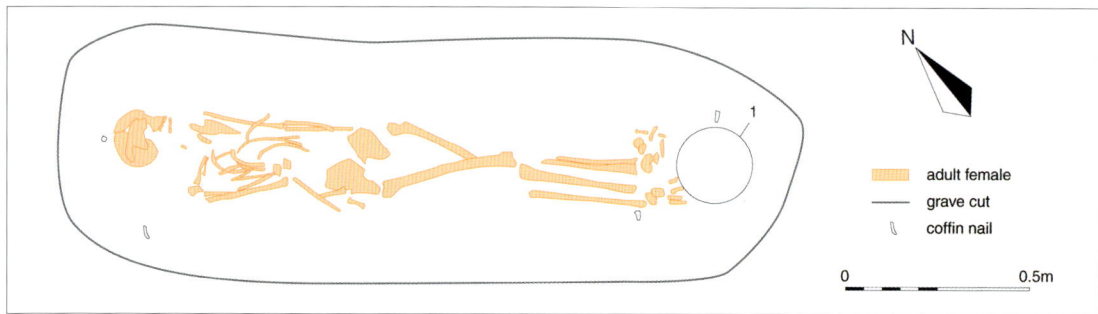

Fig. 3.52   Burial B1195

B1196 (grave 881, Sk 880) (Fig. 3.53)

Grave: north-west–south-east. Sub-rectangular with rounded corners and wider to north-west, steeply sloping sides to flattish base, 1.5m x 1.05m–0.95m x *c*. 0.15m deep. Grey-brown silty clay with common stones. The grave was just long enough to accommodate the body but wider than necessary.

Human remains: supine with hands over pelvis and decapitated, 80% skeletal recovery, age 11–12, indeterminate sex.

Coffin nails: iron x 8, including fragments. Flat-headed.

Grave fill finds: iron: strip x 1, nail fragments x 3; pottery: 2 sherds (TF 154b, 9); cbm x 2; glass x 1.

Date: ?late 3rd to 4th century on the basis of decapitation rite.

B1197 (grave 885, Sk 884) (Fig. 3.54)

Grave: west-north-west–east-south-east. Sub-rectangular, gently sloping sides to a flat base, 1.79m x 0.52m x 0.06m. Single orange-brown silty clay fill. The grave was cut by B1198 and modern truncation.

Human remains: supine, 10% skeletal recovery, age >18, female.

No artefacts recovered.

Date: not closely dateable.

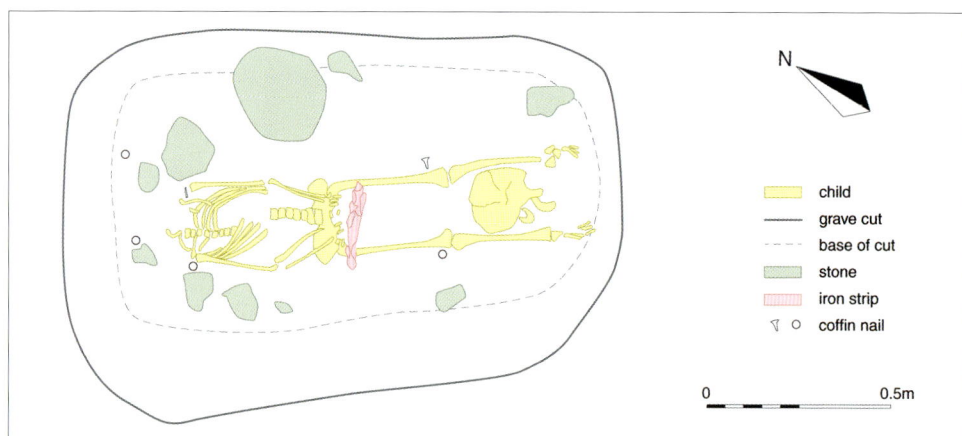

Fig. 3.53   Burial B1196

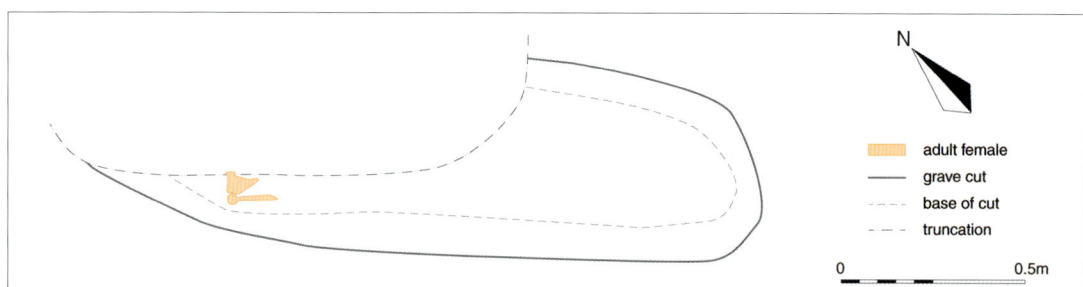

Fig. 3.54   Burial B1197

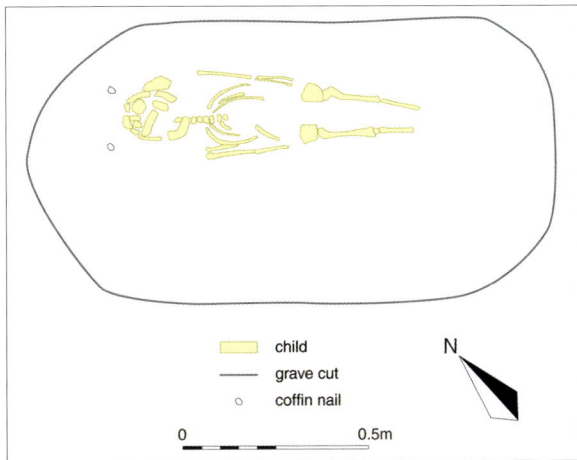

Fig. 3.55 Burial B1198

B1198 (grave 888, Sk 887) (Fig. 3.55)

Grave: north-west–south-east. Sub-rectangular with rounded corners, vertical sides to a flat base, 1.42m x 0.74m x 0.54m. Single grey-brown silty clay fill containing abundant medium to large limestones. This grave cut B1197. The grave was much larger than required to accommodate the burial.

Human remains: supine with arms at side of the body, 80% skeletal recovery, age 6–7, sex indeterminate.

Coffin nails: iron x 5, including fragments. Flat-headed.

Grave fill finds: pottery: 1 sherd (TF 6); animal bone: BOS x 1, MM x 7.

Date: not closely dateable.

B1199 (grave 902, Sk 904) (Fig. 3.56)

Grave: north-west–south-east. Sub-rectangular, steep sides to slightly curved base, 2.28m x 0.67m x 0.15m deep. Single dark brown silty clay fill. The grave was truncated by modern disturbance and heavily contaminated with hydrocarbons.

Human remains: supine with right arm by side and left arm over pelvis, 85% skeletal recovery, age 41–47, male.

Grave fill finds: pottery: 2 sherds (TF 98, 74).

Date: 2nd to 4th century (grave fill pottery).

B1200 (grave 905, Sk 906) (Fig. 3.57)

Grave: north-west–south-east. Sub-rectangular with rounded corners, vertical sides to a flat base, 2.2m x 0.6m x 0.36m deep. Single brown silty clay fill containing many medium-sized stones. The grave was heavily contaminated with hydrocarbons.

Human remains: supine with hands crossed over the pelvis, 90% skeletal recovery, age 26–35, female.

Grave goods: 1200.1: iron hobnails x 45. Location: beyond the feet at the edge of the grave cut.

Coffin nails: iron x 14, including fragments. Flat-headed; 55–76mm.

Grave fill finds: pottery: 5 sherds (TF 74, 6, 98); cbm x 1.

Date: 2nd to 4th century (grave goods/grave fill pottery).

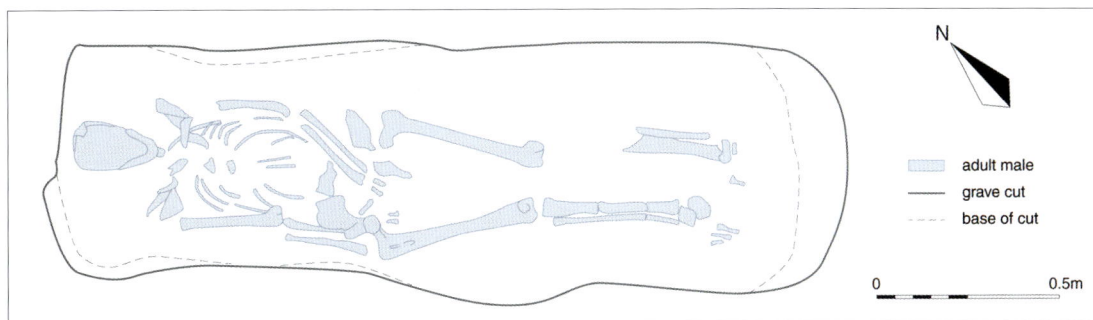

Fig. 3.56 Burial B1199

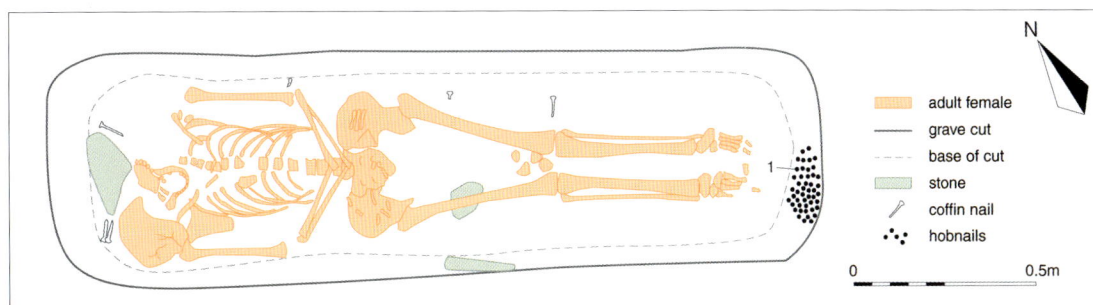

Fig. 3.57 Burial B1200

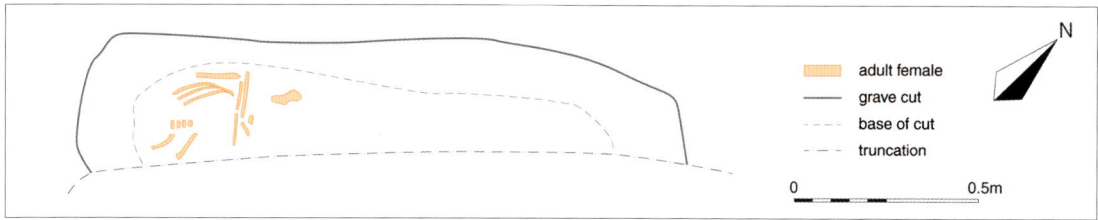

Fig. 3.58   Burial B1201

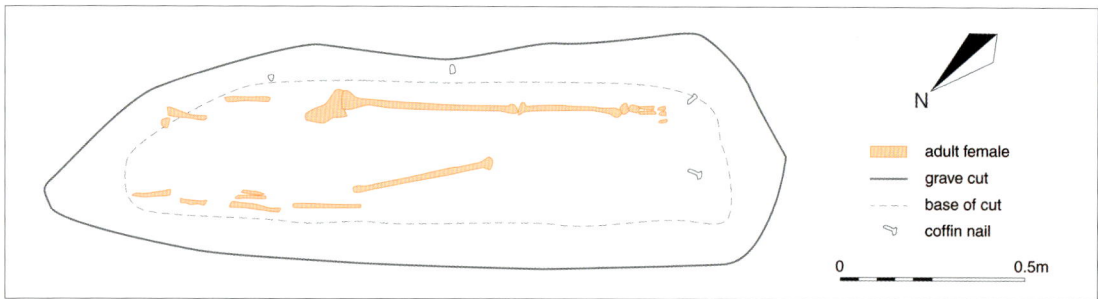

Fig. 3.59   Burial B1202

B1201 (grave 910, Sk 909) (Fig. 3.58)

Grave: south-west–north-east. Sub-rectangular, very shallow with a flat base, 1.63m x >0.29m x 0.04m deep. Dark grey silty clay fill with frequent small stones. Contaminated with hydrocarbons. This grave was cut by B1202.

Human remains: supine with left arm over lower chest, 20% skeletal recovery, age >18, female.

Grave fill finds: pottery: 8 sherds (TF 98, 35, 95, 74).

Date: 2nd to 4th century (grave fill pottery).

B1202 (grave 913, Sk 912) (Fig. 3.59)

Grave: north-east–south-west. Sub-triangular, very shallow with flat base, 1.98m x 0.57m x 0.04m. Dark grey silty clay with frequent small stones. Contaminated with hydrocarbons. This grave cut B1201 and B1206.

Human remains: supine with arms by side, 20% skeletal recovery, age 40–44, female.

Coffin nails: iron x 6, including fragments. Flat-headed.

Grave fill finds: pottery: 7 sherds (TF 74, 154b [Drag. 37]).

Date: 3rd to 4th century (grave fill pottery).

B1203 (grave 914, Sk 915) (Fig. 3.60)

Grave: north-east–south-west. Rectangular with apsidal north-east end, vertical sides to a flat base, 2.13m x 0.6m x 0.19m deep. Single brown silty clay fill with frequent small stones.

Human remains: supine with right arm by side and left arm at 90° over pelvis, 95% skeletal recovery, age 29–43, male.

Grave goods: B1203.1: iron hobnails x 44. Location: at feet; ?worn.

Coffin nails: iron x 4, including fragments. Flat-headed, none measureable.

Grave fill finds: pottery: 15 sherds (TF 98, 74).

Date: 2nd to 4th century (grave goods/grave fill pottery).

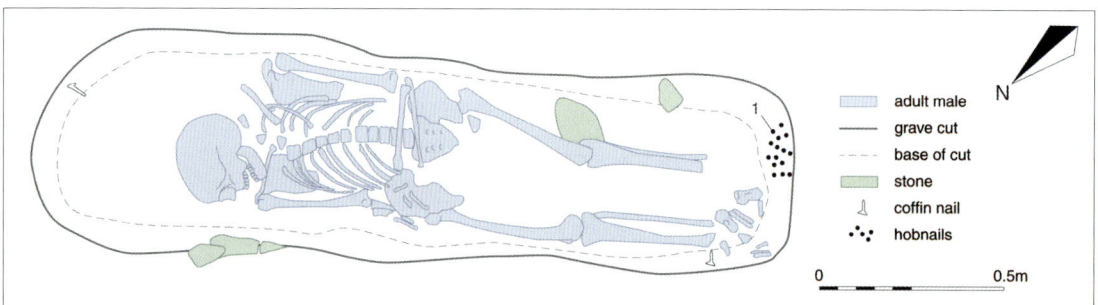

Fig. 3.60   Burial B1203

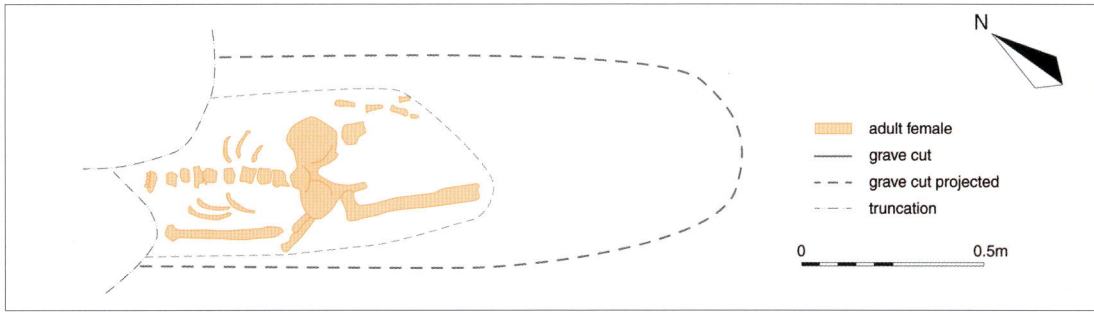

Fig. 3.61 Burial B1204

B1204 (grave 917, Sk 918) (Fig. 3.61)
Grave: north-west–south-east. Little survived of the cut, *c.* 0.9m x 0.45m x 0.1m deep. Single brown silty clay fill. The northern end of grave was cut by modern disturbance and the southern end had been truncated.

Human remains: prone with left arm beneath pelvis, 65% skeletal recovery, age 17–19, female.

No artefacts recovered.

Date: not closely dateable.

B1205 (grave 920, Sk 921) (Fig. 3.62)
Grave: north-west–south-east. Sub-rectangular with rounded ends, steep sides and a flat base, 1.35m x 0.6m x 0.17m deep.

Human remains: supine with right arm over abdomen/pelvis and left arm over pelvis and legs, the legs tightly flexed, 75% skeletal recovery, age *c.* 9, sex indeterminable.

Grave goods: B1205.1: iron hobnails x 44. Location: at feet; ?worn.

Coffin nails: iron x 4, including fragments. Flat-headed; none measurable.

Grave fill finds: pottery: 15 sherds (TF 98, 74).

Date: 2nd to 4th century (grave fill pottery).

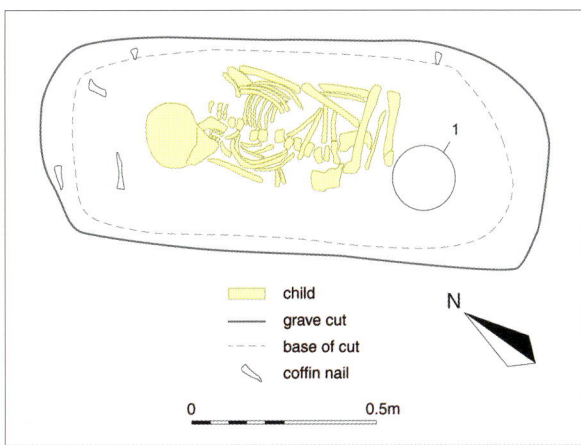

Fig. 3.62 Burial B1205

B1206 (grave 925, Sk 926) (not illustrated)
Grave: north-east–south-west. Rectangular with steep sides and a slightly uneven base, 1.8m x 0.45m x 0.2m deep. Dark grey silty clay fill. Contaminated with hydrocarbons. This grave was cut by B1202.

Human remains: supine, 75% skeletal recovery, age 42–58, male.

Grave goods: B1206.1: iron hobnail x 1. Location: at feet; ?worn or stray find.

Coffin nails: possible single iron fragment from grave fill.

Grave fill finds: pottery: 13 sherds (TF 74, 98); animal bone: O/C x 1.

Date: 2nd to 4th century (grave goods/grave fill pottery).

B1207 (grave 1000, Sk 1001) (Figs 3.63–3.64)
Grave: north-east–south-west. Rectangular with apsidal ends, vertical sides to a flat base, 2.25m x 0.84m x 0.61m deep. A 0.41m x 0.02m by 0.12m deep calcareous pinkish white deposit had two coffin nails embedded in it and appeared to represent a part of the coffin. It may either be a natural accretion or have derived from a lime coating on the coffin (Fig. 3.64). The rest of the grave backfill was a grey-brown silty clay with frequent limestone rubble. This grave was cut by the Anglo-Saxon pit 1004/5066.

Human remains: supine with hands crossed over pelvis, 80% skeletal recovery, age 31–41, female.

Coffin nails: iron x 22, including fragments. Flat-headed, none measurable.

Grave fill finds: pottery: 16 sherds. (TF 74, 9, 98, 6, 95); Anglo-Saxon pottery x 2 (F1, F5); modern pottery x 1; cbm x 6; worked flint x 1; animal bone: BOS x 2, LM x 1, MM x 2.

Date: 2nd to 4th century, but some later contamination (grave fill pottery).

B1208 (grave 1103, Sk 1104) (Fig. 3.65)
Grave: north-east–south-west. Sub-rectangular with vertical sides to a flat base, 2.26m x 0.65m x 0.26m deep. Single brown silty clay fill with common medium stones. The feet of the skeleton were *c.* 0.3m from the end of the grave cut. One coffin nail was found in this

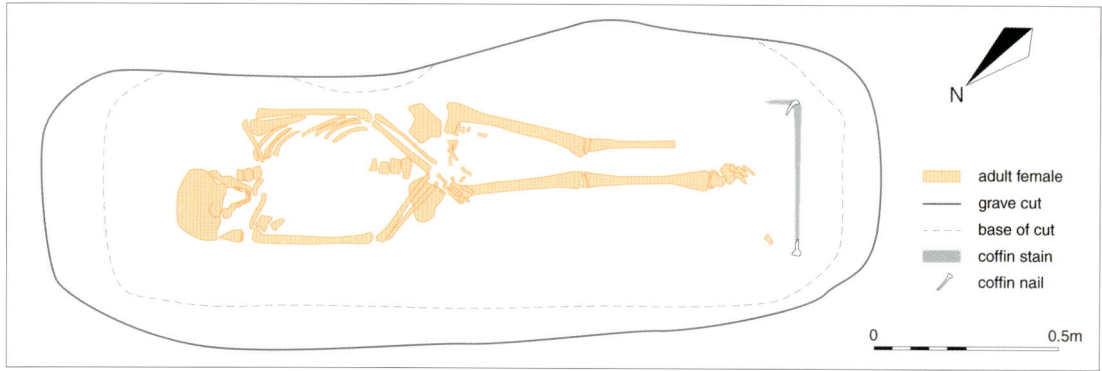

Fig. 3.63   Burial B1207

Fig. 3.64   Detail of possible lime coating to wooden coffin containing B1207

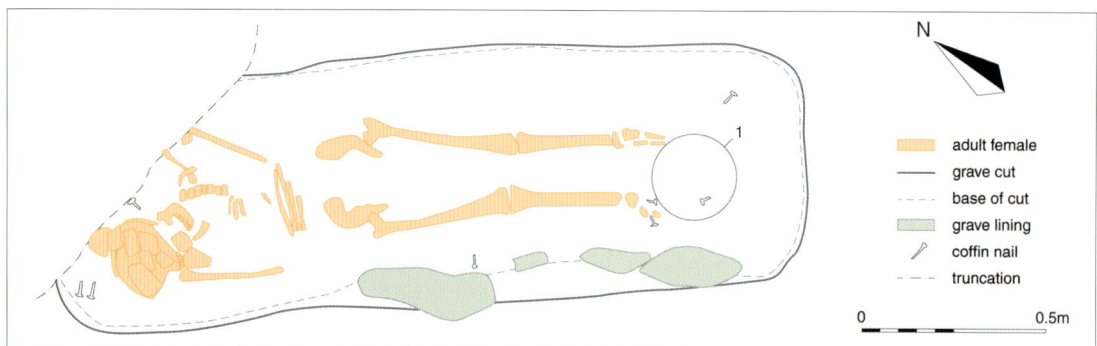

Fig. 3.65   Burial B1208

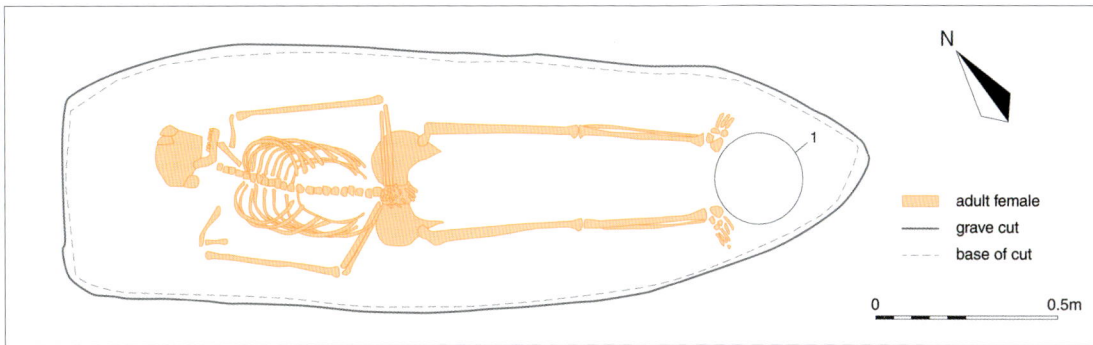

Fig. 3.66   Burial B1209

gap. The north end of the grave was disturbed by a modern intrusion.

Human remains: supine with arms crossed over abdomen, 85% skeletal recovery, age 31–37, female.

Grave goods: B1208.1: iron hobnails x 16. Location: at feet; ?worn.

Coffin nails: iron x 16 including fragments: Flat-headed; none measurable.

Date: 2nd to 4th century (grave goods).

B1209 (grave 1107, Sk 1111) (Fig. 3.66)
Grave: north-west–south-east. Sub-rectangular tapering to the south-east with vertical sides to a flat base, 2.17m x 0.71m x 0.12m deep. Very dark grey silty clay fill containing charcoal, pottery and burnt bone. This grave cut B1211 and the abundant charcoal, *c.* 200g of cremated bone and pottery in the grave backfill suggests that it had disturbed an earlier pyre or cremation burial.

Human remains: supine with both hands over pelvis, 85% skeletal recovery, age 43–66, female.

Grave goods: B1209.1: iron hobnails x 26. Location: at feet; ?worn. One hobnail from the skull area.

Coffin nails: iron x 61 including fragments. Flat-headed; none measurable.

Grave fill finds: pottery: 265 sherds (TF 74, 98, 35, 17, 9, 6, 154b, 154a, 5, 82, 88); iron sheet fragments; glass x 4 fragments; stone tessera x 1; animal bone: BOS x 2, O/C x 2, SUS x 1, LM x 1, MM x 2, AVE x 1.

Date: the bulk of the pottery from the grave fills is of mid to late 2nd-century date although there are some sherds of late 3rd to 4th-century date. The latter are conceivably intrusive.

B1210 (grave 1114, Sk 1113) (Fig. 3.67)
Grave: south-west–north-east. Sub-rectangular narrowing to north-east, sloping sides to a flat base, 1.77m x 0.52m x 0.19m deep. Grey-brown silty clay fill with frequent stones.

Human remains: supine with left arm extended and right arm bent across abdomen, 85% skeletal recovery, age 31–37, male.

Coffin nails: iron x 17, including fragments. Flat-headed, none measurable.

Grave fill finds: pottery: 13 sherds (TF 74, 5, 4, 6, 98); glass x 1; animal bone: MM x 2.

Date: 2nd century (grave fill pottery).

B1211 (grave 1117, Sk 1116) (Fig. 3.68)
Grave: south-west–north-east. Heavily truncated; possibly sub-rectangular with shallow sides to flat base, >0.5m x >0.5m x 0.08m deep. Very dark grey silty clay fill with much charcoal and cremated bone. Grave cut by B1209 and modern truncation.

Human remains: body position uncertain, 20% skeletal recovery, age 25–35, sex indeterminable.

Coffin nails: iron x 14 including fragments. Flat-headed, none measurable.

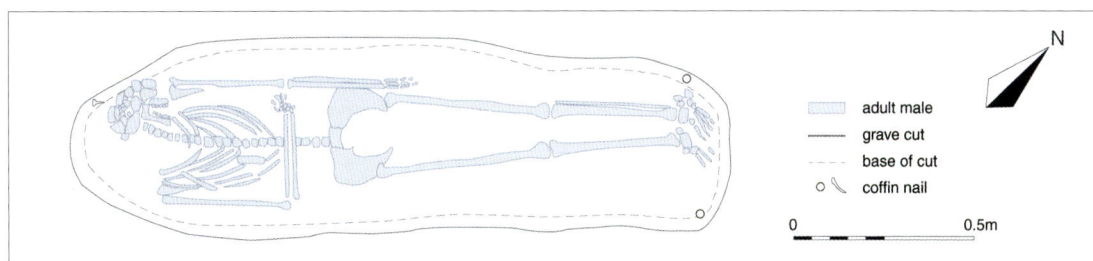

Fig. 3.67   Burial B1210

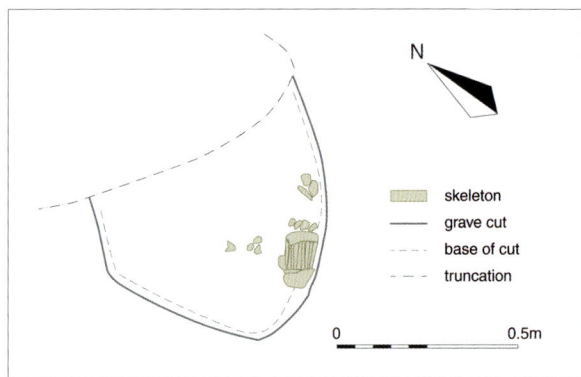

Fig. 3.68   Burial B1211

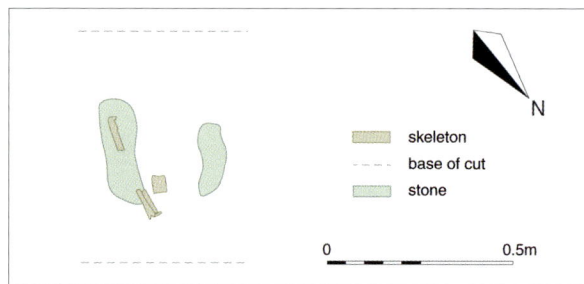

Fig. 3.70   Burial B1213

Grave fill finds: animal bone: BOS x 1.

Date: Not closely dateable, but if B1209, which it is cut by, is of mid–late 2nd-century date it cannot be any later than that.

B1212 (grave 1118, Sk 1119) (Fig. 3.69)

Grave: north-east–south-west. Sub-rectangular with steep sides and flat base, 1.99m x 0.56m–0.67m x 0.1m deep. Brown clay fill.

Human remains: supine arms crossed over pelvis, 35% skeletal recovery, age ≥46, sex indeterminate.

Grave goods: B1212.1: iron hobnails x 14. Location: at feet; ?worn.

Coffin nails: iron x 12, including fragments. Flat-headed; measurable example 72mm.

Grave fill finds: pottery: 2 sherds (TF 74); cbm x 1.

Date: 2nd to 3rd century (grave goods/grave fill pottery).

B1213 (grave 1121, Sk 1122) (Fig. 3.70)

Grave: no grave cut survived but the skeletal remains suggest a south-west–north-east orientation. Brown silty clay fill.

Human remains: supine, 10% skeletal recovery, age >18 and indeterminate sex.

No artefacts recovered.

Date: not closely dateable.

B1214 (grave 1127, Sk 1128) (Fig. 3.71)

Grave: north-west–south-east. Sub-rectangular with steep sides to a flat base, *c.* 2m x 0.65m x 0.1m deep. Brown silty clay fill with some vertically pitched limestone slabs placed at north-east end of grave. The grave was truncated by modern construction and cut by a pipe trench.

Human remains: supine with left arm by side and right arm over pelvis, 80% skeletal recovery, age 32–40, female.

Grave goods: B1214.1: copper-alloy bracelet. Penannular heavy cast type; angular oval hoop. Grooved decoration to tapering terminals. Location: at right wrist, worn. Diameter 68mm; section 3mm x 2.5mm.

Coffin nails: iron x 29, including fragments. Flat-headed, none measurable.

Grave fill finds: animal bone: LM x 1.

Date: late 3rd to 4th century (grave goods).

B1215 (grave 1132, Sk 1131) (Fig. 3.72)

Grave: north-west–south-east, rectangular with near vertical sides to a flat base, 2.49m x 0.81m x 0.19m deep. The single grey-brown sandy clay fill contained common medium-sized stones. Grave truncated by modern development.

Human remains: supine with right arm over abdomen and left arm on chest, 85% skeletal recovery, age 32–53, female.

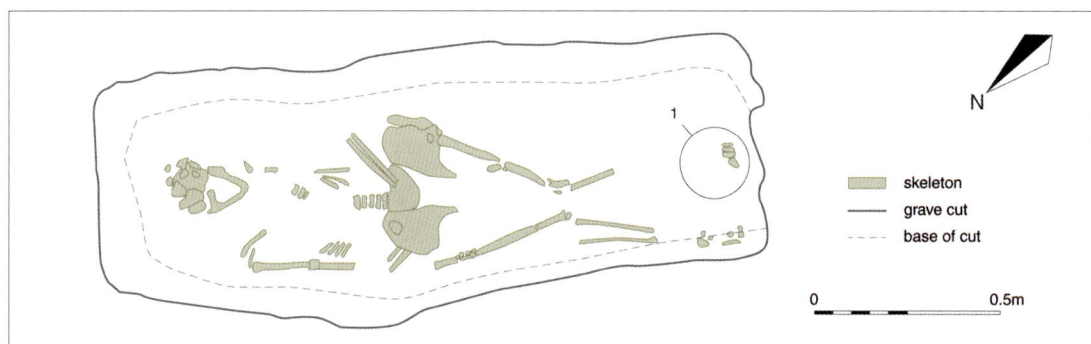

Fig. 3.69   Burial B1212

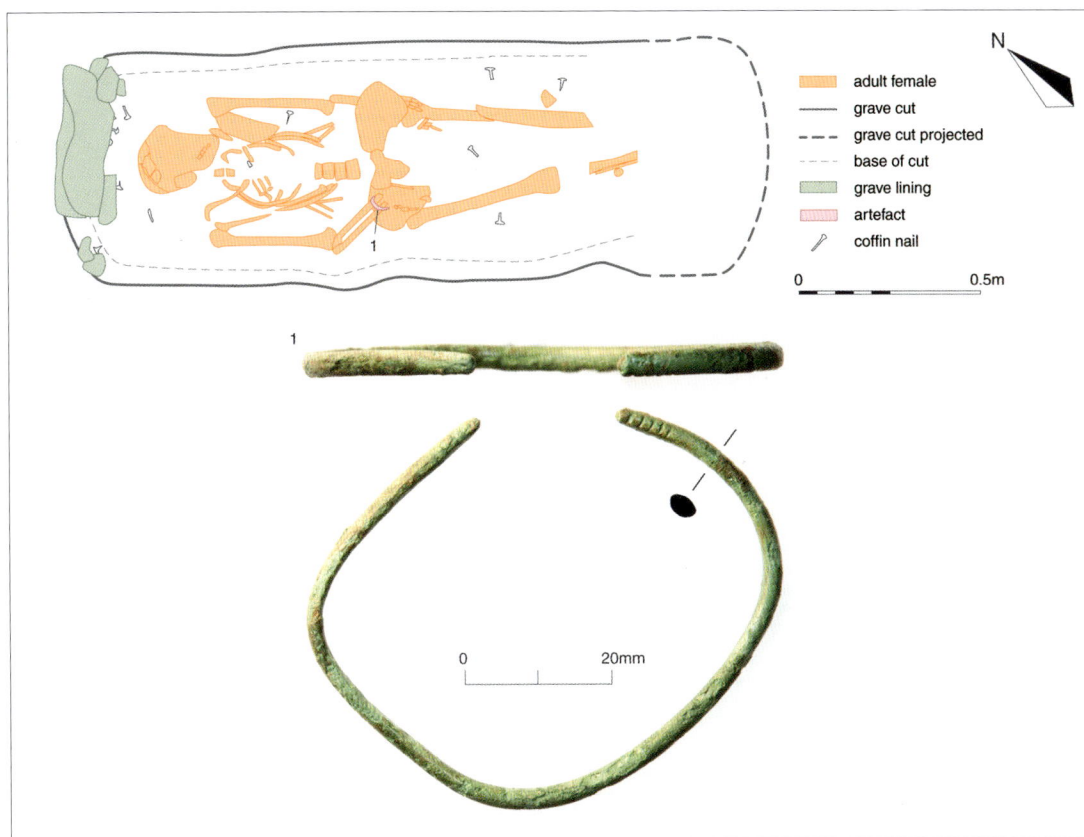

Fig. 3.71 Burial B1214

Grave goods: B1215.1: iron hobnails x 114. Location: at feet, ?worn, plus 2 from the skull area.

Coffin nails: iron x 27 including fragments: Flat-headed; measurable examples 60–67mm.

Grave fill finds: pottery: 59 sherds (TF 74, 98), with four clusters of sherds near the legs. The group includes a substantial portion of a jar in TF 74, probably a disturbed cremation vessel; animal bone: O/C x 1.

Date: 2nd century (grave goods/grave fill pottery).

B1216 (grave 1133, Sk 1134) (Fig. 3.73)

Grave: south-east–north-west. Sub-rectangular with apsidal ends, steep sides to a flat base, 1.97m x 0.73m x 0.31m deep. Grey-brown silty clay fill with frequent stones.

Human remains: supine, right arm flexed over upper chest and left arm over pelvis, 85% skeletal recovery, age 33–45, female.

Coffin nails: iron x 43, including fragments. Flat-headed; none measurable.

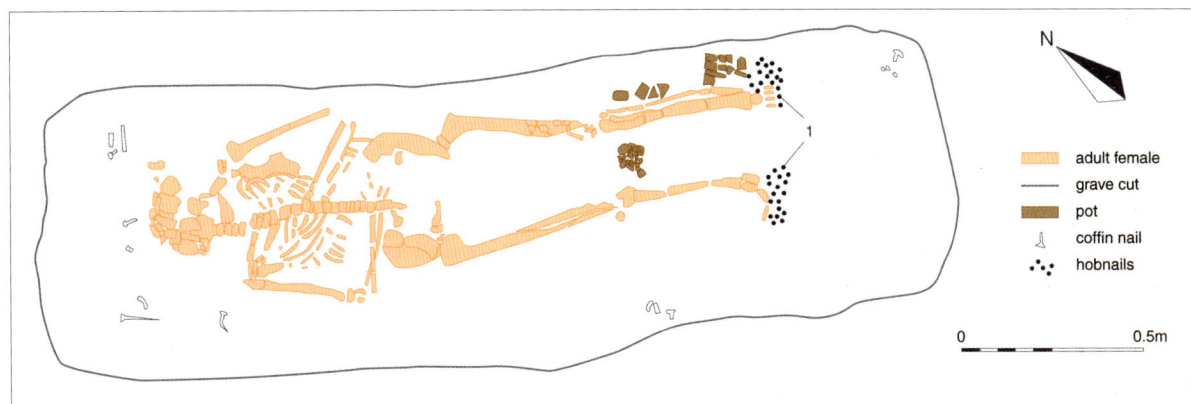

Fig. 3.72 Burial B1215

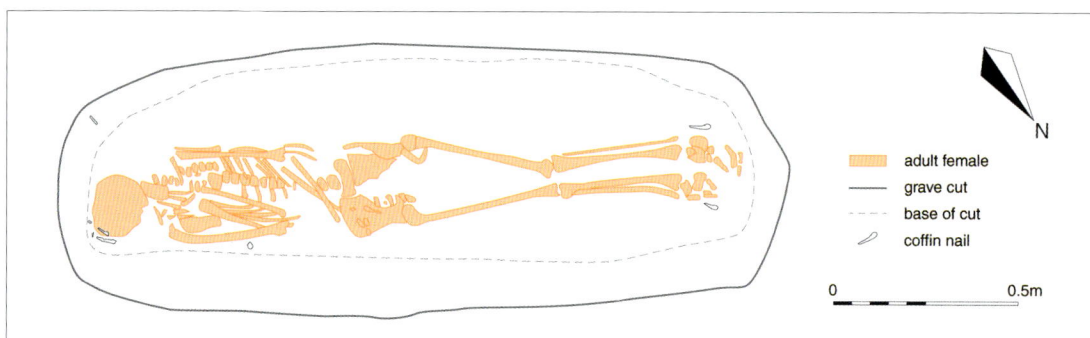

Fig. 3.73   Burial B1216

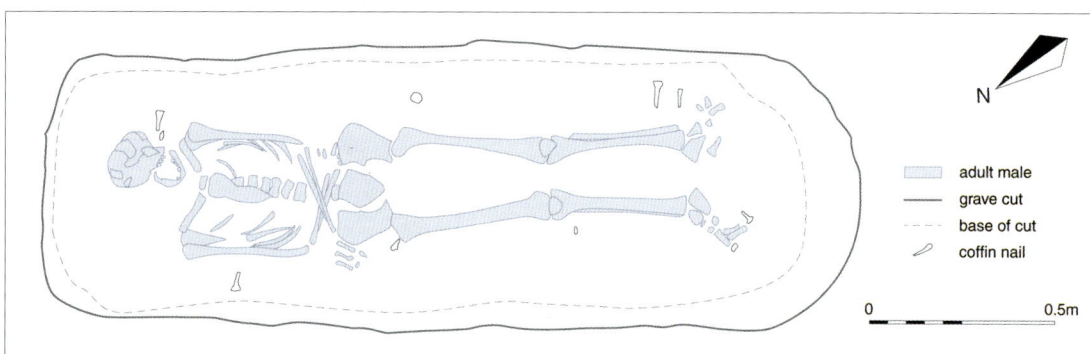

Fig. 3.74   Burial B1217

Grave fill finds: pottery: 4 sherds (TF 9, 5, 98); cbm x 1; worked flint x 1.

Date: 2nd to 4th century (grave fill pottery).

B1217 (grave 1136, Sk 1137) (Fig. 3.74)

Grave: north-east–south-west. Sub-rectangular with apsidal south-western end, vertical sides to flat base, 2.22m x 0.76m x 0.29m deep. Grey-brown sandy clay fill containing abundant limestone.

Human remains: supine with arms crossed over pelvis, 85% skeletal recovery, age 26–44, male.

Coffin nails: iron x 47 including fragments. Flat-headed; none measurable.

Grave fill finds: pottery: 6 sherds (TF 74); iron: hobnails x 2 from pelvis area; animal bone: GAL x 8, AVE x 6.

Date: 2nd to 3rd century (grave fill pottery).

B1218 (grave 1141, Sk 1140) (Fig. 3.75)

Grave: south-west–north-east. Rectangular with vertical sides to a flat base, 2.09m x 0.81m x 0.67m deep. Grey-brown silty clay fill with common stones. The grave fill was cut by a modern pipe trench.

Human remains: supine with arms by the side, 25% skeletal recovery, age 25–35, female.

Grave goods: B1218.1: copper-alloy bracelet. Hollow/ tubular form from thin sheet. Sub-square in section, with the overlapping join at the inside edge. The outside edges are indented/notched, resulting in a decorative wavy effect in elevation. The bracelet is of similar form and construction to B1177.1. External diameter approximately 65mm; section 6.5mm x 6mm. Location: in area of right hand, worn? Associated with B1218.2–3.

B1218.2: copper-alloy bracelet. Cable type from twisted wire (2 strand). Incomplete and distorted (bent to S-shape), possibly as a result of disturbance. The surviving terminal is of hooked form (as Crummy 1983, 39, no. 1628). Location: in area of right hand, worn? Associated with B1218.1 and 3. External diameter approximately 60mm; section (diameter) 2mm.

B1218.3: iron bracelet. Eight fragments of curved wire or narrow strip representing one or possibly two strip-form bracelets. The edges may be decoratively notched in the manner of copper-alloy strip bracelets (ibid., 41, no. 1656). Iron bracelets were among the grave goods from Lankhills (Cool 2010, 109, 181). External diameter approximately 55mm; section 2.5mm x 1.5mm.

Coffin nails: iron x 11, including fragments: Flat-headed, measurable examples 80–86mm.

Grave fill finds: animal bone: O/C x 1.

Date: middle to late 4th century (grave goods).

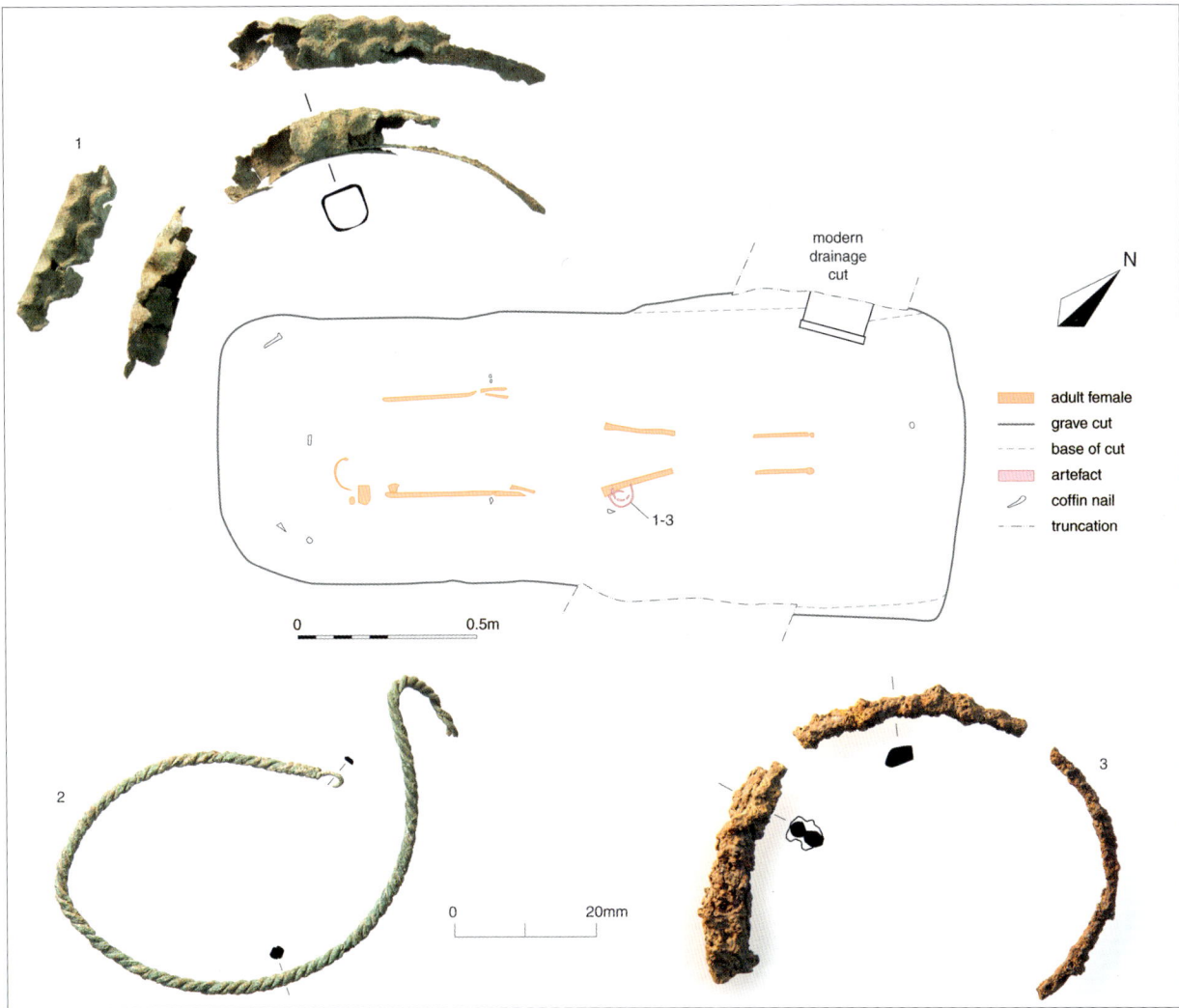

Fig. 3.75   Burial B1218

B1219 (grave 1148, Sk1147) (Fig. 3.76)

Grave: north-west–south-east. Sub-rectangular tapering to north-west, very steep sides to a flat base, 1.94m x 0.64m x 0.31m deep. Grey-brown silty clay fill with frequent small stones. The grave was cut by B1170 and modern disturbance. The grave was only just big enough to accommodate the body.

Human remains: supine with right hand over pelvis and left arm by side, 90% skeletal recovery, age 36–53, male.

Coffin nails: iron x 19, including fragments. Flat-headed, measurable example is 65mm.

Grave fill finds: pottery: 3 sherds (TF 74); iron hobnails x 4 from the skull area.

Date: 3rd to 4th century (grave fill pottery).

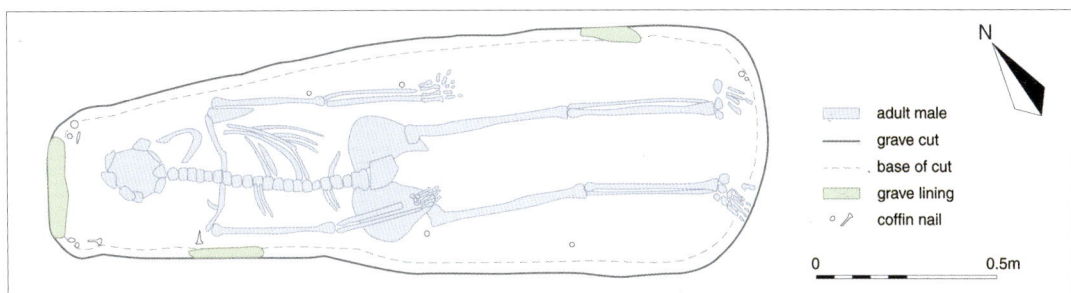

Fig. 3.76   Burial B1219

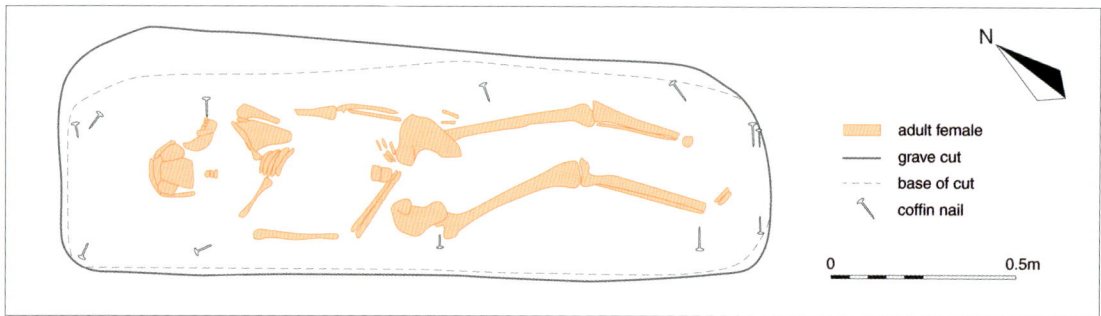

Fig. 3.77   Burial B1220

B1220 (grave 1153, Sk 1154) (Fig. 3.77)

Grave: north-west–south-east. Rectangular with vertical sides to a flat base, 1.9m x 0.6m x 0.6m deep. Brown silty clay fill with abundant limestone.

Human remains: supine with right arm over the pelvis and left arm by side, 65% skeletal recovery, age 20–30, female.

Coffin nails: iron x 29, including fragments. Flat-headed, measurable examples 89–115mm.

Grave fill finds: pottery: 2 sherds (TF 74); iron hobnail.

Date: 2nd to 4th century (grave fill pottery).

B1221 (grave 1150, Sk 1156) (Fig. 3.78)

Grave: north-west–south-east. Sub-rectangular with apsidal north-western end, south-eastern end missing as removed by modern drain, irregular south-western side, vertical sides to an undulating, broadly flat base, >1.38m x 0.45m x 0.22m deep. Orange-brown silty clay fill contained frequent limestone brash and some charcoal fragments. Coffin was placed tight into the grave cut.

Human remains: supine, right arm over pelvis and left arm over abdomen, 65% skeletal recovery, age 20–24, female.

Coffin nails: iron x 11, including fragments. Flat-headed; none measurable.

Grave fill finds: pottery: 1 sherd (TF 5). Redeposited human bones were recovered from the grave fill just above the inhumation.

Date: not closely dateable.

B1222 (grave 1161, Sk 1162) (Fig. 3.79)

Grave: north-west–south-east. Sub-rectangular with vertical sides to a flat base, >1.2m x 0.8m x 0.45m deep. Brown silty clay fill with common stones. The north-west end of the grave was heavily truncated by modern activity. There was a 0.3m-gap between the feet and the end of the grave cut.

Human remains: supine, 20% skeletal recovery, age >18, sex indeterminable.

No artefacts were recovered.

Date: not closely dateable.

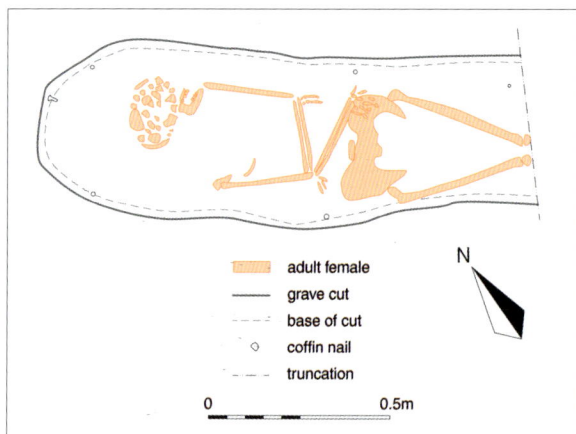

Fig. 3.78   Burial B1221

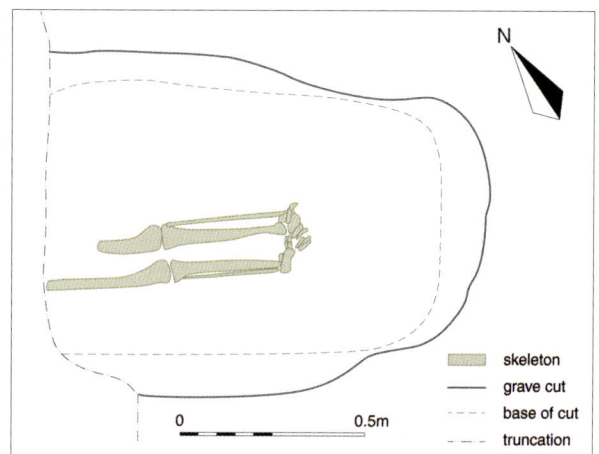

Fig. 3.79   Burial B1222

B1223 (grave 1169, Sk 1170) (Fig. 3.80)

Grave: south-east–north-west. Rectangular with vertical sides to a flat base, >1.8m x 0.84m x 0.25m. Pale orange-brown sandy clay fill containing frequent stones

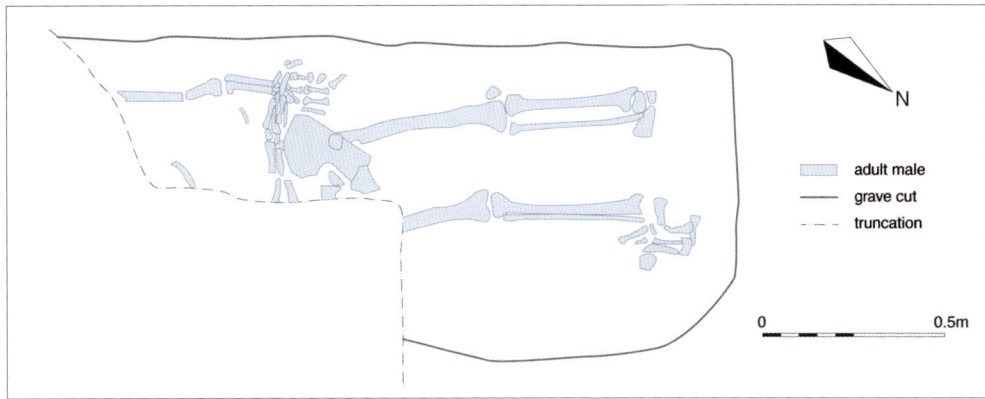

Fig. 3.80   Burial B1223

and fragments of oyster. Much of the grave cut had been truncated by modern development.

Human remains: supine with left arm by the side and the right hand near the left, 40% skeletal recovery, age 35–52, male.

Coffin nails: iron x 6, including fragments. Flat-headed, none measurable.

Grave fill finds: pottery: 3 sherds (TF 74); ironworking slag (30g); animal bone: BOS x 2, EQU x 1, LM x 3.

Date: 3rd to 4th century (grave fill pottery).

B1224 (grave 1176, Sk 1174) (Fig. 3.81)
Grave: south-east–north-west. Sub-rectangular with vertical sides to a flat base, >1.8m x c. 0.4m x 0.49m deep. Orange-brown silty clay fill containing some stone. This grave cut B1225, but this was not recognised during excavation and so there may be some mixing of finds from the fills of the two graves.

Human remains: supine with right arm by side and left arm over lower chest/abdomen, 20% skeletal recovery, age >18, sex indeterminate.

Coffin nails: iron x 5, including fragments. Flat-headed, measurable examples 90–117mm.

Grave fill finds (from fill of this grave and B1225): pottery: 5 sherds (TF 98, 17, 74, 35); cbm x 1.

Date: 3rd to 4th century? (grave fill pottery).

B1225 (grave 1184, Sk 1175) (Fig. 3.81)
Grave: north-west–south-east. Sub-rectangular with vertical sides to a flat base, >1.8m x >0.3m x 0.49m. Fill not differentiated from that of B1224 which cut it.

Human remains: supine, 10% skeletal recovery from right shoulder/arm/chest, age >18, sex indeterminable.

Coffin nails: iron x 2.

Grave fill finds: included with B1224.

Date: not closely dateable.

B1228 (grave 5024, Sk 5025) (Fig. 3.82)
Grave: south-west–north-east. Rectangular with vertical sides and flat base, 2.34m x 1.02m x 0.33m deep. Dark reddish-brown silty clay fill with frequent limestone fragments.

Human remains: supine, right arm over pelvis, left arm at side, 95% skeletal recovery, age 37–54, male.

Coffin nails: iron x 9, including fragments of shaft and flat head.

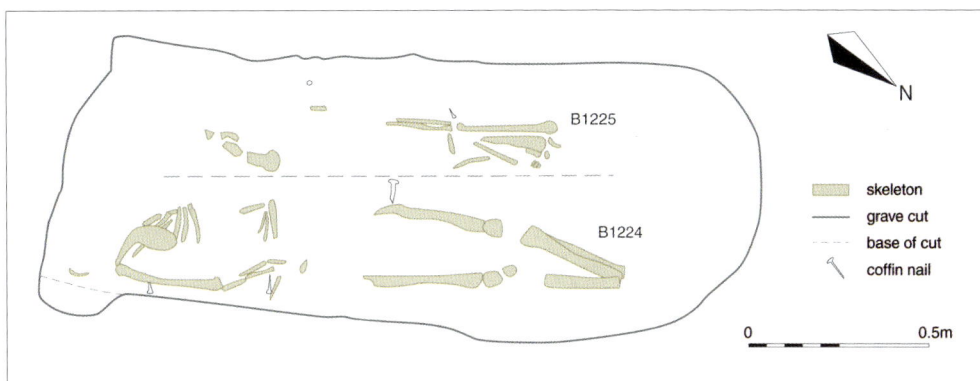

Fig. 3.81   Burials B1224 and B1225

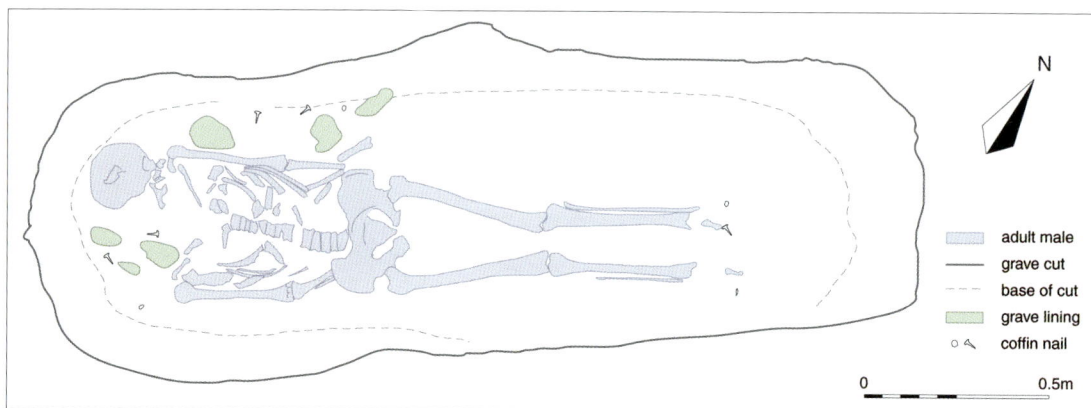

Fig. 3.82   Burial B1228

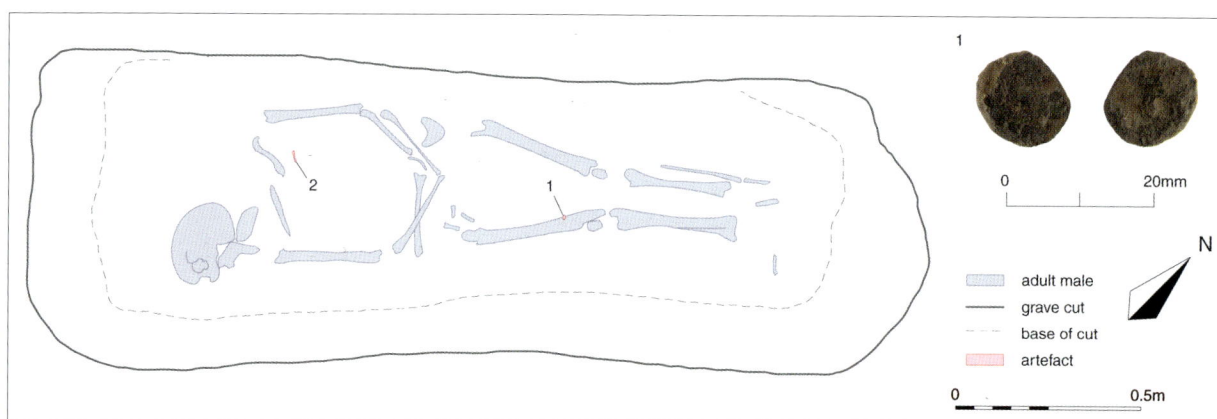

Fig. 3.83   Burial B1229

Grave fill finds: pottery: 2 sherds (TF 35, 98); animal bone: BOS x 3, O/C x 3, SUS x 2, LM x 1, MM x 2.

Date: 2nd to 4th century (grave fill pottery).

B1229 (grave 5027, Sk 5028) (Fig. 3.83)

Grave: south-west–north-east. Rectangular with vertical sides and flat base, 2.1m x 0.71m x 0.5m deep. Mixed greyish-brown and orange silty clay fill. Shrouded?

Human remains: supine, arms crossed over pelvis, 40% skeletal recovery, age 30–40, male.

Grave goods: B1229.1: copper-alloy coin, *nummus*, illegible. The reverse features an encircling wreath; however the details are unclear. Diameter 13mm. Location: in the area between the thigh bones.

B1229.2: copper-alloy strip (not illustrated). Location: in the chest area.

Grave fill finds: pottery: 4 sherds (TF 74, 98, 118); animal bone: BOS x 2, MM x 5.

Date: 4th century (grave goods and grave fill pottery).

B1230 (grave 5030, Sk 5031) (Fig. 3.84)

Grave: north-east–south-west. Sub-rectangular with steep sides and flat base, 2.24m x 0.8m x 0.36m deep. Mid brown clay fill, truncated by modern feature to north-east.

Human remains: supine, arms folded over upper part of pelvis, 90% skeletal recovery, age 38–54, male.

Coffin nails: iron x 9, including fragments of shaft and flat head.

Grave fill finds: pottery: 1 sherd (TF 74).

Date: 2nd to 4th century (grave fill pottery).

B1231 (grave 5033, Sk 5034) (Fig. 3.85)

Grave: south-west–north-east. Oval with vertical sides and flat base, 1.6m x 0.45m x 0.05m deep. Orange-brown silty clay fill with abundant limestone fragments. Heavily truncated.

Human remains: supine, arms folded over upper part of pelvis, 75% skeletal recovery, age 40–44, male.

Grave goods: B1231.1: copper-alloy coin, *nummus* copy, illegible. Diameter 10mm. Location: in the area between the thigh bones.

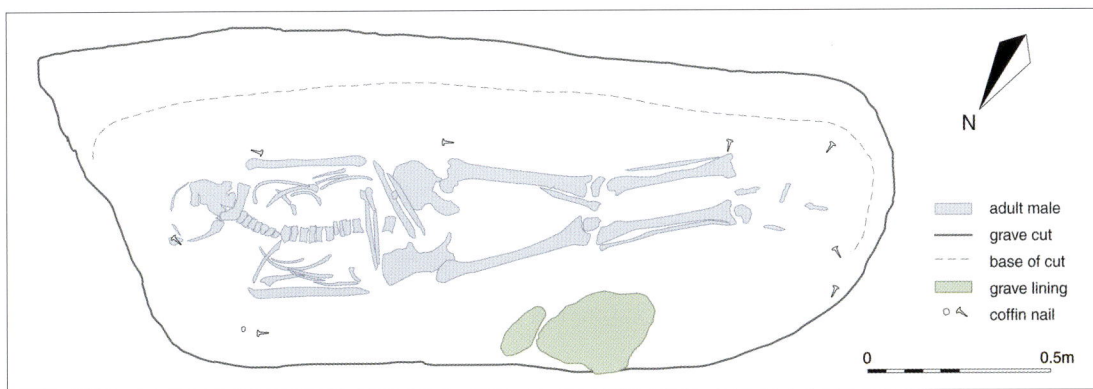

Fig. 3.84   Burial B1230

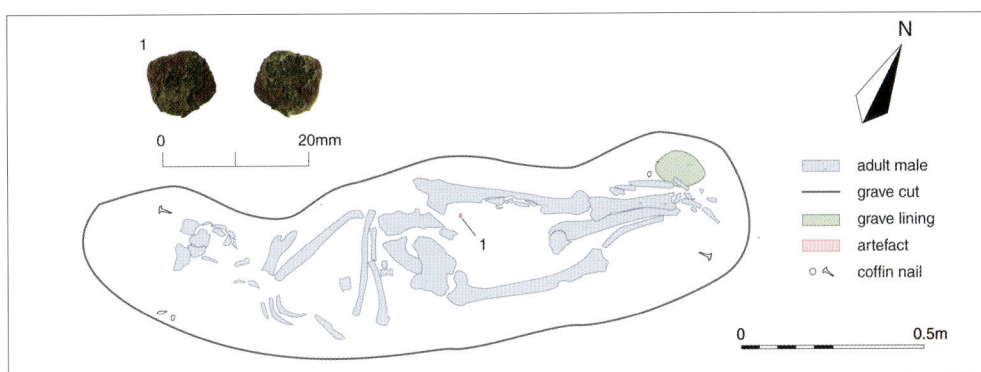

Fig. 3.85   Burial B1231

Coffin nails: iron x 5, including fragments. Flat-headed, complete example 75mm long.

Grave fill finds: animal bone: SUS x 1, MM x 1.

Date: 4th century (grave good).

B1232 (grave 5036, Sk 5037) (Fig. 3.86)

Grave: south-west–north-east. Sub-rectangular with vertical sides and flat base, 1.78m x 0.67m x 0.5m deep. Dark brown silty clay fill with occasional limestone fragments.

Human remains: supine, right arm bent over pelvis, left arm bent double at side, 60% skeletal recovery, age 6–7, sex indeterminable.

Coffin nails: iron x 9, including fragments. Flat-headed, measurable examples 45–52mm long.

Grave fill finds: pottery: 2 sherds (TF 98, 154B); animal bone: SUS x 2.

Date: 2nd to 4th century (grave fill pottery).

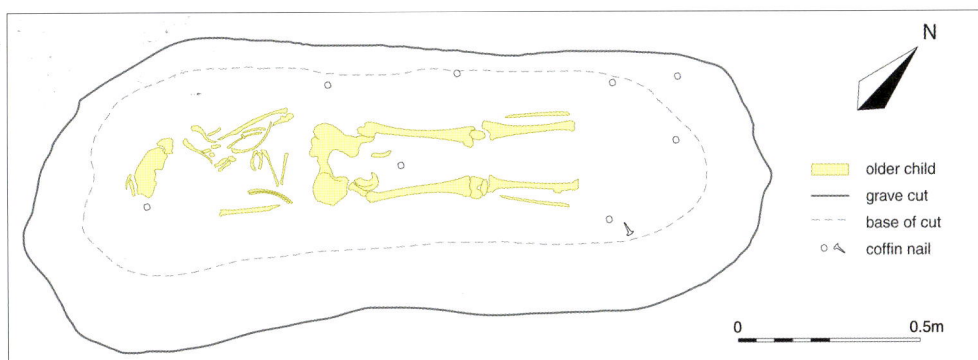

Fig. 3.86   Burial B1232

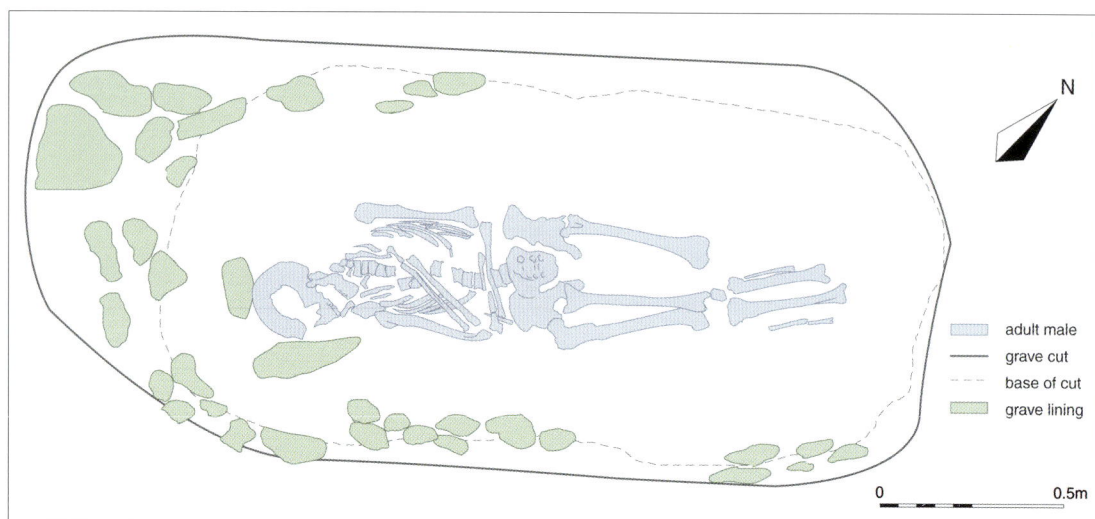

Fig. 3.87   Burial B1233

B1233 (grave 5041, Sk 5042) (Fig. 3.87)

Grave: south-west–north-east. Sub-rectangular with vertical sides and flat base, 2.35m x 1.05m x 0.55m deep. The grave cut was large compared to the size of the body. Mid orange-brown sandy clay fill with frequent limestone fragments.

Human remains: supine, right arm crossed over chest, left arm folded over pelvis, 90% skeletal recovery, age 37–49, male.

Grave fill finds: animal bone: EQU x 2, MM x 2.

Date: not closely dateable.

B1234 (grave 5020, Sk 5044) (Fig. 3.88)

Grave: north-east–south-west. Oval with shallow sides and flat base, 1.7m x 0.45m x 0.03m deep. Mid brown silty clay fill with abundant limestone fragments. Heavily truncated by modern activity.

Human remains: supine, partial left arm crossing pelvis, 10% skeletal recovery, age 40–44, female.

Grave goods: B1234.1: copper-alloy coin, *nummus* (?copy), illegible. Details unclear; possibly House of Constantine (Victory walking with wreath). Diameter 13mm. Location: at head end of grave. Uncertain if this is a deliberate placement or chance inclusion.

Grave fill finds: pottery: 21 sherds (TF 35, 74).

Date: 4th century (grave good and grave fill pottery).

B1235 (grave 5047, Sk 5048) (Fig. 3.89)

Grave: north-east–south-west. Rectangular with vertical sides and flat base, 1.92m x 0.46m x 0.08m deep. Mid orange-brown sandy clay fill with frequent limestone fragments. Heavily truncated by modern activity.

Human remains: supine, arms crossed over pelvis, 75% skeletal recovery, age 29–40, male.

Coffin nails: iron x 9, including fragments. Flat-headed, complete example 77mm long.

Date: not closely dated.

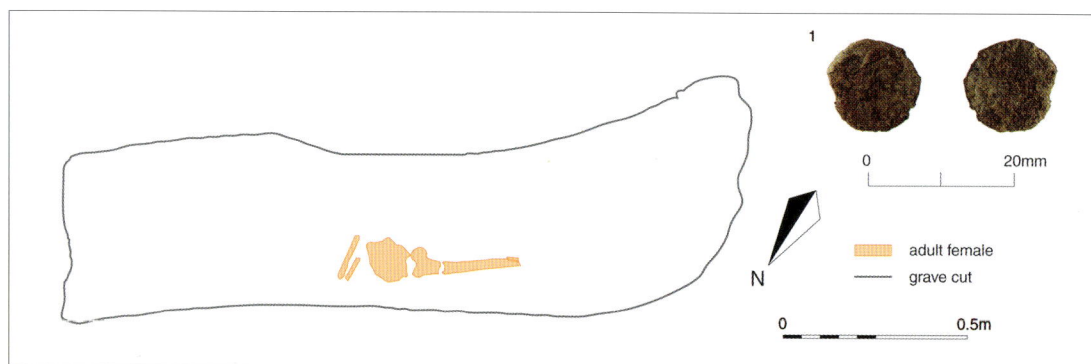

Fig. 3.88   Burial B1234

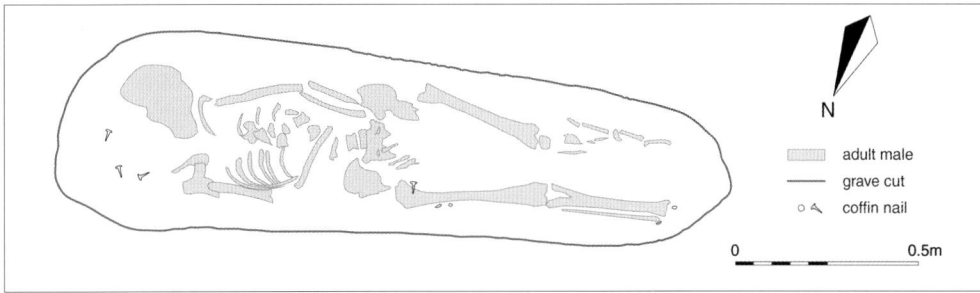

Fig. 3.89   Burial B1235

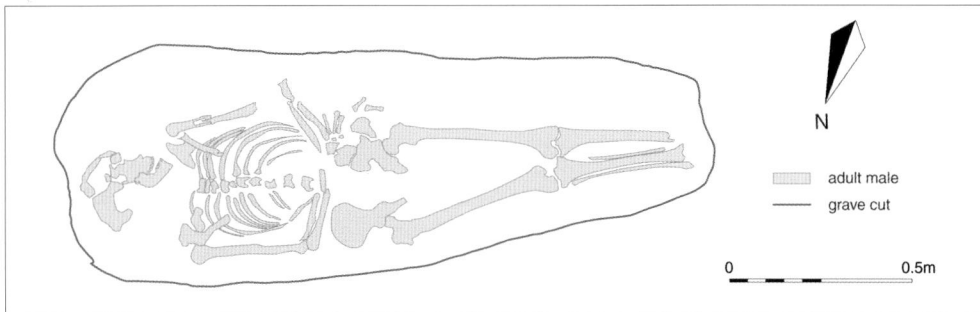

Fig. 3.90   Burial B1236

B1236 (grave 5050, Sk 5051) (Fig. 3.90)

Grave: north-east–south-west. Rectangular with vertical sides and flat base, 1.8m x 0.5m x 0.09m deep. Dark brown sandy clay fill with frequent limestone fragments. Heavily truncated.

Human remains: prone, arms crossed over lower back (bound?), ankles close together (bound?), 80% skeletal recovery, age 29–45, male.

Date: not closely dated.

B1237 (grave 5058, Sk 5059) (Fig. 3.91)

Grave: south-west–north-east. Rectangular with vertical sides and flat base, 2.32m x 0.92m x 0.8m deep. Light orange-brown sandy clay fill. Possible stone lining. Cut by Anglo-Saxon pit 1004/5066.

Human remains: supine, arms slightly bent at elbow, 85% skeletal recovery, age 22–40, male.

Grave goods: B1237.1: iron hobnails x 2, from grave fill.

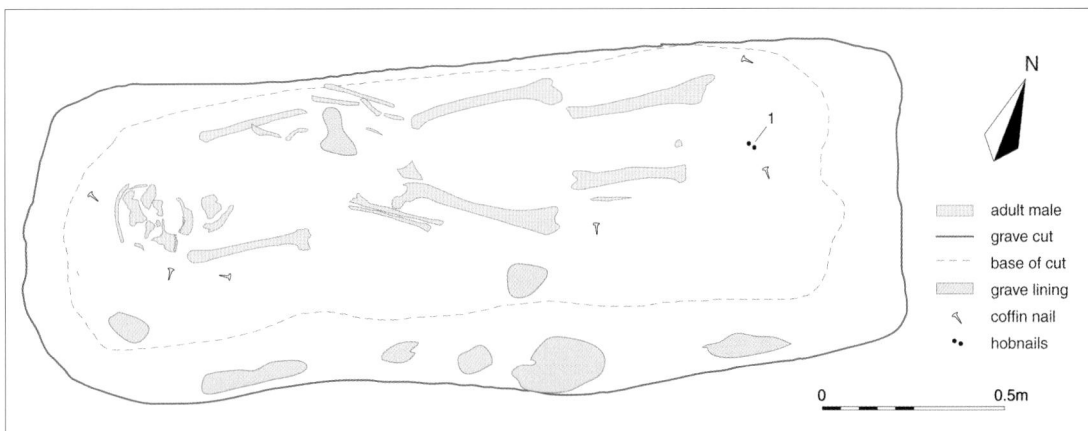

Fig. 3.91   Burial B1237

Coffin nails: iron x 6, including fragments. Flat-headed, complete example 71mm long.

Grave fill finds: Anglo-Saxon pottery x 6 sherds (SAXORG), doubtless contamination from overlying pit 1004/5066; animal bone: BOS x 1.

Date: not closely dated.

B1238 (grave 5061, Sk 5064) (not illustrated)

Grave: north-east–south-west. Rectangular with vertical sides and flat base, 1.67m x 0.56m x 0.79m deep. Primary fill of mid grey-brown sandy clay with frequent limestone fragments. Secondary fill of dark reddish-brown sandy clay with frequent limestone fragments.

Human remains: supine, skull only, 10% skeletal recovery, age 3–4, sex indeterminable.

Coffin nails: iron x 5, including fragments. Flat-headed, complete example 70mm long.

Grave fill finds: 1 sherd (TF98).

Date: not closely dated.

B1239 (grave 5070, Sk 5071) (Fig. 3.92)

Grave: north-west–south-east. Rectangular with vertical sides and flat base, 2.4m x 0.69m x 0.52m deep. Dark brown silty clay fill with frequent limestone fragments. Possible stone lining.

Human remains: supine, arms crossed over pelvis, 95% skeletal recovery, age 39–44, male.

Grave goods: B1239.1: hobnail cluster, x 72 iron nails in area of right foot (worn). B1239.2: hobnail cluster, x 30 iron nails in area of left foot (worn).

Coffin nails: iron x 18, including fragments. Flat-headed, measurable examples 78–95mm long.

Date: not closely dated.

B1240 (grave 5073, Sk 5074) (Fig. 3.93)

Grave: north-east–south-west. Rectangular with vertical sides and flat base, 1.8m x 0.53m x 0.14m deep. Mid grey-brown/orange silty clay fill with frequent limestone fragments.

Human remains: supine, arms extended, left arm under pelvis, 90% skeletal recovery, age c. 14, male.

Coffin nails: iron x 14, including fragments. Flat-headed.

Date: not closely dated.

B1241 (grave 5076, Sk 5077) (Figs 3.94–3.95)

Grave: south-east–north-west. Rectangular with vertical sides and flat base, 2.02m x 0.69m x 0.32m deep. Mid orange-grey silty clay fill with abundant limestone fragments.

Human remains: prone, decapitation, head between knees, feet at north-west end, arms flexed across body to right side, wrists together (bound?), 85% skeletal recovery, age 32–48, female.

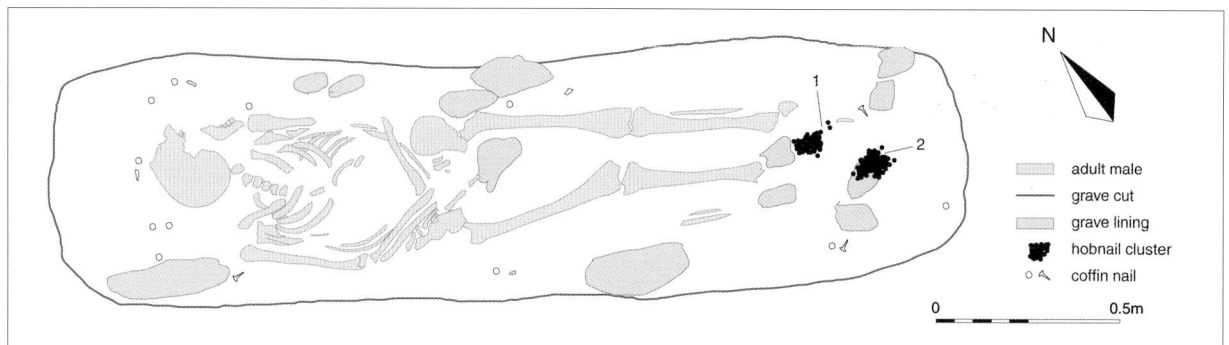

Fig. 3.92   Burial B1239

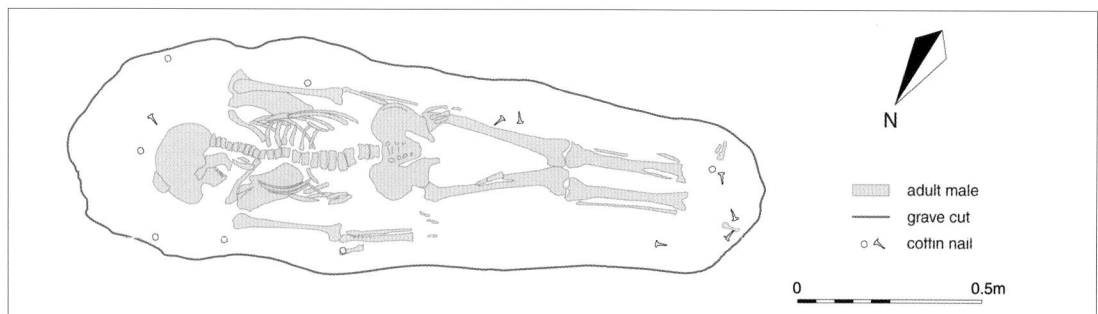

Fig. 3.93   Burial B1240

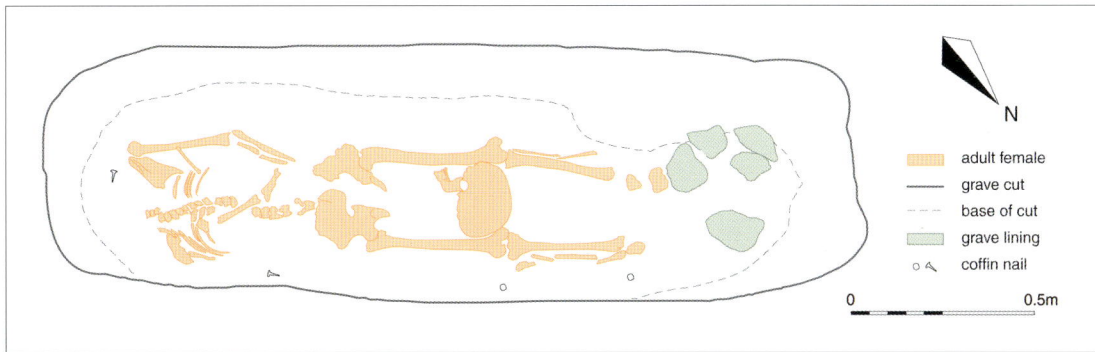

Fig. 3.94   Burial B1241

Fig. 3.95   Prone and decapitated burial B1241

Coffin nails: iron x 4, including fragments. Flat-headed.

Grave fill finds: cbm x 1.

Date: not closely dateable.

B1242 (grave 5083, Sk 5085) (Fig. 3.96)

Grave: north-east–south-west. Rectangular with vertical sides and flat base, <1m x 0.73m x 0.2m. Dark brown silty clay fill with frequent limestone fragments. Cut by a modern feature to the south-west.

Human remains: prone, upper arms extended, lower arms not surviving, 20% skeletal recovery, age 30–48, female.

Date: not closely dateable.

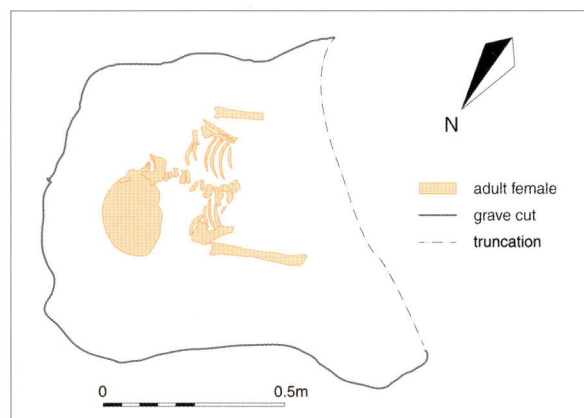

Fig. 3.96   Burial B1242

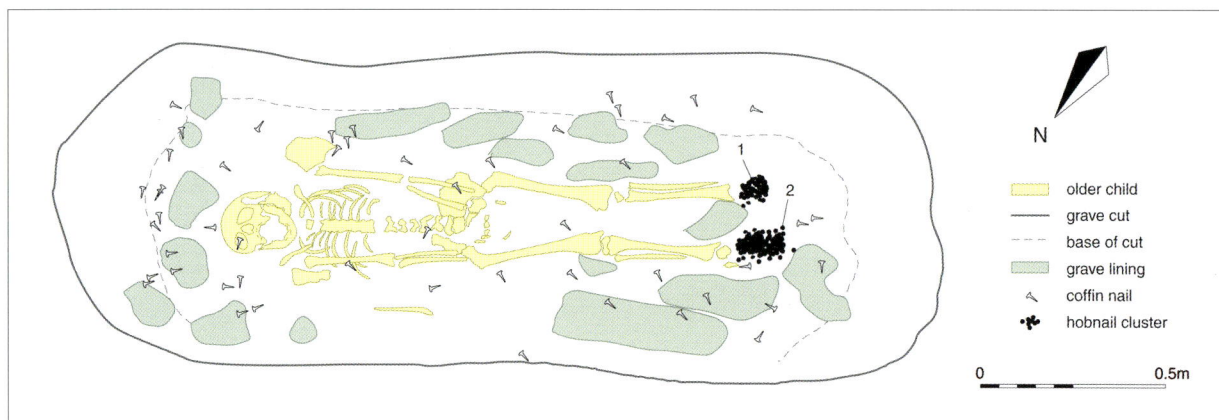

Fig. 3.97   Burial B1243

B1243 (grave 5081, Sk 5086) (Fig. 3.97)

Grave: north-east–south-west. Rectangular with vertical sides and flat base, 2.3m x 0.78m x 0.64m deep. Dark grey silty clay fill with frequent limestone fragments. Limestone slabs packed around coffin. Cut grave B1246.

Human remains: supine, arms extended over pelvis, 95% skeletal recovery, age *c.* 12, sex indeterminable.

Grave goods: B1243.1: hobnail cluster, x 22 iron nails.

B1243.2: hobnail cluster, x 73 iron nails. Location: both clusters from the feet area (probably worn).

Coffin nails: iron x 56, including fragments. Flat-headed, measurable examples 40–95mm long.

Grave fill finds: pottery: 10 sherds (TF 6, 74, 95, 98); animal bone: BOS x 1, ROD x 2.

Date: 2nd to 4th century (grave fill pottery)

B1244 (grave 5090, Sk 5091) (Fig. 3.98)

Grave: south-west–north-east. Oval with vertical sides and flat base, 2.06m x 0.52m x 0.32m deep. Orange-brown clay fill with frequent limestone fragments.

Human remains: supine, arms extended, 85% skeletal recovery, age 37–57, male.

Grave goods: B1244.1: copper-alloy coin, *nummus* (or copy), illegible. Diameter 13mm. Location: the area between the thigh bones.

Coffin nails: iron x 6, including fragments. Flat-headed.

Date: 4th century (grave good)

B1245 (grave 5093, Sk 5094) (Fig. 3.99)

Grave: south-east–north-west. Sub-oval with vertical sides and flat base, 2.36m x 1.1m x 0.55m deep. Orange-brown clay fill with frequent limestone fragments. Stone packing around coffin.

Human remains: supine, arms extended, 85% skeletal recovery, age 38–44, male.

Grave goods: B1245.1: hobnail cluster, x 28 iron nails.

B1245.2: hobnail cluster, x 26 iron nails. Location: both clusters in the feet area (probably worn).

B1245.3: iron hobnail x 1 (position not recorded).

Coffin nails: iron x 8, including fragments. Flat-headed, measurable examples 72–88mm long.

Grave fill finds: flint scraper x 1; animal bone: LM x 1.

Date: not closely dated.

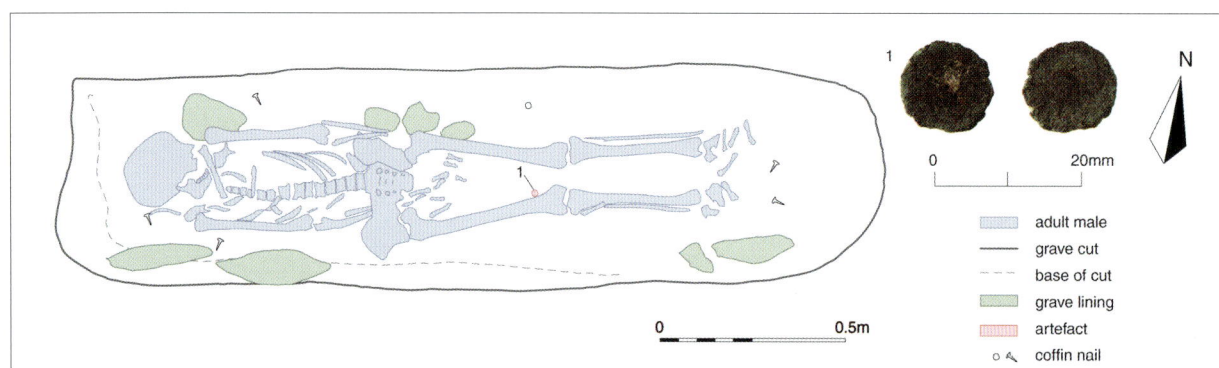

Fig. 3.98   Burial B1244

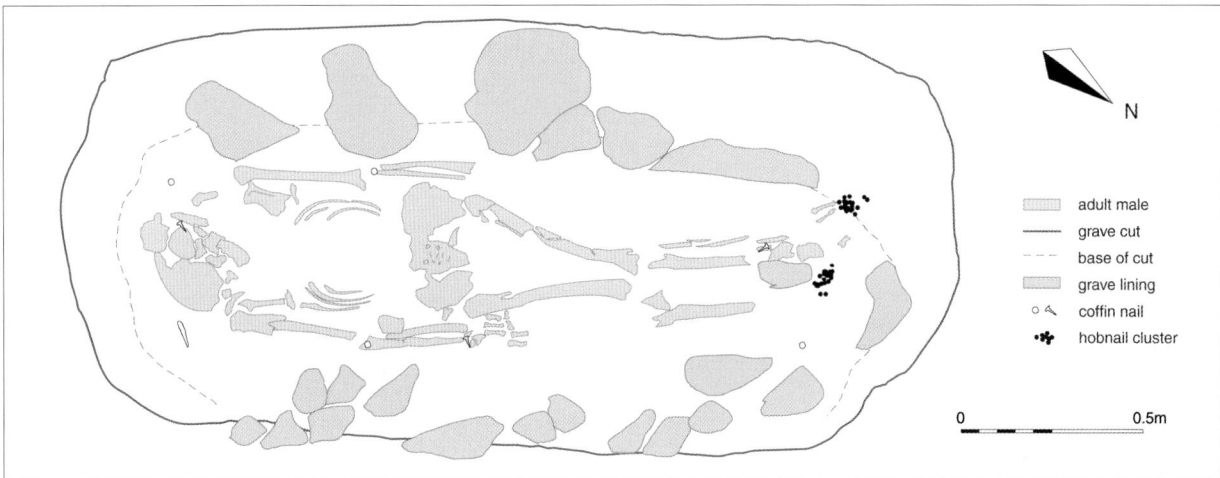

Fig. 3.99 Burial B1245

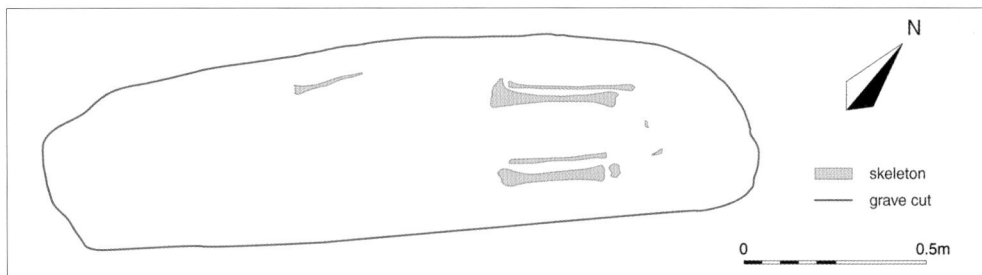

Fig. 3.100 Burial B1246

B1246 (grave 5096, Sk 5097) (Fig. 3.100)

Grave: south-west–north-east. Rectangular with vertical sides and flat base, 1.35m x 0.5m x 0.55m deep. Mid grey-orange silty clay fill. Grave cut into infilled Ditch F. Grave cut by B1243.

Human remains: supine, lower left arm extended, 15% skeletal recovery, age >18, sex indeterminable.

Date: not closely dated.

B1247 (grave 5099, Sk 5100) (not illustrated)

Grave: north-east–south-west. Rectangular with vertical sides and flat base, 0.66m x 0.56m x 0.05m deep. Orange-brown silty clay fill with frequent limestone fragments. Heavily truncated.

Human remains: supine, arms not surviving, 5% skeletal recovery, age 24–29, male.

Coffin nails: iron x 1, shaft fragment.

Date: not closely dated.

B1248 (grave 5102, Sk 5104) (Figs 3.101–3.102)

Grave: north-east–south-west. Rectangular with vertical sides and flat base, 2.15m x 0.96m x 0.31m deep. Dark brown silty clay fill with frequent limestone fragments. Stone packing around coffin.

Human remains: supine, right arm across abdomen, left arm folded over chest, left leg flexed over right knee, 80% skeletal recovery, age 20–24, female.

Grave goods: B1248.1: copper-alloy bracelet. External diameter 80mm, width 4.5mm, thickness 1mm.

B1248.2: copper-alloy bracelet. External diameter 70mm, width 3.5mm; thickness 1mm.

B1248.3: copper-alloy bracelet. External diameter 67mm; width 3.5mm; thickness 1mm.

These bracelets are of the same form, differing slightly in dimensions. They are of annular strip form (as B1185.1), with the overlapping terminals flattened and soldered. Decoration to the outside edge consists of alternating notches.

B1248.4: Iron ?bracelet, in two fragments, and of strip-like form (not illustrated). External diameter 80–100mm, width *c.* 5mm, thickness 1–3mm. Location: the copper-alloy bracelets were *in situ*, worn on the upper left arm (Fig. 3.102). B1248.4 lay in the same area and was also probably worn.

Coffin nails: iron x 17, including fragments. Flat-headed, measurable examples 50–58mm long.

Grave fill finds: animal bone: O/C x 1.

Date: 4th century (grave goods).

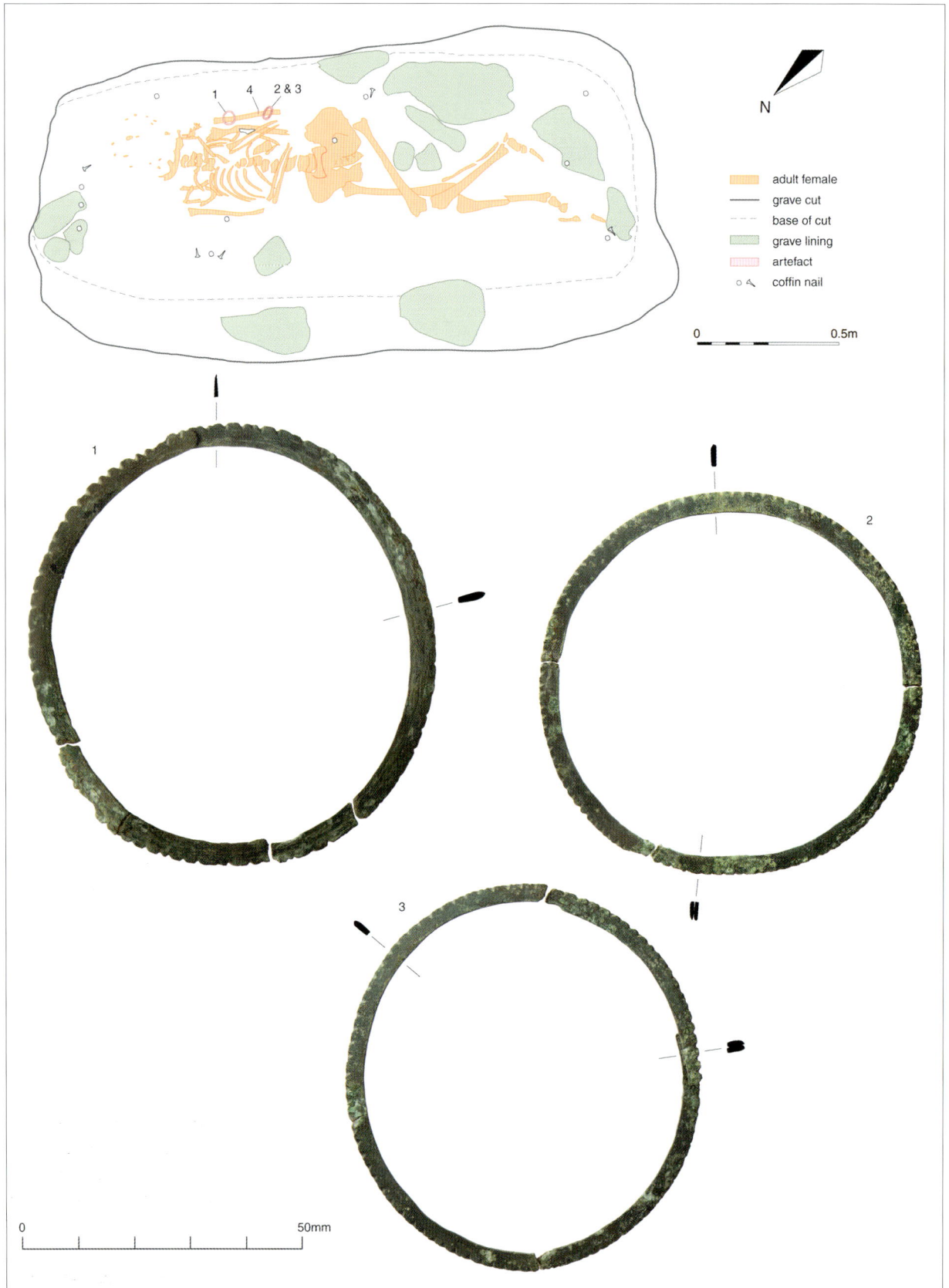

Fig. 3.101　Burial B1248

Fig. 3.102   Three copper-alloy bracelets in situ on the upper left arm of the 20 to 24-year-old female B1248. 20cm scale

B1249 (grave 5107, Sk 5108) (Fig. 3.103)

Grave: north-west–south-east. Sub-oval, 2.38m x 0.8m wide. Mid orange-grey sandy clay fill with abundant limestone fragments. Possible stone packing around coffin. Remnant of lime wash on coffin preserved in grave fill.

Human remains: supine, arms folded across lower abdomen, 90% skeletal recovery, age 29–45, male.

Coffin nails: iron x 14, including fragments. Flat-headed, measurable examples 50–68mm long.

Grave fill finds: pottery: x 3 sherds (TF5, 74); plaster x 1 fragment; cbm (tegula) x 1; animal bone: BOS x 1, O/C x 1, MM x 2.

Date: 2nd to 4th century (grave fill pottery).

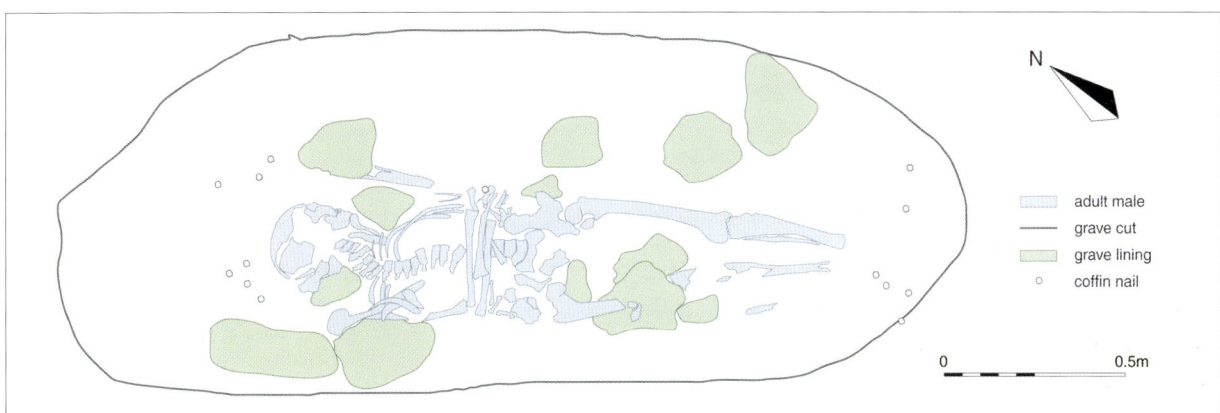

Fig. 3.103   Burial B1249

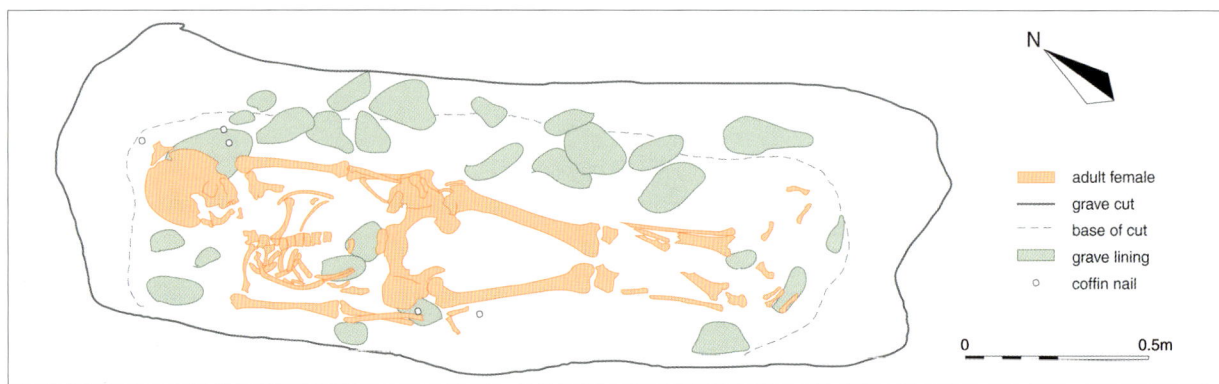

Fig. 3.104   Burial B1250

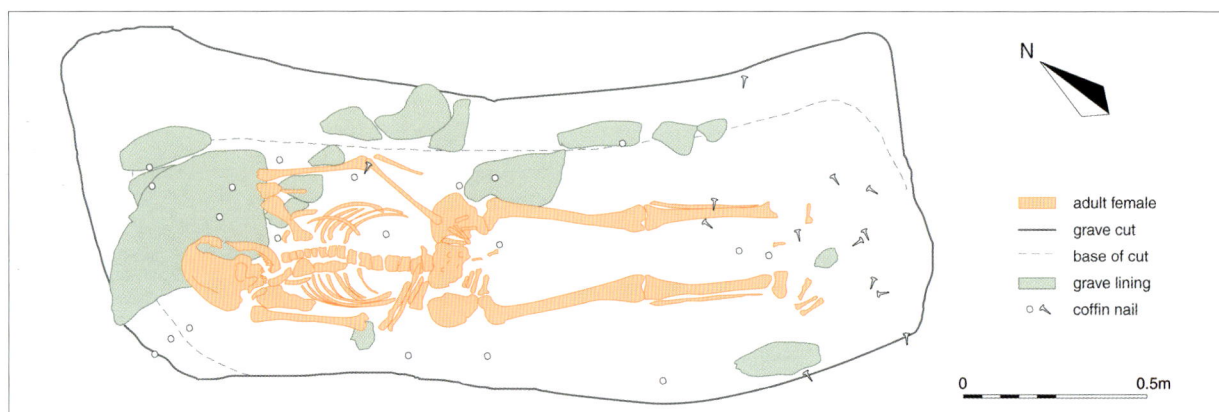

Fig. 3.105   Burial B1251

B1250 (grave 5110, Sk 5111) (Fig. 3.104)

Grave: north-west–south-east. Rectangular with vertical sides and flat base, 2.18m x 0.77m x 0.31m deep. Mid orange-brown sandy clay fill.

Human remains: supine, arms extended, left arm behind pelvis, 85% skeletal recovery, age 24–32, female.

Coffin nails: iron x 5, including fragments. Flat-headed, complete example 73mm long.

Grave fill finds: pottery: x 3 sherds (TF 5, 74).

Date: not closely dated.

B1251 (grave 5113, Sk 5114) (Fig. 3.105)

Grave: north-west–south-east. Rectangular with vertical sides and flat base, 2.38m x 0.85m x 0.43m deep. Mid orange-brown silty clay fill with frequent limestone fragments. Possible stone lining. This grave cut B1260.

Human remains: supine, arms over pelvis, 95% skeletal recovery, age 29–47, female.

Coffin nails: iron x 49, including fragments. Flat-headed, measurable examples 42–72mm long.

Grave fill finds: pottery: x 6 sherds (TF 74, 98); animal bone: IND x 1.

Date: 3rd to 4th centuries (grave fill pottery).

B1252 (grave 5116, Sk 5118) (Fig. 3.106)

Grave: north-east–south-west. Rectangular with vertical sides and flat base, 1.1m x 0.4m x 0.06m deep. Dark brown silty clay with frequent limestone fragments. Heavily truncated.

Human remains: supine, arms extended, 80% skeletal recovery, age *c.* 18 months, sex indeterminable.

Coffin nails: iron x 1, shaft fragment.

Date: not closely dated.

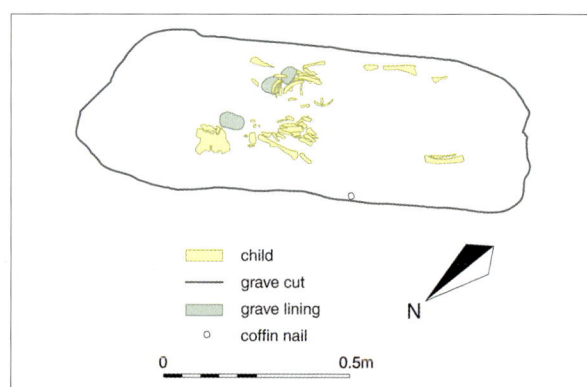

Fig. 3.106   Burial B1252

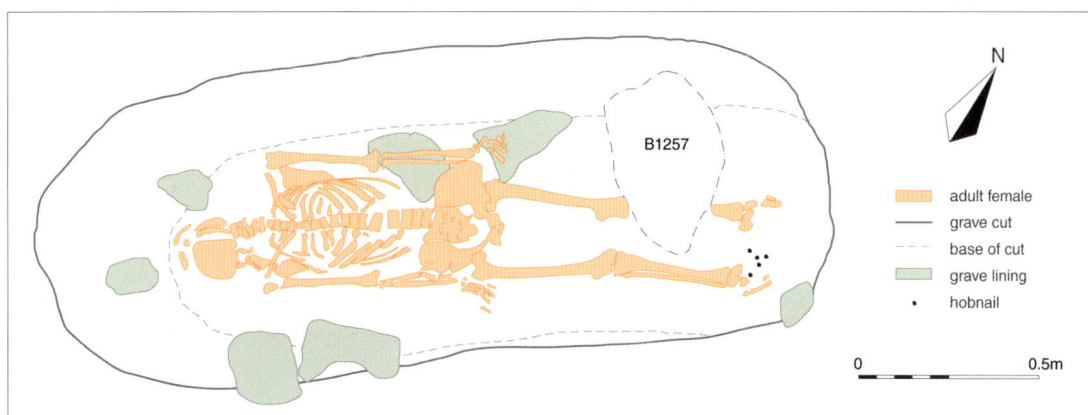

Fig. 3.107   Burial B1253

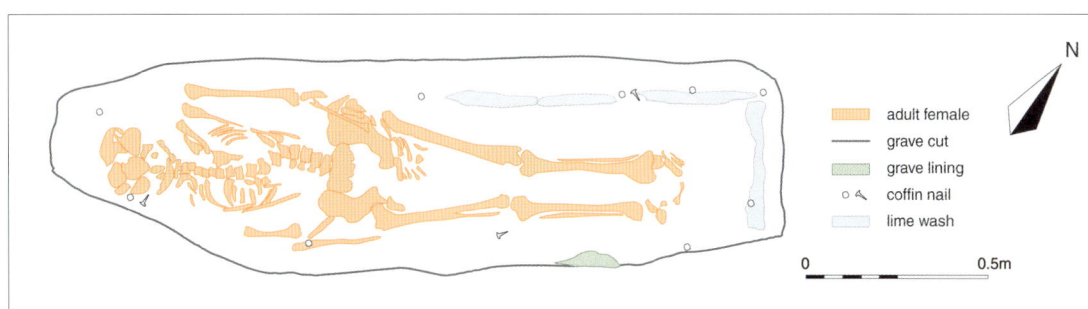

Fig. 3.108   Burial B1254

B1253 (grave 5123, Sk 5124) (Fig. 3.107)

Grave: south-west–north-east. Sub-rectangular with vertical sides and flat base, 1.72m x 0.6m x 0.1m deep. Dark brown silty clay fill with frequent limestone fragments. This grave was dug through the terminus of Ditch F which may have been at least partially visible when the grave was dug. This grave was cut by neonate grave B1257 which was located over the area of the lower left leg.

Human remains: supine, arms extended, 95% skeletal recovery, age 24–38, female.

Grave goods: B1253.1: iron hobnails x 5 (area of right foot).

Grave fill finds: pottery: x 1 sherd (TF 98); animal bone: LM x 1, MM x 1.

Date: not closely dated.

B1254 (grave 5132, Sk 5133) (Figs 3.108–3.109)

Grave: south-west–north-east. Rectangular with vertical sides and flat base, 1.94m x 0.57m x 0.17m deep. Dark brown silty clay fill with frequent limestone fragments. Remnant of lime wash on coffin preserved in grave fill (Fig. 3.109).

Human remains: supine, arms slightly flexed with hands over pelvis, 90% skeletal recovery, age 28–45, female.

Grave goods: B1254.1: hobnail cluster, x 60 iron nails (position not recorded).

Coffin nails: iron x 12, including fragments. Flat-headed, complete example 91mm long.

Grave fill finds: pottery: x 2 sherds (TF 74, 98).

Date: 2nd to 4th centuries (grave fill pottery).

B1255 (grave 5128, Sk 5135) (Fig. 3.110)

Grave: south-west–north-east. Rectangular with vertical sides and flat base, 2m x 0.7m x 0.3m deep. Mid brown clay silt fill with frequent limestone fragments.

Human remains: prone, arms extended below pelvis, 95% skeletal recovery, age 31–49, female.

Coffin nails: iron x 4, shaft fragments.

Grave fill finds: pottery: x 5 sherds (TF 5, 74, 98); animal bone: SUS x 1.

Date: 2nd to 4th centuries (grave fill pottery).

B1256 (grave 5140, Sk 5139) (Fig. 3.111)

Grave: south-east–north-west. Sub-rectangular with vertical sides and flat base, 1.75m x 0.73m x 0.18m deep. Dark grey-brown clay silt fill with frequent limestone fragments.

Human remains: supine, right arm extended, left arm

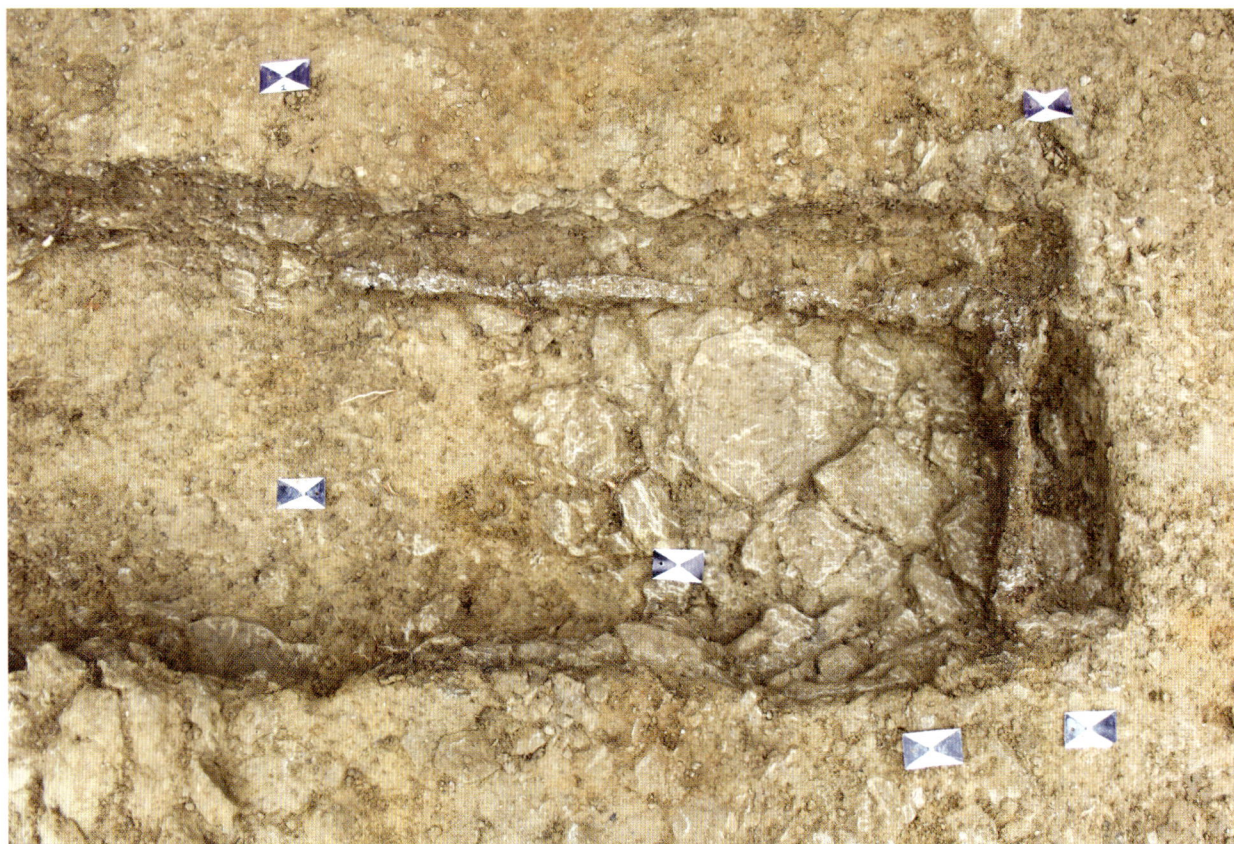

Fig. 3.109   Detail of the lime wash or plaster covering of the wooden coffin containing B1254

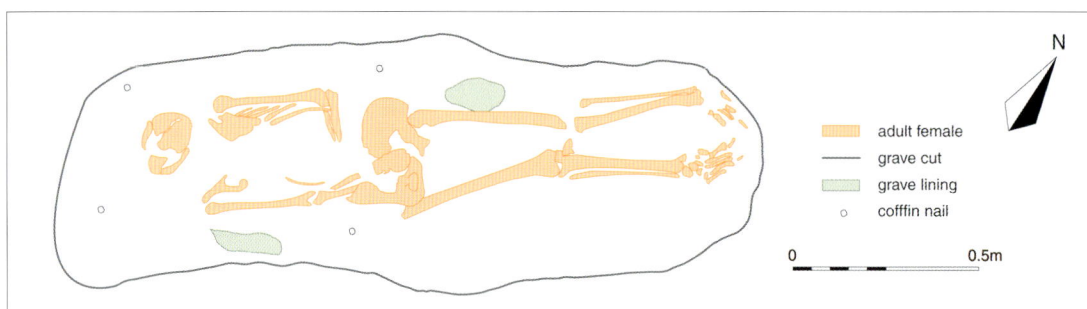

Fig. 3.110   Burial B1255

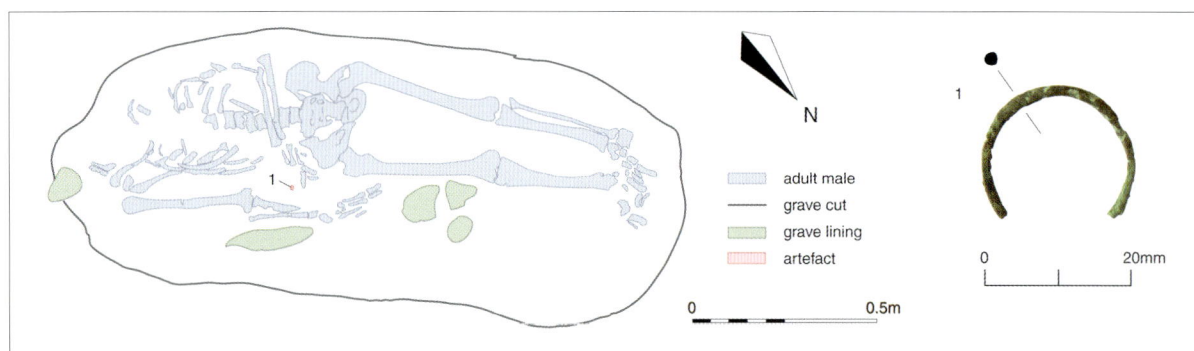

Fig. 3.111   Burial B1256

across abdomen, 85% skeletal recovery, age 26–42, male.

Grave goods: B1256.1: copper-alloy finger ring. Plain, D-sectioned hoop. External diameter 20.5mm, section 1.5 x 1.5mm. Location: worn on left hand.

Grave fill finds: pottery: x 1 sherd (TF 106).

Date: 3rd to 4th century (grave good).

B1257 (grave 5121, Sk 5141) (Fig. 3.112)

Grave: within terminus of Ditch F, approximate dimensions of 0.5m x 0.3m x 0.2m deep. The extent and shape of the grave cut are uncertain as it was dug into the backfill of B1253. Dark brown silty clay fill with frequent limestone fragments. This grave cut B1253: as there was a thin layer of grave fill between the skeleton of B1257 and lower left leg of B1253 below, it is unlikely that they were interred at the same time. It is probable that the terminus of Ditch F was at least

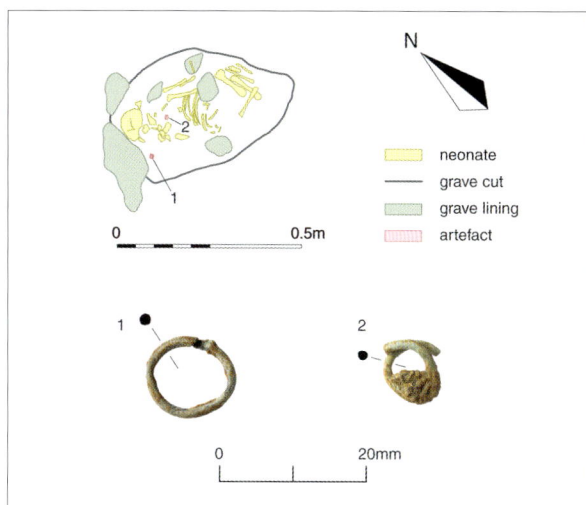

Fig. 3.112   Burial B1257

partially extant when this grave was dug, and that the location of B1253 was known, if not marked. Indeed the spatial relationship with B1253 may be more significant than its location within the terminus of Ditch F.

Human remains: crouched on left side, head at north-west end, arms and legs folded in front of body, 85% skeletal recovery, age around birth (neonate), sex indeterminable.

Grave goods: B1257.1: copper-alloy 'ring', diameter 12.5mm.

B1257.2: copper-alloy 'ring', diameter 9.5mm.

Both are simple coils of wire with butted (B1257.1) or overlapping (B1257.2) terminals. Location: close to the lower skull. Possibly earrings or hair ornaments.

Grave fill finds: pottery: x 6 sherds (TF 6, 74, 98).

Date: 2nd to 4th centuries (grave fill pottery).

B1258 (grave 5161, Sk 5163) (Fig. 3.113)

Grave: north-west–south-east. Sub-rectangular with irregular sides due to limestone bedrock and flat base, 2.1m x 0.75m x 0.4m deep. Mid orange-brown sandy clay fill with frequent limestone fragments. Possible stone lining. This grave appeared to cut the infilled terminus of Ditch B.

Human remains: supine, arms crossed on abdomen, 90% skeletal recovery, age 24–38, female.

Coffin nails: iron x 10, including fragments. Flat-headed, complete examples 75–115mm long.

Grave fill finds: pottery: x 34 sherds (TF 6, 9, 74, 98, 118, 154b).

Date: 2nd to 3rd centuries (grave fill pottery).

B1259 (grave 5172, Sk 5171) (Fig. 3.114)

Grave: south-west–north-east. Sub-rectangular with vertical sides and flat base, 2.2m x 0.98m x 0.83m deep. Mid yellow-brown clay silt with abundant limestone fragments. Possible stone packing.

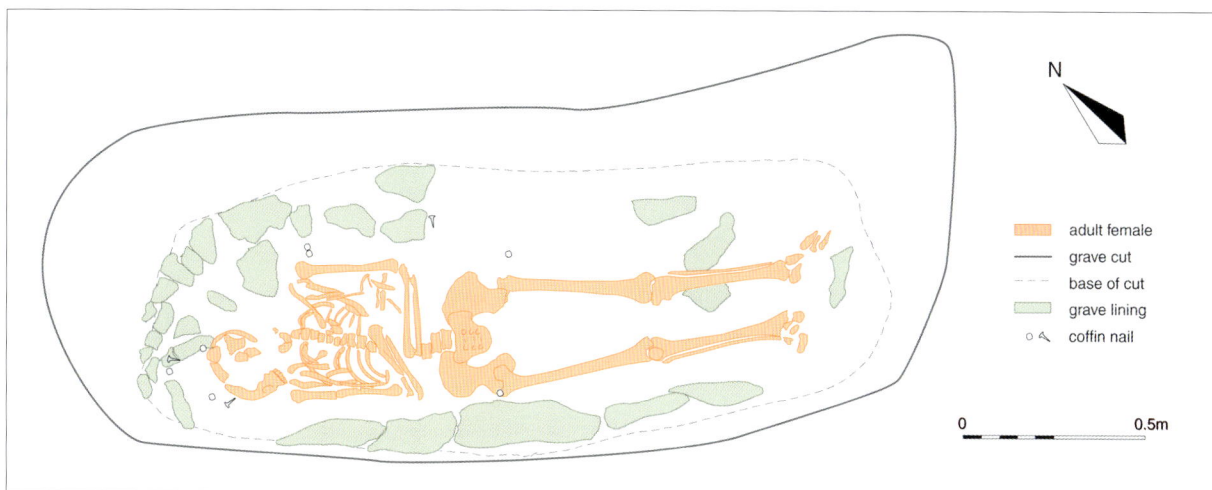

Fig. 3.113   Burial B1258

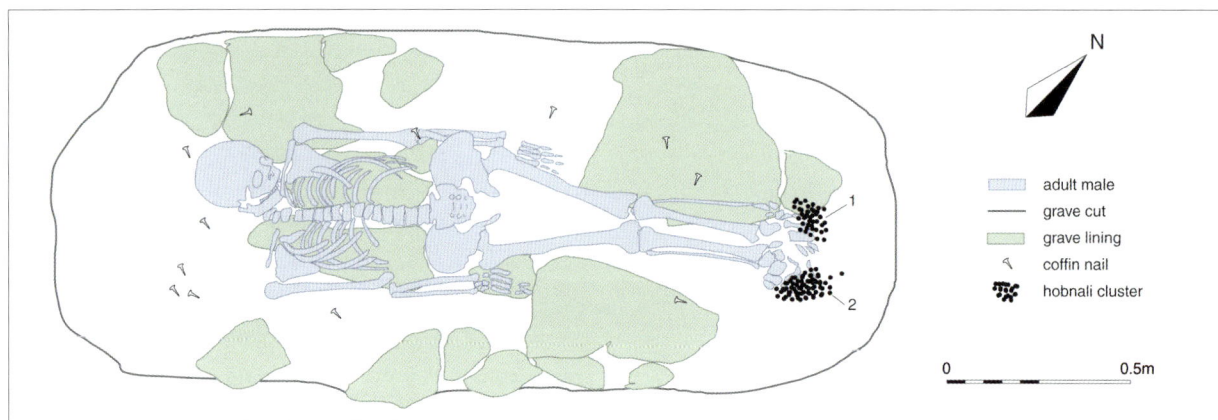

Fig. 3.114   Burial B1259

Human remains: supine, arms extended by sides of body, 95% skeletal recovery, age 26–38, male.

Grave goods: B1259.1: hobnail cluster, x 32 iron nails. Location: in area of left foot (probably worn).

B1259.2: hobnail cluster, x 31 iron nails. Location: in area of right foot (probably worn).

Coffin nails: iron x 12, including fragments. Flat-headed, complete example 65mm long.

Date: not closely dated.

B1260 (grave 5173, Sk 5174) (Fig. 3.115)

Grave: north-east-south-west. Sub-rectangular with vertical sides and uneven base due to nature of bedrock, 0.86m x 0.76m x 0.25m deep. Mid orange-brown silty clay. This grave was cut by B1251 to the south-west and to the north-east by a modern pit.

Human remains: supine, hands crossed over pelvis, 45% skeletal recovery, age 26–36, male.

Coffin nails: iron x 2, shaft fragments.

Grave fill finds: pottery: x 11 sherds (TF 9).

Date: not closely dated (grave fill pottery): while the

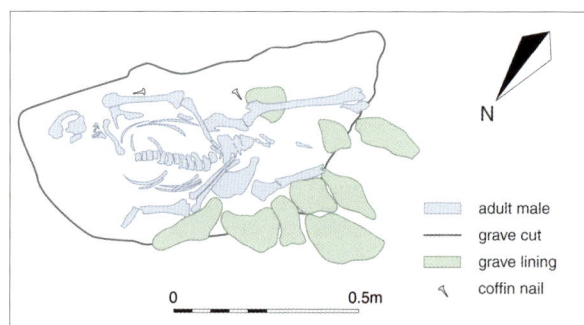

Fig. 3.115   Burial B1260

pottery is dated to the late 1st to 2nd century, there is a high risk of redeposition.

B1261 (grave 5178, Sk 5180) (Fig. 3.116)

Grave: north-west–south-east. Irregular, sub-rectangular with steep sides and flat base, 2.04m x 0.9m x 0.45m deep. Primary fill of mid yellowish-grey clay with abundant limestone fragments. Secondary fill of dark

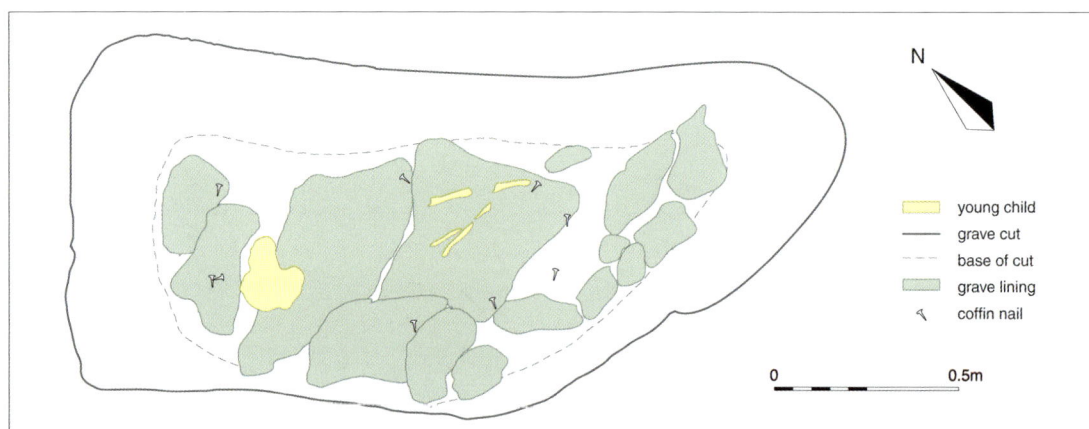

Fig. 3.116   Burial B1261

brown silty clay. Cut graves B1263 and B1274.

Human remains: supine?, extended?, position unknown due to lack of remains, 8% skeletal recovery, age *c*. 2, sex indeterminable.

Coffin nails: iron x 9, including fragments. Flat-headed, complete examples 45–75mm long.

Grave fill finds: pottery: x 3 sherds (TF 9, 98, 154b); flint blade x 1.

Date: not closely dated from the grave fill pottery, which dates to the late 1st to 2nd century, but as this grave cut B1263 it must be mid to late 4th century.

B1262 (grave 5192, Sk 5191) (Fig. 3.117)

Grave: south–north. Arbitrary cut, poorly defined, but seemingly sub-oval with shallow sides and concave base, 0.4m x 0.35m x 0.15m deep. Mid reddish-brown clay silt fill with frequent limestone fragments. Cut grave B1268 and was cut by B1267.

Human remains: crouched, arms flexed at elbow, hands near head, legs flexed at knee, 60% skeletal recovery, age around birth (neonate), sex indeterminable.

Coffin nails: iron x 15, including fragments. Flat-headed, complete examples 56–70mm long.

Grave fill finds: pottery: x 4 sherds (TF 5, 74, 98); animal bone: IND x 1.

Date: not closely dated. (grave fill pottery): while the pottery is dated to the 2nd century, there is a high risk of redeposition.

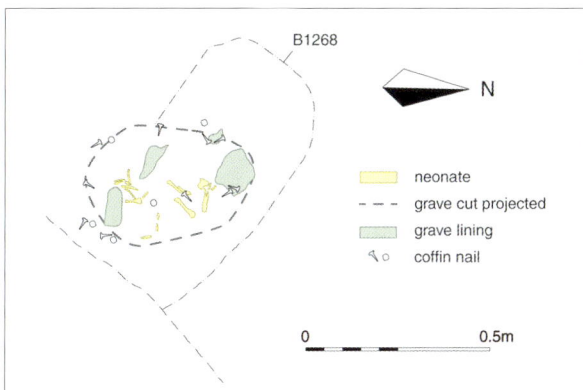

Fig. 3.117   Burial B1262

B1263 (grave 5195, Sk 5196) (Fig. 3.118)

Grave: north-west–south-east. Rectangular with vertical sides and flat base, 1.9m x 0.74m x 0.22m deep. Dark brown silty clay fill. Cut B1274 and cut by B1261.

Human remains: supine, arms flexed at elbow, hands in front of face to right, legs crossed at ankles, 90% skeletal recovery, age 12–14, sex indeterminable.

Grave goods: B1263.1: copper-alloy bracelet. Plain, round-sectioned wire hoop, the ends overlapping and coiled (two full turns) around the other to form an expanding joint of sliding knot type (*cf.* Allason-Jones and Miket 1984, 132, no. 3.249). Diameter 101–103mm; diameter of section 2.2mm.

B1263.2: glass beads string composed of 25 'appearing black' opaque glass beads of the same, sub-spherical, form. Although larger than is typical, the beads conform to Guido's (1978, 91–3) 'small segmented' type, which are known to occur in various colours including 'very dark glass, appearing black'. The use of very dark glass is a late phenomenon, current probably in the period after *c*. AD 350 and continuing into the post-Roman period. Diameter 6–7mm, thickness 5.0–5.5mm. B1263.2 was strung on a very fine copper-alloy wire, very little of which survived. Location: B1263.1 and B1263.2 were located close to the right side of the legs.

B1263.3: hobnail cluster, x 36 iron nails. B1263.4: hobnail cluster, x 41 iron nails. Footwear worn on feet.

Coffin nails: x 20. Flat-headed, complete examples 70–89mm long.

Grave fill finds: pottery: 12 sherds (TF5, 6, 9, 74, 98); animal bone: BOS x 1, SUS x 1.

Date: mid–late 4th century (grave goods).

B1264 (grave 5198, Sk 5200) (Fig. 3.119)

Grave: north-east–south-west. Sub-rectangular with vertical sides and uneven base, 1.35m x 0.5m x 0.16m deep. Dark grey-brown silty clay fill with frequent limestone fragments.

Human remains: supine, arms extended by sides of body, 15% skeletal recovery, age *c*. 4, sex indeterminable.

Coffin nails: iron x 8, including fragments. Flat-headed, complete examples 52–67mm long.

Grave fill finds: 1 sherd (TF 98).

Date: not closely dated.

B1265 (grave 5201, Sk 5202) (Fig. 3.120)

Grave: north-east–south-west. Rectangular with vertical sides and uneven base, 1.7m x 0.53m x 0.27m deep. Grey-brown silty clay fill with frequent limestone fragments.

Human remains: supine, left arm extended by side, right arm flexed at elbow over pelvis, 70% skeletal recovery, age 22–31, female.

Grave goods: B1265.1: glass vessel in 17 fragments. Sub-stantially complete convex cup (Isings 1957, form 96) in greenish colourless and bubbly glass. Self-coloured applied, arched festoon to lower third of the vessel and two bands of horizontal wheel-abraded lines below the rim, which is simple and probably ground. The lower joins of the festoon are set into deep, circular indents, which is a feature not seen with other examples of the class. Examples of this form with applied and wheel-cut decoration are known as grave finds and from 'domestic' assemblages, including the large later 4th-century group from Barnsley Park, Gloucestershire (Price 1982, 175–7).

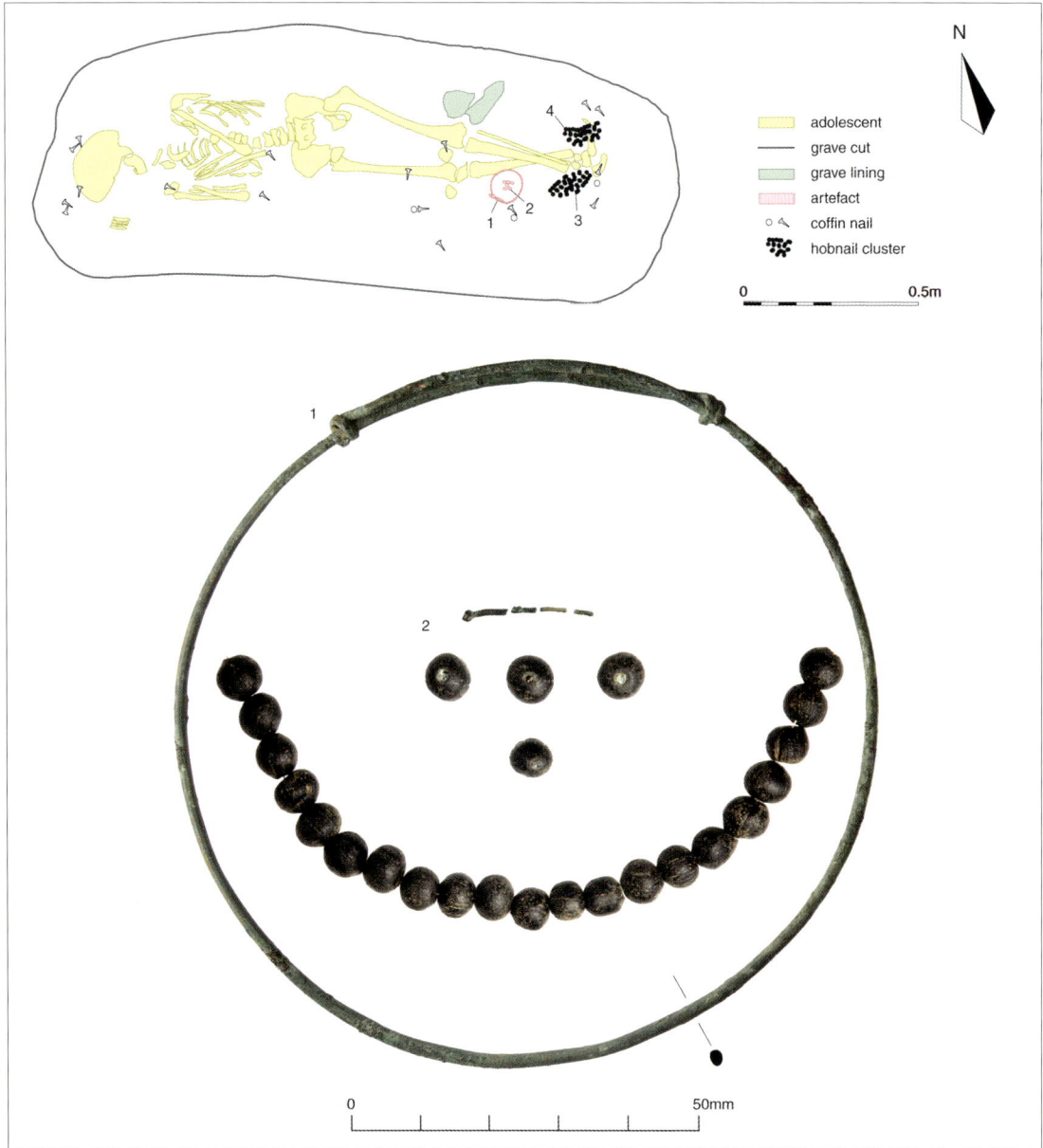

Fig. 3.118   Burial B1263

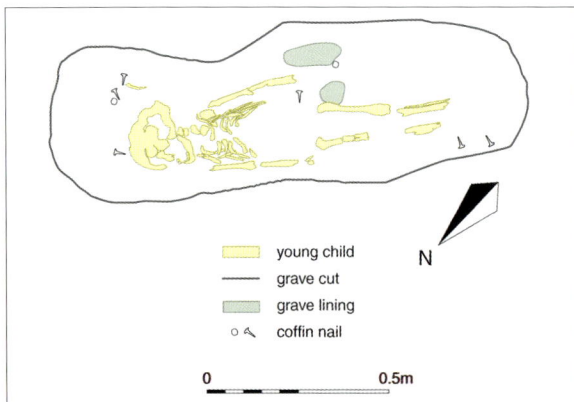

Fig. 3.119   Burial B1264

Grave finds from Lankhills (Harden 1979, 213, nos. 62, 385) also support dating in the middle or late 4th century. Location: fragments found either side of thigh bones.

Coffin nails: iron x 4, including fragments. Flat-headed, complete example 50mm long.

Date: mid/late 4th century (grave good).

B1266 (grave 5193, Sk 5204) (Fig. 3.121)

Grave: north-west–south-east. Sub-rectangular with vertical sides and flat base, 2.3m x 0.8m x 0.45m. Mid grey to yellow-brown sandy clay fill with a preserved remnant of lime wash from the wooden coffin. Slightly truncated by a modern feature to the west.

Human remains: supine, left arm extended at side under

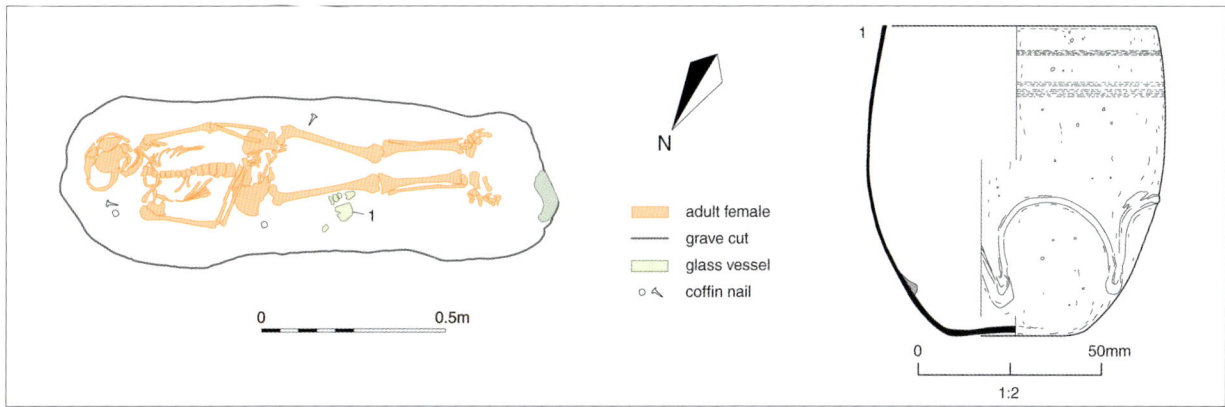

Fig. 3.120   Burial B1265

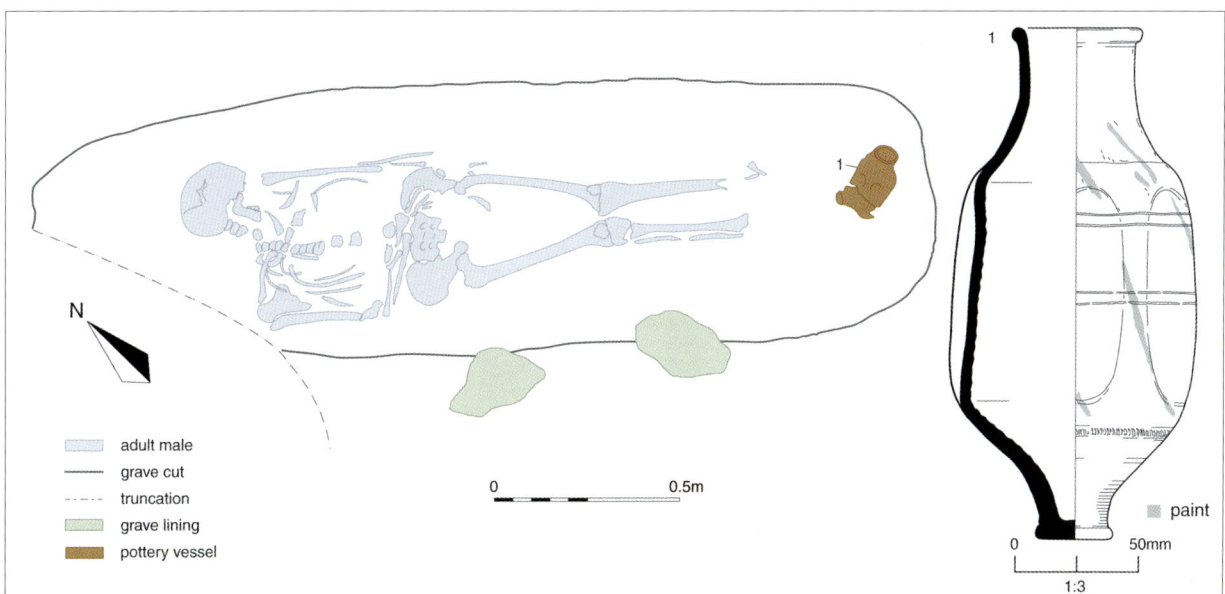

Fig. 3.121   Burial B1266

pelvis, right arm flexed at elbow across lower abdomen, 85% skeletal recovery, age 29–44, male.

Grave goods: B1266.1: complete pottery vessel. Oxford red slipped ware (TF 83). The form is a tall funnel-necked indented beaker, with horizontal grooves and rouletted bands and vertical/oblique trails of white paint. Young's (1977) corpus of Oxfordshire pottery includes a number of indented beaker types (C20, C31, C32), none of which match exactly the form of this example. The use of white paint is commonly a late trait and dating after *c*. AD 325 is probable. Location: at feet, outside of the coffin stain.

B1266.2: iron hobnails x 3.

Coffin nails: none.

Grave fill finds: fragment of prismatic glass bottle.

Date: mid/late 4th century (grave good).

B1267 (grave 5205, Sk 5207) (Figs 3.122–3.123)

Grave: south-west–north-east, but noticeably misaligned compared to the prevailing alignment of other graves. Rectangular with vertical sides and flat base, 1.87m x 0.67m x 0.37m deep. Mid grey-brown clay silt fill with frequent limestone fragments. Possible stone lining. The grave cut contained a carved and inscribed reused limestone tombstone laid face down on top of grave fill. The gable end of the slab pointed to the north-east, the foot end of B1267 (Fig. 3.123). The tombstone had tilted to the south-east, possibly as a result of the collapse of the underlying coffin, which resulted in the crushing of parts of the right arm of the skeleton. The tombstone had been placed central to the grave cut with a gap of 0.25m between the north-east and south-west ends of the slab and the grave cut. The edges of the stone were flush against the sides of the grave cut. This burial

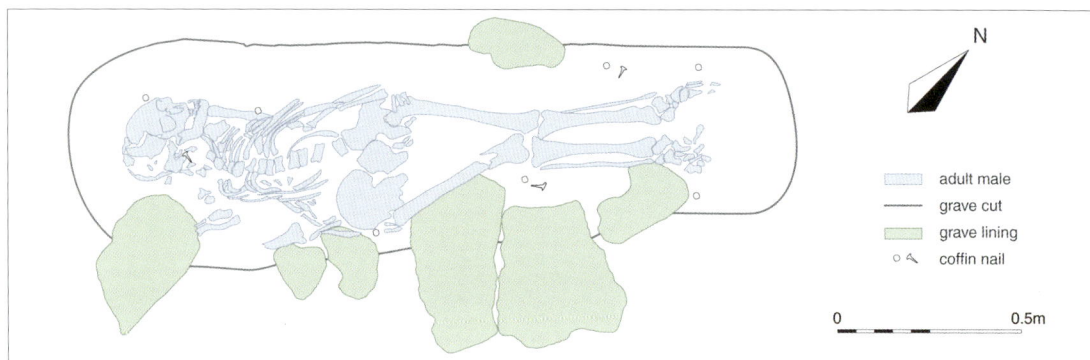

Fig. 3.122   Burial B1267

Fig. 3.123   *The underside of the reused tombstone of Bodicacia covering B1267. The skull of the skeleton can be seen beneath the right end of the slab. In the foreground are the unexcavated graves of neonate, infant and young child B1262, B1268 and B1271 cut through by B1267. 1m scale*

cut neonate, infant and young child graves B1262, B1268 and B1271.

Human remains: supine, left arm extended under ribs, right arm extended under pelvis, 90% skeletal recovery, age 45–58, male.

Coffin nails: iron x 16, including fragments. Flat-headed.

Grave fill finds: pottery: 18 sherds (TF 5).

Date: not closely dated, but later than the mid 2nd century given that the tombstone was reused in the grave.

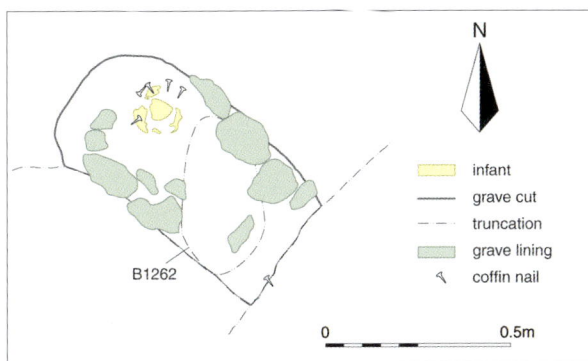

Fig. 3.124   Burial B1268

B1268 (grave 5210, Sk 5209) (Fig. 3.124)

Grave: north-west–south-east. Rectangular with vertical sides and flat base, >0.68m x 0.4m x 0.16m deep. Mid grey-brown clay silt fill with frequent limestone fragments. Possible stone packing around coffin. Cut by graves B1262 and B1267. Cut B1271.

Human remains: supine, arms extended?, 5% skeletal recovery, age *c.* 9 months, sex indeterminable.

Grave goods: B1268.1: hobnails, x 68 iron nails. Location: not recorded.

Coffin nails: iron x 12, including fragments. Flat-headed, complete examples 35–52mm long.

Grave fill finds: pottery: 18 sherds (TF 5, 6, 74, 98).

Date: 2nd to 4th centuries (grave fill pottery).

B1269 (grave 5213, Sk 5212) (Fig. 3.125)

Grave: north-east–south-west. Sub-rectangular with vertical sides and flat base, >0.9m x 0.8m x 0.5m deep. Mid grey-brown clay silt fill with frequent limestone fragments. Possible stone packing. The grave was only partially exposed within the excavation area, and the upper part of its fill had been truncated by a modern service trench. The grave possibly respected the terminal of Ditch F which would suggest that the ditch was at least partially extant when B1269 was interred.

Human remains: supine, arms crossed over pelvis, 40% skeletal recovery, age 39–49, male. Probably decapitated, but insufficient evidence for certainty.

Possible grave goods: B1269.1: copper-alloy coin, *nummus*/AE3 (LRBC 790): Siscia mint, Constantius/Victories with wreaths, AD 341–6;

Coin B1269.2: copper-alloy coin, *nummus*/AE3. Probably House of Constantine, FEL TEMP REPARATIO (soldier leading barbarian from hut), AD 348–50; Trier mint (TRS). Location: neither coin was precisely located, but recorded as loose in the grave fill.

Coffin nails: iron x 2, fragments. Flat-headed.

Grave fill finds: pottery: 2 sherds (TF 74, 98); animal bone: BOS x 2.

Date: mid 4th century (grave goods).

B1270 (grave 5215, Sk 5217) (not illustrated)

Grave: north-east–south-west. Precise grave cut indiscernible in the field, so arbitrary number attributed, *c.* 0.2m x 0.2m x 0.05m deep. Mid grey-brown silty clay fill. Grave cut heavily truncated by modern activity. Potentially laid within Ditch E rather than having an individual grave cut.

Human remains: right tibia and fibula only, so position of the body could not be established, 5% skeletal recovery, age 1–2, sex indeterminable.

Date: not closely dated.

B1271 (grave 5222, Sk 5221) (Fig. 3.126)

Grave: north-west–south-east. Sub-rectangular with shallow sides and flat base, >1m x 0.45m x 0.1m deep. Mid brown-grey clay silt fill. Cut by graves B1268 and B1267.

Human remains: prone, upper arms only: extended?, legs slightly flexed at knee, 50% skeletal recovery, age *c.* 2, sex indeterminable.

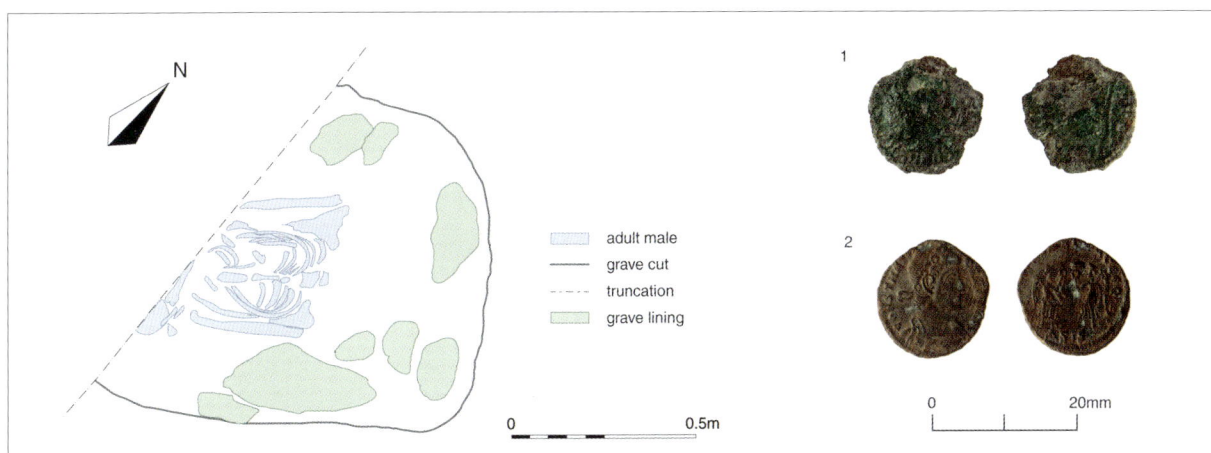

Fig. 3.125   Burial B1269

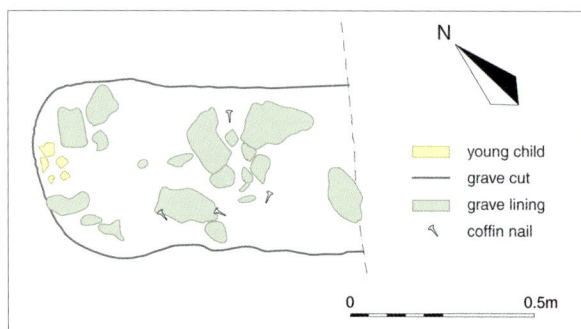

Fig. 3.126   Burial B1271

Coffin nails: iron x 4, shaft fragments.

Grave fill finds: pottery: 1 sherd (TF 5).

Date: not closely dated.

B1272 (grave 5223, Sk 5224) (Figs 3.127–3.128)

Grave: south-west–north-east. Sub-rectangular with vertical sides and flat base, 1.68m x 0.58m x 0.19m deep. Dark brown-grey sandy clay fill with frequent limestone fragments. Pitched limestone slabs around the edge of the body (Fig. 3.128).

Human remains: supine, left arm extended, left hand on pelvis, right arm flexed at elbow, right hand on pelvis, 70% skeletal recovery, age 41–45, female.

Coffin nails: iron x 9, including fragments. Flat-headed.

Grave fill finds: animal bone: O/C x 1.

Date: not closely dated.

B1273 (grave 5226, Sk 5228) (Fig. 3.129)

Grave: north-west-south-east aligned. Rectangular with vertical sides and irregular base, >1.4m x 0.47m x 0.1m deep. Mid brown clay fill with frequent limestone fragments. Truncated to the north-west by a modern feature.

Human remains: supine, right arm only, extended alongside body, 80% skeletal recovery, age *c.* 2, sex indeterminable.

Grave goods: Locations not recorded. B1273.1: copper-

Fig. 3.128   B1272 showing packing stones around the outside of the wooden coffin. 1m scales

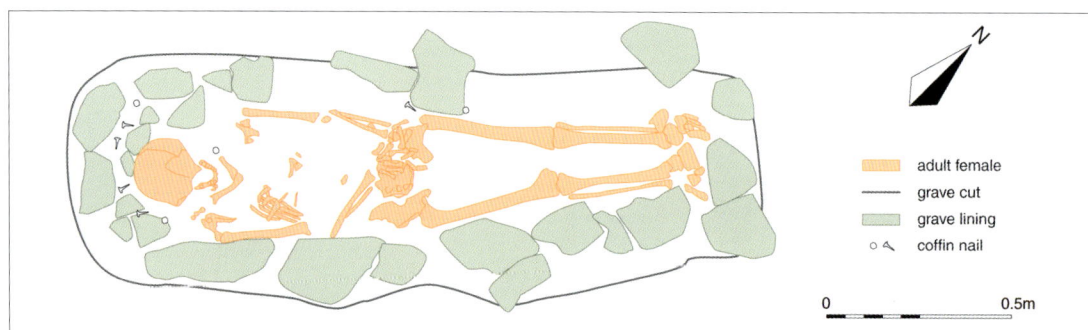

Fig. 3.127   Burial B1272

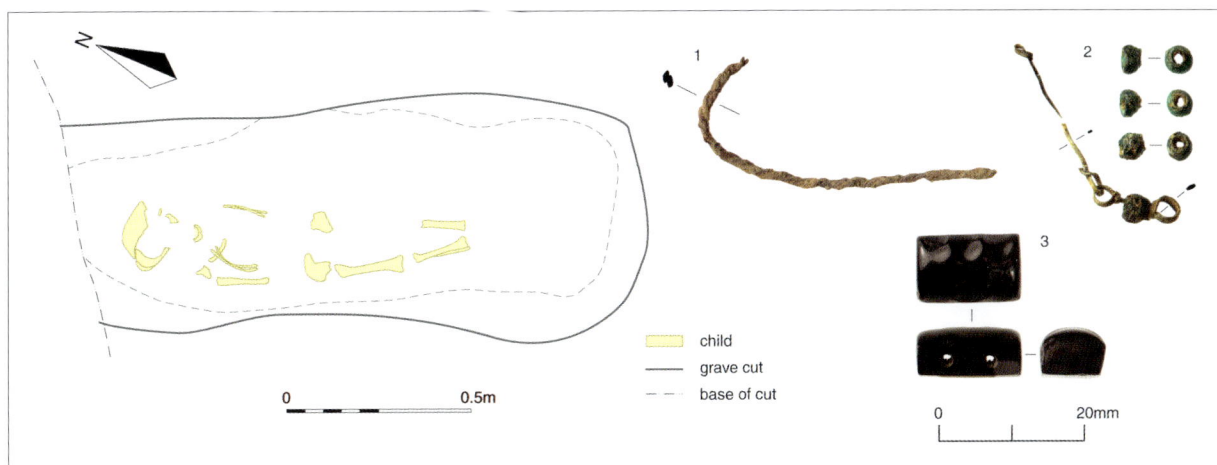

Fig. 3.129   Burial B1273

alloy ?bracelet. A length of (2 strand) twisted wire, length 42mm, section 1.5mm.

B1273.2: copper-alloy/glass articulating beaded ornament. Fragment. The surviving portion consists of a single link of flat-sectioned wire, with terminal loops created by twisting the ends around the centre strand, on which is an opaque green bead of small segmented type. There are a further three detached beads of the same type and two fragmentary links of flat-sectioned wire. Length (link) 12.5mm; bead diameter 4mm. Parallels for B1273.2 include B1177.6 and better-preserved examples from Lankhills (Cool 2010, 1360, fig. 3.191, no. 101/b) and Poundbury (Guido and Mills 1993, fig. 72, no. 5). Dating in the second half of the 4th or early 5th centuries would seem probable.

B1273.3: jet bead. Rectangular 'spacer' bead with two parallel perforations. The upper face features shallow grooves/ridges and in this respect B1273.3 resembles a shale bead from South Shields (Allason-Jones and Miket 1984, 309, no. 7.78). Length (link) 14mm, width 8mm, thickness 5.5mm.

Coffin nails: iron x 1, flat-headed.

Date: mid to late 4th century (grave goods).

B1274 (grave 5229, Sk 5230) (Fig. 3.130)

Grave: south-east–north-west. Sub-rectangular with shallow sides and flat base, 0.97m x 0.4m x 0.13m deep. Dark grey-brown silty clay fill. Cut by graves B1261 and B1263.

Human remains: supine, left arm extended, right arm flexed at elbow across lower abdomen, 25% skeletal recovery, age 45–49, male.

Grave fill finds: animal bone: MM x 1.

Date: not closely dated.

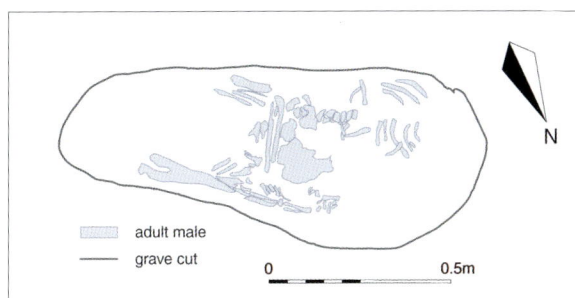

Fig. 3.130   Burial B1274

B1279 (a, b and c) (Sk 5187 (a); Sk 5188 (b); Sk 5189 (c) within Ditch F) (not illustrated)

Grave: three fragmented skulls in a cluster at the base of Ditch F at the point where it cut through infilled Ditch B. No evidence of a cut through the fill of Ditch F was observed, and the skulls may have been placed on the base of the ditch whilst it was still open. Alternatively they have been placed in a pit dug through infilled Ditch F which was not detected in the field. Animal bone was also present on the base of the ditch adjacent to the skulls.

Human remains: B1279a: adult female, frontal bone only. B1279b: older adult male, skull vault only. B1279c: male, frontal bone and left parietal bone only, with possible sharp-force trauma suggesting decapitation.

Feature 5079, on the western edge of the excavation area, may be the north-eastern end of another grave, although not enough of the feature was exposed to confirm this, and no human remains were recovered. The feature appeared to be on a similar alignment to surrounding burials B1252, B1248 and B1240.

Chapter 4
Artefacts

4.1 The Tombstone
K.M.J Hayward, Martin Henig and
Roger S.O. Tomlin

The tombstone comprises a single block of local limestone, 1.34m long by 0.54m wide, and up to 0.23m in thickness (Figs 4.2–4.4, 7.6–7.8). It was found in a reused context: face down covering the skeleton of B1267, a 45 to 58-year-old man (Fig. 3.123). The stone was placed in the grave and covered with backfill, and so would have lain entirely below contemporary ground level. For this reason it escaped the attention of later stone robbers. Whilst the face of the stone has been finely worked, the sides and rear have only been very crudely dressed, as if they were never intended to be seen. Interestingly Mark Hassall also noted that the back of another inscribed tombstone from the Bath Gate Cemetery (RIB III, 3063) 'is rough, as if broken or built into some structure' (CEII, MF2, E11–12). As will be seen, whilst the carving of the epitaph is of high quality and evidently the work of a skilled local sculptor, the inscription has been incompetently rendered: only five of the six marking-out lines were used in the inscription, and the spacing between letters (such as the separation of the S from the rest of ANNOS shows either miscalculation or disregard). It is quite likely therefore that the tombstone was purchased with a blank panel, and that the inscription was added by a much less gifted craftsman after Bodicacia's death. Adcock (2015) provides a preliminary discussion of the tombstone and its significance, and the inscription has been previously published by Roger Tomlin in the journal *Britannia* (Tomlin 2015).

Petrology
K.M.J. Hayward

Hand specimen and thin-section petrographic analysis was conducted to determine what type of limestone the tombstone was made from and, where possible, to determine its geological source. Petrological comparison has been made with a reference collection of outcrop samples from the Cirencester area, as well as samples from Roman military and civilian tombstones and fragments of monumental architecture from Cirencester. These were prepared during earlier research and have improved the chances of finding a successful match for the source of the stone used in the new tombstone (see Hayward 2006; 2009; Coombe *et al.* 2015 and see the listing of comparative samples in the Technical Details section below).

Methodology
The macroscopic character of the tombstone was examined using a hand lens (Gowland x10). The retained sample underwent further visual analysis using a long arm stereo-microscope and the texture, colour (Munsell Color Group 1980) and inclusions were recorded. Treatment of dilute hydrochloric acid determined whether the rock had a calcareous composition or not.

A 20mm-long by 15mm-thick sub-sample was selected for thin-section preparation and analysis. Although destructive, this method ensured that the maximum amount of information could be obtained from the smallest possible sample size thus fulfilling the museum's sampling policies. Further details of the procedural implications and sample preparation can be found in Hayward 2009. The sample was additionally embedded in coloured araldite resin (CY1301) which was necessary for two reasons. First, the process of embedding with the addition of a hardener (HY951) strengthened the sample. Second, the addition of a green colouring agent (BW1034) during this process highlighted the pore spaces in the sample enabling the overall porosity to be determined. Staining is a necessary process (Adams and Mackenzie 1998) during the production of the more lime-rich thin sections. It picks out the variability in colour between ferroan and non-ferroan calcite as well as dolomite, with the addition of Alizarin Red C and Potassium Hexocynoferrate.

This high resolution petrographic approach enabled

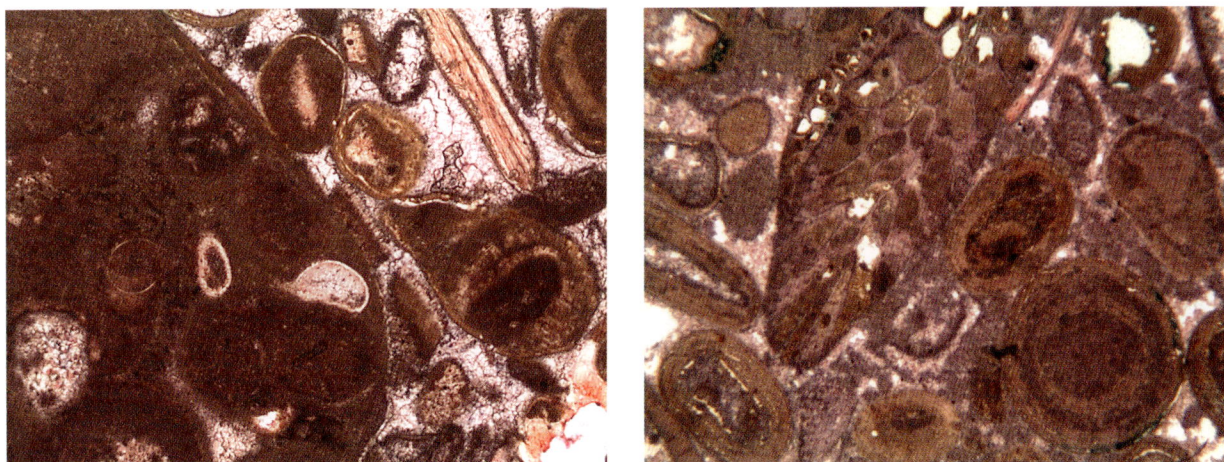

Fig. 4.1 Comparative photomicrograph showing textural and palaeontological similarities of the limestone slide from the Bodicacia tombstone (left) and Bibury Stone Outcrop Middle Jurassic White Limestone Formation (Bathonian) (right). Plane polarised light. Slides stained with Alizarin Red C and Potassium Hexocynoferrate to pick out variability in colour between ferroan and non-ferroan calcite. Field of view 2.4mm

a 30 micron-thick slice of stone to be viewed under the polarising microscope at magnifications greater than x400 (Leica DMLP). Thin sections can help distinguish between different types of calcite grains, minerals, cements and microfossils. Finally, a series of photomicrographs of the tombstone, as well as comparative archaeological and geological samples, were produced using a Leica DFC 320 Digital Camera (Fig. 4.1) of the fabric and successful geological and archaeological matches.

Geological background

The underlying geology of Cirencester and its immediate environs are defined as a series of Middle Jurassic (Bathonian) shelly, sandy and oolitic limestones (BGS Sheet 235; Sumbler *et al.* 2000). Some of these are freestones, even-grained oolitic and shelly limestones with an open porous texture (Leary 1989) suitable for fine carving and inscription in funerary, architectural and religious sculpture. These include dimension stones from the Taynton Limestone Formation (e.g. Taynton stone) as well as the White Limestone Formation (Bibury stone; Barnsley stone), made all the more accessible by the presence of the nearby Fosse Way which cuts through many of these outcrops. On a wider regional scale still, Cirencester also acted as a major road hub for material supply with connections to Gloucester, the River Severn, Bath and Akeman Street, thus greatly increasing the potential number of suitable material types.

Results

Hand specimen

Banded oolitic limestone (shelly) Middle Jurassic (Bathonian); South Cotswolds. Initial visual inspection

of the tombstone surface determined that it was carved from a compact, fine flaggy-banded shelly oolitic grainstone (Dunham 1962). The external surface on all faces of the epitaph had been weathered pale yellow-brown (2.5 YR 8/6) to a depth of 5mm, whilst fresh surfaces revealed a paler fine cream-white (2.5 Y 8/1) to pale yellow (2.5 Y8/2) hue. The outer face was pitted with sparse to intermittent large (0.5–1mm) hollowed ooids along with a varied group of fossils, including small (0.1–0.4mm) black and grey oyster fragments, occasional ribbed rhynchonellid brachiopods, and white coral or bryozoan colonies, which together are diagnostic of a Middle Jurassic faunal assemblage. Along the sides of the tombstone this shelly material formed discrete narrow (20mm thick) pale cream-grey bands inter-bedded with thicker bands (50–70mm) of fawn-coloured ooids. Imperfections in the choice of stone, however are shown by the presence of a sizeable (130cm long by 20mm thick) bifurcating calcite vein or *watermark* (Jope 1964) on its underside.

Together these features (oyster-rich, pitted ooids, banding, watermarks) are characteristic features of the Middle Jurassic (Bathonian) rocks of the South Cotswold escarpment between Cirencester and Bath, seen in all the Roman architectural fragments and tombstones from Cirencester at the Corinium Museum (Hayward personal observations) and in many other towns in south-central England including the provincial capital of London (Coombe *et al.* 2015) and Silchester (Hayward 2009).

Thin-section

Oo-biosparite (Folk 1959; 1962): In order to reinforce and refine characterisation, a prepared thin-section of the tombstone was compared with a petrographic reference collection of slides obtained from 150 freestone outcrop samples and early Roman sculptural samples collated from earlier research (see Technical Details). A photomicrograph (Fig. 4.1 left) of the slide shows it to contain large (1mm) round ooids, with a thick pale-yellow coating or cortex and large bivalves. This and the presence of ferroan purple microcrystalline cement, but no quartz; oyster and bryozoan rich fauna as well as grapestones not only verifies a limestone from the Middle Jurassic (Bathonian) escarpment of the South Cotswolds but illustrates some important textural and palaeontological similarities with some thin sections taken from local outcrop samples (Fig. 4.1 right) and other examples of religious and funerary sculpture from late 1st-century AD London and Cirencester prepared and analysed in this way.

Identifying a more precise source for the Cirencester stone needs to be considered with great caution on account of an absence of exposures of Roman quarries, the lateral and vertical lithological variability at out-crop of these building stones (even within a single exposure), and a number of different Bathonian units close by containing freestone conforming to this generic description (Chipping Norton Limestone Formation; White Limestone Formation; Taynton Limestone Formation; Sumbler *et al.* 2000).

A thin section (CHED 1) of Bibury stone (Middle Jurassic Bathonian - Ardley Member, White Limestone Formation; Sumbler *et al.* 2000, 65) obtained from Bibury village, 5 miles north-east of Cirencester displays similar though not identical petrological affinities (Fig. 4.1 right) with the tombstone. Both the tombstone and the outcrop contain the well-rounded large ooids coated in a thick brown iron oxide matrix with ferroan cement. Given that outcrops of White Limestone lie even close to Cirencester than this, in particular those exposed along the valley side outcrops along the River Churn and Ampney Brook within 1 mile of the Roman town, then a ready supply of relatively high quality local stone could be supplied to the town.

Petrology of other Cirencester tombstones

Although none of the other thin-sectioned tombstones from Cirencester have an identical petrological character to the present example, they too bear the same hallmarks of locally acquired Middle Jurassic (Bathonian) rocks including Bibury stone, especially the presence of thickly coated well-rounded ooid fragments. The quality of stone varies. Two military tombstones bearing the 'horseman with fallen enemy motif' (Mackintosh 1986), associated with the presumed Claudio-Neronian to early Flavian fort: Dannicus (RIB 108) and Genialis (RIB 109), have the best quality, more open textured, stone (Hayward 2009). The later civilian tombstones, on the other hand, such as that of Julia Casta (RIB 113), are characterised by slabbier shellier units of rock more akin to that used for Bodicacia. The fact that the Bodicacia tombstone has

imperfections (see above) would suggest that it was not quarried from the most pristine grade of stone.

Tombstones from Early Roman London

Taking this petrological study one step further, the stone used in some of the early Roman tombstones from London is comparable with that used for the better-quality Cirencester monuments, Examples from London include a tombstone depicting a state official and a probable early funerary sculpture depicting a lion overcoming a stag, both from Arthur Price's 1876 excavations from bastion 10 of the town defences (Price 1880; Coombe *et al.* 2015), and the recent discovery of an eagle from the Minories site (Lerz *et al.* 2017). Cotswold limestone was by far the most common stone type used for late 1st to 2nd-century religious and funerary sculpture in London, having been identified in 40 examples, and would suggest that the Cirencester region was a major focal point for the quarrying and provincial distribution of these stones.

Technical details

One 20mm hand specimen was taken mechanically on 22 July 2015 using a hammer and chisel on the underside of the tombstone already scored by the mechanical digger. Thin-section SMR was produced in October 2015 using the thin-section preparation facilities at the School of Archaeology, Geography and Environmental Sciences at the University of Reading.

The following selected comparative thin sections were used:

1. *Archaeological samples:* Cirencester: KH52 Sextus Valerius Genialis (RIB 109); KH53 Dannicus (RIB 108); KH110 Philus (RIB 110); KH192 miniature Corinthian capital Class B (Blagg 2002, Cirencester 44–9); KH264 Corinthian capital Class C (Blagg 2002, Cirencester 20); civilian tombstone KH55 Aurelius Igennus (RIB III, 3030); KH56 Nemmonius (RIB III, 3061); KH57 Julia Casta (RIB 113). London: KH38: tombstone of a *beneficiarius consularis* (Bishop 1983; Hayward 2006; 2009; Coombe *et al.* 2015); funerary sculpture of a lion (Bishop 1983; Hayward 2006; 2009; Coombe *et al.* 2015); Claudia Martina tomb (RIB 21). 2. *Geological samples*: CHED 1 Outcrop (Bibury stone) (Hayward in prep.); KH124 Forest marble Cirencester amphitheatre; KH159 Minchinhampton Coarse Bed GR (SO 857015) Taynton stone (Hayward 2006; 2009); KH148 Taynton stone GR (SP 236152).

Sculpture
Martin Henig

The upper part of the tombstone, the pediment, is a superb example of Cotswold-school sculpture (Figs 4.2–4.4). The pediment is embellished with cresting, and surmounted by a finial, a very rare feature. It is inhabited by a mask of Oceanus, which in this context is again virtually unique.

The two rows of cresting, or *cima* ornament, meet at the apex with a finial of curving acanthus tendrils. The nearest parallel in Britain to this sort of cresting is upon the sides of the pediment of a tomb from Chester with cresting of confronted S-shaped elements (Henig 2004, 33, no. 10, pl. 29), which probably dates to the early 3rd century. Similar cresting is also a feature of the pediment of a tomb from Bonn (Bauchhenss 1979, 27–8, no. 21, Taf. 12); on a tombstone from Entrains in Gaul (Esperandieu 1910, 273, no. 2310), and on the limestone pediment of a late 1st-century AD *lararium* from the Severinstrasse, Cologne, within which are figures carved in relief, the central image being Mercury, who is flanked by Fortuna and Felicitas(?), while in the spandrels river gods recline (Schoppa 1959, 55, no. 41, Taf. 39). On a miniature scale there is indeed cresting represented on the pipe-clay shrines generally containing an image of 'Venus' from the Allier region of Gaul (Rouvier-Jeanlin 1972, 142–9, especially nos 228, 230 (Saint-Bonnet near Moulins, Allier), no. 249 (Toulon-sur-Allier), no. 258, all with tongue-like cresting; no. 257 is a case of a semi-circular top to the shrine with confronted S cresting). It is probable that slabs with S-shaped motifs from Chedworth and Great Witcombe (Blagg 1993, 74, no. 236, pl. 57; RCHME 1976, 61, pl. 28 bottom left) are actual examples of such cresting from full size architectural features. A pediment with a roof finial in the form of a pine-cone is a feature of the tombstone of Philus likewise from Corinium (Henig 1993, 49, no.141, pl. 36). These roof finials can be matched by real examples, notably those from Chedworth with vegetal ornament (Blagg 1993, 75, no. 237, pl. 57) and more stylishly from Gloucester in which curving tendrils emerge from behind a tragic mask (Henig 1993, 58, no. 173, pl. 42).

Within the pediment, carved with great panache in low relief, is a mask of Oceanus, identified by the two crab claws springing from each side of the crown of his head. From here two long strands curve away to near the edge of the pediment where they fold over themselves. On one side of the head (on the left as seen by the viewer) a second strand emerges curving at its terminal. From the sides of the mouth, with its rather thick lips, spring two long moustachios and there is a short beard below the mouth, which rests on the lower edge of the pediment. All of these features can be read as hair or as sea-weed as befits the great god of the Ocean (Cahn 1997). Other features have been defaced and probably deliberately. A chisel would seem to have been employed to score across the crab claws, the ends of the two major curving tendrils and, most unfortunately of all, the face. It is suggested that this was the result of Christian iconoclasm when the stone was reused as a grave cover in the 4th century. Enough, however, remains to demonstrate its refinement. The Chester pediment contains a male mask which seems to be a conflation of Neptune or Oceanus with Medusa,

Fig 4.2   The tombstone dedicated to Bodicacia

The cresting consists of five ball-and-crescent motifs on each of the sides, the crescents in each case being very full with only a short gap between the two ends. However, the deep cutting of the grooves marking the break between the ends of each crescent gives to the ornament the impression of openwork, characteristic of some jewellery from the late 2nd century and especially the 3rd century (see two disc brooches with cymation surrounds respectively from the Hauran, Syria and Cologne, Germany, Yeroulanou 1999, esp. 151–2, figs 279–80, and 230, nos 149–50) and even the surrounds of a few pieces of silver plate from the 3rd and 4th centuries (cf. Baratte *et al.* 1989, 177, no. 124).

on the lines of the centrepiece of the Temple of Sulis Minerva at Bath. Medusa masks occupy the pediment of the tombstone of Placida and Deuccus from Chester (Henig 2004, 49, no. 150, pl. 41) and occur within a pediment from Bonn mentioned above. There is a mask which might be an Oceanus mask in the pediment of a civilian tombstone from Bonn (Bauchhenss 1979, 23, no. 11, taf. 7) but this is nowhere near as fine.

Oceanus is not commonly depicted in sculpture from Roman Britain. A head of Neptune or Oceanus from Southwark, probably funerary (Coombe *et al.* 2015, 37–8, no. 63a, pl. 38), and from Cirencester itself, the head of another watery deity, variously identified as Oceanus, Neptune or simply a river god (Henig 1993, 30, no. 89, pl. 25), both of them carved in the round in Cotswold limestone (presumably by sculptors from the region) deserve to be noted. A mask of Oceanus or a river god is preserved amongst the unpublished Roman sculpture evidently from a mausoleum demolished and employed in the 4th century as post-packing at a villa at Stanwick, Northamptonshire (Frere 1991, 252–3; Taylor and Flitcroft 2004, fig. 5.4). From northern Britain the statue of a river god (presumably the Tyne) from the commandant's bath-house of the fort at Chesters is of interest as he leans on a mask which may represent Oceanus into which the river debouches (Coulston and Phillips 1988, 35, no. 94, pl. 26).

Mosaics provide the best iconographic parallels for the head. The 2nd-century mosaic depicting the head of Oceanus from Verulamium is very close in date and it too is identified by crab claws in the hair (Cahn 1997, 909, no. 22, pl. on p. 602; Neal and Cosh 2009, 326–7, mosaic 348.22). There are two masks, plausibly of Oceanus, figured on a 2nd-century mosaic from Dyer Street, Cirencester, though they lack the crab claws (Cahn 1997, 909, no. 19 = Cosh and Neal 2010, 107–10, mosaic 421.45). And, of course, from the 4th century we may note the Oceanus masks on the Woodchester and Withington mosaics (Cosh and Neal 2010, 221, mosaic 456.1; 204–6, mosaic 455.4 = Cahn 1997, 909, no. 21, pl. on p. 602), both with the distinctive crab claws.

Although Cirencester is far inland, Oceanus may have had a particular resonance in Britain, traditionally thought to lie on the other side of Ocean, and which both Caligula and Claudius claimed to have conquered (Suetonius, *Caligula* 46; Dio Cassius LIX, 1–3 (Caligula); Suetonius, *Divus Claudius* 17 and see Barrett 1991, 12, fig. 3 (Claudius)). Oceanus, replete with his distinctive crab claws, appears on several coins which have direct reference to Britain; thus a denarius of Hadrian struck between AD 119 and 122 refers in all probability to that emperor's visit to the province (Cahn 1997, 907, no. 3, pl. on p. 600) and almost two centuries later, the god is figured on the reverses of coins struck *c.* AD 293 by the British usurpers Carausius and Allectus, where he holds a trident and strides from the sea with one foot resting

on the back of a dolphin and the other on the deck of a war galley (Robertson 1978, 266, no. 127, pl. 60 (described as Neptune); Mairat 2015, 19; Henig 2015). Interestingly a gold medallion of Maximian of the same date figures Virtus crowning Maximian-Hercules who is portrayed with a figure of Oceanus (identified by his distinctive crab claws) at his feet, urging him on (Cahn 1997, 908, no. 8, pl. on p. 600) and thereby attesting an abortive attempt to reconquer Britain.

A few final thoughts on this most fascinating tombstone spring to mind. Pedimented tombs such as this one or that of Philus, likewise from Cirencester, or other simpler pedimental tombs (e.g. Henig 1993, 50, nos 143–5 and pls 36–7) were doubtless intended to represent much grander temple tombs or mausolea where the dead might reside in a private chamber, as of course Trimalchio in Petronius's *Satyricon* intended to spend his afterlife. If the stone was originally set in the wall of a funerary enclosure where annual or seasonal feasting took place on the *Parentalia* or at other times, such indeed might not be too far from actuality. It is likely that such buildings, temples and civic buildings as well as tombs existed in Cirencester.

It is legitimate to ask why iconoclasm may have taken place on this relief and not on mosaic images of Oceanus. A plausible answer, if it was not simply the choice of a single fanatic, is that as it was *carved* in relief, it was regarded as the 'graven image' of a god, of a 'demon', which might demand worship or in some way harm the occupant of the late Roman grave. Oceanus, figured on a mosaic, was simply a two-dimensional personification of the sea.

Even though damaged this is a masterly work of art by a skilled local sculptor, and a very important addition to the repertoire of the Cotswold school.

Inscription
Roger S.O. Tomlin

The text is inscribed upon a recessed rectangular panel 0.66m high, 0.41m wide at the top, 0.425m at the bottom, defined on all sides by a simple moulding. This panel was prepared by scribing seven pairs of horizontal setting-out lines at regular vertical intervals of 52–55mm between one pair and the next (Fig. 4.4). The first pair is located 42mm below the top moulding, and a single, incomplete line was scribed below the seventh and last pair at the appropriate interval, as if to begin another pair. Six horizontal bands for lettering were thus defined, but only the first five were actually used, whereas letter-cutting began *above* the bands, a single letter (line 1) being inserted between the top moulding and the first pair of setting-out lines, in a space which was surely intended to be an upper border. Line 1 is either an error or an addition, therefore, and how it relates to the rest of the text is unclear: see further below (note to line 1).

Fig 4.3   Detail of the inscription and sculpture

The failure to use all six bands might suggest that some text was accidentally omitted, whether in the drawing or the subsequent cutting, but it seems more likely that it was simply due to miscalculation or disregard of how much space the text would require. This is further implied by the apparent beginning of a redundant seventh band (see above). Other signs of miscalculation and disregard are noted below, at the end of the note to line 2.

The text was probably first drawn with a brush and

pigment, letter by letter, without any conscious attempt at line-centring or symmetry. A brush-drawn original is suggested by the sinuous serifs and the treatment of the letters A, M and N, which are made entirely with diagonal (not vertical) strokes, these strokes meeting below the apex and A being left 'open' (unbarred). These characteristics are typical of pen-written 'rustic capitals' rather than formal 'monumental' lettering. The letter-heights respect the setting-out lines: apart from the incongruous line 1, which is only 42mm high, line 2 is 53mm; line 3 is 52mm; line 4 is 50mm; line 5 is 53mm; and line 6 is 50mm.

Except for line 1, the reading is straightforward:

I
D M
BODICACIA
CONIVNX
VIXIT ANNO
S XXVII

<I> | D(is) M(anibus) | Bodicacia | coniunx | vixit anno|s XXVII

'To the Shades of the Dead. Bodicacia, spouse, lived 27 years.'

Line-by-line notes

1. There is only one letter, a single vertical stroke, which was either a mistake or a subsequent addition, since (as already noted) it was cut *above* the first pair of setting-out lines, in what was surely intended to be a border. It might be seen as an unfinished D, as if the letter-cutter began to cut the usual tombstone-heading D M, but soon realised his mistake. But the letter is clearly I, being quite carefully formed with serifs top and bottom like the first I in BODICACIA (3) and XXVII (6). Was it then an afterthought, the letter-cutter having intended the heading to be *D(is) I(nferis) M(anibus)*, 'To the Shades of the Dead below'? This formula is widespread, but it has occurred only once in Britain, far away in Papcastle (RIB III, 3221). At Cirencester, apart from three tombstones which have no heading because they are so early (RIB 108, 109, 110), the tombstones which retain their heading are all headed D M (RIB 111, 112, 113, III 3060, 3061, 3062). Moreover, if I were inserted to make D M into D I M, it would surely have been placed between D and M on the same line (there would have been just enough space); or even if above them, then midway, but surely not above the middle of M.

2, *D(is) M(anibus)*. This tombstone formula, which is very frequent, is almost always abbreviated to D M after the first quarter of the 2nd century, which is thus a *terminus post quem* for the inscription; the lettering is not diagnostic, but would suit a 2nd-century date. However, D M has been set oddly to the left, raising the possibility that a third letter was drawn (but not cut), or at least intended: D M S, *D(is) M(anibus) S(acrum)*,

Fig. 4.4   Drawing of the tombstone (1:10)

'Sacred to the Shades of the Dead'. This formula is typical of North African epitaphs, but is not common in Britain, which has about 28 examples; and except for a possible one from Caerleon (RIB 392), they all come from Chester, Lincoln, and the northern frontier-zone. Another guess would be that Bodicacia bore an abbreviated imperial nomen such as VLP (*Ulpia*), AEL (*Aelia*) or AVR (*Aurelia*), but that there was some uncertainty about using it. However, it is much more likely that the draughtsman (or stone-cutter), working letter by letter, simply drew the two letters of the heading and turned at once to the next line, rather than divide the important BODICACIA, which received a line to itself. The inept placing of D M would be in keeping with his disregard of layout elsewhere: compare the crowding of IA at the end of 3, the failure to centre CONIVNX (4), the failure to separate VIXIT from

ANNOS (5), and the equally inept postponement of S to the next line (6).

3, *Bodicacia*. This feminine Celtic name, that of the deceased, is the most interesting part of the epitaph. It is hitherto unattested in this form, but it must be a development of *Bodica*, an alternative spelling or transliteration of Celtic *Boudica* ('victorious'), famously the name of the rebel Queen of the Iceni. There is no need, though, to suppose that it was a conscious reminiscence. In this alternative form, it occurs in the name of Lollia Bodicca, who was a Roman citizen more than a century after Boudica's revolt, but also the British-born wife of a centurion who had served many years in Britain. Appropriately, they named their sons *Victor* and *Victorinus* (ILS 2653): they knew what *Bodicca* meant. The sense of the termination *acia* is uncertain, but like some Celtic masculine names in *acus* it may be hypocoristic (an affectionate diminutive) or be patronymic, indicating derivation from the father's name; see further Russell 1988, 136–8.

4–5, *coniunx | vixit*. *Bodicacia* is the subject of the verb *vixit* ('lived'), the object of which is *anno|s XXVII*, ('27 years', her age at death). The only word between *Bodicacia* and *vixit* is the nominative *coniunx* ('spouse', whether husband or wife) which, since it is without further qualification, must refer grammatically to her, as a 'wife'. This is difficult, since the term *coniunx* is usually applied in epitaphs to the named dedicator, the surviving widow or widower, rather than to the deceased. In this epitaph, however, no dedicator is named, even though Bodicacia was explicitly married. This might be a hint that the widower's name (and some funerary formula

indicating his responsibility) has been accidentally omitted, but the continuity of sense between *Bodicacia* and *vixit*, of which she is undoubtedly the subject, make this hypothesis remote. There is in fact a good parallel from Cirencester itself for this use of *coniunx* (but in the dative case), in the text of another gabled tombstone (RIB 113): *D(is) M(anibus) | Iuliae Castae | coniugi vix(it) | ann(os) XXXIII*, 'To Julia Casta, spouse, (she) lived 33 years'. This stone is broken here, but just enough of the surface remains to show that the text is complete. The case is dative, to imply that the stone was dedicated 'to' Casta, but her husband, like Bodicacia's, is not named.

The reason for this reticence may be that the husbands of Casta and Bodicacia were already dead, or had at least made provision for their own commemoration, so that these women's tombstones would have been erected beside that of the husband. The relationship would then have been explicit. The original location of Bodicacia's stone is unknown, since it seems to have been reused face downward to cover someone else's grave, a man's. The lack of finish to the gable where it would not have been seen suggests that it was not intended to be free-standing, but rather to be inserted into a larger funerary structure. This might well have incorporated other epitaphs.

4.2 Discussion of Selected Grave Goods
E.R. McSloy

A concordance of all artefacts made from metal, glass, pottery, jet/shale and worked bone/ivory recovered from the grave fills is presented in Table 4.1.

Table 4.1 Summary of grave goods and coffin fittings.
N = number of items; TG = total incidence (number of graves)

Material>		Fe		Cu alloy		Glass		Pottery		Jet/shale		Bone/ivory		Total
Quantities/incidence>		*N*	*TG*	*N*	*TG*	*N*	*TG*	*N*	*TG*	*N*	*TG*	*N*	*TG*	*N*
Function	**Description**													
Dress	bracelet/armlet	2	2	13	9	-	-	-	-	3	3	3	2	**21**
(jewellery)	finger ring	-	-	1	1	-	-	-	-	-	-	-	-	**1**
	?hair ring	-	-	2	1	-	-	-	-	-	-	-	-	**2**
	beads	-	-	-	-	109	5	-	-	341	4	5	1	**455**
(footwear)	hobnails	2240	53	-	-	-	-	-	-	-	-	-	-	**2240**
	shoe rivets	-	-	57	3	-	-	-	-	-	-	-	-	**57**
Household	vessels	-	-	-	-	3	3	3	3	-	-	-	-	**6**
	key	1	1	-	-	-	-	-	-	-	-	-	-	**1**
'Religion'	cockerel figurine	-	-	1	1	-	-	-	-	-	-	-	-	**1**
Currency	coins	-	-	7	6	-	-	-	-	-	-	-	-	**7**
Fixtures	nails (coffin)	1879	99	-	-	-	-	-	-	-	-	-	-	**1879**
Indet.	fragments	15	8	5	4	-	-	-	-	-	-	-	-	**20**

The cockerel figurine (B1163.1) (Figs 4.5–4.7)

There are now at least ten known examples of enamelled cockerels of similar configuration, which include four or possibly five further examples from British sites: two are recorded on the Portable Antiquities Scheme database (http://finds.org.uk/database), from Slyne with Hest, Lancashire (LANCUM-361F75) and Cople, Bedfordshire (SOM-745EA2; Worrell 2012, 81–2). A further possible but very fragmentary example recorded in this way, is that from Drayton Bassett, Staffordshire (WMID-D965B4). The other British examples are un-published fragments from Corbridge, Northumberland (Corbridge Museum Acc. No. CO 833) and Leicester (Acc. No. A116·1992·295), and from the Royal Exchange, London (Smith 1922, 94, fig. 116). Those known from the Continent are from Cologne (Menzel 1986, 59); Tongeren, Belgium (De Schaetzen and Vanderhoeven 1956), Buchten, Netherlands (Bloemers 1977; Hoss *et al.* 2015) and Ezinge, Netherlands (Zadoks-Josephus Jitta *et al.* 1967, 114, no. 47). With the exception of the London figurine, which is idio-syncratic in its construction, the known examples can be ascribed to two distinct forms conforming in size,

patterns of enamelling and the presence or not of a separately moulded or cast-in 'wattle'. The Cirencester example belongs to the larger Group 1 form (typically *c.* 130mm in height) and is near-identical to the figurines from Cologne and Buchten, and almost certainly that from Corbridge. Where all these features survive the Group 1 examples share characteristics of lozenge-pattern enamelling to the breast and crescentic/kidney-shaped cells to the wing plate. None of the other known examples have retained a tail, although all exhibit the open, blunt-ended terminal suggesting they were originally equipped in this manner. It is possible that detached tails survive unrecognised in museum collections; a possible example of this comes from Balkerne Lane, Colchester (Crummy 2006), significantly a site associated with the cult of Mercury (see further below).

The function of the Cirencester figurine and the other similar objects remains uncertain. Menzel (1986, 59) recognised that their attribution as lamps or incense burners was improbable, at least for examples where the wing and body portions were fixed in place by soldering. Description as containers is inaccurate for the same reasons. If it is accepted that all were originally equipped with a tail and 'closed', then a function other than as figurines seems unlikely. Solid casting appears not to have been practical for enamelled bronzes and composite

Fig. 4.5   The bronze cockerel figurine from B1163 during excavation

Fig. 4.6   The enamelled bronze cockerel figurine from B1163

Fig. 4.7   Various views of the enamelled bronze cockerel figurine from B1163

construction was preferred more for technical reasons than the economy of metal (Ralph Jackson pers. comm.).

The examples from Tongeren and Buchten survive complete with pedestal bases of bronze; those from Cople and Ezinge, where the feet are preserved, appear to have been intended for mounting above a base of different design. Given the cultic associations of the subject, use as portable objects in ceremonial activities or as votive offerings is most plausible. Evidence for the latter is recorded on the example from Buchten where the base carries an inscribed dedication to the little known local goddess Arcuana by a veteran of the Sixth Legion Victrix.

Origin and dating

The Rhineland and the area of modern Belgium have been acknowledged as centres of bronze and enamel working in the north-western provinces and the discovery of four of the known cockerel figurines from the Low Countries and northern Germany might on face value support an origin in this area. However, it is now clear that Britain was also an important source of richly enamelled bronzes, the best known of which being the 'souvenir' pans inscribed with the names of the forts of Hadrian's Wall (Breeze 2012). The discovery of moulds for vessels with complex enamelled decoration from Castleford, West Yorkshire, has lent weight to the suggestion that northern Britain was the premier source for vessels with complex enamelled decoration and for objects which are known across the western empire (Künzl 2012). The presence of two of the five known British finds of enamelled cockerels of the type described here from north Britain may also be significant in pointing to a manufacture in this wider area. The dating of the Castleford moulds was thought to be in the decades either side of AD 100 (Bayley 1998) and the *floruit* for the tradition of elaborately enamelled vessels/objects would seem to be the 2nd century (Künzl 2012, 15).

If, as seems likely, the cockerel figurines originate in Britain, the number known from the Low Countries and Germany may be rare evidence of reciprocal trade between Britain and the Rhineland, and indeed extending as far as the Maas Valley. Cultural or religious preferences, reflected also in terracottas known from graves, may be a further reason for the seeming popularity of these figurines in this area. The Buchten cockerel may have arrived not by trade, but as a personal possession. Its dedicator, one Ulpius Varinus, was a veteran of the Legio VI Victrix, plausibly recruited to this unit when it was stationed at Xanten in Lower Germany (Derks 2015, 150–2). The transfer of the legion to York *c.* AD 120/122 could suggest that Varinus acquired the figurine whilst in Britain and dedicated it to a local deity on his return to his homeland. Such a hypothesis, given the 25 years' service usual for a legionary, refines the date of cockerel figurines of this type, placing its manufacture in the second quarter of the 2nd century.

Mercury associations

Many smaller and simpler cockerel figurines and enamelled cockerel brooches are known from across the north-western provinces. A reason for this significance as a subject is very probably the well-known association with the classical god Mercury, a connection probably stemming from his role as messenger to the gods and that of the cockerel as announcer of the dawn. There is good evidence from Cirencester in the form of stone reliefs for the veneration of Mercury (Henig 1993, nos 63–5, 68–71, 81) which may point to it being a centre for the cult. Indeed there may be another enamelled example from Cirencester, now apparently lost, but mentioned in the 1922 Corinium Museum guidebook: 'During the last thirty or forty years, however, several enamelled ornaments have been disinterred here. One of these, a small bronze figure of a cock, found in 1870, in an excavation in Cricklade-street, has found a resting place in the collection of the late Sir John Evans. It was particularly interesting as an example of Roman translucid enamel' (Church 1922, 15). John Evans' collection of antiquities passed to the Ashmolean Museum in Oxford, but the figurine is not listed in their collections.

Bracelets/armlets

Bracelets of metal, jet/shale or bone/ivory are the most common form of jewellery accompanying graves (Tables 4.1–4.2). Nine burials contained a total of 21 bracelets of copper alloy (13); iron (2); bone/ivory (3); jet (1) or shale (2). In addition, burials B1171, B1177 and B1263 included items (B1171.8; B1177.5–6; B1263.2) thought to represent jewellery items made from beads of jet or other materials and worn at the arm or wrist (Table 4.3).

Among the metal bracelets there is a marked degree of variability of form, with duplication rare except within individual graves.

Table 4.2 Summary of bracelets/armlets by material and form. Quantities as number of complete objects.
For key to Age group see Table 5.11

Burial number			B1171	B1173	B1177	B1185	B1214	B1218	B1248	B1263	B1273
Sex			?	?	F	F	F	F	F	?	?
Age group			OC	YA	YA	YA	LMA	EMA	YA	Adol.	YC
Material	**Description**	**Reference**									
Copper alloy	Cable (twisted wire)	Crummy 1983	-	1	-	-	-	1	-	-	1
	Cast, penannular	Cool 2010	2	-	-	-	1	-	-	-	-
	Hollow/tubular	Cool 2010	-	-	1	-	-	1	-	-	-
	Strip	Crummy 1983	-	-	-	1	-	-	3	-	-
	'expanding joint'	Allason-Jones and Miket 1984	-	-	-	-	-	-	-	1	-
Iron	uncertain		-	-	-	-	-	1	1	-	-
Shale	Octagonal	Crummy 1983	1	-	-	-	-	-	-	-	-
	Plain annular		-	-	1	-	-	-	-	-	-
Jet	Plain annular		-	-	-	-	1	-	-	-	-
Bone	with cu al. collar		-	-	2	-	-	-	-	-	-
Ivory?	'cable'		-	-	-	1	-	-	-	-	-

Table 4.3 Summary of the beads by material and form. Quantities shown as number of beads.
Us = unstratified; for key to Age group see Table 5.11

Burial number			B1171	B1173	B1177	B1180	B1263	B1273	Us
Sex			?	?	F	F	?	?	
Age group			OC	YA	YA	LMA	Adol.	YC	
Material	**Description**	**Reference**							
Jet	'baluster/toggle'-shaped	Crummy 1983, no. 1507	7	-	-	-	-	-	-
	sub-spherical	Allason-Jones 1996, no. 48	1	-	-	-	-	-	-
	cylinder/segmented	Crummy 1983, no. 1042	49	-	-	38	-	-	1
	tubular/ribbed	Allason-Jones 1996, no. 25	7	-	-	-	-	-	-
	small segmented	Allason-Jones 1996, no. 9	200	-	-	-	-	-	6
	ribbed/pillar (2 transverse perfs)	Crummy 1983, no. 974	19	-	-	-	-	-	-
	Spacer; plano-convex (2 perfs)	Allason-Jones 1996, no. 50	-	-	13	-	-	-	-
	Spacer; ridged (2 perfs)	Allason-Jones and Miket 1984, no. 7.78	-	-	-	-	-	1	-
Glass	Small segmented	Guido 1978	40	5	23	-	25	4	-
	Cylinder	Guido 1978	-	-	12	-	-	-	-
Bone/ivory	faceted	Clarke 1979	-	-	5	-	-	-	-

The metal strip-form (B1185.1; B1248.1–3), penannular (B1171.1–2 and B1214.1), cable (B1173.1; B1218.2; B1273.1) and 'expanding joint' (B1263.1) bracelets are representative of well-known types recorded from cemeteries or non-funerary contexts. Similarly, those of materials other than of metal belong to known styles, with the cable form bracelet B1185.3 reproducing a form in bone/ivory more frequently seen in metal, shale or jet. The use of iron for bracelets B1218.3 and B1248.4 is also unusual, though it is easy to appreciate that site finds of this nature have been overlooked in the past. All of the bracelets can be expected to date to the late 3rd to 4th centuries, a period when the wearing of bracelets appears to have been common. Bone or bone/ivory bracelets B1177.3–4 and B1185.3 probably belong to the later part of this range, the second half of the 4th century or a little later (Stephen Greep pers. comm.).

Most unusual of the metal bracelet forms are the hollow/tubular types: B1177.1 (young adult, female) and B1218.1 (early middle adult, female). Differently decorated, the two examples are similarly constructed from thin sheet metal with an overlapping seam on the inside edge. Bracelets of this type are rare from Roman Britain, though absence in circumstances other than as grave finds may be due to their insubstantial construction. The closest parallel is from Lankhills (Cool 2010). This and a second example from Winchester support dating in the second half of the 4th century and a related find from Cannington, Somerset (Rahtz *et al.* 2000, 355–9), hints at continuation into post-Roman

material culture. The Continental origins claimed for the type on the basis of finds from the Rhineland and Danubian provinces (Swift 2000) now seem less likely and Cool (2010) suggests that the type has insular origins.

Interpretation of groups of jet beads (B1171.8 and B1177.5), bone and glass-bead group B1177.6 and 'appearing black' glass group B1263.2 as arm ornaments rests largely on location within the grave (close to the wrist) or an association with a metal bracelet/armlet (B1263.2). In the case of B1177.5–6 this is also supported by association with conventional bracelets in other materials. B1263.2 was threaded on thin copper-alloy wire and B1177.6 on a chain of copper alloy which survives only as fragments. The condition of the wire chain is very poor, though a number of double loops and figure-of-eight form elements are identifiable. Glass cylinder beads retaining copper-alloy wire are known from Uley (Woodward and Leach 1993, fig. 126, no. 17) and comparable chain necklaces are known from 4th-century graves at Dunstable (Matthews 1981, fig. 30, no. 29) and Poundbury (Guido and Mills 1993, fig. 72, no. 5). The use of bi-perforated jet beads as armlets is evidenced from York and other locations, although in the form of articulating or trapezoid-form beads (Allason-Jones 1996, 27–8).

Separation by determinable sex (Table 4.2) shows a pattern consistent with most Late Romano-British cemeteries where bracelets typically occur in female graves of divergent age groups (Cool 2010). One burial recorded by Reece (1962, 53–4, BK3) which was accompanied by bracelets of jet and copper alloy was described as male, although this sexing has not been subject to more recent re-examination. In five of the nine instances where bracelets occur from the Bridges Garage site, these are as multiples of three or more and there would appear to be a preference for the combining of differing designs and materials (Table 4.2).

Poor condition or disturbance to some burials makes the location of objects uncertain in some instances. In only one instance, B1214.1, was a bracelet worn at the wrist, although in other examples (B1171.8; B1177.1–6; B1185.3; B1218.1–3) proximity to the wrist might be significant. B1185.1–2 and B1248.1–3 were probably worn at the upper (left) arm making designation as 'armlets' most appropriate. Some objects of this class were clearly not worn, but 'placed' at the foot of the grave (B1171.1–2), near the legs (B1263.1–2) (an alternative use as 'anklets' might perhaps be considered), or at the chest (B1171.3).

The fragmentation/distortion of 'cable' bracelets/armlets B1173.1, B1218.2 and 1263.1 is notable; the damage is unlikely in all instances to have been as the result of disturbance. It perhaps points to the deposition of unserviceable 'token' items, where functionality is implied; or a form of object 'killing' that made items unserviceable as part of the burial ritual.

Necklaces

Beads of jet or glass were recorded from six burials (Table 4.3), and of these, only those from B1171, B1173 and B1180 appeared to be worn at the neck. Of these three, the sex of the burial could only be determined for B1180 (late middle adult, female). B1171 (older child, indeterminate sex) included as many as four separate strings of jet and glass (B1171.4–7).

The glass beads and most of the jet bead forms compare with known types recorded from York (Allason-Jones 1996, 26–9) and elsewhere. Jet 'toggle' forms (B1171.5/6) differ in detail to examples from Butt Road, Colchester, from 4th-century graves (Crummy 1983, 35, no. 1507).

The use of jet and shale is well known from Roman Britain (Allason-Jones 1996; 2011). The utilisation of jet from the North Yorkshire coastal region is evidenced from the later 2nd century, although finds of jet jewellery most commonly date to the later 3rd and 4th centuries. Jet finds are relatively well known from later Roman burials, including from the large municipal cemeteries associated with the principal Roman towns. Evidence for its use in Cirencester is however, to date, limited. The magical and curative properties described by Roman writers may have enhanced its popularity as a decorative material. Its 'exotic' nature and the time-intensive working is likely to have made jet a relatively expensive commodity. The multiple jet items associated with B1171 may therefore signify an individual of some status. The close association of 'cockerel burial' B1163

and the richly furnished, though seemingly much later B1171, raises the possibility that burials were sited near earlier, but still marked, higher status graves.

Thirty-eight beads of similar cylinder segmented form were associated with B1180 (late middle adult, female). Most (35) were recovered from the head area of the grave and would seem to represent a necklace.

Rings

Only one finger ring was recorded (B1256.1); this was a simple hoop of copper alloy and worn on the left hand of a male. The function of two small copper-alloy wire coils (B1257.1–2), associated with a neonate is uncertain. Location close to the skull may suggest use as hair ornaments or earrings, although adornment of neonates in this way would be uncommon (Philpott 1991, 99–100).

Glass vessels

Three glass vessels were recorded. B1171.10 and B1186.1 were incomplete and highly fragmentary, most likely as the result of truncation. They probably represent the remains of vessels deposited in the grave during backfilling or possibly placed on the coffin. Both appear to comprise single vessels of greenish colourless glass of the type characteristic of the 4th century (Cool and Price 1995, 218). The third vessel, B1265.1 is also of the same greenish colourless glass. It is fully reconstructable and there can be little doubt that it was whole at the time of its inclusion within the grave. It is of a type dating to the second half of the 4th century or a little later. The three grave finds show no bias towards age/sex groupings, being associated with a young adult female (B1265), an early middle adult male (B1186) and an older child of indeterminate sex (B1171).

A further 28 fragments of glass recovered from the fills of 12 graves are considered stray finds accidentally integrated into the grave fills. A prismatic bottle fragment of the type common across the 1st to 2nd centuries was present from B1266. The remainder comprised featureless fragments mainly of natural green coloured glass. Fragments from the fills of B1160, B1179 and B1209 and a further unstratified (clear glass) fragment are heat-distorted and perhaps represent the remains of pyre activity.

Iron key

One of very few 'utilitarian' items recorded from a burial is iron 'lift' key B1164.1 which accompanied an adult female. The position of the key in the grave suggests that it hung from a belt. Keys are not uncommon from Romano-British burials and their presence may denote 'status', being indicative of property ownership, or may symbolise a religious adherence as the key was an attribute of the Celtic goddess Epona (Philpott 1991, 187; Ross 1975, 336). The significance of the key may be entirely symbolic; as able to unlock the gates of the afterlife or representative of 'hope in the face of death' (Black 1986, 222).

Pottery vessels

Complete pottery vessels B1160.1, B1163.2 and B1266.1 were placed as grave goods with inhumation burials. Further vessels (C1153.1, C1154.1–2, C1226.1, C1275.1 and C1276.1, C1277.1 and C1278.1–3), surviving in varying levels of completeness, were recovered from *in situ* or disturbed cremation burials. Two fragmented but substantial portions of vessels were recovered from graves B1177 and B1215; they are likely to have been disturbed from earlier cremation burials. Vessels B1160.1 and B1163.2 each occur in a North Wiltshire oxidised fabric (TF 9). No detailed study of the North Wiltshire industry or the chronological development of its products has yet been undertaken; however, there seems no reason to doubt that the ring-necked flagon B1160.1 can be placed within a date range *c.* AD 70–150/70. Such dating is typical, for example, for equivalent forms in Verulamium region whiteware (Davies *et al.* 1994, 42). Ring-necked flagons are abundant among earlier Roman groups (to *c.* AD 150) from Cirencester and Wanborough, Wiltshire (Seager-Smith 2001, 277, fig. 91).

Tettine B1163.2 is a rare example of a form usually interpreted as a feeding vessel for infants. No previous occurrences appear to be recorded from Cirencester. Philip Crummy (1993, 273) first noted the association with infant burials, a pattern repeated at Pepper Hill, Springhead, Kent (Biddulph 2006). That B1163.2 accompanied a child (indeterminate sex) of approximately 2–3 years lends further weight to this interpretation and to Crummy's comparison to modern spouted cups suitable for toddler-aged children. Incidence elsewhere suggests a dating for the form across the 2nd and 3rd centuries (Cool 2010, 271). Although lacking a handle B1163.2 is closer in form to globular or bi-conical examples from Colchester (ibid.), than to the beaker-like vessels found in 3rd-century deposits (Barber and Bowsher 2000, 228, B713).

Notwithstanding evidence elsewhere for anachronistic vessel use in cemetery sites (Biddulph 2006), B1160.1 and B1163.2 appear likely to have been deposited not long following manufacture and almost certainly in the 2nd century. The third vessel, Oxford red slipped ware indented beaker B1266.1 from adult male burial B1266 is certainly later, probably dating after *c.* AD 325. As such B1266.1 provides rare evidence for pottery grave goods from this period from Cirencester, with no other examples from either the Western or Bath Gate cemeteries save an indented fineware beaker (perhaps a New Forest product) recorded by Reece in association with his BK3, an adult male (Reece 1962, 59). 'Functionally' however, it can be included with the glass vessels B1171.10, B1186.1 and B1265.1. Adult

male associations can be demonstrated for this grouping of receptacles in three out of the five instances.

Cirencester would seem typical of Late Romano-British cemeteries where pottery grave goods are generally scarce (Philpott 1991, 103–113). An obvious exception is Lankhills, where 83 of the 444 4th-century inhumation burials contained pottery vessels (Booth *et al.* 2010, 486–7). At Lankhills and at other 4th-century sites, there is a clear preference for drinking-related forms with fineware (colour-coated) beakers most common (ibid., 109).

Cremation burials C1153, C1154, C1226 and C1275–8 were contained within pottery vessels, adding to the 45 (urned) burials recorded from the Oakley Cottage excavation. In common with the Oakley Cottage group, most of the urned burials are associated with single vessels, the badly truncated C1154 being one of only two burials from the combined group containing ancillary vessels.

Urns/accessories C1153.1, C1154.2, C1226.1, C1275.1 and C1278.1–3 are Dorset Black-burnished ware (fabric TF 74) vessels, demonstrating the same preference for this ware type apparent in the Oakley Cottage group. A further two vessels in this fabric have been interpreted as disturbed urns or accessories. Urn C1226.1 exhibits evidence for former use for cooking as it has an internal carbonised residue, and C1278.1 had been repaired using a lead rivet. The dating of individual vessels is hindered by the levels of truncation, particularly for C1154 where only the lower portion of each vessel survived. Typologically C1226.1 is earliest, exhibiting the barrel-like profile, short rim and acute-angled lattice consistent with Hadrianic or earlier Antonine vessels (Holbrook and Bidwell 1991, 95–6). Urn C1275.1, of which only the lower portion survives, exhibits burnished lattice decoration which is close to 'right-angled' and may date to the late 2nd or earlier 3rd century (ibid., 96). Later dating, probably in the range *c.* AD 220–280/300, is likely for C1153.1, based on its wide flaring rim and obtuse-angled lattice (ibid.), and possibly also for the more fragmentary C1278.1.

Footwear in graves

The presence of footwear in graves was evidenced mainly from iron hobnails which were noted from 53 individual graves (44.2%). In nine graves the number of hobnails was fewer than five and there is a high likelihood that these resulted from stray finds or were intrusive from other features. Graves with good evidence for nailed footwear amount to 33% of the total. Metrical study of the hobnails was not undertaken, although all were of the typical conical-headed or dome-headed form typical of Roman forms (Manning's 1985 Type 10). No examples of the cleat/boot plate type objects noted from some Roman sites were recorded. Details of the total number of hobnails and their position in the grave, where recorded, are provided in the grave catalogue.

Evidence for footwear other than from the hobnails was also present as groups of small (2–3mm) double-headed copper-alloy studs, which were recorded from bulk soil samples taken from the foot area of burials B1161 and B1164. A total of 56 studs of this type was recorded, associated with two adjacent female burials to the north-east of the walled cemetery. A decorative use seems certain and there are parallels with the ornamented vamps seen on some 3rd-century shoes (Quita Mould pers. comm.).

Hobnails occurred in equal proportions from burials where sex could be determined (17 were male and 16 were female) and a number were burials of infants and children (B1160, B1163, B1171, B1205 and B1268). The number of individual hobnails was very variable (1–244), averaging 42. Four graves (B1165, B1167, B1190 and B1215) produced in excess of 100 individual hobnails; however, there were no indications that multiple (pairs of) footwear were deposited in any one grave. Position within the grave was not always apparent as some hobnails are only recorded as having been found in the general grave fill. In the majority of instances (77%) where location was determinable, hobnails were recovered at the foot of the grave close to the feet, and from the degree of 'disarticulation' it is apparent that in the majority of instances footwear was probably worn. In a small number of graves hobnail clusters were more cohesive and probably placed: over the legs (B1167), to each side of the thigh bones (B1176), and at the base of the grave (B1171, B1200 and B1203).

The incidence (33.3%) of nailed footwear is significantly higher in this assemblage compared to the Bath Gate Cemetery, where only five of the 450 inhumation burials (1.1%; Table 7.1) included hobnails (CE II, 1982, 129–32). This is a substantially higher prevalence than at Poundbury (Mills 1993a, 99) where only *c.* 3% of burials included nailed footwear, but is comparable to Lankhills (36.1%) where incidence was considered untypically high for a large urban cemetery (Powell 2010a, 318). Inhumed burials with hobnails are common in the Roman period across southern Britain, Philpott (1991, 167) noting that incidence aggregated to rural sites with a relative paucity from the large urban cemeteries. The practice appears to have begun by the early or mid 2nd century and continues into and throughout the 4th century (ibid.).

The untypically high incidence of nailed footwear in the Western Cemetery, in particular when set against the evidence from the (at least partially contemporaneous) Bath Gate collection, requires some explanation. Philpott (1991, 172) observed that nailed footwear occurs rarely in the graves of high-status individuals, and this together with the weighting to rural sites lead him to suggest that use was largely confined to a 'middle ranking rural population'. There is no basis for considering the Western Cemetery population of lower status compared to that of the Bath Gate group, and

indeed the contrary is likely. The two 'stand-out' richly furnished burials from the Western Cemetery (B1163, B1171) were both accompanied by nailed footwear. Explanations for the inclusion of nailed footwear may therefore be more nuanced than a straightforward reflection of high or low status. It should also be considered that hobnailed shoes or boots will have accounted for only some of the footwear in use, some of which will have decayed without trace. For such reasons it was concluded at Lankhills (Powell 2010a, 318) that burial with footwear may have been the dominant rite, but that evidence for this survived in only a fraction of cases.

When examined spatially (Fig. 7.4) hobnail incidence per grave is distributed across the site, although some tendencies are evident. Few burials to the east of Ditch A contained hobnails (2 out of 17). More striking is the association with the walled cemetery and the area immediately to the north-east of it: all eight of the undisturbed burials inside the walled cemetery included hobnails, together with 15 of the 21 burials to the north-east which shared the same orientation. The incidence of hobnails from the burials to the south-west of the walled cemetery was more variable, although a majority (60%) contained none. The reasons for the concentration in and around the walled cemetery may relate to a common set of beliefs or a division of society electing or selected for burial in this location. Chronology may also be a factor, with this group of burials representative of fashions or traditions from a particular timespan. There are good indications that the walled cemetery and the area to its north-east were used for burial in the 2nd century, and support for a mainly early or middle Roman date range for this grouping of burials comes from finds from individual burials (B1160, B1163 and C1227).

Coffin nails

Iron coffin fittings of the kind relatively well known from cemeteries, including that outside the Bath Gate (CE II, 89, fig. 36) were not recorded and evidence for wooden coffins survived only as nails (or rarely as staining to the base of the grave). Incidence of coffin nails per grave is set out in the grave catalogue. From a total of 1,879 nail fragments, only 144 nails were sufficiently complete to be measurable and the count of fragments will significantly overstate the true number of individual nails used. Nail position, where recorded, is shown in individual grave drawings; however, no analysis was undertaken of their position as evidence for coffin construction.

Details of nail form/size are also included in the catalogue. The majority were flattened or conical-headed forms similar to 'standard' Roman carpentry nails (Manning 1985: Class 1b). From the measurable sample, length is in the 30–150mm range, with most (116 nails or 81%) between 50mm and 100mm.

Nails (including fragments) were recorded from 84% of all graves. This figure is close to that estimated for Lankhills (Table 7.1; Powell 2010b, 322: 78) and higher than the 72% estimated for Poundbury (Mills 1993b, 114). Incidence is very much higher than for the Bath Gate Cemetery where only *c.* 25% of the graves included one or more nail (CE II, 86–8). The number of nails per grave averaged at 15.8, with the highest proportion (70%) producing up to 30. Six graves produced 50 or more nails (to a maximum of 99) and a further 9 between 30 and 50 nails.

The variability in nail incidence may be due to a number of factors relating to the form and construction of the coffin. In addition some nails may have come from boxes or other items deposited within the grave, although none were recognised during excavation. The graves producing the largest number of nails show no clear age/sex comparability but do show spatial tendencies. Most (B1161, B1164, B1167, B1171 and B1176) clustered to the north-east of the walled cemetery, with B1159 and B1209 located within its projected limits (B1243 is an outlier). Two burials among this group, B1171 (99 nails) and B1243 (56 nails), were juveniles of ages *c.* 6 and *c.* 12 years, an indication that the number of nails is not a direct reflection of larger coffin size.

4.3 Other Finds
E.R. McSloy

Small finds from non-grave deposits

Seven jet beads of small segmented (6) and cylinder form (1) were recovered from an unstratified context. They almost certainly represent grave goods from a disturbed burial. Metalwork from non-grave contexts amounted to 47 items, 46 of iron and one of copper alloy. The ironwork comprises mainly fragmentary nails (8) or hobnails (35). The remainder consists of unidentifiable fragmentary objects and a hook fitting from a post-medieval deposit. Most of the ironwork was derived from ditches, including a group of 34 hobnails from Ditch A, probably representing discarded footwear. The single copper-alloy object was a conical-headed stud or rivet (not illustrated), probably of Roman date, from the robber trench of Wall C.

Whetstone
Fiona Roe

A whetstone fragment (not illustrated) was recovered from the Anglo-Saxon pit 1004/5066. The whetstone is broken at both ends and is approximately oval to sub-rectangular in cross-section, with wear on all surfaces. It now measures 63.5 x 24 x 22mm and weighs 68g. The stone, which is not local, is a quartz sandstone now weathered to a greyish brown and has proved to be calcareous, so that it can be suggested that the source area is in a Jurassic sandstone, the Corallian Lower Calcareous Grit, in this case possibly from around Calne, Wiltshire (Arkell 1970, 395). This is a known whetstone material and a mid Saxon find was recorded, for example, from Eynsham Abbey, Oxfordshire (Roe 2003, 293).

Architectural stone
Peter Davenport

A large block of oolitic limestone with a concave moulding along one edge was retrieved from the upper fill of Ditch B. The maximum dimensions of the block are 0.5m x 0.47m x 0.16m, but it is broken on all but two of its six faces. It may have been about two Roman feet square originally. One almost complete face is the upper face with broad chisel and either adze or hollow-ground-chisel working evident. Two distinct zones of working are apparent which reflect the position of another block on top, set back some 150mm. The other surviving face is the front face which has a narrow fascia over a simple cavetto moulding. Both these faces show traces of working. The cavetto is incomplete toward the base as the entire lower face of the block has sheared off. The other faces appear to have been chopped off.

The block is a fragment of an architectural moulding from a high-status masonry structure, of monumental scale, possibly funerary, but if so very grand. The scale of the moulding is comparable to those in the baths at Bath, around the Great Bath or the Sacred Spring enclosure (Cunliffe 1969, fig. 38; Cunliffe and Davenport 1985, fig. 30) but it is somewhat more crudely finished. The indications of another block having sat on the upper face, but set back, suggest this might have been part of a composite entablature, or a deep string course in a wall face.

Building stone

Four fragments of possible building stone and two stone tesserae were recovered. Three flat fragments of lias from Ditch A might have been used for roofing or possibly paving; a fragment of oolitic limestone from B1209 exhibits no evidence for working though might represent building rubble. Two stray stone tesserae were recovered from the fills of two graves within the walled cemetery: in fine white limestone from B1155 and in blue lias from B1209.

Ceramic building material

A total of 168 fragments (5.2kg) was recorded. With the exception of nine fragments of modern brick fragments, which were intrusive within a Roman context, the assemblage all dates to the Roman period. The majority was derived from grave fills (85 fragments), with most of the remainder from ditch (83 fragments) and pit fills (1 fragment). The assemblage is well-fragmented, the largest proportion (129 fragments) comprising tile/brick fragments of indeterminate form. Identifiable forms consist of 16 fragments of imbrex, 10 of tegulae and 3 of brick.

Prehistoric worked flint

Twenty pieces of worked lithic weighing 86g were recovered. All were redeposited, coming from Roman grave (13 pieces) or ditch fills (5 pieces), Roman pyre deposits (3 pieces) or the modern subsoil. The condition of the flint is variable, though most pieces exhibit some edge damage and/or breakage. The raw material consists of grey flint with varying levels of white cortication. Cortex where present is unworn and this is suggestive of flint from primary (chalkland) areas. Three pieces exhibit secondary working: a piercer from the fill of burial B1155, and scrapers from Ditch F and Burial B1245. Of these the piercer and the (thumbnail type) scraper from B1245 probably date to the late Neolithic or earlier Bronze Age. A well-worked-down blade/bladelet core from the grave fill of B1216 is probably Mesolithic, as may be a broken blade from B1261. The remainder comprises flakes or chips (small flakes) without secondary working, for which no dating can be suggested.

Roman pottery

The assemblage amounts to 2,529 sherds (20kg; Table 4.4). The bulk of the material was hand recovered, although 424 sherds (0.91kg) was collected from soil samples taken from the graves. Including the cremation burials, 1,517 sherds or 60% of the total were derived from funerary contexts, including the three vessels deposited with inhumations as grave goods and from seven urned cremations discussed above. Some 1,405 sherds derived from grave fills. Of the latter group most was recovered from graves within the projected confines of the walled cemetery. Moderately large groups were recovered from ditches (222 sherds), with most coming from Ditch A. The mean sherd weight for the hand-recovered group is on the low side for a Roman group at 9.3g. The surface condition of the sherds is typically poor, a product of local soil conditions, and has resulted in the removal of surface slips. Evidence for burning is most readily apparent with the small samian group, some 11 sherds (33%) exhibiting this to varying degrees.

Methodology

The pottery was sorted by context and quantified by sherd count and weight, together with rim EVEs (estimated vessel equivalents based on a percentage measure of rim circumference) per fabric. Recording was directly to an Access database. Fabric nomenclature (prefixed by the letters TF) is taken from the Cirencester pottery type series (CE I–V) and a concordance matches certain fabrics with those of the National Roman Fabric Reference Collection (Tomber and Dore 1998).

Composition

The overall composition of the Roman assemblage is set out in Table 4.4, and for graves within the walled cemetery in Tables 4.5–4.6. The bulk of the pottery comprises coarsewares of local (North Wiltshire/Gloucestershire) origin and common traded coarseware types, in particular Dorset Black-burnished ware. The samian constitutes a surprisingly small proportion of the group (1.8% by count). Among the South Gaulish component are a Dragendorff 15/17 platter (Ditch B) and Ritterling 12 bowl (grave backfill of B1157), both probably of pre-Flavian date. The majority Central Gaulish component dates to the 2nd century; most comprises plain dish or cup forms and includes forms dating after *c.* AD 150 (see Chapter 2, dating evidence). Non-samian fineware imports are scarcely present, though sherds from a Central Gaulish black-slipped ware beaker with appliqué decoration from grave fill of B1161 are notable. Amphora types, particularly Gallic, flat-based wine amphorae (TF 35), appear to be well represented, in particular from grave fills in the area of the walled cemetery (below).

Backfills of graves inside the projected extent of the walled enclosure (Tables 4.5–4.6)

Pottery from eight graves (B1155, B1156, B1157, B1158, B1159, B1160, B1168 and B1209) which are assumed to have lain within the projected bounds of the walled cemetery amounts to 704 sherds, 57% of the total recovered from grave fills. No pottery was recovered from a ninth grave (B1211) from within the walled area, although this feature was heavily truncated. Both the quantity and composition of the pottery groups contrast with material from graves outside of the enclosure.

Only B1160 was accompanied by grave goods (other than hobnailed footwear): the pottery flagon B1160.1 discussed above. The pottery from the grave fills is consistent in composition and, with some exceptions, supports a 2nd-century date range, with some indications suggesting a date in the middle decades of that century. Samian is uncommon (11 sherds; 1.4%), occurring as South and Central Gaulish types, none of which need be later than *c.* AD 150. Other vessels useful for dating are the fine greyware (TF 17), ovoid or globular beaker with barbotine dot-panel decoration from B1155 (Fig. 4.8, no. 8), and a sherd from a Cologne colour-coated ware beaker from B1159. In both instances dating is unlikely to extend beyond the first half of the 2nd century. Dorset Black-burnished ware (TF 74) is present ubiquitously, a factor encouraging dating after *c.* AD 120. Identifiable forms in Black-burnished ware are early style jars with acute-angled lattice and flat-rimmed dishes. Savernake ware (TF 6) or early wheel-made black-burnished wares (TF 5), both dominant types in 1st and earlier 2nd-century assemblages from Cirencester, are poorly represented.

Most striking compositionally are the quantities

Table 4.4 Summary quantification of the Roman pottery by stratigraphic period (shown as sherd count (Ct)/weight (Wt) in grammes). Ciren TF refers to the type fabric codes in the Cirencester pottery type series (CE I–V); NRFRC is the concordance with the codes used by the National Roman Fabric Reference Collection (Tomber and Dore 1998).

Source	Description	Ciren TF	NRFRC	Period > 1		1/2		2		3		Unph.		Total	
				Ct	Wt	Ct	Wt	Ct	Wt	Ct	Wt	Ct	Wt	Ct	Wt
Local/North Wilts	Limestone-tempered	25	-	1	1	-	-	-	-	-	-	-	-	1	1
	Grog-tempered	3/24	-	8	140	5	18	1	4	-	-	-	-	14	162
	Savernake grog-tempered	6	SAV GT	34	920	17	291	45	522	1	26	2	6	99	1765
	Late BB imitations	102-4	-	-	-	8	88	8	53	-	-	-	-	16	141
	Greywares (North Wilts)	17/98	-	232	1564	100	442	23	101	6	13	19	113	380	2233
	Greywares (fine)	41	-	42	146	2	13	2	9	-	-	-	-	46	168
	Greywares (gritty)	117	-	1	5	1	13	-	-	-	-	-	-	2	18
	Black sandy	5	-	73	324	39	169	7	57	-	-	-	-	119	550
	Black sandy (coarser)	15		8	24	10	268							18	292
	Local colour-coated	85	-	-	-	-	-	7	8	-	-	-	-	7	8
	Oxidised	9/98	-	202	552	19	109	25	129	1	2	16	51	263	843
	Oxidised (flagons)	9	-	79	835	23	136	7	24	-	-	3	22	112	1017
	Oxidised/white-slipped	95	-	49	480	10	50	12	91	4	17	9	119	84	757
	South-west white-slipped	88	SOW WS	1	29	2	76	-	-	-	-	-	-	3	105
	Severn Valley ware (early)	1-4	-	2	68									2	68
	Severn Valley ware	106-9	SVW OX2	2	61	1	16	2	13	-	-	-	-	5	90
	Kingsholm flagons	29	-	1	12	-	-	-	-	-	-	-	-	1	12
	Gloucester mortaria	-	-	-	-	1	62	-	-	-	-	-	-	1	62
Regional	South-east Dorset BB1	74	DOR BB1	351	1836	382	2103	351	1869	6	20	25	135	1115	5963
	New Forest slipped	82	NFO CC	1	2	-	-	1	6	-	-	-	-	2	8
	Oxford red-slipped	83	OXF RS	-	-	2	20	5	288	6	90	-	-	13	398
	Oxford whiteware	90	OXF WH	2	25	1	17	-	-	-	-	1	20	4	62
	Oxford? whiteware	90?	OXF WH?	24	131	10	55	7	22	1	2	2	4	44	214
	Oxford white-slipped	84	OXF WS	1	3	1	6	-	-	-	-	-	-	2	9
Imports (samian)	South Gaulish	154a	LGF SA	9	75	1	11	-	-	-	-	-	-	10	86
	Central Gaulish	154b	LEZ SA	7	39	10	79	10	117	-	-	1	3	28	238
	East Gaulish	154c		-	-	3	81	4	38	1	1	-	-	8	120
Imports (other fine)	Cologne colour-coated	81a	KOL CC	2	12	-	-	1	6	-	-	-	-	3	18
	Central Gaulish black-slip	80a	CNG BS	-	-	4	6	-	-	-	-	-	-	4	6
Imports (amphorae)	South Gaulish (flat-based)	35	GAL AM	90	1847	6	251	6	211	-	-	3	10	105	2319
	Baetican	40	BAT AM	2	99	7	1709	1	26	-	-	1	42	11	1876
	Baetican?	40?	-	4	262	2	91	-	-	-	-	-	-	6	353
	Campanian	-	CAM AM	-	-	1	76	-	-	-	-	-	-	1	76
Total				1228	9492	668	6256	525	3594	26	171	82	525	2529	20038

Table 4.5 Summary composition of the pottery by fabric from the backfills of graves within the projected extent of the walled cemetery (shown as sherd count (Ct)/weight (Wt) in grammes/estimated vessel equivalents (EVEs)). No pottery was recovered from the heavily truncated fill of B1211.

Ciren TF	B1155			B1156			B1157			B1158			B1159			B1160			B1168			B1209			Total		
	Ct	Wt	EVEs	Ct	Wt	EVEs	Ct	Wt	EVEs	Ct	Wt	EVEs	Ct	Wt	EVEs	Ct	Wt	EVEs	Ct	Wt	EVEs	Ct	Wt	EVEs	Ct	Wt	EVEs
6?	-	-	-	-	-	-	1	8	0	-	-	-	-	-	-	-	-	-	-	-	-	-	-	-	1	8	0
6	1	36	0	-	-	-	-	-	-	4	58	0	-	-	-	3	111	0	-	-	-	3	10	0	11	215	0
17/98	47	166	0.03	3	18	0	25	347	0.22	14	83	0	7	77	0.30	6	40	0.03	3	12	0	70	250	0.28	175	993	0.86
5	13	67	0.05	-	-	-	12	34	0.20	-	-	-	2	17	0.06	1	7	0	-	-	-	2	15	0	30	140	0.31
15	3	9	0	-	-	-	-	-	-	-	-	-	-	-	-	5	15	0	-	-	-	-	-	-	8	24	0
9/98	6	38	0.07	1	7	0	7	31	0.02	-	-	-	3	82	0.17	5	51	0.10	4	6	0	43	146	0.20	69	361	0.56
9	5	14	0.11	1	1	0	14	154	0	5	24	0.11	30	301	0.42	15	128	0	-	-	-	15	34	0	85	656	0.64
95	3	13	0	-	-	-	5	17	0.10	3	5	0	-	-	-	14	264	0.40	-	-	-	16	109	0.09	41	408	0.59
88	-	-	-	-	-	-	1	14	0	-	-	-	-	-	-	-	-	-	-	-	-	-	-	-	1	14	0
74	33	79	0	7	35	0.05	16	83	0.29	22	127	0.14	9	88	0	1	1	0	7	13	0	89	170	0.08	184	596	0.56
82	-	-	-	-	-	-	-	-	-	-	-	-	-	-	-	-	-	-	-	-	-	1	2	0	1	2	0
90	-	-	-	-	-	-	-	-	-	-	-	-	-	-	-	2	25	0	-	-	-	-	-	-	2	25	0
90?	2	34	0	-	-	-	-	-	-	-	-	-	-	-	-	2	27	0	-	-	-	2	10	0	6	71	0
84	-	-	-	-	-	-	-	-	-	1	3	0	-	-	-	-	-	-	-	-	-	-	-	-	1	3	0
81a	-	-	-	-	-	-	-	-	-	1	1	0	-	-	-	-	-	-	-	-	-	-	-	-	1	1	0
154b	-	-	-	1	1	0.02	1	8	0.06	1	10	0	-	-	-	1	2	0	-	-	-	2	8	0	6	29	0.08
154a	-	-	-	-	-	-	2	60	0.12	-	-	-	-	-	-	-	-	-	-	-	-	3	6	0.05	5	66	0.17
40?	1	157	0	-	-	-	-	-	-	-	-	-	-	-	-	2	42	0	-	-	-	-	-	-	3	199	0
40	-	-	-	-	-	-	-	-	-	1	17	0	-	-	-	-	-	-	-	-	-	-	-	-	1	17	0
35	4	89	0	2	9	0	20	373	0.09	4	29	0	10	525	0	10	382	0	4	94	0	19	172	0	73	1673	0.09
Total	118	702	0.26	15	71	0.07	104	1129	1.1	54	353	0.25	63	1094	0.95	67	1095	0.53	18	125	0	265	932	0.7	704	5501	3.86

of amphorae sherds, almost all comprising flat-based Gallic wine carrying types (such as Gauloise 4; TF 35: 73 sherds; 10% of the total; Fig. 4.8, no. 6). These were noted in each of the eight graves in quantities ranging from 2 to 20 sherds. Cross-context joins were sought but none were found and it is clear from the multiple handle sherds that several vessels are represented. Flagons are well represented (1.19 EVES; 30% of the EVEs total), the forms recorded being ring-necked or triangular rimmed varieties (Fig. 4.8, no. 5). Drinking receptacles, by contrast, are uncommon (beakers: 0.20 EVEs; 5%), as are platters/dishes or bowl forms (0.63 EVEs; 16%; Fig. 4.8, no. 3). The vessels most suggestive of a 'special' character of this group are sherds from no fewer than six tazze (Fig. 4.8, nos 1, 2, 4, 7, 9 and 10). These distinctive vessels are generally considered to have functioned as incense burners and have religious or ceremonial associations (Mackinder 2000, 37).

The representation of wine amphorae, flagons and, particularly, tazze are untypical characteristics of 2nd-century pottery groups from elsewhere in Cirencester. Given its location, the most plausible interpretation is that the special character of the pottery incorporated into the grave fills relates to funerary or post-funerary ceremonies, possibly involving the consumption of wine or pouring it as libations.

There is some evidence for the use of tazze in rituals associated with the dead from funerary sculpture (Toynbee 1971, 45, pl. 9). The purpose may have been purification, to counter the polluting influence of the dead (Philpott 1991, 192). Tazze are relatively rare finds from Romano-British graves, although examples are recorded from York and London (ibid., 193; Hall 1996, Appendix 1; Mackinder 2000, 37). In the latter instance, from Great Dover Street, Southwark, six complete tazze dating to the late 1st or 2nd century were associated with a *bustum* burial. The levels of fragmentation of the pottery from the group considered here argue against it relating to individual graveside rituals and it is more plausible that this material was originally deposited on the ground surface within the walled cemetery and subsequently incorporated into individual graves at the time of backfilling. If this was so the graves need not be as closely contemporaneous as is implied by the compositional similarities across grave fills. The conspicuously late sherds from the backfills of B1156 and B1209 (Black-burnished ware flanged bowls and a New Forest beaker sherd) are considered intrusive.

Table 4.6 Summary composition of the pottery by fabric from the backfills of graves within the projected extent of the walled cemetery (shown as sherd count (Ct)/weight (Wt) in grammes/estimated vessel equivalents (EVEs)). No pottery was recovered from the heavily truncated fill of B1211.

	Amphora		Flagon		Jar		Beaker		Bowl		Bowl/tazza		Dish		Mortarium	
Ciren TF	*No.*	*EVEs*	*No.*	*EVEs*	*No.*	*EVEs*	*No.*	*EVEs*	*No.*	*EVEs*	*No.*	*EVEs*	*No.*	*EVEs*	*No.*	*EVEs*
17/98	-	-	-	-	9	0.78	3	0.05	1	0.03	-	-	-	-	-	-
5	-	-	-	-	3	0.11	1	0.15	2	0.05	-	-	-	-	-	-
9/98	-	-	-	-	1	0.10	-	-	1	0.08	6	0.38	-	-	-	-
9	-	-	7	0.64	-	-	-	-	-	-	-	-	-	-	-	-
95	-	-	5	0.55	-	-	-	-	-	-	-	-	-	-	-	-
74	-	-	-	-	5	0.34	-	-	3	0.22	-	-	-	-	-	-
90	-	-	-	-	-	-	-	-	-	-	-	-	-	-	1	-
88	-	-	-	-	-	-	-	-	-	-	-	-	-	-	1	0.04
35	3	0.9	-	-	-	-	-	-	-	-	-	-	-	-	-	-
(Glos mort)	-	-	-	-	-	-	-	-	-	-	-	-	-	-	1	0.10
102–4	-	-	-	-	2	0.10	-	-	-	-	-	-	1	0.07	-	-
154b	-	-	-	-	-	-	-	-	2	0.06	-	-	1	0.02	-	-
154a	-	-	-	-	-	-	-	-	1	0.12	-	-	1	0.05	-	-
Total	**3**	**0.9**	**12**	**1.19**	**20**	**1.43**	**4**	**0.2**	**10**	**0.56**	**6**	**0.38**	**3**	**0.14**	**3**	**0.14**

Evidence from Cirencester for funerary ceremonial in the earlier Roman period is largely confined to grave goods or deposits of pyre debris. Evidence for the latter, associated with small, gully-defined enclosures has been recorded elsewhere in the Western Cemetery (CE VI, 110–13). The importance of wine (or similar) to funeral rites has been demonstrated at other sites where functional analysis has been undertaken for burial groups; drinking-related vessels (beakers and flagons) typically dominate and the pattern can be exaggerated with pyre goods assemblages (Biddulph 2006, 24). The scarcity of beakers/cups in the present group, however, appears inconsistent with derivation from drinks consumption as part of funerary ceremonial and there is no evidence for the use of glass or other receptacles. However, another possibility is that the amphorae and flagons relate to post-funerary rituals, to libation and ceremonial making use of tazze. Classical sources mention graveside ritual at intervals following the funeral and including libation and the lighting of lamps (Toynbee 1971, 51). Libation pipes enabling the pouring of liquids directly into the burial container are known from a number of British sites such as Caerleon (Wheeler 1929).

Other grave fills

Few of the graves outside the walled cemetery produced large pottery groups and this suggests that most sherds are accidental inclusions. Two larger groups from the grave fills of B1177 and B1215 (67 and 59 sherds respectively) comprise substantial portions of jars in Black-burnished ware (TF 74). They probably represent disturbed cremation urns.

The grave-soil pottery rarely provides reliable or discrete dating evidence, although *termini post quo* are provided for some burials by later Roman fabrics or forms. Among the more notable pottery finds are three sherds from a Central Gaulish black-slipped vessel (TF 80a) which features moulded, applied decoration (Fig. 4.8, no. 11). The vessel form is distinctive and uncommon and is dateable to the Hadrianic or Antonine periods (Simpson 1957; 1973).

Illustrated vessels (Fig. 4.8)

Backfills of graves inside the projected extent of the walled cemetery

1	B1159. TF 9/98; tazza.
2	B1159. TF 9/98; tazza.
3	B1159. TF 17/98; carinated bowl or jar.
4	B1160. TF 9/98; tazza.
5	B1160. TF 9/98; ring-necked/triangular rim flagon.
6	B1160. TF 35; flat-based (Gauloise 4?) amphora.
7	B1155. TF 9/98; tazza.
8	B1155. TF 17/98; beaker; barbotine dot-panel decoration.
9	B1157. TF 9/98; tazza.
10	B1209. TF 9/98; tazza.

Backfill of B1161

11	B1161. TF 80a; beaker (Déchelette 74?).

Ditch B

12	Period 1 Ditch terminal 5186 (fill 5184). TF 17. Shouldered, necked bowl; out-curved rim.

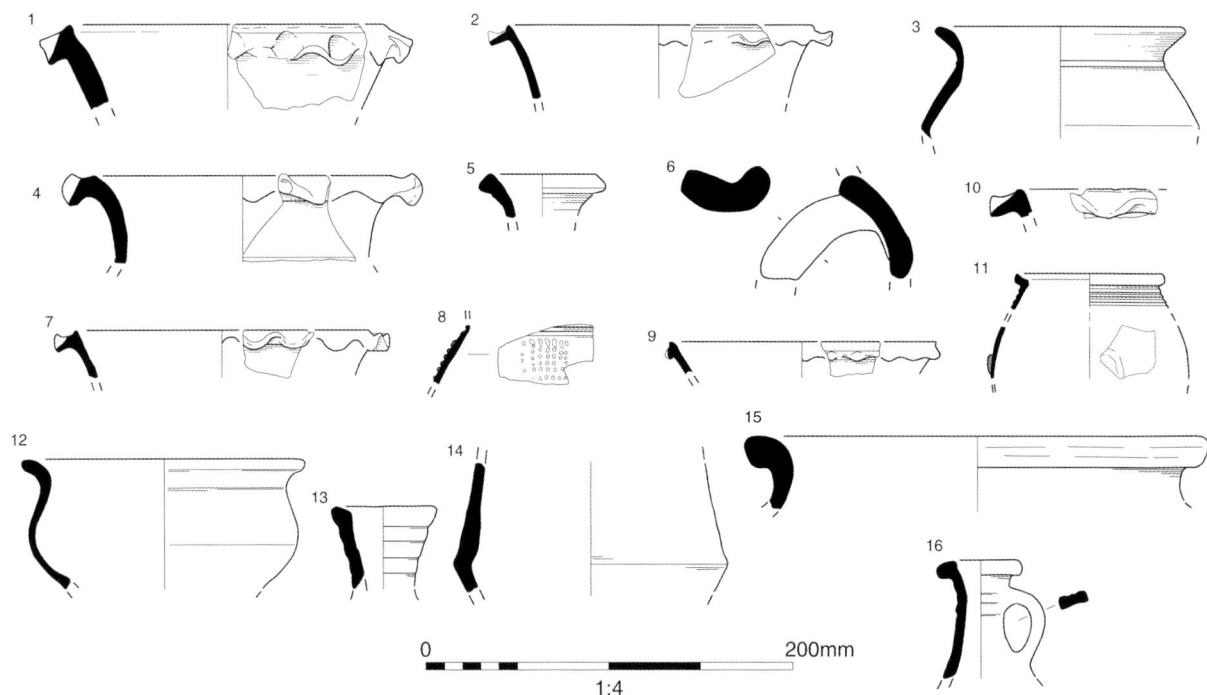

Fig. 4.8   Roman pottery

Ditch F

13   Period 1 Ditch 5149 (fill 5148). TF 9. Ring-necked flagon.

14   Period 1 Ditch 5126 (fill 5127). TF 1–4. Carinated cup/bowl (Webster 1976; Class H).

15   Period 1 Ditch terminal 5121 (fill 5122). TF 6. Large jar, out-curved rim.

Ditch A

16   Period 1/2 Ditch 5011 (fill 5012). TF 95. Ring-necked flagon (vestigial lower rings/grooves). Heavily distorted 'second'.

Anglo-Saxon pottery

A total of 61 sherds of Anglo-Saxon pottery (511g) was recovered, all likely derived from a single pit 1004/5066 (53 sherds). In addition some sherds were identified from Roman burials truncated by, or close to, the pit (B1207, 2 sherds, and B1237, 6 sherds). They are doubtless intrusive from that feature. The fill of pit 1004/5066 also produced 21 sherds of Roman pottery and a whetstone (see Roe, above). The pottery was sorted by fabric and quantified according to sherd count and weight, with rim EVEs recorded for rim sherds. The condition is moderately good with no surface loss. Fragmentation is however relatively high and mean sherd weight is low at 8g.

Fabrics

The pottery fabrics are described below; all are hand-made. Organic-tempered types are most common, the remainder comprising a few sherds in sandy and limestone-tempered types. The range of fabrics is typical for the early to middle Saxon period in the region and all could be local in origin.

F1: *Organic-tempered.* Typically dark grey throughout and micaceous. Moderate to dense organic voids up to 7mm. 32 sherds, 218g; 0.27 EVEs.

F2: *Organic-tempered with quartz.* Grey throughout. Moderate organic voids 3–5mm; sparse, ill-sorted rounded quartz sand. 21 sherds, 187g; 0.16 EVEs.

F3: *Quartz.* Dark grey throughout; common, well-sorted sub-angular quartz (0.3–0.5mm). 3 sherds, 22g; 0.02 EVEs.

F4: *Quartz with organic and sparse limestone.* Dark grey with patchy grey/brown surfaces; common, well-sorted sub-angular quartz (0.3–0.5mm); moderate organic voids 3–5mm and sparse moderately-sorted oolitic limestone 1–2.5mm. 1 sherd, 54g.

F5: *Limestone.* Dark grey with light brown exterior surface. Common, moderately-sorted oolitic limestone 1–3mm. 4 sherds, 30g.

Forms and decoration

The assemblage includes eight rim sherds, most of which are probably representative of jars with globular or slacker profiles. None were decorated. Rims are upright or slightly everted and with simple/rounded or slightly thickened rim tops (Nos 1–3 and 5). Vessel No. 4 is carinated and might be bowl-proportioned.

Discussion and dating

This group is among the largest from this period recognised from the Cirencester environs. In the absence of decoration and with the forms representative

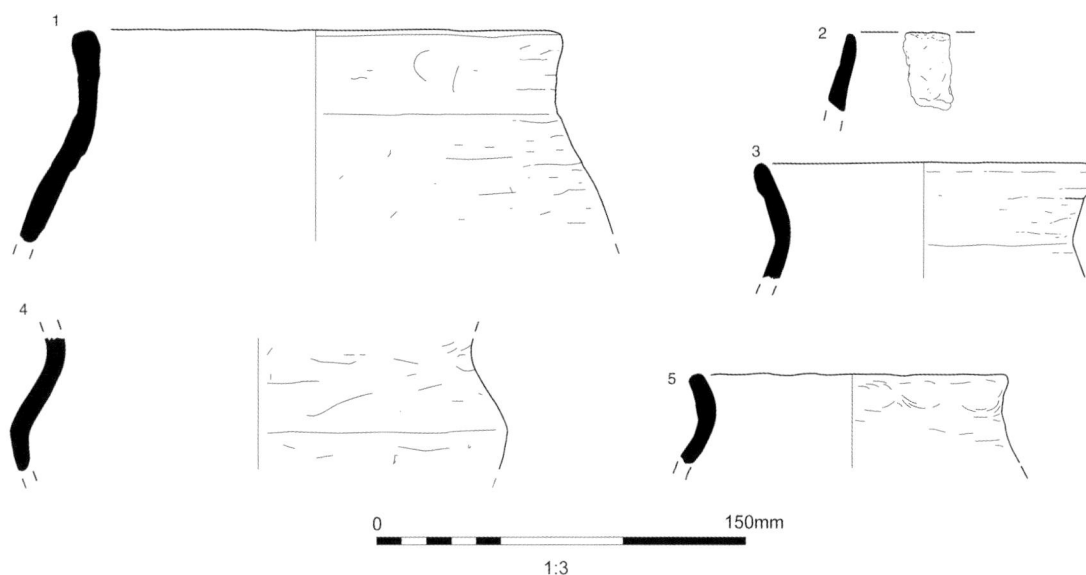

Fig. 4.9   Anglo-Saxon pottery

of utilitarian vessels seen across the early and middle Anglo-Saxon period (*c.* AD 450–850), dating on stylistic grounds is not possible. The range of fabrics is typical of the Anglo-Saxon groups which have emerged from Gloucestershire in recent decades, most notably those from Lower Slaughter (Timby 2006), Sherborne House, Lechlade (Timby 2003), Bourton-on-the-Water Business Park (Timby 2011) and All Saints, Cheltenham (McSloy forthcoming). A mix of calcareous, quartz-tempered and (mainly) organic-tempered fabrics characterises these groups. The abundant representation of organic (grass or chaff-tempered) types may be significant in respect of chronology; the increased use such fabrics is a feature noted with 6th to 7th-century assemblages from central and eastern England (Hamerow *et al.* 1994, 14–16).

The scant finds of Anglo-Saxon/post-Roman pottery recorded from Cirencester come from immediately outside of the walled circuit (Holbrook 2013, 44). A group from Grove Lane on the eastern ring road is similar to that described here in its range of fabrics (ibid., note 61), although it included at least one stamped sherd. Stamped sherds were also present among pottery associated with burials just outside the walls at Barton Farm which Brown dated to the first half of the 6th century (Brown 1976). Material from excavations at the amphitheatre comprised four sherds of 'grass-tempered' pottery from the turf-line overlaying the latest Roman deposits (CE V, 171).

Illustrated vessels (Fig. 4.9)
Pit 1004/5066 (fills 1005 and 5065)

1   Fabric F2. Jar with globular profile and simple, upright rim.

2   Fabric F3. Small jar with simple rim; slack profile.

3   Fabric F1. Jar with globular profile and simple, upright rim.

4   Fabric F1. Bi-conical vessel.

5   Fabric F1. Jar with simple, upright rim.

Chapter 5
Human Remains

by Jonny Geber

In this discussion of the human remains the skeletal material is considered in the context of previous osteoarchaeological analyses from the Western Cemetery, which in addition to this author includes studies undertaken by Calvin Wells, Teresa Gilmore and Annsofie Witkin (CE VI, 109–31; Reece 1962) (Table 5.1). Wells' study dates back to the early 1960s, but it is assumed here that his observations are comparable to those from a modern osteological analysis. Wells was throughout his career recognised as an exceptionally skilled osteologist and palaeopathologist, albeit with sometimes rather innovative interpretations (Roberts and Manchester 2012; Waldron 2014). The term Western Cemetery is used here to describe burials in the vicinity of Tetbury Road, and to the north-west of the dry valley which separates this area of burial from the Bath Gate Cemetery further to the south-east. This chapter presents the most significant aspects of the human remains from the former Bridges Garage site. A full osteological catalogue of the burials, which provides the supporting data for the analyses and conclusions presented in this chapter, can be found in the online archive which is available at http://www.cotswoldarchaeology.co.uk/publications-2/monographs/.

5.1 Cremation Burials
with contributions by Emily Carroll

The largest previous analysis of cremation burials from the Western Cemetery was that of the 44 burials analysed by Calvin Wells found at Oakley Cottage in 1960 (Reece 1962). The analysis was a pioneering study in British osteoarchaeological research, as very few skeletal studies of cremation burials had been undertaken at that time (see Herrmann 1980). Wells' analysis focused on determining the age and sex of the cremated individuals, and he also made some notes on observed pathologies and the efficiency of the cremations. The publication report did not, however, include any systematic description of the quantity or degree of fragmentation in these deposits. These burials were not available for a reanalysis as part of this study. A further seven cremation burials discovered at the former Cattle Market in 2002 and Old Tetbury Road in 2002–4 have also been reported on (CE VI, 109–31).

Osteological methodology

The five cremation burials with extant human remains from the present site were block-lifted on site and

Table 5.1 *The number of human burials discovered during archaeological investigations of the Western Cemetery.* * = preserved *in situ* and not made subject to skeletal analysis

Project name	Type of investigation	Year	Inhumation burials	Cremation burials
Oakley Cottage	Salvage recording	1960	9	44
Former Cattle Market	Evaluation	2002	1*	1
Old Tetbury Road	Excavation	2004	0	1
Former Cattle Market	Watching brief	2004–6	1	5
Former Bridges Garage	Excavation	2011, 2014–15	118	5
Total			**129**	**56**

excavated within a controlled laboratory environment by 5cm spits and quadrants, as recommended by McKinley (2004). In addition, the lower portion of a lead vessel (C1227.1) was discovered and is believed to constitute an urned cremation burial. This vessel however did not contain any bones, although these may have lost due to horizontal truncation. The same applies to disturbed cremation burials C1277–C1278. The deposits of human bone were sorted, and, as part of the osteological analysis, dry sieved in a four mesh-size category subdivision (<2mm, 2–5mm, 5–10mm and >10 mm) for the purpose of assessing the general degree of fragmentation. Measurements on cremated bones were taken according to the descriptions by Gejvall (1948).

Age and sex

When taking the osteological analyses of all cremation burials discovered on the site into account, a total of six non-adult and 43 adult burials and six burials of individuals of unknown age have been identified (Table 5.2). Four of the juvenile cremation burials were of young children, and these were identified in burials from the Oakley Cottage and former Cattle Market excavations. One older child and one individual aged generally as a non-adult were also present at Oakley Cottage. Of the adult burials, 14 were aged by Wells as young adults and one by Witkin as 20–30 years old at the time of death. The five cremation burials at the present site were all of adults likely to have been aged less than 45 years at the time of death. The sex could be determined in 28 adult burials, which included 13 males and 15 females. Females dominated in Wells' analysis of the young adult age groups and two females were also identified at the present excavation (C1153 and C1154). The majority of the males could not be aged more precisely than as adults. Although based on a small sample, there is no indication to suggest differential treatment based on social factors such as age and sex in the cremation burial practice at the Western Cemetery.

Pathology

Due to heat distortion and considerable fragmentation, it is virtually impossible to assess skeletal health from burnt remains in cremation burials. However, some bones in these burials displayed pathological lesions. Witkin observed active periostitis on a long bone fragment in burial C1150 at the former Cattle Market. The periostitis indicates a periosteal inflammatory reaction to conditions such as infection, metabolic disease or trauma (Ortner 2003), but due to the fragmentary nature of the burial it was not possible to determine its most likely aetiology.

Wells identified vertebral osteophytosis in two males and one adult female from the Oakley Cottage excavation, two of which he aged as young adults. Considering that vertebral osteophytosis is a general degenerative condition of the spine – which results in build-up of bone along the margins of the vertebral bodies (see Rogers and Waldron 1995) – it seems unlikely that these two individuals were young adults at the time of death; they are more likely to be aged more than 30 years of age. There is therefore reason to believe that some of Wells' age estimations of the adult cremated material may have been inaccurate. Another degenerative pathology was observed in female burial C1154 at the present site. She displayed a slight marginal osteophyte (bone formation) along the superior margin of the right sacro-iliac joint. The age of this individual was estimated at 18–44 years, and considering the presence of this degenerative pathological condition is seems most likely that she belonged to the upper end of this age range.

Quantity, anatomical completeness and fragmentation

As Wells only gave brief descriptions of the quantities in the burials he analysed, which range from 'a few dozen' to 'many hundreds of fragments', his quantifications cannot be further discussed. The remaining burials (N = 12) ranged between 48g to 904g in quantity,

Table 5.2 The age and sex profile of the cremation burials recovered from the Western Cemetery to date.

Age group	Males	Females	Indet.	Total	%All
Young child (2–5 years)	-	-	4	4	7.27
Older child (6–12 years)	-	-	1	1	1.82
Non-adult (< 18 years)	-	-	1	1	1.82
Young adult (18–25 years)	4	8	2	14	25.45
Young/Early middle adult (18–35 years)	0	0	1	1	1.82
Young/Middle adult (18–45 years)	1	2	2	5	9.09
Indet. adult (> 18 years)	8	5	10	23	41.82
Indet. (? years)	0	0	6	6	10.91
All	**13**	**15**	**27**	**55**	**100.00**

Table 5.3 The most common anatomical region identified in the cremation burials in relation to anatomical completeness.

	Total	Skull		Axial		Upper limb		Lower limb	
		No.	%	No.	%	No.	%	No.	%
1 region (25%)	8	3	37.50	4	50.00	1	12.50	0	0.00
2 regions (50%)	14	11	78.57	12	85.71	2	14.29	3	21.43
3 regions (75%)	8	8	100.00	5	62.50	7	87.50	3	37.50
4 regions (100%)	10	10	100.00	10	100.00	10	100.00	10	100.00
Any	**40**	**32**	**80.00**	**31**	**77.50**	**20**	**50.00**	**16**	**0.40**

with a mean weight of 262g (SD = 253.8). These quantities should be compared with the 1,000–2,400g of bone that is expected to be generated from an adult cremation (McKinley 1993, 285). Only C1147 from the former Cattle Market is close to this size, although it is clear in that case that this burial had indeed suffered truncation and that it did not represent the whole of the original deposit. Horizontal and vertical truncation was also clearly the major factor causing relatively low quantities of bones recovered in the rest of these burials, and further discussion on the quantity of bone in each burial is therefore of little value.

The osteological analysis quantified the number of elements present from each of four anatomical regions: the skull, the axial skeleton (the vertebral column, ribs and sternum), the upper limb (scapulae, clavicles, humeri, radii, ulnae, wrist and hand bones), and the lower limb (coxal bones, femora, patellae, tibiae, fibulae, ankle and foot bones). The quantity of bones from each region is specified in the osteological catalogue. Overall, elements from the skull and the axial region of the skeleton were most frequently identified in the deposits followed by bones from the upper and lower limbs (Table 5.3). There is in general even anatomical representation observed in these burials, with about half of all burials containing identifiable fragments of bones from three or four anatomical regions. Identified bones

from two or less anatomical regions were identified in 22 burials. Many of these include the Oakley Cottage burials. Wells often made reference to large amounts of long bones being present in the deposits, which he was however unable to identify to skeletal element. These included both upper and lower limb bones, and many of his analysed burials are therefore likely to be 'anatomically complete' and the proportion of poorly anatomically represented burials in Table 5.3 is probably a misrepresentation (cf. Table 5.4, which states the representation of anatomical representation of cremated bone weights from the Bridges Garage site). Overall, the distribution of identified skeletal elements in the cremation burials from the Western Cemetery indicates that no selection of particular bones was likely to have taken place, and that the remains were collected from the pyre at random.

Wells made no reference to the degree of fragmentation in his analysis of the Oakley Cottage cremation burials. The bone fragmentation in the other burials from the Western Cemetery has however been assessed using the same methodological approach by subdividing the material by weight into four different size categories (see Osteological methodology above). The results indicate a great variation in the degree of fragmentation, with the most heavily fragmented burials being C1145 and C1148 from the former Cattle Market, and the

Table 5.4 The relative distribution of identified skeletal elements from the four main anatomical regions of the body in cremation burials, the pyre debris deposit, and backfills in graves, ditches and pits at former Bridges Garage site.

Context type	No.	Total weight (g)	% identified	Cranial		Axial		Upper limb		Lower limb	
				Weight (g)	%	Weight (g)	%	Weight (g)	%	Weight (g)	%
Cremation burials	3	549.38	66.35	75.65	20.75	36.65	10.05	66.24	18.17	185.97	51.02
Pyre debris	1	324.20	20.09	30.68	47.11	4.95	7.60	12.98	19.93	16.52	25.36
Inhumation burial backfill	31	1,004.46	15.73	53.57	33.91	6.75	4.27	18.68	11.82	78.98	49.99
Ditch fill	2	3.39	0.00	0.00	-	0.00	-	0.00	-	0.00	-
Posthole fill	1	2.03	0.00	0.00	-	0.00	-	0.00	-	0.00	-
Pit fill	1	0.32	0.00	0.00	-	0.00	-	0.00	-	0.00	-
Unstratified / Other	2	20.18	57.63	0.00	-	0.00	-	0.00	-	11.63	100.00
Total	**41**	**1,903.96**	**31.47**	**159.90**	**26.68**	**48.35**	**8.07**	**97.90**	**16.34**	**293.10**	**48.91**

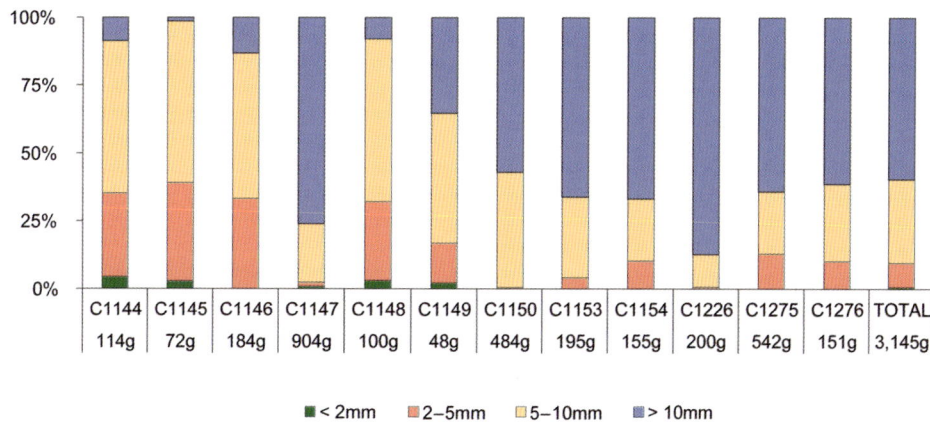

Fig. 5.1   The relative fragmentation of the cremation burials from the Western Cemetery assessed by weight proportions in mesh-size categories

least fragmented burial C1226 from the present site (Fig. 5.1). In total, more than half of the weight in the deposits measured more than 10mm in linear size, and only about 9% of the weight was comprised of fragments measuring 2–5mm in size. The samples therefore appear to have suffered a relatively minor degree of fragmentation (see Geber 2009).

The degree of fragmentation in cremation burials is dependent on a variety of factors, such as the age and sex of the deceased, the cremation process and collapse of the pyre, the post-cremation handling and actual burial of the remains, and a multitude of post-depositional factors such as ground pressure, bioturbation and truncation. In addition, even the most careful archaeological excavation of a cremation burial will inevitably cause further damage to the remains (Geber 2009). However, a common interpretation has been to explain the often considerable degree of fragmentation in ancient cremation burials as a result of having been manually crushed as part of the funerary ritual prior to deposition (e.g. Lynch and O'Donnell 2007; Sigvallius 1994). This interpretation was suggested by Witkin in her analysis of the cremation burial C1150; however, this author is more inclined towards suggesting natural factors causing fragmentation in all of these burials. In fact, due to the numerous factors that may cause fragmentation in a cremation burial, it is almost impossible to determine with any certainty that they have been intentionally crushed or pounded (Geber 2009).

Animal bones

Wells identified animal bones in five burials, which included bird bones, a possible cattle rib and cockle shells in four non-adult burials, and a caprovine talus amongst the remains of a young adult male. Caprovine remains, including a hind limb of a juvenile sheep, were identified in burials C1147 and C1148 and a

bone from an unknown mammal in C1149. Burial C1150 contained one burnt bird bone of unknown species. These clearly represent intentional inclusions, and as they were burnt it can be concluded that they were present on the pyre. The significance of these is discussed further in Section 6.1.

Cremation technology

The actual process of cremation would have been a significant undertaking in ancient societies which would have taken several hours and possibly even lasted for days (Holck 1997, 33; McKinley 1989, 65). The rite of cremation would have involved the collection of large amounts of fuel, the construction of the pyre and starting and maintaining the cremation itself (McKinley 1997; Piontek 1976; Sigvallius 1994). The wood species identified from the anthracological analysis of the Western Cemetery burials revealed that primarily oak was used as fuel, with inclusions of hawthorn/rowan/crab apple, ash and cherry (see Chapter 6).

The general efficiency of a cremation can be assessed by the colours of the burnt bone, as these will range from brown/black/grey-blue nuances in lower temperatures around 200–300°C to bright white in temperatures exceeding 650–800°C which is when human bone commences incineration (Herrmann 1988). Wells made reference to the efficiency of the cremation in his analysis of the Oakley Cottage burials, of which nine were described as good, nine as fair to moderate and seven as poor. He did not, however, explain the criteria on which he based his assessment. The colour of the burnt bone in the remaining burials ranged from grey to white, which would suggest that they had all been successfully cremated, although at varying temperatures. The efficiency and outcome of a cremation depends on several factors, such as the construction of the pyre, the position of the corpse upon it, and on the quality and quantity of the wood fuel (McKinley 2000). To maintain high temperatures, the fire must also be tended and supplied with oxygen by stirring the pyre from time to time (see Østigård 2000, 27). McKinley (2000) has observed that the efficiency in Romano-British cremations was generally poorer than their prehistoric equivalents, and she explains this as possibly reflecting a difference in what was considered an accepted degree of incineration, or that cremations were undertaken by paid attendants who were less concerned about the result of the cremation than immediate family members would have been.

The cremation of bone involves a chemical process, in which the organic content of the bone is destroyed and calcium salts transformed into calcium apatite (Herrmann 1988; Hiller *et al.* 2003; Hummel and Schutkowski 1986; Iregren and Jonsson 1973). Along with the fragmentation occurring during this process, bones that are largely trabecular, such as as vertebrae and coxal bones, tend to shrink. Compact bones such as the cranial bones, the long bone and tubular bones warp and distort in the heat. Bones that are defleshed, however, display a fracture pattern different from the typical curvilinear deep transverse fissures that are evident in bones from cremated bodies (Binford 1963; Buikstra and Swegle 1989; Schutkowski 1991). None of the burials from the Western Cemetery excavations have reportedly included cracking patterns which would indicate that any of the elements had been defleshed prior to the cremation.

Pyre debris and redeposited cremated human remains

In addition to the burials described above, 14 Roman contexts contained varying amounts of cremated human bone. Three of these have been interpreted as deposits of pyre debris in pits. These included two features (Pit 128 and Pit 133) from the Old Tetbury Road site, which included a mixture of cremated human remains, charcoal, glass and pottery. The bones in these deposits derived from adult individuals, were grey/white in colour, and weighed a total of 56g and 42g respectively. A third such deposit was recovered from Pit 1179, 0.98m by 0.48m and 0.12m deep, at the present excavation. It contained a total of 324g of cremated human bone mixed with charcoal and was the remains of a minimum of one adult individual. It included identifiable fragments of cranial vault, teeth, fragments of ribs and vertebrae, scapula, long bone fragments and phalanges and tarsals. Most of these remains displayed a grey shade in colour, and appear to have been much less oxidised that the bones in the formal cremation burials found on site. One cranial vault fragment was also only partly burnt. This difference in oxidation may indicate that well-cremated bones were particularly selected for burial, while the remainder were deposited with the general debris from the cremation. This disparity is a

contrast to what was observed in the cremation burials and pyre debris deposits at the Eastern Cemetery in London, where no indication of any intentional selection of bones prior to burial based on cremation efficiency could be argued (McKinley 2000). No evidence of a pyre site has been identified within the excavated portions of the cemetery; however, the presence of pyre debris deposits indicates a nearby location. Cremations during the Romano-British period generally occurred at the cemetery to judge from the frequent finds of pyre sites and dumps of pyre debris (ibid.).

In addition to these contexts, cremated human remains were also found as inclusions in the backfill of 31 inhumation burials. These ranged in quantities from only 0.10g to 301.80g with a mean weight of 32.40g (SD = 63.49), and do not appear to have been deliberate inclusions. Considering the truncation that has occurred on the site, it appears most likely that these are remains of earlier features disturbed when later graves were dug. The highest quantities of these backfill deposits were found in burials located in the central and north-east area of the excavation. The most noteworthy amongst these deposits was the backfill of B1209, which contained the highest quantity of burnt bone. Considering also the relatively high proportion of of burnt wood remains in the same deposit, this fill is likely to primarily contain pyre debris. Overall, however, the anatomical distribution of identified elements in these deposits, i.e. no apparent bias related to anatomical region, is more similar to the pattern observed in the cremation burials (Table 5.4).

Discussion

Reece's observations make plain that many more cremation burials once existed within the bounds of the former Bridges Garage site. Unlike the majority of the inhumation burials, several cremation burials are likely to have been truncated while the cemetery was still in use. This may indicate that these graves lacked markers, or possibly that later inhumation burials were intentionally placed in plots where previous burials of urned cremated remains had taken place. Although the outcome of the osteological analyses of the cremation burials from the Western Cemetery was limited due to truncation and the small number of surviving examples, it can be concluded that cremation was undertaken for both the non-adult and adult sections of the population and there is no indication that any differentiation relating to other social factors such as sex and age took place.

5.2 Inhumation Burials

The discussion of the inhumation burials recovered from the various excavations within the Western Cemetery is based on the results of Wells' original analysis of the Oakley Cottage skeletons and this author's analysis of the former Bridges Garage skeletons and reanalysis of

Table 5.5 The minimum, mean and maximum dimension of six post-cranial measurements in morphologically sexed adult males and females.
For definition of measurements, see Bräuer 1988

Variable	Males					Females					t	df	p
	min.	mean	max.	SD	N	min.	mean	max.	SD	N			
Scapula 12	34.61	39.18	44.08	2.26	31	29.50	33.66	37.12	1.89	29	-10.217	58	< 0.001
Humerus 10	42.22	48.20	55.58	2.81	29	37.32	41.78	49.42	2.81	30	-8.783	57	< 0.001
Humerus 4	59.58	65.00	70.74	3.15	29	50.00	56.35	61.83	3.41	22	-9.373	49	< 0.001
Femur 19	39.00	49.70	56.05	3.12	31	38.11	42.53	49.15	2.67	32	-9.800	61	< 0.001
Femur 21	74.20	82.36	86.15	3.26	21	69.20	74.44	83.91	3.79	19	-7.101	38	< 0.001
Tibia 3	72.94	76.84	82.51	3.05	20	64.85	69.06	72.67	2.27	18	-8.838	36	< 0.001

skeleton B1151 from the former Cattle Market. While Wells' osteological descriptions of the Oakley Cottage skeletons are relatively detailed it was not possible to fully incorporate some of these results into the overall statistical analysis of the data. It is also anticipated that his analysis, which was undertaken more than 50 years ago, would have missed some pathological lesions; particularly those relating to metabolic diseases which were not well understood at that time. This fact was taken into account when prevalence frequencies of various conditions were calculated. The skeletons from Oakley Cottage were unfortunately not available for reanalysis in this study.

Osteological methodology

Wells gave no description of the methods he employed for ageing and sexing the five skeletons from Oakley Cottage. His results are however assumed to be accurate, and due to the fact that he only assessed a small number (N = 9) of largely incomplete inhumation burials, no attempts to revise his determinations have been undertaken. The methods employed for the osteological analyses of the other skeletons followed recommendations and standard practice in Britain and internationally (Brickley and McKinley 2004; Buikstra and Ubelaker 1994; Ferembach *et al.* 1980; Rösing *et al.* 2007; Sjøvold 1988; Szilvázzy 1988).

Non-adult skeletons were aged from the stage of dental development and eruption (Broadbent *et al.* 1975; Liversidge *et al.* 1998; Moorrees *et al.* 1963; Smith 1991), and epiphyseal bone fusion (Scheuer and Black 2000). Adults were aged from the morphology of the auricular surfaces of the ilia (Lovejoy *et al.* 1985b), the pubic symphysis (Brooks and Suchey 1990; Todd 1921a; 1921b), suture obliteration (Meindl and Lovejoy 1985), sternal rib morphology (İşcan *et al.* 1984; 1985) and dental attrition (Brothwell 1981). A multifactorial determination of the age at death, using all of the aforementioned methods above, was conducted for the adult skeletons (Lovejoy *et al.* 1985a). The use of this method assured that the most consistent age determination was applied to the population sample.

The mid-value for the estimated age-ranges determined which age group each individual was assigned to, which were defined as: neonate (N) = less than 4 weeks; infant (I) = 1–12 months; young child (YC) = 1–5 years; older child (OC) = 6–12 years; adolescent (Adol.) = 13–17 years; young adult (YA) = 18–25 years; early middle adult (EMA) = 26–35 years; late middle adult (LMA) = 36–45 years; older adult (OA) = ≥46 years; and indeterminable adult (Indet. A) = >18 years.

Sex determinations can only be reliably performed in skeletons of post-pubertal individuals. These followed from the descriptions by Buikstra and Ubelaker (1994) and Sjøvold (1988), with a primary focus on pelvic features followed by cranial traits. Sexual dimorphism was scored according to the following division: hyperfeminine (-2), feminine (-1), indeterminable sex (0), masculine (+1), and hypermasculine (+2). For cases where the pelvis and skull were absent, sex was determined from metrical analysis. The discriminatory values are based on the mean range values of seven measurements of morphologically sexed adult males and females within the population, which were all significantly different between the sexes (Table 5.5). The section point between male and female dimensions was determined from the middle value of the two mean estimates for each variable (Table 5.6). The bicondylar

Table 5.6 The sectioning point, and accuracy, of six post-cranial measurements employed for sexing adult skeletons.
For the definition of measurements see Bräuer 1988

Variable		% Sexed correctly		
	M > F	Males	Females	All
Scapula 12	36.42	93.75	96.43	95.00
Humerus 10	44.99	89.21	83.33	84.75
Humerus 4	60.68	86.67	82.61	84.91
Femur 19	46.12	90.32	87.50	88.89
Femur 21	78.40	90.48	89.47	90.00
Tibia 3	72.95	95.00	100.00	97.37

breadth of the tibia (3), the greatest length of the glenoid cavity of the scapula (12) and the bicondylar width of the femora (21) were most reliable for metrical sexing in this population, and good values were also given from the transverse diameter of the head (19) of the femora. The epicondylar width of the humeri (4) gave poor discriminatory values, and was therefore not used for sexing. Unsexed skeletons that had a majority of the remaining measurements indicating a particular sex, and where at least three variables were present, could be sexed using this methodology. In total, however, these only comprised three out of 15 morphologically unsexed adult skeletons, which were sexed as one male (B1172) and two females (B1197 and B1204).

Generic bone measurements were taken following the descriptions by Bräuer (1988). Estimation of living stature was calculated from long bone lengths following the equations developed for Caucasian populations by Trotter and Gleser (1952; 1958) and Sjøvold (1990). Additionally, the stature of seven individuals was estimated from metacarpal lengths (Meadow and Jantz 1992), and from the calcaneus and talus (Holland 1995) in eleven individuals. The results of these are presented in the detailed skeletal catalogue contained in the digital archive, and not considered for the overall statistical assessment of the mean stature of the population. Statistical analyses were performed using the IBM SPSS Statistics for Windows, Version 22.0 software package.

Bone preservation and skeletal completeness

The preservation of the skeletons recovered from the former Cattle Market and former Bridges Garage ranges from very poor to very good, with the majority being of moderate to good preservation, although usually quite fragmented. Non-adult skeletons were the least well preserved in this cemetery. This result is expected, as juvenile skeletons are smaller and less mineralised, and therefore more prone to damage caused by post-depositional taphonomical factors such as water erosion, bioturbation and truncation (Lyman 1994). No significant difference was observed in bone preservation between adult male and female skeletons ($\chi^2(4) = 3.932$, $p = 0.415$).

The majority of the skeletons were in general anatomically complete, although the bone preservation of the same single skeleton often varied when the remains of trabecular bones such as the vertebral column and coxal bones were particularly fragile, and in some cases absent. As well as being partly dependent on the degree of bone preservation, incompleteness of skeletons is also the result of intercutting burials observed in several cases at the present site. In total, 29 skeletons were less than 20% complete, which in most cases was due to post-depositional truncation. The skeletons recovered from the Oakley Cottage excavation were all very incomplete, which is likely to relate to hurried excavation under salvage conditions.

Metrical indices and stature

Considering that the population of Corinium is likely to have been mixed, with various ethnicities represented, as well as the wide range of occupations and professions to be expected in an urban community, some aspects of the variation of physical build and shape are worth exploring. For example, the variance in overall shapes of the adult crania, using the cephalic index, can be used (Schwartz 1995, 324). In this analysis, this assessment could only be undertaken from a few skeletons recovered from the present excavation. Amongst these, male skulls ranged from 64.49 to 80.74 with a mean value of 74.66 (SD = 4.27; N = 20), while female skulls ranged from 69.04 to 82.97 and had a mean value of 75.86 (SD = 3.90; N = 18). By type, most skulls were dolichocranic and mesocranic (Table 5.7). This distribution is similar to the cranial types observed at the Bath Gate Cemetery, although the skeletons interred in that burial ground had a lesser proportion of brachycranic skulls (CE II, 137–9). Overall, however, there is nothing to suggest that there would have been a difference between the two population samples in terms of physical appearance.

Table 5.7 The rate of cranial indices by categories (Schwartz 1995), based on an individual count.

	Males		Females		All	
	N	%	N	%	N	%
Dolichocranic (< 75.0)	9	45.00	5	27.78	14	36.84
Mesocranic (75.0–79.9)	10	50.00	9	50.00	19	50.00
Brachycranic (80.0–84.9)	1	5.00	4	22.22	5	13.16
Hyperbrachycranic (> 84.9)	0	0.00	0	0.00	0	0.00

The general flattening of the proximal shaft of the femora and tibiae are assessed using the platymeric and platycnemic index, which can also be used as a comparative measure. Both these indices are calculated by multiplying the antero-posterior diameter by 100, and dividing it by the medio-lateral diameter at the same point, which is at the subtrochanteric area of the femur and the level of the nutrient foramen on the tibia. The explanations as to why this flattening occurs vary, and include proposed factors such as mechanical adaptation, abnormal physiological strain during childhood and adolescence, and calcium or vitamin deficiencies (Buxton 1938; Cameron 1934; Parsons 1914; Turner 1887). By type, the majority of the adult individuals displayed flattened platymeric femora and broad and wide eurycnemic tibiae (Table 5.8). While there was no statistical difference in platymeric indices between the sexes ($\chi^2(1) = 0.007$, $p = 0.993$), the much higher proportion of eurycnemic tibiae in females than males was statistically significant ($\chi^2(2) = 14.170$, $p = 0.001$). This may reflect differences in activity patterns between the sexes where females possibly undertook

Table 5.8 The rate of platymeric and platycnemic indices in adult skeletons by categories (Schwartz 1995). Based on an individual count, with a preference to left-sided elements.

	Males		Females		Unsexed		All	
	N	%	*N*	%	*N*	%	*N*	%
Platymeric index								
Platymeria (< 85.0)	28	77.78	28	77.78	3	75.00	64	78.05
Eurymeria (85.0–99.9)	8	22.22	8	22.22	1	25.00	18	21.95
Stenomeria (> 99.9)	0	0.00	0	0.00	0	0.00	0	0.00
Platycnemic index								
Hyperplatycnemia (< 55.0)	0	0.00	0	0.00	0	0.00	0	0.00
Platycnemia (55.0–62.9)	0	0.00	3	8.82	0	0.00	3	4.05
Mesocnemia (63.0–69.9)	18	51.43	4	11.76	1	20.00	23	31.08
Eurycnemia (> 69.9)	17	48.57	27	79.41	4	80.00	48	64.86

more diverse physical tasks than the male proportion of the population (see Lovejoy *et al.* 1976).

The maximum obtained stature achieved in an individual is dependent on multiple factors, such as environment, genetic background, diet and general health. As such, stature has frequently been used as a measure of socioeconomic status in both anthropological and historical research. However, a direct correlation between stature and social and economic status is not likely to have been the case in pre-modern populations. Access to wealth did not necessarily mean access to a healthier lifestyle, as what were considered 'high-status' indicators such as diet may have had a negative impact on the general well-being of an individual. Variations in stature are also known to relate to general living conditions, such as housing standards and whether people lived in a rural or urban environment, and demographic changes (see Arcini *et al.* 2012; Lantzsch and Schuster 2009; Maat 1990).

When only taking the results given from the Trotter and Gleser equations into account, the living stature of the adult male population is estimated to have been between 156cm (5ft 1in) to 182cm (6ft), with a mean height of 170cm (5ft 7in). Females measured on average 158cm (5ft 2in) in height, ranging from 146cm (4ft 9½in) to 171cm (5ft 7in). The Sjøvold method gave slightly shorter statures by the minimum and mean height values and higher statures for the tallest individuals (Table 5.9). The heights of the adults at the Western Cemetery are similar to contemporaneous Romano-British populations (Table 5.10). It is interesting to observe, nonetheless, that males from the Western Cemetery are the tallest in this comparison. The females, however, are within the mean range given from the other populations. The mean stature in the Roman period increased slightly for the male population and decreased for the female population in comparison with previous centuries (Roberts and Cox 2003, table 8.1), and may relate to either a new population influx or a physiological change

Table 5.9 The range and mean value of estimated living statures (cm) in the adult male and female population buried at the Western Cemetery (former Bridges Garage and former Cattle Market sites).

Sex	Estimated living stature (cm)				
	min.	mean	max.	SD	*N*
Males					
Trotter and Gleser (1958)	155.78	169.87	181.90	5.74	38
Sjøvold (1990)	146.62	168.41	189.69	8.29	38
Females					
Trotter and Gleser (1952)	145.67	158.33	170.93	5.96	29
Sjøvold (1990)	138.97	158.21	172.04	7.72	30

relating to new living patterns and lifestyles (see Redfern 2008). After the Roman period, during the 5th to 11th centuries, there are osteoarchaeological indications that stature increased in Britain by approximately 3cm (1½in) for both sexes (Roberts and Cox 2003, table 8.1).

Age and sex distribution of the burial sample

The excavated portions of the Western Cemetery have generated 127 inhumation burials to date, comprising 21 non-adults and 106 adults. Forty-eight of these could be sexed as males, and 47 as females (Table 5.11). As the cemetery has been considerably truncated in the past, and owing to the fact that only a small proportion of it has been excavated, it is difficult to discuss the demographic profile in this group, as the excavated skeletons may not truly represent the buried population. The male to female ratio was even and close to the expected value of 1.05:1 in a modern population (Jacobsen *et al.* 1999), and there is therefore no indication of a differential spatial placing of the adult population based on sex.

The sex ratio of the inhumation burials at the Bath Gate Cemetery, which were also analysed by Wells, was dominated by males with a ratio of 2.45:1. Wells

Table 5.10 Estimated living statures (cm) in Roman-period skeletal populations from Britain, all based on the methods by Trotter and Gleser (1952; 1958).

Site/Population	Period	Males			Females		
		mean	SD	N	mean	SD	N
Western Cemetery, Cirencester	Roman	169.87	5.74	38	158.33	5.96	29
Bath Gate, Cirencester (CE II)	Roman	169.10	n/a	107	157.90	n/a	44
Cotswold School, Bourton-on-the-Water (Geber 2016)	Late Roman	166.81	4.91	5	158.30	5.66	4
London Road, Gloucester (Márquez-Grant and Loe 2008)	Early Roman	169.00	7.98	4	160.00	2.69	4
Hucclecote, Gloucestershire (Waldron 2003)	Early Roman	163.00	-	1	156.00	3.46	4
Cannington, Somerset (Brothwell *et al.* 2000)	Late Roman	168.00	n/a	n/a	163.50	n/a	n/a
Great Barford (Sites 4 and 8), Bedfordshire (Geber 2007)	Roman	169.61	n/a	5	169.28	-	1
Poundbury, Dorset (Molleson 1993)	Roman	166.17	5.92	341	160.86	4.15	360
Various sites, Dorset (Redfern 2008)	Roman	169.00	-	71	153.00	-	32
Brough, East Yorkshire (Holst 2007)	Roman	164.80	5.23	2	-	-	0
Lankhills, Winchester (Clough and Boyle 2010)	Late Roman	168.99	n/a	38	157.13	n/a	31
Long Melford, Suffolk (Anderson 1997)	Late Roman	168.90	4.93	4	158.10	5.66	2
Bradley Hill, Somerset (Everton in Leech 1981)	Late Roman	168.84	6.51	10	158.68	5.81	10

Table 5.11 Age and sex profile of the inhumation burials recovered from the Oakley Cottage, former Cattle Market and former Bridges Garage excavations in the Western Cemetery.

Age code	Age group	Males	Females	Unsexed	Total
N	Neonate (< 1 month)	-	-	2	2
I	Infant (1–12 months)	-	-	2	2
YC	Young child (1–5 years)	-	-	6	6
OC	Older child (6–12 years)	-	-	7	7
Adol.	Adolescent (13–17 years)	2	0	2	4
YA	Young adult (18–25 years)	1	7	1	9
EMA	Early middle adult (26–35 years)	11	18	3	32
LMA	Late middle adult (36–45 years)	24	16	0	40
OA	Older adult (≥ 46 years)	9	3	1	13
Indet. A	Indet. adult (> 18 years)	1	3	8	12
	All	**48**	**47**	**32**	**127**

interpreted this as a cultural reflection, where he hypothesised that the majority of the males must have been 'retired legionaries' or 'Roman officials, many whom lacked regular wives and whose sexual partners, if any, were probably drawn from the professional prostitutes who were no doubt an abundant and pleasant amenity of the town' (CE II, 135). Wells' often sexist and vulgar over-interpretations of human skeletal remains are notoriously well known in British osteoarchaeology (see Waldron 2014), and his interpretations of Roman burials from Cirencester were no exception.

Pathological changes

The palaeopathological analysis of ancient human bones gives the greatest insight into past life experiences and living conditions. The published results of Wells' analysis of the few inhumation burials discovered during the Oakley Cottage excavation are basic in comparison with current osteological and palaeopathological analytical practices. Therefore, it was only possible to amalgamate his diagnoses of dental caries and occasional descriptions of spinal degenerative joint disease into the analysis of skeletal health of this population. As most of the Oakley Cottage skeletons were incomplete, it is not believed that this will alter the general prevalence rates of identified pathologies. Nevertheless, as several skeletons from the former Bridges Garage excavation displayed cortical erosion, most likely due to a fluctuating ground-water table and rain water percolation, many periosteal lesions may have been destroyed in the ground and therefore not been identifiable in the palaeopathological analysis of the human remains from the Western Cemetery.

Dental disease and anomalies

Poor oral health can result in serious negative health consequences. Dental decay, for instance, may provide the entry point for serious infections with possible mortal outcomes, and loss of teeth may result in an inadequate nutritional intake, as certain foods may become too difficult to digest due to impaired mastication. In the skeletons from the Western Cemetery, the observed dental pathologies include caries, antemortem tooth loss, periodontal disease, periapical lesions and dental calculus. Some dentitions did also display enamel defects, which related to an underlying poor health condition during childhood (see below). True disease prevalences for the dentitions are calculated as much as possible and the rates are based on cases where at least one quarter of the original dentition was available for examination.

Dental caries

Caries, or tooth decay, is the most common chronic dental pathology. It results from a demineralisation process of the enamel matrix of the teeth, due to bacterial fermentation of dietary carbohydrates contained in plaque (Hillson 1996; Selwitz *et al.* 2007). Other than being indicative of a diet rich in carbohydrate food stuffs, high frequencies of caries generally reflects a poor oral hygiene (Featherstone 2000). For this analysis, caries frequencies were assessed by number of teeth and dentitions, following the Comparable Dental Index (Brinch and Møller-Christensen 1949) for all teeth (CDI_t) and molar teeth only (CDI_m). By total tooth count, the highest frequencies were observed in the older adult age group (Fig. 5.2), and there is a clear increase in dental caries by age. This progression with advancing age is also observed when quantified by dentition, and more than half of all individuals aged over 35 years displayed evidence of tooth decay (Table 5.12).

Table 5.12 Crude prevalence rate of dental caries based on observable dentitions by age groups.
For key to Age group see Table 5.11

Age group	CDI_t		CDI_m	
	No./Total	%	No./Total	%
YC	0/5	0.00	0/6	0.00
OC	3/6	50.00	3/6	50.00
Adol.	0/3	0.00	0/4	0.00
YA	3/9	33.33	3/9	33.33
EMA	13/29	44.83	11/30	36.67
LMA	22/33	66.67	20/33	60.61
OA	10/10	100.00	10/10	100.00
All	**51/95**	**53.68**	**47/98**	**47.96**

The only non-adult dentitions with caries belonged to three older children (B1171, B1205 and B1243), which involved cavities in the maxillary deciduous molars and mandibular permanent molars.

The frequencies of caries differed between the sexes in the adult population. Males were more affected than females, with dentitions being 1.3 times more commonly affected by CDI_t and CDI_m (Table 5.13). Amongst the young adults, the only male individual did not display any carious teeth, while three of the seven females were affected. In the older adult population, all males and females had at least one tooth affected by caries. In comparison with contemporaneous populations, the caries frequency by total tooth count is slightly above average (Table 5.14). Males, in particular, had a relatively higher rate and frequency of teeth affected by caries which is interesting in this comparison. Generally, the female rate of caries is expected to be higher compared to males due to biological factors (see Lukacs 2017). In this case, however, the higher proportion of late middle and older adults amongst the males compared to the females in the Western Cemetery (see Table 5.11)

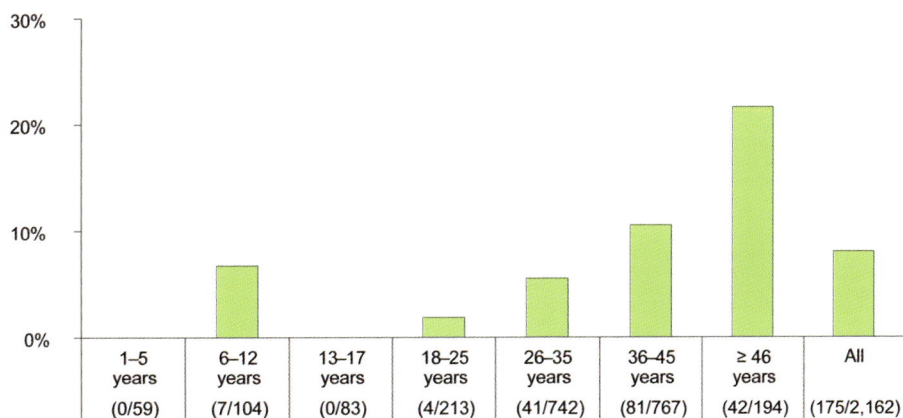

Fig. 5.2   Prevalence rate of dental caries (total tooth count) by age group

Table 5.13 Crude prevalence rate of caries in total dentitions (CDI$_t$) and molar dentitions (CDI$_m$) in adult males and females by age groups and in total.
For key to Age group see Table 5.11

	Males		Females				
	No./Total	%	No./Total	%	χ^2	df	p
CDI$_t$							
YA	0/1	0.00	3/7	42.86	0.686	1	0.408
EMA	6/11	54.55	7/15	46.67	0.158	1	0.691
LMA	13/19	68.42	9/14	64.29	0.062	1	0.803
OA	8/8	100.00	2/2	100.00	-	-	-
All	**27/39**	**69.23**	**21/38**	**55.26**	**1.599**	**1**	**0.206**
CDI$_m$							
YA	0/1	0.00	3/7	42.86	0.686	1	0.408
EMA	5/11	45.45	6/16	37.50	0.171	1	0.679
LMA	12/19	63.16	8/14	57.14	0.122	1	0.727
OA	8/8	100.00	2/2	100.00	-	-	-
All	**25/39**	**64.10**	**19/39**	**48.72**	**1.877**	**1**	**0.171**

Table 5.14 Frequency of teeth affected by caries in adult skeletons from Romano-British populations.
For references see Table 5.10. [1] Including unsexed adults

	Males		Females		All	
Population	No./Total	%	No./Total	%	No./Total	%
Western Cemetery, Cirencester	85/923	9.21	83/975	8.51	168/1,916[1]	8.77
Bath Gate, Cirencester	120/2,382	5.04	47/869	5.41	167/3,251	5.14
Cotswold School, Bourton-on-the-Water	24/188	12.77	22/93	23.66	46/281	16.37
London Road, Gloucester	41/1,148	3.57	35/560	6.25	207/2,367[1]	8.75
Cannington, Somerset	96/1,145	8.38	81/1,488	5.44	177/2,633	6.72
Great Barford (Sites 4 & 8), Bedfordshire	12/169	7.10	4/7	57.14	17/190[1]	8.95
Lankhills, Winchester	79/1,665	4.74	132/1,764	7.48	214/3,631[1]	5.89

explains why this deviation is apparent, as dental caries rates and frequencies increase with age.

Dental calculus

The most common dental pathology was calculus, often referred to as tartar. Calculus is calcified dental plaque, consisting of calcium phosphate mineral salts, and is clearly visible as dense clay-like mineral deposits on the teeth (White 1997). It is particularly prevalent in individuals with soft diets, while food particles in a fibre rich diet generally provide a tooth surface cleaning action and therefore generate less calculus plaque build-up (Anekar 2011). Dental calculus irritates the gums, and may lead to gingivitis and periodontal disease, and could therefore, through extension, cause considerable oral health problems. The condition was observed in all age groups of the Western Cemetery population, with the exception of the dentition of the young child individuals (Table 5.15). There is a clear increase with

Table 5.15 Crude prevalence rate by dentition and frequency by teeth of dental calculus in different age groups.
For key to Age group see Table 5.11

	Dentitions		Teeth	
	No./Total	%	No./Total	%
YC	0/4	0.00	0/59	0.00
OC	5/6	83.33	33/104	31.73
Adol.	3/4	75.00	20/83	24.10
YA	5/9	55.56	47/213	22.07
EMA	27/28	96.43	442/699	63.23
LMA	30/31	96.77	581/745	77.99
OA	9/10	90.00	161/194	82.99
All	**79/92**	**85.87**	**1,284/2,097**	**61.23**

age, which however appears to decrease slightly in the older adult age group. A significant decrease in the prevalence of calculus is also observed between the older child and adolescent age categories, but this is likely to relate to the change from deciduous to permanent dentition. In the adult population, 97% (35/36) of males were affected and 89% (34/38) of all females ($\chi^2(1) = 1.762$, $p = 0.184$).

Periodontal disease
Inflammation of the gums, so-called gingivitis, can result in a progressive condition which involves the periodontal bone (Hillson 2005, 304–7). In severe cases, the alveolar support structure of the teeth is affected which can result in antemortem loss of teeth. In dry bone, periodontitis is evident from a porous appearance of a reduced alveolar bone process with rounded margins, and should not be confused with normal physiological bone loss (Clarke 1993). As with all dental pathologies, the frequency of periodontal disease increased with age in the Western Cemetery population, from no young adults affected (0/7), 25% of all early middle adults (6/24), 55% of late middle adults (17/31) and 73% of all older adults (8/11). There were 50% (18/36) of male dentitions affected, and 37% (13/35) of female dentitions ($\chi^2(1) = 1.193$, $p = 0.275$). No non-adult dentitions displayed evidence of periodontal disease.

Periapical lesions
The diagnostic criteria described by Dias and Tayles (1997) were consulted for diagnosing periapical lesions, which included granulomae, chronic periapical abscesses and dental cysts. Granulomae occur as a consequence of granulation tissue around the apex of the root of teeth, and are usually asymptomatic (Hillson 2005, 308). An abscess is potentially a very painful condition, and is often the result of progressed granulomae, which results in a considerable accumulation of pus at the apex of the dental root which eventually erupts through the bone through a fistula (Hillson 1996, 285). Dental cysts, which are larger than both granulomae and abscesses, are commonly a progressive but slow continuation of granulomae, and are usually asymptomatic (Reichart and Philipsen 2000, 215–18). Periapical lesions were identified in 13 adult dentitions (17.11%; 13/76), which belonged to six males (15.79%; 6/38) and seven females (19.44%; 7/36) ($\chi^2(1) = 0.171$, $p = 0.680$). By type, cysts were most common with two male (5.26%; 2/38) and three female dentitions (8.33%; 3/36) affected. Granulomae were present in two males (5.26%; 2/38) and two female dentitions (5.56%; 2/36), and abscesses were diagnosed in two male (5.26%; 2/38) and three female (8.33%; 3/36) dentitions.

Antemortem tooth loss
In vivo loss of teeth has a multifactor background. It is generally the result of dental caries, but can also be caused by progressive periodontal disease, tooth wear and other factors such as trauma. In total, 31% (24/77) of all adults had lost at least one tooth prior to death. In the adult male population, 41% (16/39) were affected, and amongst the females 19% (7/36), a difference which was statistically significant ($\chi^2(1) = 4.101$, $p = 0.043$). When broken down to age groups, it is clear that the risk of losing teeth prior to death increased with age: none in the young adult age group were affected (0/7), 8% in the early middle adult age group (2/26), 42% in the late middle adult age group (14/33) and 73% of all older adults (8/11). The risk of antemortem tooth loss is likely to have been associated with the age-related increase in the frequencies of dental caries and periodontal disease in this population.

Enamel hypoplasia
Periods of childhood stress during the first seven years of life are potentially permanently manifested as linear or pitted defects on the enamel of the teeth, and these could relate to conditions such as fever, starvation, infection and low birth weight (Lewis and Roberts 1997). Enamel hypoplasia was recorded as observable when at least 25% of the teeth (incisor, canine and premolar) were present, as these are those most commonly affected. The result would indicate that one third of the adult population had suffered periods of stress as children (Table 5.16). The lower frequencies observed in the non-adult age groups is likely to reflect that they died before any enamel defects took form, and that they constituted the weakest proportion of the non-adult population. When assessing the time during childhood when these episodes generally formed (method by Goodman and Song 1999), the majority occurred during the fourth year for both males (N = 25) and females (N = 18). No considerable difference in rates is observed between the sexes, although boys appear to have been affected earlier by physiological stress than girls (Fig. 5.3).

Table 5.16 Crude prevalence rate by dentition and frequency by teeth of enamel hypoplasia in different age groups.
For key to Age group see Table 5.11

	Dentitions		Teeth	
	No./Total	%	No./Total	%
YC	0/4	0.00	0/59	0.00
OC	2/6	33.33	5/104	4.81
Adol.	1/4	25.00	4/83	4.82
YA	1/9	11.11	1/213	0.47
EMA	13/28	46.43	44/699	6.29
LMA	10/31	32.26	21/745	2.82
OA	2/10	20.00	6/194	3.09
All	**29/92**	**31.52**	**81/2,097**	**3.86**

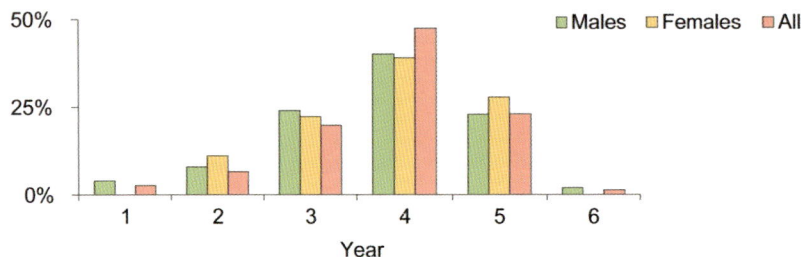

*Fig. 5.3   The proportion of stress episodes as indicated by enamel hypoplasia by year
in life it occurred in adult skeletons*

Dental anomalies

Various epigenetic dental anomalies were observed in the adult dentitions, which included parastyles (2.56%; 2/78), Carabelli's cusps (1.28%; 1/78), enamel pearls (2.56%; 2/78), foramen caecum (12.82%; 10/78) and enamel extensions (25.64%; 20/78). Three individuals had particularly interesting dentitions: adolescent male skeleton B1192 displayed an accessory peg-shaped maxillary incisor tooth, which was impacted within the bone in a horizontal angle. This tooth may have continued to erupt, and if so would have been exposed through the bone just inferior of the nasal margin. Another peg-shaped tooth was observed in the dentition of late middle adult female skeleton B1207, which involved the right third maxillary molar. Late middle adult female skeleton B1161 displayed impacted maxillary canine teeth, which were both positioned behind the first incisors.

Joint disease

Diseases of the joints were diagnosed in 62 adult skeletons (63.92%; 62/97), and represent the most commonly observed pathological condition in the population. Typical osseous reactions at the synovial joints include marginal osteophyte formation, porotic pitting and eburnation. The latter condition, which occurs when joint surfaces rub against each other in direct contact, is a pathognomonic trait of osteoarthritis, as well as a combination of marginal osteophytosis, pitting of the joint surface and alteration of the joint contour (Rogers 2000; Rogers and Waldron 1995; Rogers *et al.* 1987).

Spinal degenerative joint disease

Degeneration of the vertebral column is usually attributed to normal wear-and-tear, and is therefore a condition progressing with advanced age. Disease of the joints in the spine was diagnosed in 65 adult skeletons (74.71%; 65/87), with a clear increase in occurrence with age. Identified pathologies included eburnation of the uncal processes of the cervical vertebrae, vertebral osteophytosis, osteoarthritis of the apophyseal joints, intervertebral osteochondrosis, Schmorl's nodes and ossification of the ligamentum flavum.

Eburnation of the uncal processes occurs as a progression of degenerative joint disease of the cervical spine, and is indicative of osteoarthritis and chronic pain in the neck (Briney 2001; Orofino *et al.* 1960). The condition was identified in two late middle adults (11.76%: 2/17) and two older adult individuals (22.22%; 2/9). Of these, three individuals were male (14.29%; 3/21) and one skeleton female (4.35%; 1/23) ($\chi^2(1)$ = 1.312, p = 0.252).

Vertebral osteophytosis is characterised by marginal bone proliferation of the vertebral bodies, and is primarily observed in the mid and lower cervical, upper thoracic and lower lumbar vertebrae. It is usually attributed to normal wear-and-tear of the spine, but can also occur as a consequence of several additional conditions such as intervertebral disc disease, diffuse idiopathic skeletal hyperostosis, trauma, psoriatic arthropathies and more (Rogers and Waldron 1995). In a modern population, it is present in 60–80% of all individuals over the age of 50 years, and is often asymptomatic and considered a normal and expected variation in older adults (Arcini 1999, 86–7). In total, 45.71% (32/70) of the adults displayed this spinal pathology in the Western Cemetery population, which increased in occurrence with age. There was a significant difference in prevalence rates between the sexes where males (69.44%; 25/36) were more affected than females (21.88%; 7/32) ($\chi^2(1)$ = 15.387, p < 0.001).

Osteoarthritis of the spine was identified in 24% (18/75) of all adult spines, which comprised 40% (14/35) of all males and 8% (3/36) of all females. This difference was statistically significant ($\chi^2(1)$ = 9.772, p = 0.002). It increased in prevalence with age, and the most common spinal segments affected were the cervical vertebrae (32.56%; 14/43) followed by the lumbar (25.49%; 13/51) and thoracic (22.22%; 12/54) segments.

Pitting of the intervertebral surfaces of the bodies, and sometimes with new bone formation, is characteristic of intervertebral osteochondrosis. This condition is frequently observed in the cervical, upper thoracic and lower lumbar region of the spine (Rogers 2000, 169) and it has been suggested that it occurs as a progression of vertebral osteophytosis (Kelley 1982). It was present in 19% (12/62) of all adult spines from the Western Cemetery. The prevalence in male spines (36.67%; 11/30) was significantly higher than in female spines (3.33%; 1/30) ($\chi^2(1) = 10.417$, $p = 0.001$).

Schmorl's nodes are impressions observed on the bodies of the thoraco-lumbar vertebrae, and it is a common spinal pathology with a reported frequency of 75% in modern populations (Gallucci *et al.* 2005). It is usually described as a focal depression of a portion of intervertebral disc tissue, due to a hernia, into the trabecular bone (Aufderheide and Rodríguez-Martín 1998, 97). The condition has been observed in association with vertebral trauma, Scheuermann's disease and osteoporosis (Saluja *et al.* 1986), but appears in most clinical cases to be generally asymptomatic (Faccia and Williams 2008). Schmorl's nodes were identified in the spine of 54% of all adults (35/65), where males (83.87%; 26/31) were significantly more affected than females (30.00%; 9/30) ($\chi^2(1) = 18.092$, $p < 0.001$).

Ossification of the ligamenta flava (longitudinal ligaments in the spine) can cause myelopathies and radiculapathies and is a frequently observed pathological condition in archaeological skeletons. However, its aetiology is currently largely unclear. It is considered to be a degenerative enthesopathy of the ligaments, the main function of which is to provide spinal stability, due to mechanical stress. It is also found in association

with other conditions such as diffuse idiopathic skeletal hyperostosis (Yoshida 2006). The condition was identified in 65% (47/72) of all observable adult spines, with more males (67.65%; 23/34) than females (65.71%; 23/35) affected. This difference was not statistically significant ($\chi^2(1) = 0.029$, $p = 0.865$).

Extra-spinal joint disease
Of the extra-spinal articulations, the shoulder and hip joints were most commonly affected by degenerative joint disease, with a significantly higher frequency of the former observed in males. Following the shoulders, high frequencies of degeneration were thereafter noted in the hips, hands and ankles and wrists in males. In females, the high frequency in the hips was followed by shoulders, wrists, hands and ankles (Table 5.17). When assessing evidence of eburnation only, the shoulder was particularly affected in males, followed by elbow and wrist joints. In females, wrists were most commonly affected, followed by feet and hip joints. Possibly due to the small empirical data (Table 5.17), no significant differences in extra-spinal osteoarthritis frequencies were observed between the sexes.

Bilateral tarsal ankylosis
An adult individual of unknown sex (B1166) displayed bilateral massive tarsal ankylosis (Figs 5.4–5.5). This skeleton, which only comprised the lower legs and feet, revealed partial and complete fusion between

Table 5.17 The prevalence rates of degenerative joint disease (DJD: osteophytes, porosity or eburnation) and osteoarthritis (OA: eburnation) of the major joints in adult males and females (individual count), and chi-square test values.

	Males		Females				
	No./Total	%	No./Total	%	χ^2	df	*p*
DJD							
Shoulder	18/38	47.37	5/38	13.16	10.537	1	0.001
Elbow	4/36	11.11	1/35	2.86	1.847	1	0.174
Wrist	6/36	16.67	4/33	12.12	0.287	1	0.592
Hand	12/37	32.43	3/33	9.09	5.644	1	0.018
Hip	13/39	33.33	7/37	18.92	2.034	1	0.154
Knee	3/37	8.11	0/35	0.00	2.961	1	0.085
Ankle	7/36	19.44	2/33	6.06	2.719	1	0.099
Foot	5/33	15.15	1/35	2.86	3.191	1	0.074
Any	**21/41**	**51.22**	**13/44**	**29.55**	**4.154**	**1**	**0.042**
OA							
Shoulder	2/38	5.26	0/38	0.00	2.054	1	0.152
Elbow	1/36	2.78	0/35	0.00	0.986	1	0.321
Wrist	1/36	2.78	2/33	6.06	0.446	1	0.504
Hip	1/39	2.56	1/37	2.70	0.001	1	0.970
Foot	0/33	0.00	1/35	2.86	0.957	1	0.328
Any	**5/41**	**12.20**	**2/44**	**4.55**	**1.643**	**1**	**0.200**

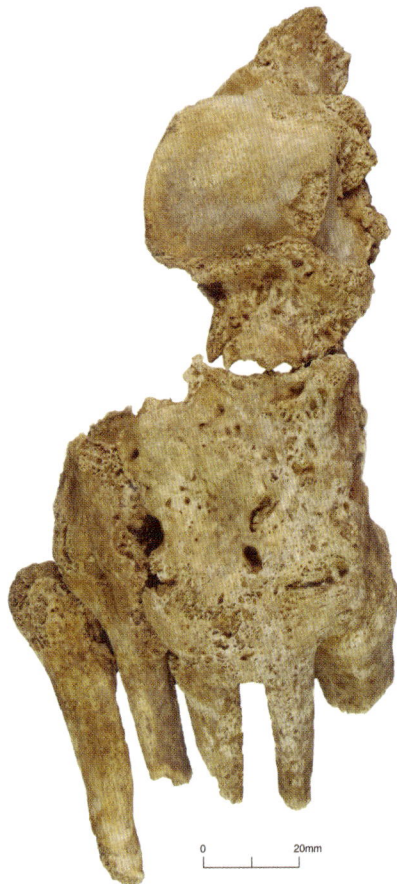

Fig. 5.4   The right foot of adult skeleton B1166, display-ing considerable tarsal ankylosis possibly due to psoriatic arthritis

Fig. 5.5   Radiograph of the right foot of adult skeleton B1166

the tarsal and metatarsal bones in both feet, and also included considerable erosive arthropathy of the distal tibiae. Enthesophyte formation was also noted on the plantar surface of the tarsal bones, particularly on the cuboid bones. The case is likely to be a bilateral erosive arthropathy involving more or less all the joints in the foot, of which psoriatic arthritis is the most probable aetiology (see Isidro *et al.* 2000). This condition is associated with the chronic skin disease psoriasis, and equally affects both males and females particularly within the ages of 20 and 50 years (Ortner 2003, 577–80). Typical symptoms of this condition are pain and swelling of the joint (Amherd-Hoekstra *et al.* 2010) and it is likely to have considerably reduced the quality of life for this individual. A diagnosis of this condition is argued from the presence of both ankylosis and enthesophyte formation of the tarsal bones, which is a non-feature in the alternative diagnosis of rheumatoid arthritis. The absence of the distal ends of the metatarsals and proximal foot phalanges in this skeleton does however inhibit a confident diagnosis of this condition (see Aufderheide and Rodríguez-Martín 1998, 104; Rogers *et al.* 1987).

Neoplastic disease

Neoplastic disease was diagnosed in nine individuals (7.56%; 9/119). Late middle adult female skeleton B1155 displayed a large bony growth (43mm × 14mm) on the posterior surface of the mid-diaphysis of the left tibia, at the interosseous border. This lesion is likely to be an osteoid osteoma, which is a benign accumulation of poorly mineralised bone in the cortex or the trabecular part of the bone with dense reactive ossification as a consequence (Ortner 2003, 506–7). A 6mm by 6mm large button osteoma was present on the squama of the occipital bone of early middle adult male B1237, on the frontal bone (4mm × 4mm) of late middle adult male B1245, on the occipital bone (21mm × 21mm) of older adult male B1267, and on the lateral surface of the left ramus of the mandible (10mm × 8mm) belonging to an unsexed adolescent individual (B1156). An osteoma is a lesion consisting of dense lamellar bone. The mandible is a rare location for these lesions, and it has been suggested that they are triggered by trauma (Ertas and Tozoglu 2003). Osteomata was also present on older adult female skeleton B1209, which displayed multiple bone growths (approximately 6mm × 4mm in size) on the visceral surface of three left ribs, and on the antero-medial surface of the proximal diaphysis of the left femur (4mm × 2mm).

An early middle adult female (B1258) displayed a 23mm-long inferiorly extending exostosis at the medial metaphyseal junction of the left tibia, which is likely to be a case of unilateral osteochondroma. This is a relatively common benign bone tumour that is initiated in childhood while the skeleton is still growing (Ortner 2003), and it is likely to have been asymptomatic in this individual.

Two late middle adult males (B1229 and B1245) displayed cranial lytic lesions which are indicative of multiple myeloma, which is a malignant type of tumour generally most often diagnosed in older males (Ortner 2003). B1229 displayed three or four craters: a large circular lesion (19mm × 19mm and 5mm deep) was present on the posterior portion of the left half of the frontal bone, at the mid-coronal suture. This crater displays sharp lateral, posterior and medial edges, and a more diffuse anterior edge margin. The floor of the cavity is smooth and is comprised of exposed diploë (the middle porous bone layer within the skull vault). No signs of pathological changes are noted on the corresponding surface of the endocranial side. A second crater (18mm × 11mm) was located on the anterior portion of the right parietal bone, at the mid-coronal junction. This lesion is oval shaped (4mm deep) with more rounded margins; however this may be due to taphonomical erosion. The floor is smooth and comprised of exposed diploë, and no endocranial involvement is seen. The anterior margin of a third osteolytic lesion (more than 17mm × 7mm) was present on the tuber of the right parietal bone; however most of this portion of the bone is fragmented and missing. The surviving lesion displays a sharp margin, and a floor surface comprised of smooth exposed diploë. A possible fourth lesion (or possibly belonging to the third osteolysis) is represented by an irregular margin (more than 14mm × 11mm) noted on the posterior portion of the tuber of the right parietal bone; however this area of the bone is marked by considerable taphonomic damage, and may be due to post-depositional cortical erosion. The second individual (B1245) displayed a circular (12mm in diameter) osteolytic crater just anterior of the tuber on the mid portion of the right parietal bone. The lesion was concave with sharpish margins, and exposes a diploë that is deeper in the supero-lateral portion (5mm × 4mm and 3mm deep). No reactive bone is noted adjacent to the lesion. As no endocranial involvement is present in these two cases, it seems unlikely that these lesions are due to trauma. Taphonomic damage can be ruled out, as the margins are very sharp and well defined as round or oval lesions. No reactive bone is noted near any of the lesions, which is why metastatic carcinoma, or even an infectious process – such as tuberculosis – seem unlikely. It is also unlikely that they represent

trephinations as only the ectocranial surface is involved, and no evidence of mechanical modification is noted. The post-cranial elements in both skeletons are very poorly preserved, and it is not possible to assess these elements for any additional osteolytic neoplasms.

Trauma

Fractured, and possibly fractured, bones were identified in 19 skeletons (14.96%; 19/127), which included 14 adult males (30.43%; 14/46) and five adult females (10.64%; 5/47) ($\chi^2(1)$ = 4.625, p = 0.032) (Table 5.18). The male cases included multiple healed fractures identified in the skeleton of late middle adult male B1157. A blunt and shallow compression injury (30mm × 26mm and approximately 1mm in depth) was present on the tuber of the right parietal bone and indicates healed blunt force trauma (see Hart 2005). The lesion is well defined on the ectocranial surface, but no endocranial injuries were observed. This probably means that the injury was relatively minor in terms of secondary consequences. The distal phalanx for the left first metatarsal (big toe) displayed a healed articular fracture of the proximal articular surface, with a diagonal fracture line running across the lateral half of the surface. This individual also displayed healed rib fractures, with one right rib being fractured at the angle and a left rib at the mid body. These may relate to the pathological compression fractures due to generalised osteopenia which was evident in five thoracic vertebrae of this skeleton. Rib fractures in other males were also observed in older adult B1230, and late middle adults B1239 and B1249. There was also an additional case of healed blunt force trauma observed on the right parietal bone of older adult B1267. The injury measured 12mm by 16mm, and was located on the postero-medial portion of the bone. A third case of possible cranial trauma was noted in older adult male B1244. This individual displayed a possible fracture line across the right nasal bone, which may be indicating interpersonal violence. However, the bone was poorly preserved, and a confident diagnosis is difficult to establish.

A healed compression fracture was observed on the lower back of a late middle adult male (B1233), which affected the tenth and eleventh thoracic vertebrae. Both vertebrae displayed clear fracture lines across the superior intervertebral surfaces of the bodies, and the injury would have resulted in a permanent slight anterior kyphosis of the spine (forward hunch of the back) of this individual. Slight degeneration of the hip joints was also observed in this skeleton, and that may be a secondary consequence of the spinal injury.

A late middle adult male (B1231) displayed considerable degeneration of the right hip joint, which is likely to have been caused by trauma. The superior portion of the lunate surface is pitted and eburnated. A possible fracture line is visible across the mid portion of the acetabulum, although it is unclear whether this is a

Table 5.18 Identified bone fractures in skeletons from the Western Cemetery.
For key to Age group see Table 5.11

Skeleton	Age group	Sex	Injured region(s)	Fractured elements
B1155	LMA	F	Right lower arm	Right ulna
B1157	LMA	M	Head, thorax, back, left foot	Right parietal, 1 left rib, 1 right rib, T7–T10, T12, left Ph3 Mt I
B1168	LMA	M	Left foot	Left talus
B1183	OA	M	Right shoulder and thorax	Right clavicle, right rib
B1193	EMA	F	Thorax, chest	4 left ribs, 1 right rib
B1200	EMA	F	Left thorax	1 left rib
B1214	LMA	F	Head, upper back	Left parietal, T4
B1219	LMA	M	Left hand	Left Mc I
B1230	OA	M	Chest	1 left rib, 1 right rib
B1231	LMA	M	Right hip joint?	Right acetabulum?, and right femoral neck
B1233	LMA	M	Lower back	T10–T11
B1239	LMA	M	Thorax	1 right rib
B1240	Adol.	M	Left leg?	Left tibia?
B1244	OA	M	Nose?	Right nasal bone?
B1245	LMA	M	Right wrist	Right Mc I
B1249	LMA	M	Thorax	3 left ribs, 2 right ribs
B1253	EMA	F	Left wrist	Left triquetral
B1267	OA	M	Head	Right parietal
B1274	OA	M	Right shoulder, right hand?	Right clavicle, 1 right Ph1 Mc?

true manifestation or not. The corresponding change to the femoral head is characterised by severe build-up of irregular new bone and osteophytic growth on the postero-inferior aspect, and patches of eburnated bone are observed in the middle of this new bone build-up. The original bone surface is clearly visible underneath the bone build-up section, along its superior margin, which is why it is probable that the lesion is the result of trauma, possibly concussion fracture, a neck fracture, or a slightly superior dislocation of the joint. Alternative diagnoses are slipped femoral capital epiphysis or Perthe's disease; however the head appears to be aligned properly with the neck of the bone. In articulation, the joint appears to have been more or less fixed in a slight anterior angle with limited movement possible.

Late middle adult male skeleton B1168 displayed evidence of healed trauma affecting the left foot. A well-healed transverse fracture across the posterior process and a compression fracture of the middle calcaneal articular facet were evident on the talus. A typical mechanism for this type of foot fracture includes falling from a height and hitting the ankle when in a hyperdorsiflexion; it would have been an extremely painful event (Koval and Zuckerman 2002, 257). Fractures to the right shoulder and a right rib was identified in a third male, an older adult (B1183). Here the clavicle in this skeleton displayed an unhealed and long-standing fracture of the mid diaphysis, probably oblique, where muscle pull had

pushed the lateral and medial ends together and resulted in a pseudo-joint between the two portions. The fracture would have been unstable, and probably resulted in chronic pain of the shoulder. In most reported modern cases, fractures of the clavicle occur in falls (Koval and Zuckerman 2002). The rib fracture was identified from a fragment displaying a healed transverse fracture line. The fourth male individual was the skeleton of a late middle adult (B1219), which displayed a healed fracture of a portion of a palmar marginal osteophyte running along the rim of the head of the left first metacarpal. It is clear that this would have occurred secondarily to degeneration of the joint, and may have been initiated by a muscle pull.

One of the female cases, a late middle adult (B1155), displayed a well-healed oblique fracture of the distal portion of the right ulna. This is a so-called 'parry fracture' which generally occurs from direct force applied to the bone (Judd 2008). While numerous circumstances can result in this type of fracture, it has often been interpreted as an indication of interpersonal violence, when the arm would have been fractured in attempts to shield the face against an aggressor (see Lovell 1997, 165). It would, however, be too speculative to suggest such an aetiology from this single case. Some degenerative changes were present in the elbow joint, which suggests that she may have suffered some secondary ailments following the injury. These were however minor, and may not have affected the use of her right arm. A second female case was that of early middle adult B1193 that displayed multiple rib fractures. An unhealed transverse fracture was observed on the mid body of the twelfth right rib. This injury would have occurred sometime before death, as build-up of bone around the fractured portions was evident which had resulted in a pseudo-joint. Healed transverse fractures were observed at the sternal end of four left ribs.

One single healed transverse fracture of the mid-body of a left true rib was identified in the skeleton of early middle adult female skeleton B1200. Secondary new bone formation on the visceral surface was observed at the fracture point. The fourth female case was that of a late middle adult (B1214), which displayed a well-healed avulsion fracture of the spinous process of the fourth thoracic vertebra. When occurring at the level between the sixth cervical and third thoracic vertebrae, these types of injury are typically referred to as a 'clay-shoveler's fracture' and are generally the result of continuous stress and muscle pull of the supraspinous ligaments (Feldman and Astri 2001). The mechanisms are likely to have been the same in this case and probably indicate that this individual had once been exposed to heavy and straining labour. These types of fractures are generally stable, and the condition may not have affected the well-being of this individual once it was thoroughly healed. This individual did also display a 10mm by 6mm and *c.* 1mm-deep impression on the tuber of the left parietal bone, which indicated well-healed blunt force trauma to the left part of the skull vault.

No child skeletons displayed any clear evidence of trauma; however an adolescent male (B1240) displayed a slight lateral curvature of the proximal diaphysis of the left tibia which may be the result of a healed green-stick fracture. This type of fracture occurs in childhood when the bones are still relatively soft and flexible, and is characterised by an incomplete fracture that only affects one side of the bone (Ortner 2003). In this case, the fracture line would have been present on the medial portion of the proximal diaphysis. A bony nodule (13mm × 6mm) was observed on that location of the curvature, which may relate to this condition.

In addition to these cases with bone fractures, there was also a late middle adult male skeleton (B1223) that displayed evidence of soft-tissue trauma. This was observed on the right lower leg, and indicated an ankle injury. A marked enthesophytic tubercle (9mm × 12mm) is present on the interosseous margin of the proximal articular surface of the right fibula, and a 15mm by 12mm-large exostosis on the interosseous surface of the distal metaphysis of the same bone. Sclerotic bone had formed around this proliferation (38mm × 20mm and *c.* 4mm thick), and reveals that ossification as a consequence of a rupture of the interosseous ligament between the tibia and fibula had occurred. In the clinical literature, these types of injuries are usually attributed

to the forcing of the foot upwards and outward (external rotation with abduction and dorsiflexion), resulting in severe sprains of the foot and ankle (Porter 2009).

There was also a possible case of osteochondritis dissecans diagnosed in the population. This is a circulatory disorder which is generally triggered by trauma. It is the result of subchondral bone fragmentation of the articular joint surface, which results in necrotic bone tissue which may become loose and permanently lodged as an intra-articular body in the joint. It is identified as a pit in convex joint surfaces (Aufderheide and Rodríguez-Martín 1998, 81–3; Ortner 2003, 351–3; Rogers and Waldron 1995), and diagnosis was suggested from a blunt fovea (8mm × 8mm) at the base of the malleolus process of the right tibia of a late middle adult male (B1157).

Metabolic disease

Most metabolic diseases in bone occur as a consequence of deficiencies in nutrients and minerals, and are likely to have very much been omnipresent in past populations. Only a few conditions are however potentially diagnosable in the human skeleton, and they generally only produce non-specific pathological changes which often makes solid diagnoses difficult (Brickley and Ives 2008). The most common pathology relating to a metabolic disorder identified in the population was cribra orbitalia. This pathology is manifested as porotic lesions due to marrow expansion of the roof of the orbitae. Much of the palaeopathological literature has traditionally attributed this pathology to iron deficiency anaemia (Stuart-Macadam 1989), although its true aetiology is still largely unclear. In a recent article by Walker *et al.* (2009) it was argued that it is physiologically impossible for iron deficiency anaemia to cause these lesions, as a lack of iron would inhibit any marrow expansion. Instead, they suggested that a more likely primary cause is nutritional megaloblastic anaemia caused by Vitamin B_{12} deficiency. Criticism of these suggestions was however made by Oxenham and Cavill (2010) who pointed out, when taking the current clinical understanding of iron metabolism into account, that iron deficiency can indeed cause these lesions, with the exception of anaemia of chronic disease. Hence, there are currently arguments in place to suggest that both vitamin deficiencies and iron deficiency anaemia can result in cribra orbitalia. In this population, the condition was identified in adult skeletons only (18.18%; 12/66), with a prevalence of 16% (5/31) in males and 23% (7/30) in females ($\chi^2(1) = 0.501$, $p = 0.479$). The frequency of cribra orbitalia in the Western Cemetery skeletons is slightly less than in comparable Roman populations (Table 5.19).

There were four individuals (B1156, B1171, B1205 and B1255) displaying skeletal lesions which suggest scurvy. This condition has been increasingly identified in palaeopathological analyses of archaeological skel-

Table 5.19 Prevalence of cribra orbitalia in Romano-British populations.
For references see Table 5.10

Population	Non-adults		Adults		All	
	No./Total	%	No./Total	%	No./Total	%
Western Cemetery, Cirencester	0/15	0.00	12/66	18.18	12/81	14.81
Cotswold School, Bourton-on-the-Water	2/4	50.00	4/11	36.36	6/15	40.00
London Road, Gloucester	2/9	22.22	11/51	21.57	13/60	21.67
Great Barford (Sites 4 and 8), Bedfordshire	0/4	0.00	1/5	20.00	1/9	11.11
Poundbury, Dorset (Stuart-Macadam 1991)	74/128	57.81	143/548	26.09	217/676	32.10
Lankhills, Winchester	14/61	22.95	27/200	13.50	41/261	15.71
Total	**92/221**	**41.63**	**198/881**	**22.47**	**290/1,102**	**26.32**

etons in more recent years. Scurvy is caused by the lack of Vitamin C, which is a prerequisite for mature collagen formation and bone remodelling process in the skeleton. Skeletally it is primarily manifested as periosteal new bone formation or porotic pittings at the sites of muscle attachments, which is a reflection of microtrauma and haemorrhage due to impaired collagen formation. Other clinical traits include bleeding gums, which potentially is identifiable as abnormal porosity of the alveolar margins and palatal processes. All four individuals displayed porotic lesions to the medial surface of the rami of the mandible (Fig. 5.6), which is considered a typical skeletal trait of the disease (see Ortner and Ericksen 1997). This particular lesion relates to microtrauma of the musculature used during mastication. The combination of the other cranial and post-cranial lesions in these individuals, all of which are similar to, or the same as, those observed in skeletons with lesions indicative of Vitamin C deficiency from other archaeological populations (e.g. Geber and Murphy 2012), confirms that scurvy most likely was a disease that was present in Roman Cirencester.

Periostitis

Periostitis is an inflammation of the outer surface membrane (periosteum) surrounding the bone, and is manifested as a layer of new bone on the original bone surface (Ortner 2003). This pathology has generally been attributed to infectious processes, and is often described as non-specific when no clear aetiology has been ascertained. While infection is a major causative agent for periostitis, it can also occur in metabolic conditions, of which scurvy is perhaps the most common. In the Western Cemetery population periostitis was observed in post-cranial elements of two non-adult (9.09%; 2/22) and twenty adult individuals (19.23%; 20/104), comprising eight males (17.39%; 8/46), nine females (20.00%; 9/45) and three unsexed individuals (23.08%; 3/13). One non-adult and eleven adult skeletons displayed periostitis to the medial and interosseous surfaces of the tibiae, which are commonly involved in Vitamin C deficiency. The tibia is, however, also the element most commonly affected by

periostitis caused by infection as the bone surface lies close to the skin, and is therefore at greater risk of being affected in an injury (Ortner 2003).

Osteomyelitis

Osteomyelitis is a severely painful condition which is the result of an infection of the internal medullar cavity of the bone, and is usually the result of pyogenic bacteria. It can occur as a consequence of direct trauma or surgical wounds (acute), directly from soft-tissue infections, or indirectly via the blood flow (haematogenous) from a remote focus (Ortner 2003, 181). The infection produces pus, which eventually breaks through the bone via a cloaca opening. Other skeletal reactions include the considerable build-up of reactive bone (involucrum) and accumulation of dead bone tissue (sequestra) (Aufderheide and Rodríguez-Martín 1998, 172–81). Two adult individuals buried in the Western Cemetery were affected by this condition. An osteomyelitic infection was observed in the left elbow joint of older adult male B1187, which had also caused the bones to fuse at a fixed 90° angle (Fig. 5.7). The distal humerus displays dense sclerotic and porotic new bone formation across the entire anterior and posterior surfaces of the epiphysis and metaphysis, and nodular new bone formation is present on the interosseous margin. The entire fossa and trochlea of the humerus is destroyed, and a 14mm by 11mm-large cloaca is present on the medial surface of the original location of the epicondyle. Considerable damage due to the infection is also evident on the olecranon of the ulna and the head of the radius. The full extent of the osteomyelitic abscess, positioned within the elbow joint, would have measured approximately 35mm by 35mm. Osteomyelitis of the elbow is a common skeletal manifestation of smallpox in children (Aufderheide and Rodríguez-Martín 1998), and although this disease is a possible aetiology, it seems most likely that direct trauma is the primary cause for this infection.

The second individual was a late middle adult female (B1272) who was affected in the lower portion of the right thigh bone. A healed oval-shaped (32mm × 11mm × 7mm deep) lytic cloaca lesion is present on the

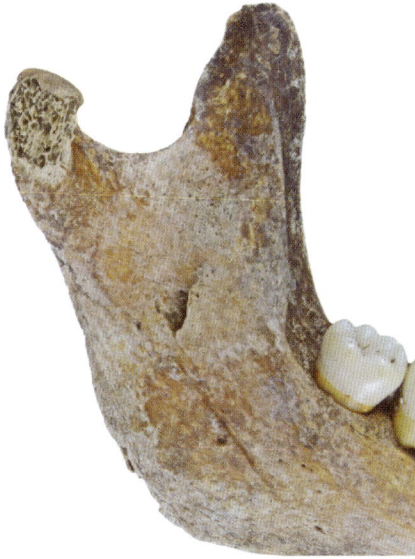

Fig. 5.6 *Patch of active new bone on the medial surface of the left ramus of the mandible of adolescent skeleton B1156, suggestive of haemorrhage due to microtrauma relating to scurvy*

Fig. 5.7 *Severe osteomyelitic infection of the left elbow joint in older adult male skeleton B1187*

anterior surface of the distal metaphysis of the femur, just superior of the condyle. The lesion displayed very smooth edges, smooth base and rounded margins, with a seemingly slightly sclerotic area at the inferior portion, and is likely to have occurred long before death, possibly even during childhood.

Congenital disease and anomalies
Eleven adult individuals displayed congenital abnormalities in the skeleton. The most common anomaly was sacralisation, which was present in three adults (B3 from the Oakley Cottage excavation and B1187 and B1203 at the present site) (6.98%; 3/43). This is a condition when the last lumbar vertebra is assimilated to the sacrum, and is typically a congenital abnormality which occurs during embryogenesis. It has a reported frequency of approximately 7.5% in modern populations, and is believed to be primarily asymptomatic (Bron *et al.* 2007). One case of lumbarisation was also noted (B1255), which is a condition when the first sacral segment assimilates the shape of a lumbar vertebrae as a contrast to sacralisation. Three individuals displayed a supernumerary lumbar vertebra (B1178, B1216 and B1235) (4.48%; 3/67), one skeleton (B1159) displayed only eleven thoracic vertebrae, and one individual (B1228) an additional thoracic vertebra. The most interesting anomaly, however, was a case of congenital fusion of the last cervical and first thoracic vertebrae in late middle adult female skeleton B1162 and late middle adult male B1229. This condition, usually referred to as Klippel-Feil syndrome, is a congenital anomaly of the neck, which results in physical symptoms such as a short and stiff neck with a low posterior hairline (Jeffreys

1993, 48–50). The female individual also displayed a slight scoliosis of the cervical spine (the neck).

One adult female (B1255, buried prone) displayed a significantly malformed mandible, and it is unclear whether this is a congenital anomaly or a developmental disorder that occurred after birth. The bone displayed a substantial medial angulation affecting its right half: the right head is deformed into a round articular surface (with corresponding articular malformation in the temporomandibular joint fossa) with an anterior osteophytic overhang (*c.* 5mm). The right ramus is pushed about 18mm superiorly compared to the left side, and the right angle has a different, more slender, shape than the left counterpart. The deformity has resulted in a left lateral malocclusation, with the midline of the mandibular incisors being positioned in axis with the junction between the right maxillary second incisor and canine teeth. More noticeable dental attrition on the right side of the dentition suggest that this condition had been in place for a very long time prior to death, and this individual is likely to have had difficulties speaking and possibly even masticating properly. A slight scoliosis of the upper spine noted in this skeleton may also be a secondary consequence of this condition.

Decapitations
Three individuals displayed clear evidence of decapitation, and a fourth case (B1269) was possibly beheaded. The head was placed by the feet in B1178, between the legs in B1196, and in the third case (B1241) between the

knees. Osteological evidence of these procedures was scarce due to poor bone preservation and surface erosion, and it is not possible to determine whether they are likely to have been performed perimortem or postmortem. The first case was that of a late middle adult female B1178, with the head placed below the feet. This burial was moderately well preserved. There was no clear evidence of cut marks observed on the neck vertebrae of this skeleton, although a possible diagonal and shallow knife cut mark present on the posterior margin of the right ramus of the mandible may relate to the beheading event.

Disarticulated skulls

In addition to the articulated remains in the inhumation burials, there were also partial skull remains from a minimum of three individuals found adjacent to each other within Ditch F (B1279). They were either laid on the base of the open ditch, or else contained within a pit dug through the infilled ditch (which escaped detection in the field). These included a frontal bone from an adult female (B1279a), the skull vault (occipital bone, parietal bones, frontal bone and the left temporal bone) from an older adult male (B1279b), and the frontal bone and left parietal bone from a male (B1279c). The skull fragments did not display any clear evidence of trauma, which, if present, could have suggested that they are depositions of decapitated heads. A possible exception is B1279c which displayed a sharpish edge on the lateral margin of the coronal suture on the frontal bone. Unfortunately poor bone preservation and fragmentation make a suggestion that this is a case of intentional sharp-force trauma difficult to prove.

Discussion

The recovery of a relatively large number of burials from the Western Cemetery has provided a significant new insight into the population of Corinium. Some restrictions on the quality of the evidence do, however, need to be acknowledged. The skeletons and cremated remains recovered from the Western Cemetery cannot be considered a fully representative sample of the buried population due to the substantial truncation that has occurred to cemetery deposits after it went out of use. The small proportion of non-adults to adults in the cemetery (0.14:1) does imply that most children were either buried elsewhere beyond the exposed portion of the cemetery, or that their skeletal remains have not survived. In comparison, the non-adult to adult ratio at the Bath Gate Cemetery was higher at 0.19:1 (CE II), and the ratio at Lankhills, Winchester, where the bone preservation was generally excellent, was 0.29:1 (Booth *et al.* 2010, 324). Unlike the age-at-death distribution of the exposed burials, the sex ratio amongst the adults is even and there does not appear to be a sex bias in the excavated portion of the cemetery.

The overall moderate bone preservation and fragmentation of the skeletal remains are likely to have prohibited positive diagnoses of inflammatory disease processes in many of the skeletons, and thus the calculated crude prevalence rate of periostitis at 17% in this population is likely to be an underestimation. This rate is nevertheless higher than the *c.* 7% that has been reported from Roman human skeletal remains across Britain as a whole, which however include interments from both rural and urban burial contexts (Roberts and Cox 2003, 124). Wells reported periostitis on the leg bones (tibiae and fibulae) of 24 adults and 2 non-adults from the Bath Gate Cemetery, which represents crude prevalence rates of 7% (24/344) and 3% (2/63) (CE II, 182). At the Western Cemetery, periostitis on the leg bones was observed in adults at a prevalence rate of 23% (15/64). This may indicate that the early Roman population of Corinium experienced more health stress than in later periods.

Unlike the osseous lesions, the dental pathological changes are more likely to reflect a true skeletal representation which is particularly valuable for inter-population analogies, as dental enamel is stronger than bone and therefore survives much better in the ground. The oral health of the Western Cemetery appears to be neither particularly good nor poor for the period: all observed frequencies of dental pathologies are similar to the values noted in contemporaneous populations. In terms of oral health, the individuals interred at the Western Cemetery exhibit the expected frequencies and disease pattern for the period. The same can be said about the frequency of joint disease and trauma, as well as the maximum obtained statures for both males and females in this population, which all correspond well to what has been observed in other Romano-British groups.

The study of archaeological human remains provides the only direct line of evidence relating to living conditions in the past, which is approachable from both a population and an individual level. The skeletal evidence of disease, trauma and disability (such as the possible case of psoriatic arthritis in B1166) demonstrates the physical hardship that people endured during their lives, but often in many cases also how they were treated and cared for in society (see Tilley 2015). This care for the living was also emulated through the care of the dead, which is reflected in how the funerary rites were undertaken. At the Western Cemetery, the earliest rites included cremation, which would have been a very resourceful and time consuming (and probably communal) effort. During the later use of the cemetery, the dead were inhumed in coffins in large grave cuts, some with grave goods. The practice of decapitation, which was evidenced from three cases, indicates that the concept of the afterlife was an integral aspect of the funerary rite that related to the treatment of the dead.

Chapter 6
Environmental Evidence

6.1 Animal Bones
Jonny Geber

Introduction

The animal bone assemblage from the former Bridges Garage site comprises 1,091 fragments (4,934.57g) from 96 contexts. The majority of the assemblage derives from Roman deposits although a proportion of the material was found in an Anglo-Saxon pit. The bones were identified to species and skeletal element with the aid of a reference collection and relevant literature (Cohen and Serjeantson 1996; Iregren 2002; Schmid 1972). The majority of the bones were hand collected although some derived from sieved samples (see Section 6.2, below).

The assemblage was in general moderately well preserved, with many bones displaying cortical erosion and often considerable fragmentation. A relatively large proportion of the remains could be identified to species. A total of thirteen species was identified (Table 6.1). Material from modern, unstratified or undated contexts is not discussed further. Bones from Roman ditch fills or the backfill of graves dominated the assemblage. As the latter has the potential to include intentional ritual depositions, these two types of context are discussed separately. There were clear differences in the species identified in the material from these two groups, with the burials containing a very high proportion of bird bones, of which the majority could be identified as fowl (Fig. 6.1). The present assemblage adds to previous

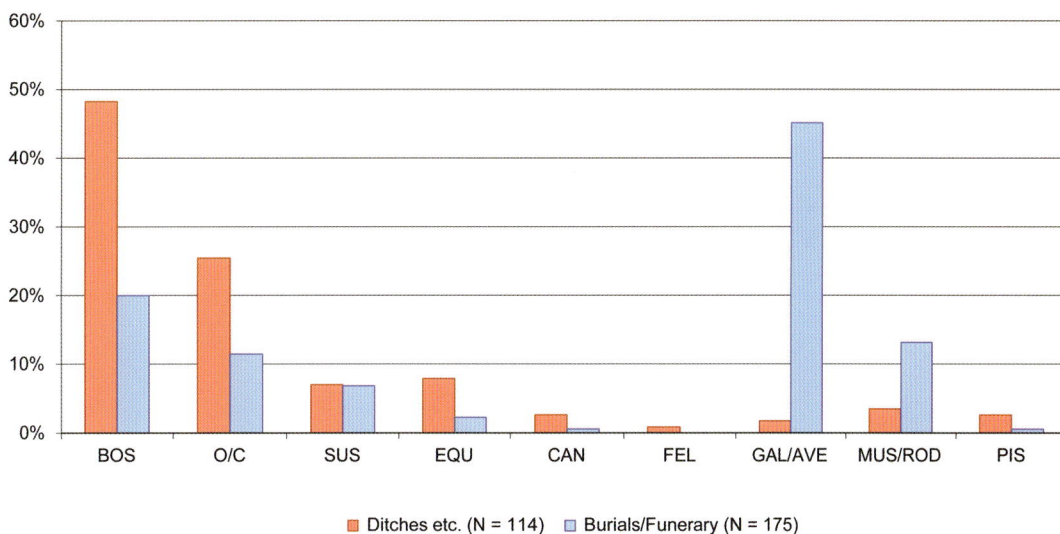

Fig. 6.1   *The relative representation of identified animal species from Roman deposits by fragment count (NISP) in types of contexts. BOS = cattle; O/C = sheep/goat; SUS = pig; EQU = horse; CAN = dog; FEL = cat; GAL/ AVE = fowl/bird; MUS/ROD = mouse/rodent; PIS = fish*

Table 6.1 Identified animal species by fragment count (NISP) and Period.
Period 1 = Early Roman; 2 = Late Roman; 1/2 = Roman; 3 = Anglo-Saxon;
4 = post-medieval/modern; U = undated

Species	Period						
	1	**2**	**1/2**	**3**	**4**	**U**	**Total**
MAMMALS							
Cattle (*Bos taurus*)	22	14	54	15	4	10	119
Sheep/Goat (*Ovis aries/Capra hircus*)	11	6	30	1	4	7	59
Pig (*Sus scrofa dom.*)	6	2	12	1	-	1	22
Horse (*Equus caballus*)	2	4	7	-	-	1	14
Dog (*Canis familiaris*)	1	1	2	-	-	1	5
Cat (*Felis catus*)	-	-	1	-	-	-	1
Red deer (*Cervus elaphus*)	-	-	-	1	-	-	1
Rabbit (*Oryctolagus cuniculus*)	-	-	-	-	1	-	1
House mouse (*Mus musculus*)	-	-	2	-	-	-	2
Rodent (*Rodentia sp.*)	20	4	1	1	-	2	28
Large-sized mammal	17	22	89	13	4	17	162
Medium-sized mammal	7	4	67	21	-	7	106
Small-sized mammal	-	-	1	-	-	1	2
Indeterminable (*Mammalia sp.*)	21	58	23	353	-	24	479
Subtotal:	*107*	*115*	*289*	*406*	*13*	*71*	*1,001*
BIRDS							
Fowl (*Gallus gallus*)	1	23	16	-	-	-	40
Indeterminable (*Aves sp.*)	3	27	11	-	-	-	41
Subtotal:	*4*	*50*	*27*	*0*	*0*	*0*	*81*
FISH							
Herring (*Clupea harengus*)	-	1	3	-	-	-	4
Subtotal:	*0*	*1*	*3*	*0*	*0*	*0*	*4*
AMPHIBIAN							
Toad/frog (*Anura sp.*)	-	1	4	-	-	-	5
Subtotal:	*0*	*1*	*4*	*0*	*0*	*0*	*5*
TOTAL	**111**	**167**	**323**	**406**	**13**	**71**	**1,091**

records of animal bones associated with cremation burials at Oakley Cottage and the former Cattle Market.

Ditches and pits

The largest proportion of the bones recovered from ditches was from cattle (N = 55), followed by caprovine (N = 29), pig (N = 8) and horse (N = 9). These deposits also included three dog bones, one cat bone, two unidentified bird bones and two herring vertebrae. Most of these fragments were from meat-rich elements and represent food waste. The herring vertebra indicates that there was a trade in preserved fish between Cirencester and the coast as it is a marine species (Cool 2006, 105).

Of seven animal bone fragments recovered from pits, four were identified as frog and one as a herring vertebra. In addition there was also a medium-sized mammal vertebra identified. The seventh fragment could not be identified to species.

Burials and funerary contexts

Animal remains were recovered from 51 burials (one cremation and 50 inhumation burials; Table 6.2). In no case during excavation was the deliberate placement of part of an animal in association with a human burial identified, with the bones being recovered during the removal of the grave fill. Some of the bones could therefore be incidental inclusions within the grave fill rather than deliberate placements (see further Section 7.4). In addition, five cremation burials from the Oakley Cottage excavation included cattle, caprovine, bird and cockle remains. Caprovine, unidentifiable mammal bones and burnt bird bones were present in

Table 6.2 Burials containing animal bones (fragment count).
BOS = cattle; O/C = sheep/goat; SUS = pig; EQU = horse; CAN = dog; ROD = rodent; GAL = fowl; AVE = bird; LM = large-sized mammal; MM = medium-sized mammal; SM = small mammal. For key to Age group see Table 5.11

Burial	Age group	Sex	BOS	O/C	SUS	EQU	CAN	LM	MM	SM	ROD	GAL	AVE	IND	Total
C1153	Indet. A	F	-	-	-	-	-	-	-	-	-	-	-	5	5
B1155	LMA	F	1	-	1	-	-	-	-	-	-	-	-	-	2
B1156	Adol.	?	-	-	-	-	-	-	1	-	-	-	-	-	1
B1157	LMA	M	1	3	-	-	-	3	1	-	17	-	-	7	32
B1158	OA	F	1	-	-	-	-	1	-	-	-	-	-	-	2
B1159	EMA	M	-	-	-	-	1	-	-	-	-	-	1	-	2
B1160	OC	?	5	2	1	1	-	-	-	-	2	1	-	-	12
B1161	LMA	F	-	1	-	-	-	-	-	-	-	-	-	-	1
B1162	LMA	F	-	-	-	-	-	-	1	-	-	-	-	-	1
B1163	YC	?	-	-	1	-	-	-	-	-	-	-	-	-	1
B1165	Indet. A	?	-	-	-	-	-	3	-	-	-	7	4	-	14
B1168	LMA	M	1	-	-	-	-	-	-	-	1	-	1	-	3
B1170	EMA	M	-	-	-	-	-	-	-	-	-	1	-	-	1
B1171	OC	?	-	-	-	-	-	-	-	-	-	22	25	-	47
B1172	Indet. A	M	1	-	-	-	-	-	-	-	-	-	-	-	1
B1175	EMA	?	1	-	-	-	-	-	-	-	-	-	-	-	1
B1176	EMA	?	-	-	-	-	-	-	2	-	-	-	-	-	2
B1177	YA	F	-	1	-	-	-	-	-	-	-	-	-	1	2
B1179	EMA	F	-	-	-	-	-	-	-	1	-	-	1	-	2
B1181	LMA	F	-	-	-	-	-	-	-	-	-	1	-	-	1
B1182	EMA	F	-	-	1	-	-	-	-	-	-	-	-	-	1
B1193	EMA	F	-	1	-	-	-	-	-	-	-	-	-	-	1
B1198	OC	?	1	-	-	-	-	-	7	-	-	-	-	-	8
B1206	OA	M	-	1	-	-	-	-	-	-	-	-	-	-	1
B1207	LMA	F	2	-	-	-	-	1	2	-	-	-	-	-	5
B1209	OA	F	2	2	1	-	-	1	2	-	-	-	1	-	9
B1210	EMA	M	-	-	-	-	-	-	2	-	-	-	-	-	2
B1211	EMA	?	1	-	-	-	-	-	-	-	-	-	-	-	1
B1214	LMA	F	-	-	-	-	-	1	-	-	-	-	-	-	1
B1215	LMA	F	-	1	-	-	-	-	-	-	-	-	-	-	1
B1217	EMA	M	-	-	-	-	-	-	-	-	-	8	6	-	14
B1218	EMA	F	-	1	-	-	-	-	-	-	-	-	-	-	1
B1223	LMA	M	2	-	-	1	-	3	-	-	-	-	-	-	6
B1228	OA	M	3	3	2	-	-	1	2	-	-	-	-	-	11
B1229	LMA	M	2	-	-	-	-	-	5	-	-	-	-	-	7
B1231	LMA	M	-	-	1	-	-	-	1	-	-	-	-	-	2
B1232	OC	?	-	-	2	-	-	-	-	-	-	-	-	-	2
B1233	LMA	M	-	-	-	2	-	-	2	-	-	-	-	-	4
B1237	EMA	M	1	-	-	-	-	-	-	-	-	-	-	-	1
B1243	OC	?	1	-	-	-	-	-	-	-	2	-	-	-	3
B1245	LMA	M	-	-	-	-	-	1	-	-	-	-	-	-	1
B1248	YA	F	-	1	-	-	-	-	-	-	-	-	-	-	1
B1249	LMA	M	1	1	-	-	-	-	2	-	-	-	-	-	4

Table 6.2 (cont.) Burials containing animal bones (fragment count).

Burial	Age group	Sex	BOS	O/C	SUS	EQU	CAN	LM	MM	SM	ROD	GAL	AVE	IND	Total
B1251	EMA	F	-	-	-	-	-	-	-	-	-	-	-	1	1
B1253	EMA	F	-	-	-	-	-	1	1	-	-	-	-	-	2
B1255	LMA	F	-	-	1	-	-	-	-	-	-	-	-	-	1
B1262	N	?	-	-	-	-	-	-	-	-	-	-	-	1	1
B1263	Adol.	?	1	-	1	-	-	-	-	-	-	-	-	-	2
B1269	LMA	M	2	-	-	-	-	-	-	-	-	-	-	-	2
B1272	LMA	F	-	1	-	-	-	-	-	-	-	-	-	-	1
B1274	OA	M	-	-	-	-	-	-	1	-	-	-	-	-	1
	TOTAL		30	19	12	4	1	16	32	1	22	40	39	15	231
	%Total		*12.99*	*8.23*	*5.19*	*1.73*	*0.43*	*6.93*	*13.85*	*0.43*	*9.52*	*17.32*	*16.88*	*6.49*	*100.00*

four cremation burials from the former Cattle Market. None of the bones from these investigations were systematically recorded and are therefore omitted from further discussion. Of the inhumation burials containing animal bones at the present site, nine were non-adults (42.83%; 9/21) and 41 adults (41.84%; 41/98). Of the adults 18 were males (45.00%; 18/40) and 19 females (45.24%; 19/42). Mammal bones were found in 39% (46/119) and bird bones in 8% (10/119) of all the inhumation burials.

Animal bones are not an uncommon occurrence in Romano-British burials. Philpott (1991) reports on a particular occurrence of domestic fowl across the whole Roman period, while mammal bones were more common with 3rd and early 4th-century burials. While some of these remains are evidently food offerings placed with the interred in the grave during the burial, an unknown proportion of the bones may be later inclusions brought into the deposit by burrowing animals. This can be further argued from the find of rodent bones in four burials (B1157, B1160, B1168 and B1243). Rodent remains are not uncommon finds in grave fills, and indirect indications of rodents in graves are often represented by gnaw marks on human bones. This was not evident in any of the Western Cemetery burials, but was, for instance, reported from several burials within the Bath Gate Cemetery (CE II, 194–6). The possibility that some of the rodent remains were of edible dormice, considered a delicacy by the Romans, cannot be completely discounted (Dobney 2001, 37).

Cattle bones were present in 19 burials. These included both meat-rich elements such as fragments of a scapula, ribs, coxae and vertebrae which may derive from meat joints and meat-poor elements such as cranial bones, carpal/tarsals, metapodial and phalanges. The latter may not be from meat joints, and could instead be token ritualistic depositions within graves (Philpott 1991, 203). However, as none of these bones displayed any evident butchery cut marks it is unclear whether or not they were deliberate placements within the grave backfill.

Caprovine bones were present in 13 burials; all were from meat-rich elements, with the exception of an astragalus found with B1209, cranial fragments in B1157 and the anterior portion of a mandible in B1160. As such, the majority of these are potentially mutton meat-cut food offerings. Pig bones were identified in ten burials. These included a single tooth fragment in the grave backfill of B1209 and a phalanx from B1155, both of which are more likely to be chance inclusions. Probable meat cuts were however represented by a diaphyseal fragment of a humerus in B1182 and a lumbar vertebra in B1163. Philpott (1991) reported that pig bones in Romano-British burials primarily dated to the early Roman period, although this conclusion was based on a very small data set.

Four horse bones were found in burial contexts. These included a cervical vertebra in the grave backfill of B1223, a cranial fragment within the grave fill of B1160 and a maxillary molar tooth with B1233. The occurrence of horse bones with human burials has been interpreted as the votive deposition of selected portions (Luff 1982; Philpott 1991). An interesting find was an almost complete dog mandible in the grave backfill of B1159. It is uncertain whether this bone should be interpreted as an intentional inclusion. Dog remains in Roman burials are usually part of complete skeletons, although there are also reported finds of dismembered and decapitated dogs having been interred within human graves in inhumation cemeteries which have been interpreted as sacrifices (Philpott 1991, 204). No cut marks were observed on the specimen from the present site, which makes it difficult to argue for this interpretation in the present case.

The clearest evidence of intentional inclusions of food offerings with the inhumation burials was the bird bones present in ten burials, of which fowl could be identified in six cases. Philpott (ibid.) observed a particularly high frequency of bird bones in urban cemeteries and the finds from the burials within the Western Cemetery further supports this observation. These bones provide

Table 6.3 Identified skeletal elements by fragment count (NISP) of fowl remains found in graves.

Element	B1160	B1165	B1170	B1171	B1181	B1217	Total
Coracoid	-	-	-	1	-	1	2
Cerv.vert.	-	2	-	1	-	-	3
Synsacrum	-	-	-	1	-	-	1
Scapula	-	-	-	-	-	1	1
Humerus	1	-	-	3	-	1	5
Radius	-	-	-	2	-	1	3
Ulna	-	-	1	2	-	1	4
Carpo-metacarpus	-	1	-	2	-	1	4
Femur	-	2	-	2	-	1	5
Tibio-tarsus	-	2	-	-	1	1	4
Tarso-metatarsus	-	-	-	3	-	-	3
Phalanx 1	-	-	-	4	-	-	4
Phalanx 2	-	-	-	1	-	-	1
TOTAL	1	7	1	22	1	8	40
MNI	*1*	*2*	*1*	*2*	*1*	*1*	*8*

an interesting parallel to the copper-alloy cockerel figurine found with child burial B1163, which is likely to reflect ritualistic aspects relating to the cult of Mercury (see Section 4.2, above). The most abundant number of fowl remains was present with older child burial B1171, where bones from a minimum of two birds are represented (Table 6.3). A minimum number of two individuals was also evident from the fowl remains with adult burial B1165. The remaining burials included bones from a minimum of only one bird.

Twenty-four fragments of unburnt animal bone were also present alongside deposits of pyre debris in Pit 1179. This included a cattle carpal bone, a fragment of a caprovine scapula, a mouse humerus and a herring vertebra. Whether these are intrusive or possible remains of food offerings on the pyre is unclear.

Discussion

The difference in species representation from the animal bones retrieved from burial deposits compared to those from non-funerary contexts is most clearly marked by the presence of fowl (Fig. 7.5). This clearly indicates the deliberate ceremonial inclusion of food offerings as part of the burial rite at the Western Cemetery (see further Section 7.4). The significance of fowl remains in Roman burials from a wider European perspective has been discussed by Lauwerier (1993), who interprets them as having been prepared food portions, based on the fact that they in general lack the heads and feet which had been cut off prior to deposition. This anatomical distribution is also evident with the present burials; the most common fowl element was limb bones, which may indicate that meat-rich portions of fowl carcasses

(such as the wing and leg) were deliberately selected for this purpose (Table 6.3). Lauwerier interpreted these meat cuts as food for the deceased, either literally or symbolically, rather than as food consumed by mourners or attendees. He also argues for a distinction between fowl bones and bird figurines in graves, with the former representing food offerings in a more functional sense, and the latter a symbolic inclusion.

The significance of the remainder of the animal bones from burial contexts is equally interesting as very few pig bones were present. This is noteworthy as pig remains in general are reportedly the most abundant find from burials in Romano-British and Continental cemeteries (Lauwerier 1983; 1993; Philpott 1991, 203–6). At the Bath Gate Cemetery, however, pig bones were also reportedly rare and fowl bones abundant (CE II, MF2, E13–G09), and perhaps this reflects a particular local practice at Cirencester. It should be noted, however, that not all meat-cut food offerings, either prepared or not, would necessarily have included bones (Lauwerier 1983), and a relatively low proportion of pig remains in the Cirencester burials may reflect a differential preparation of pork in these offerings. The animal bones also reveal that beef and mutton were included as food offerings in the graves. The few finds of horse and dog bones in these burials are likely to represent symbolic inclusions relating to religious practices, or possibly merely chance incidental inclusions within the grave backfill.

Anglo-Saxon

The majority of the animal bones from an Anglo-Saxon context were those found within the fill of pit

1004/5066. The 396 fragments of bone from the pit included fragments of a mandible, ribs, scapula and metatarsal of cattle, a femur fragment from a pig and one fragment from a rodent. No cut marks were observed on these bones. There were also 169 burnt bone fragments in this feature, of which one could be identified as a caprovine carpal bone, and a second as a tine fragment of a red deer antler. This may indicate that they represent burnt waste, and that the bone in this pit should be interpreted as domestic, or possibly even partly industrial, refuse. Given the presence of Roman pottery in this pit some of these bones might also be residual.

6.2 Plant Macrofossils and Charcoal
Sarah Cobain

Introduction

Some 236 bulk soil samples were collected from the excavation. Of these, 176 samples were taken from inhumation burials for human bone retrieval whilst the remaining 60 samples were recovered from cremation burials, cremation urns, inhumation grave backfills (containing pyre material), ditches and pits for osteological analysis and plant macrofossil and charcoal assessment. Following flotation the residues were dried and sorted by eye. The floated material was scanned and seeds identified using a low power stereo-microscope at magnifications of x10 to x40. The carbonised plant macrofossils from the excavation were recovered in small quantities and were poorly preserved. Those present were located in features containing pyre material and are likely to have become incorporated into pyre debris from kindling material or from small plants/residual material lying on the surface where the pyre was placed. The poor preservation and ambiguous origin of these remains means that little further can be usefully said about these deposits. Three samples from pit 1179, which contained pyre debris, were however suitable for charcoal analysis to provide information regarding fuel selection for cremation activities together with evidence for woodland management. The results are presented in Table 6.4.

In total 100 charcoal fragments (>2mm) were fractured by hand to reveal the wood anatomy on radial, tangential and transverse planes and identified using an epi-illuminating microscope (Brunel SP400) (x40 to x400 magnifications). Identifications were carried out with reference to images and descriptions by Gale and Cutler (2000), Schoch *et al.* (2004) and Wheeler *et al.* (1989). Nomenclature of species follows Stace (1997).

Discussion

Pit 1179 (fill 1160) contained charcoal identified predominantly as oak (*Quercus* spp) and hawthorn/rowan/crab apple (*Crataegus monogyna/Sorbus* spp/*Malus sylvestris*), with smaller quantities of ash (*Fraxinus*

Table 6.4 Charcoal identifications.
Key: r/w = round wood; h/w = heartwood (tyloses present)

Family	Species	Common Name			
		Feature number	1179	1179	1179
		Fill number	1160	1160	1160
		Quadrant (Q)/Spit (S) Number	QA, QB, QC & QD	QC	QB
		Sample number	190	194	200
		Flot volume (ml)	3	4	82
		Sample volume (l)	9	7	20
		Charcoal quantity (>2mm)	++++	++++	++++
		Charcoal preservation	Moderate	Good	Good
Fagaceae	*Quercus petraea* (Matt.) Liebl./*Quercus robur* L.	Sessile Oak/Pedunculate Oak	15	3	24
	Quercus petraea (Matt.) Liebl./*Quercus robur* L.	Sessile Oak/Pedunculate Oak h/w	-	-	9
Oleaceae	*Fraxinus excelsior* L.	Ash	7	-	-
Rosaceae	*Crataegus monogyna* Jacq./*Sorbus* L./*Malus sylvestris* (L.) Mill.	Hawthorn/rowans/crab apple	11	26	-
	Crataegus monogyna Jacq./*Sorbus* L./*Malus sylvestris* (L.) Mill.	Hawthorn/rowans/crab apple r/w	-	4	-
	Prunus L.	Cherries	1	-	-
		Number of Fragments	**34**	**33**	**33**

excelsior) and cherry (*Prunus* spp) also present. There was no evidence of any pyre sites within the limits of this excavation, but the charcoal was recovered in sufficient quantities to suggest it originates from pyre debris. The charcoal would have been collected alongside the cremated bone and deposited within the pit (for the human bone from this pit see Section 5.1, above).

The charcoal was not of sufficient preservation to ascertain whether the pyre was constructed from older heartwood timbers or younger sapwood branches, although a small number of fragments with tyloses (indicating heartwood) were identified. It is however likely that oak made up the bulk of the cremation pyre frame. Oak would have been chosen as a dominant fuel wood as it has dense heartwood, and if properly seasoned, burns slowly at a high and constant temperature (Gale and Cutler 2000, 205). This would be ideal for pyre fuel where temperatures in 650–800°C are required for efficient cremation of human remains.

Hawthorn, rowan and crab apple all have a relatively dense grain and are therefore good fuel woods, although would not reach temperatures as high as oak (ibid., 184). This may provide an explanation for the incomplete oxidation of the human bone in this deposit. The presence of ash and cherry species may indicate additional species utilised as poles within the pyre construction, or they may have been used as kindling or the remnants of grave goods.

The charcoal associated with cremation activity at the Old Tetbury Road site differed from that in pit 1179 as it was dominated by oak with only a single fragment of hawthorn/rowan/crab apple and a small amount of lime present (CE VI, 129). This is not thought to be significant as there are examples of oak dominating Roman cremation burials at sites such as Westhampnett bypass, West Sussex (Gale 1997) and Cotswold Community, Gloucestershire (Challinor 2010, 201). Examples of species other than oak (hawthorn/rowan/crab apple, alder (*Alnus glutinosa*), birch (*Betula* spp)) dominating cremation burial assemblages include Baker's Wood, Sevenhampton, Gloucestershire (Cobain 2016, 155), Latton Lands, Wiltshire (Challinor 2009, 97) and Brougham, Cumbria (Campbell 2004, 268–70). The reason for this difference in species selection, in particular selection of less efficient fuel wood is currently unclear. There has been discussion as to whether different species were used for men and women (Campbell 2004, 270), although there were insufficient well-preserved cremation burials on the present site to examine this assertion. An additional explanation (depending on which species was present) for the use of crab apple wood may be its pleasant aroma when burnt, which might have helped to counter-act the pungent smell produced during the cremation process (Challinor 2010, 201).

Chapter 7
Discussion

by Neil Holbrook

7.1 Cemetery Location, Layout and Chronology

For the reasons stated in the Introduction it is reasonable to suppose that a Roman road or track underlies Tetbury Road, although whether this was ever actually constructed as the primary metalled course of the Fosse Way is more problematical (CE V, 11–16; Reece 2003). The large earthen barrow known as Grismond's Tower would have been an imposing monument next to the road, and a highly visible landmark for travellers on the Fosse Way as they started their descent into the Churn valley on the approach to Cirencester. Whether Grismond's Tower is a prehistoric barrow reused in the late Iron Age or early Roman period, or a newly constructed monument of that date, must remain conjecture until fresh evidence is forthcoming, but either way it would have been a prominent feature throughout the Roman period (Darvill 2014). The former Bridges Garage site lies opposite Grismond's Tower on the other side of the road or track and there is no certain evidence for pre-cemetery activity here. Ditches A and B/E served as a boundary to the earliest phases of funerary activity, with burial spreading beyond them in the later Roman period, but whether this was a case of burial simply filling up a former agricultural plot, or whether the ditches were dug as part of the laying out of the funerary landscape, is uncertain. The limited dating evidence indicates that Ditch B fell out of use relatively quickly, and its infilled course was cut by Ditch F which itself seems to have been infilled by the end of the 2nd century at the latest. The reuse of agricultural plots for burial is suggested at the Old Tetbury Road excavation where ditched land plots were utilised for cremation burial from the Flavian period, shortly after the establishment of the Roman town (CE VI, 109–31). Whether burial started this early at the present site is unclear. It is possible that some of the cremation vessels could date to the late 1st century AD, but precision is not possible as these coarseware vessels are not susceptible to close dating. Nevertheless it is clear that the area adjacent to the south-east frontage of the road was intensively utilised for cremation burial in the late 1st/earlier 2nd centuries AD to judge from the 46 cremation burials recorded by Reece (what proportion of the original total he managed to retrieve is impossible to determine). Indeed it is possible that the walled cemetery, which dates no later than the middle of the 2nd century, was set back from the road frontage to avoid the densest area of pre-existing cremation burial. Walled cemeteries were not always positioned immediately adjacent to a road frontage: at Derby Racecourse for instance the frontage was occupied by five mausolea, with the walled cemetery 28m to the rear (the intervening area was used for both cremation and inhumation burial; Wheeler 1985). Ditch D/F was conceivably dug at the same time as the walled cemetery was built, as along with Ditch A it defined a zone *c.* 14m wide which contained both the walled cemetery and the area immediately to its south-west. Perhaps Ditch D/F served to demarcate a familial or corporate group burial area which included the walled cemetery, and thus separated this from a pre-existing zone of dense cremation burial adjacent to the road frontage?

There is little reason to suppose that burial was not continuous at the former Bridges Garage site and in the Western Cemetery generally. While it has been possible to separate burials which appear from associated artefacts to date to the late 1st to early 3rd century (Period 1) from those which are late 3rd century or later (Period 2) (Fig. 2.3), many have no close dating and there is no reason to suppose that burial did not continue throughout the 3rd century. Cremation burial certainly continued on the site until at least the earlier 3rd century, to judge from the cremation vessels which accompanied burials C1153 and C1278, and the deposit of pyre debris contained within pit 1179 which was cut into the backfill of Ditch A. By the later Roman period burial had spread beyond the, by now, backfilled ditches A and B/E, a common enough event as the encroachment of late Roman inhumation cemeteries over suburban areas formerly used for other purposes is well attested in the major towns of Roman Britain.

Despite the partial nature of the plan of the cemetery available to us, it is evident that the layout of the graves displays obvious traces of planning, with the predominant orientation of the inhumation burials dictated by the alignment of the road or track beneath Tetbury Road. The walled cemetery would also have remained a prominent monument throughout the Roman period. It is likely that the great majority of inhumation graves were marked above ground, as instances of intercutting were uncommon. Whether the cremation burials were also marked, or otherwise respected by later inhumation burials, is difficult to determine due to the level of truncation that took place in the zone adjacent to Tetbury Road. Some inhumation graves clearly disturbed earlier cremation burials, however, as demonstrated by the inclusion in some grave backfills of cremation debris and disturbed fragments of cremation urns (the fills of B1177 and B1215 for instance). The cemetery therefore displays a level of order and management not apparent at the Bath Gate Cemetery where intercutting was prevalent (CE II, 100–1). Conceivably this is another reflection of the greater status of the occupants of the Western Cemetery compared to those at the Bath Gate, which finds its best expression in the differential quantities of grave goods in the two cemeteries (below, and Table 7.1). Limited intercutting of graves is a common facet of many Romano-British urban cemeteries, and the seemingly random nature of burial at the Bath Gate Cemetery is more uncommon than the order apparent here (Pearce 2015, 148).

There is some evidence for how long the cemetery continued in use, but it is not conclusive. Six graves contained the following coins: AD 270–90 (B1171); *nummus*, ? House of Constantine (B1234); AD 341–6 and AD 348–50 (B1269), and unidentifiable *nummi* from B1229, B1231 and B1244. With so few coins it is hard to draw firm conclusions, but we might note the absence of coins of the second half of the 4th century from the site (these are prevalent elsewhere in the town). The latest grave goods recovered from the graves date broadly to the mid–late 4th century, although the absence of shell-tempered ware from the grave backfills could be significant. This fabric was prevalent in Cirencester from the mid 4th century and its earliest well-dated occurrence in the town is from a pit containing a coin hoard of *c*. AD 340–50 (AFI Pit 3; CE V, 208, 291–2). The absence of this fabric from the site might lend support to the notion that burial did not continue until the very end of the 4th century, unlike

the Bath Gate Cemetery where a coin of Honorius from beneath the vertebrae of an inhumation demonstrates that burial continued after AD 395 at least (CE II, 103, 127). Burial in this part of the Western Cemetery therefore conceivably ceased around the middle of the 4th century.

There is no doubt that the land either side of Tetbury Road was an important zone from the late 1st to at least the mid 4th century for burial of the inhabitants of Corinium. Much of that evidence on the south-east side of the road has now been removed by 19th, 20th and 21st-century development, although pockets of preservation doubtless still remain. Indeed the present excavation has ably demonstrated how high-quality evidence can survive the effects of previous development. Very little is known of burial on the opposite side of the road, however, as this area lies within the bounds of Cirencester Park and archaeological deposits have thus been spared the effects of recent development. It is reasonable to assume, however, that there will be excellent preservation of important remains there and that it is a valuable resource for furthering our future understanding of the health and burial rituals of the population of Corinium.

7.2 The Walled Cemetery

Wall C is interpreted as the corner of a walled cemetery as its internal area is too large for a roofed mausoleum. Wall C was 0.8–1m wide and the minimum north-east/south-west dimension of the enclosure was 8.7m and the maximum 14.5m. A width at the higher end of this range gains support from the location of B1209. This burial contained abundant pottery in its grave fill, which links it with the other graves that clearly lay within the enclosure. To have contained B1209 as well, therefore, the enclosure would have had to be close to the maximum possible size. The Cirencester walled cemetery can be compared with similar examples which occur predominately in the south-east of England (Jessup 1959; Black 1986, 205–10). For instance at Great Dover Street in Southwark two walled cemeteries (Structures 1 and 3) built in the mid 2nd to early 3rd century formed part of a group of burial monuments fronting onto Watling Street (Mackinder 2000). Structure 3 had dimensions of 9m by 7m; was defined by a wall 0.7m wide, and contained a central structure, 2.4m by 2.1m. Structure 1 was 11m by 9.2m across and defined by a wall 0.7–0.9m wide. It contained a central plinth 4.5m by 4.2m and had an amphora set into the ground (perhaps to accept libations?). Like the Cirencester walled cemetery, the inhumation burials were set close to, and parallel with, the perimeter wall. We may reasonably suppose therefore that the centre of the Cirencester walled cemetery was, like those in Southwark and elsewhere, occupied by some manner of monument. The crudely dressed sides and rear of the tombstone commemorating Bodicacia, reused in B1267, suggest that they were never intended to be seen, and Tomlin wonders whether the stone was originally designed to be part of a larger funerary structure, rather than a free-standing memorial. The fresh condition of the carving on the stone does suggest that it was not subject to prolonged weathering, and was perhaps afforded some protection from the elements, conceivably within a monument. Whilst the date of the tombstone cannot be determined closely, the quality of the carving and lettering suggest that it is unlikely to be later than the earlier 3rd century. Conceivably therefore, the tombstone might have originally formed part of a central monument within the walled cemetery. No dedicator is named on the epitaph, and Tomlin suggests that one explanation could be because the tombstone was originally intended to sit alongside that of her husband, thus making the relationship explicit (Bodicacia's husband might already have been dead, or at least made provision for his own commemoration). A small fragment of a second inscribed tombstone was recovered from the site in 1960 (RIB III, 3065). Might this also have come from a monument inside the walled cemetery, as perhaps did the moulded block from the upper fill of Ditch B which must have come from a substantial structure?

How many burials once lay within the walled cemetery is impossible to determine given the amount of later disturbance, but it was in excess of nine. Structures 1 and 3 at Southwark contained two and four inhumation burials respectively, while at Derby Racecourse the 12m-square walled cemetery contained 61 inhumation and at least 39 cremation burials dating predominantly to 2nd and 3rd centuries (there was no suggestion of a central monument; Wheeler 1985). There is no certain evidence for cremation burials within the undisturbed portion of the Cirencester walled cemetery, although the amount of disturbed cremation material contained within the grave backfills inside the enclosure suggests that pyres might have been lit within it. This seems to have been the case at Derby Racecourse where a large quantity of charcoal and cremated human bone was found both on the ground surface within the walled cemetery and in the backfill of inhumation graves (ibid., 231–4).

Table 2.1 presents the principal attributes of the burials within the walled cemetery. Most, if not all, of the burials were buried wearing hobnailed footwear and contained within wooden coffins. McSloy's insightful analysis of the pottery groups from these grave fills isolates them as a group distinct from the graves outside of the enclosure, not only in terms of the quantity of pottery sherds present but also the composition of the assemblage which has a clear emphasis on wine amphorae, flagons and tazze (Tables 4.5 and 4.6). We may reasonably reconstruct funerary ceremonies within the walled cemetery which involved the consumption of

wine, or the pouring of it as libations, and the burning of substances contained in tazze. These vessels were then broken and scattered on the ground surface, this material being incorporated into the backfill when subsequent graves were dug. The levels of fragmentation and lack of cross-context joins within individual grave fills argues against this material being deliberately introduced into the backfill as part of graveside rituals.

The significance of the walled cemetery for richer burial seems not to have been restricted solely to those interred within it. Two adjacent burials just outside the perimeter wall are notable as they contained the richest grave goods from the whole cemetery. B1163, a 2 to 3-year-old child, contained a pottery feeding bottle and a magnificent enamelled figurine of a cockerel, both dateable to the 2nd century, while the grave goods accompanying B1171, a child of *c*. 6 years, included three bracelets, a glass vessel and six strings of jet or glass beads, the largest number of grave goods from any burial in the cemetery. These grave goods are no earlier than the late 3rd century at earliest and Burial B1171 was therefore at least a century later than B1163, unless the grave goods in the latter are considered as heirlooms, which seems unlikely given the good evidence from other nearby graves for burial in the 2nd century. Presumably the site of the earlier burial was marked above ground and the locality retained some continuing significance. A further sign of the significance of this particular part of the cemetery is the nearby burial of a lead cremation vessel of probable 1st or 2nd-century date (C1227). This is the first lead cremation urn recorded from Cirencester. They were a Roman introduction to Britain and finds of such vessels concentrate around the major centres of Colchester, London and York (Toller 1977, 27, 45–6, map 6). More recent finds from Gloucestershire comprise a lead cylindrical canister within a 1st-century AD ditched burial enclosure at 167 Barnwood Road, Barnwood, 2.5km distant from the legionary fortress at Kingsholm, Gloucester (CA 2017); a lead container housed within a hollow cut into a pair of stone blocks from Well's Bridge, Barnwood (a probable villa site; Ellis and King 2016; Ellis *et al.* forthcoming), and a lead box from a villa at Harnhill, 6km east of Cirencester (Wright 2008). There can be little doubt that the tradition of lead cremation vessels was brought to western Britain by the Roman army and that they are another manifestation of wealth and status. Perhaps the walled cemetery contained an élite family, with more distant relatives or descendants buried outside?

It is surely significant that wealthy inhumation burials B1163 and B1171 were both of children (and we may also observe that the only grave good from inside the walled cemetery was a pottery flagon which accompanied an 8-year-old child (B1160)). Gowland's (2001) analysis of the later Roman Lankhills cemetery in Winchester revealed that the number of grave goods buried in any one grave peaked for juveniles in the 8–12 years age category, and a similar association has been detected at other cemeteries (Pearce 2015, 150). The only two burials furnished with grave goods other than footwear within the walled cemetery at Derby Racecourse were also children (a 3 to 4-year-old child with two copper-alloy bracelets and *c.* 9-year-old child with a copper-alloy finger ring). Perhaps the artefacts were imbued with a significance associated with particular childhood events, and death prior to adulthood increased the likelihood that they would be put in the grave with the deceased?

The walled cemetery forms one of a small number of burial monuments known from the Western Cemetery. Grismond's Tower has already been mentioned. It may be no coincidence that the walled cemetery was constructed directly opposite it on the other side of the road. Could the walled cemetery have contained the descendants or relations of those interred in or around the barrow? Other monuments comprised a small masonry mausoleum at Cirencester Hospital, 6.7 by 6.4m across, which would have been readily visible to travellers on the Fosse Way (Fig. 1.2, B1103; CE II, MF5, B10–11), and a masonry wall at the Old Tetbury Road site which conceivably, but far from certainly, formed part of another walled cemetery (CE VI, 113, 130–1). Further monuments are likely in the other cemeteries of Cirencester as geophysical survey on the opposite side of Cirencester in the area around Tar Barrows, just to the north-west of the Fosse Way, has revealed anomalies which could be interpreted as masonry mausolea and/or walled cemeteries (Holbrook 2008, 308–11; Booth 2009, 267–9). No such features were found during excavation on the opposite side of the Fosse Way hereabouts, however (Biddulph and Walsh 2011). Pearce (2013, 111–15; 2015, 143) has discussed the evidence for burial monuments from Britain as a whole. In some cases small groups of monuments (masonry or timber structures or enclosures, and more rarely earthen barrows) are found distributed over several hundred metres along roads traversing cemeteries, and this bears comparison with several cities in Gaul and Germany. Distinct clusters of monuments are much more rarely found, although Great Dover Street in Southwark (Mackinder 2000) is an example of a 'street of tombs' akin to those found on a much larger scale in southern France.

The selection of inhumation burial during the 2nd century in the Western Cemetery now occasions little surprise, as Pearce (2015, 146) has demonstrated that the simple narrative of cremation as the dominant urban burial ritual until it was replaced by inhumation in the early 3rd century must be set aside. Extended supine inhumation burial is now commonly attested as an early Roman ritual, as at Great Dover Street in Southwark where in the mid 2nd century two and three inhumations were buried with walled cemeteries Structures 1 and 3 respectively, with a further 16

inhumation burials outside them. Inhumation was also an indigenous burial tradition in the Cotswold-Severn region in the late Iron Age, and this persisted into the early Roman period (Holbrook 2006, 121).

7.3 Burial Rituals

Cremations

Detail on cremation rituals is limited, given that the great majority of cremation burials lay in the zone closest to the Tetbury Road frontage and thus we are dependent upon the information which Reece was able to salvage from his hurried recording programme. Only eight cremation burials were revealed in the recent excavation, and some of those had been heavily disturbed by later activity. The prevailing burial practice was to place cremated bone within a pottery jar or cooking pot which was set vertically within a small cut. Not all cremated bone was contained in urns, however, as Reece's Cremation V, which comprised hundreds of fragments of bone, was not thus contained (although the bone might conceivably have been placed in an organic bag or wooden box of which no trace survived). Reece (1962, 53, 70) also found some neatly cut small pits, *c.* 0.2–0.4m across with vertical sides, which contained ash, charcoal and many fragments of cremated bone. It is unclear whether these pits also held un-urned cremation burials, or rather a deposit of pyre debris such as that contained in pit 1179 on the present excavation, or pits 128 and 133 at the Old Tetbury Road site (CE VI, 111). Jars or cooking pots were the exclusive pottery form used to contain the cremated remains. In one case, C1278.1, the vessel had been repaired with a lead rivet, proving that this vessel had been in domestic use and that it was not a new purchase specifically for use in a funerary ritual. In C1154 a second jar accompanied a cremation urn; it may have been an ancillary vessel unless this was a double cremation burial (the second vessel had been heavily truncated). Nor is it clear whether the three vessels grouped together as C1278 were all cremation vessels, or whether at least one of them was an ancillary vessel. A more certain example of an ancillary vessel accompanied C1144 at the Old Tetbury Road site (CE VI, 121–2) and Reece's Cremation XG at this site was accompanied by a flagon which had a distorted rim and was a distinct 'second' (as indeed was another cremation vessel he recovered; Reece 1962, fig. 3, nos 6 and 2).

Both adults and children were cremated, and no sex bias is apparent in the very small sample. Fragments of animal bone mixed with the human bone must reflect the presence of animals or joints of meat on the funeral pyre. Other than that no grave goods accompanied the cremation burials found on this site, although this occurred elsewhere in the Western Cemetery. One cremation vessel discovered at the Cattle Market in 1867 contained, alongside cremated bone, a ceramic lamp, a brooch, a glass 'tear bottle' and four coins (CE II, MF5,

Burial 1060). The cremation burial probably dates to the 1st century AD to judge from the surviving grave goods. Another marker of status for cremation burials found in both the Western and Southern Cemeteries of Cirencester was the use of a square block of limestone with a hollow scooped out to take either the ashes or a pottery cremation vessel (CE II, 207). Eleven such examples are recorded from the town, and in one notable case in the Southern Cemetery a glass cremation vessel was apparently wrapped in lead sheeting (CE II, MF5, Burial 2002). The only example of a high-status cremation burial at the present site is the lead cremation vessel C1227.1 found adjacent to the walled cemetery and discussed above, but overall there is little evidence for differential status display amongst the cremation burials.

Grave pits

The typical form of the graves was as rectangular pits with straight, steep sides and square or rounded corners, the latter giving rise in some cases to a slightly apsidal end to the cut. In many cases the precise form of the grave was determined by the bedding of the natural limestone through which it was dug. The depths recorded in the excavation varied considerably, and must have done so in the Roman period, but little store can be placed on these data given the variable degrees of truncation that have occurred across the site. In some cases the grave cut was noticeably larger than required to accommodate the coffin (B1167, B1188, B1193, B1208, B1222, B1233); in others it was a tight squeeze (B1219, B1221). In two cases a layer of silt had accumulated in the base of the pit before the coffins were laid in the grave (in B1162 the silt was up to 0.14m deep, and B1185 up to 0.15m thick). This suggests that the graves had been dug and left open for a period of perhaps at least several days before the funeral took place.

As discussed above it is likely that the positions of the graves were mostly marked above ground in some form, given the relatively limited instances of intercutting. Indeed the relationship of B1257, a neonate, dug into the backfill of B1253, a 24 to 38-year-old female, may be more than just coincidence and could be further evidence for the marking of graves. Perhaps the woman died in childbirth, with the child dying somewhat later? Given the level of truncation it is unsurprising that little evidence survived for any such markers, although in two cases (B1157 and B1168) postholes adjacent to the graves might conceivably have held upright marker posts.

Coffins

The overwhelming majority of burials were contained in wooden coffins to judge from the presence of iron nails in the base of the grave pits (*c.* 83% of well-preserved graves produced this evidence). Indeed there were only ten examples where no nails were recovered from graves

where preservation was such that they would have been expected to be found had they been present. That said, the number of nails varied considerably between graves, ranging from less than five nails to considerable numbers (six graves produced 50 or more, with a maximum number of 99). For instance B1176 had 73 nails and it was subsequently cut by grave B1171 which produced 99 nails. High numbers of nails presumably denote a more elaborate constructional technique for the coffin, or the attachment of some form covering that has left no trace, and it may not be mere coincidence that B1171 was well-furnished with grave goods. Whilst earlier burial B1176 had no grave goods, it is conceivable that some of the nails recovered from the fill of this grave were in fact intrusive from overlying B1171. Burial B1171 dates to the late 3rd or 4th century to judge from its accompanying grave goods. McSloy (Section 4.2) observes that the coffins with the highest number of nails cluster outside of the walled cemetery, with one (B1209) within it.

At Lankhills the number of nails used in coffins formed a continuum up to the low thirties, although four coffins had more (the maximum was 62; Booth *et al.* 2010, 483). Of the ten burials without evidence of coffins at the present site, two were laid prone (B1204, B1236). Of course an absence of nails, or just a few examples, need not mean that no coffin was present, as wooden pegs or joints could have been used. One notable example (B1193) where the distribution of nails allows the form of the coffin to be determined shows that either the coffin was 0.3m longer than the body, or else that a separate nailed box was placed above the head. If the former, this implies that this coffin was pre-fabricated.

In five cases a thin calcareous covering of the coffin timbers was preserved within the grave fill (B1169, B1207, B1249, B1254 and B1266, representing both male and female adult burials), and with B1207 this pinkish white deposit was 20mm thick and had two iron nails embedded in it (Fig. 3.64). Whilst the infilling of coffins with plaster or chalk is a well-known facet of Romano-British funerary practice (Philpott 1991, 90–6), the covering of the external faces of a timber coffin in this manner is less attested. It cannot be excluded that these deposits are the product of a natural mineralisation of the decaying wood of the coffin, although the writer has not come across this effect in Cirencester before. If not, and these represent the deliberate covering of the exterior of a coffin with a lime-rich coating, perhaps this was an attempt to imitate the appearance of stone coffins formed from white Cotswold limestone? The only useful dating is for B1266 which contained a 4th-century grave good.

The common use of coffins in the Western Cemetery is reflected at a number of other urban cemeteries such as Lankhills and Butt Road, Colchester (Table 7.1) but contrasts with a poor showing at the Bath Gate Cemetery where only around a quarter of burials were

Table 7.1 Approximate comparative occurrence of different finds categories in inhumation burials from selected late Roman cemeteries in southern Britain.
Source: Booth *et al.* 2010, table 8.2, with the addition of Western Cemetery data. Footwear at the Western Cemetery is taken to be indicated by the presence of five or more iron hobnails

	Cirencester Western Cemetery	Cirencester Bath Gate Cemetery	Lankhills Winchester	Butt Rd Colchester Period 1	Butt Rd Colchester Period 2	East London
No. excavated graves	120	450	751	44	669	*c.* 362
Coffins	84.0%	?*c.* 25%	78.3%	100%	90.9%	?*c.* 65%
Footwear	33.3%	1.1%	36.1%	25.0%	1.0%	6.1%
Vessels	5.0%	0.7%	17.0%	36.4%	2.2%	13.3%
Coins	5.0%	0.7%	8.8%	–	0.1%	4.7%
Jewellery	10.0%	0.9%	7.5%	11.4%	3.3%	7.7%
Brooches	–	–	2.0%	–	0.1%	0.8%
Belt sets	–	–	2.7%	–	0.1%	0.3%

placed in coffins. Perhaps this reflects a difference in the prevalent burial ritual between the two cemeteries, with coffins signifying greater visibility of the funerary ritual, including the formal procession of the burial party to the graveside?

Packing

There were 23 examples of stone lining or packing around the edge of a grave pit in the Western Cemetery. In some cases this was a very distinct occurrence and clearly intentional (Burial B1272 for instance; Figs 3.127–8); in others more ambiguity attaches to how deliberate an act this was, given that many graves were rock cut and the backfills thus frequently contained lumps of limestone. The trait occurs with both males and females, infants and children, and in one case (B1178) a decapitated burial. Packing was adopted as a technique from early in the life of the cemetery as two of the burials within the walled cemetery were so treated (B1159 and B1160).

The function of the packing is uncertain. In some cases it clearly filled the gap between the edge of the grave pit and the coffin, and whilst in some cases such packing could have served to hold the boards of a non-nailed coffin together, that cannot be the case here as coffin nails occur alongside the packing. It may rather just be a local tradition, in an area where stone is abundant, that had no obvious functional purpose. The presence of rough stone packing in graves is well attested in the Cotswolds. It was found at the Bath Gate Cemetery for instance, although less frequently than in the Western Cemetery (6% of graves had this treatment in that cemetery compared to 19% here; CE II, 92–7). Stone lining or packing also occurs with rural burials in the Cotswolds, as at Bourton-on-the-Water, although in some cases burials were contained in more fully-developed stone cists (Hart *et al.* 2016; RCHME 1976, xlix).

Body positions

Bodies were found lying in a variety of positions which encompass variation in the dispositions of arms and legs. In some cases post-depositional displacement will serve to confuse the picture revealed in excavation, but this is unlikely to create significant bias. The great majority of burials lay in a supine position with legs extended (there were just three examples where legs were crossed rather than extended; this trait is unlikely to be significant). Exceptions to this were burials laid prone, which are considered below, and those on their sides in a crouched position. There were six examples of crouched burials: two were neonates; one an older child; and three adults, of which two were males (B1157 laid on his right side and Reece B4 laid on the left side) and B1175 of indeterminate sex laid on the right side. B1157 was buried within the walled cemetery and so is of 2nd-century date. The low representation of crouched burials can be compared to the Bath Gate Cemetery where ten flexed burials were found, of which seven were adults (CE II, 81). Late Iron Age and early Roman inhumations in the Cotswold-Severn region were often buried in a crouched posture, and such burials occur sporadically in the urban cemeteries of Gloucester as well as Cirencester, and indeed some other towns as well. They are likely to represent a survival of an indigenous tradition (Heighway 1980, 57; Philpott 1991, 55; Holbrook 2006, 121; Booth *et al.* 2010, 478–80).

The greatest variation in burial posture was in the disposition of the arms. In all 97 bodies survived sufficiently well for this to be established. A basic five-fold categorisation was established as follows, with the numbers of examples in brackets: both arms straight beside body (18 examples); one or both arms flexed with hand(s) over pelvis (46 examples); one or both arms bent at right angle with hand(s) across the waist/abdomen (12 examples); one or both arms tightly flexed with hand(s) on chest or shoulder (6 examples); other dispositions (15 examples). As can be appreciated over half of the burials either had one or both hands placed on the pelvis, by far the most common arrangement. In no case was there an obvious correlation of age or sex with any arm position. At the Bath Gate Cemetery the most common arm positions were those with one or both arms laid straight beside the body (44%), or semi-flexed with hand(s) on the pelvis (43%), with combinations of these positions accounting for 87% of all burials (CE II, 85). The same is true at Lankhills where combinations of these positions accounted for almost three-quarters of the burials (Booth *et al.* 2010, 473). The two positions accounted for slightly less of the burials in the Western Cemetery (66%) but the general correspondence in body positions with Bath Gate and Lankhills is apparent. Of the 15 burials with arms placed in other positions, most are just variations on the basic arrangements already defined. In two cases the left arm was placed under the pelvis (B1240 and B1266) while B1267, the burial that was covered with the reused tombstone, the left arm lay under the ribs while the right arm was extended beneath the pelvis, an usual arrangement reminiscent of the arm positions of prone burials B1236 and B1241 where the wrists may have been bound behind the back. B1263, an adolescent, is notable as the only example where the arms were placed in front of the face. This burial was accompanied by a bracelet and bead string placed by the lower right leg.

Clothing

There is virtually no evidence for clothing other than footwear amongst the burials. In some cemeteries textile impressions are preserved on the corrosion products of grave goods, but not here. More frequently a constriction or hunching of the shoulders observed during excavation has been taken as evidence that the body was tightly bound in a shroud, although this is far from conclusive and a narrow coffin would produce the same effect. Only one example of a possible constriction of a body was noted in the field (B1229), but this is not evident from the burial plan (Fig. 3.83) and little weight can be attached to this possible identification. Given that many burials had evidence for nailed footwear, it might reasonably be wondered whether the presence of footwear is compatible with wrapping in a shroud.

Nailed footwear has been recovered from 53 graves (44.2%), but if heavily disturbed graves and instances of less than five hobnails are omitted the number reduces to 40 graves (33.3%). This is still a very high proportion of individuals buried with nailed footwear, and contrasts dramatically with the Bath Gate Cemetery where only four burials (1%) were so accompanied (CE II, 129–32). Of the main Romano-British urban cemeteries, only Lankhills has an equivalent provision of nailed footwear (36%; Table 7.1; Booth *et al.* 2010, 535). In the Western Cemetery footwear accompanied burials

of a *c.* 9-month-old infant (B1268), children and adult females and males, the latter including prone burial B1188. In most cases the shoes were probably worn at the time of burial, although in five instances they were apparently placed in the grave (B1167, B1171, B1176, B1200 and B1203). The tradition of placing hobnailed footwear with burials began in the 2nd century to judge from the concentration in the walled cemetery and area immediately to the north-east (Fig. 7.4 and McSloy Section 4.2). Other evidence for footwear derives from copper-alloy studs used to decorate later Roman shoes, which were recovered from the foot area of two adult females (B1161 and B1164).

'Deviant' practice

There were nine examples (7.5%) of so-called 'deviant' burials in the Western Cemetery: seven laid prone (B1188, B1204, B1236, B1241, B1242, B1255, B1271), of which B1241 was also decapitated, and two other supine decapitations (B1178, B1196). Burial B1269 is another possible example of a supine decapitation, but there is insufficient evidence for certainty. These practices were used with one young child (B1271), one older child (B1196), six adult females and one adult male (B1236). The bias towards adult females is notable, and finds reflection in the Eastern Cemetery of London where females and sub-adults were twice as common amongst prone burials as they were in the rest of the cemetery (Barber and Bowsher 2000, 87). The prone burial of adult female B1255 had a significantly malformed mandible. This appears to have been a long-standing condition, possibly congenital, and the woman is likely to have had difficulties in speaking and perhaps even masticating properly. Conceivably it was this deformity that led to the decision to bury her in a prone position. The nine examples of deviant practice from the Western Cemetery compare with 33 prone burials and six decapitated burials at the Bath Gate Cemetery (8.7%; 39/450). Whilst the overall representation is comparable at the two sites, the bias towards female prone burials was not represented at Bath Gate where of the 31 prone burials that were anatomically examined, 14 were adult females, 13 adult males, 1 unsexed adult and 3 children (CE II, 78).

It has been suggested that some prone burials may have been bound when they were placed in the grave (cf. the discussion of the Lankhills evidence; Booth *et al.* 2010, 477–8). Burial B1236 may have had his hands tied behind his back; B1241 may also have been bound, while B1188 and B1255 had both hands beneath the pelvis and were conceivably tied. B1236 also looks to have had his ankles bound, as may also have been the case with certain individuals at Lankhills and the Bath Gate Cemetery (CE II, 78, fig. 13, burial 224; the right clavicle and parts of the cranial vault of this man had apparently been exposed to fire). In five out of nine cases these deviant burials were placed in wooden coffins, and in one case (B1188) an adult female wore nailed footwear. No other grave goods were deposited with this type of burial.

Prone and decapitated burials often occur in close proximity in late Roman cemeteries (Philpott 1991, 73–6), and this is the case here with adjacent burials B1178 and B1188 and B1241 and B1242 (Fig. 7.5). The prone burials were concentrated in the south-west side of the site, and this is notable as prone burials often occur close to the edge of managed cemeteries, as at Lankhills where they cluster close to the north and east boundary ditches (Booth *et al.* 2010, 476–9). The significance and interpretation that should be placed upon prone and decapitated burials has been widely discussed (Philpott 1991, 71–87; Taylor 2008; Pearce 2015, 148).

The most obvious example of an abnormal burial rite was the placement of a complete, but clearly reused, tombstone face down within a grave pit, directly above a wooden coffin, with the stone then being covered with backfill (B1267). Such an occurrence is unparalleled in Roman Britain, although this is hardly surprising given that so few tombstones have been recovered from known archaeological contexts. Funerary markers were certainly reused as building material within the Roman period in Britain, as is shown for instance by their incorporation within the late Roman town defences of London and Lincoln (Blagg 1983, 130–1), although the British evidence is slight in comparison with that from the Continent where the reuse of funerary monuments is widely attested. In Cirencester part of a tombstone was reused in the foundations of a stone building constructed *c.* AD 280 just outside the Bath Gate (CE II, MF2, E11–12; RIB III, 3063) and three tombstones found during building work at the rear of the earthen rampart of the town defences at Stepstairs Lane might have been either destined for reuse in an external tower or, more likely, been reused as a consolidation for the surface of the rampart like that found in a nearby excavation trench and elsewhere on the defensive circuit (CE V, 59–62; RIB III, 3060–62). Reuse of tombstones in funerary contexts is rarer, but not unknown as fragments of smashed-up tombstones were reused in the linings of three later Roman cist graves outside the fort at Brougham in Cumbria (Cool 2004, 36–8; RIB III, 3231, 3238, 3247, 3248) and the packing of a grave in the Eastern Cemetery of London (Barber and Bowsher 2000, 338–9; RIB III, 3004). The Cirencester tombstone probably dates to the later 2nd century to judge from the stylistic affinities of its sculpted decoration, and it may have been built into some manner of funerary monument rather than being a free-standing epitaph. As discussed above one possible location for such a monument might have been within the walled cemetery. While burial B1267 is not closely dated from internal evidence, it doubtless belongs to the 4th-century expansion of the cemetery when burial spread south-westwards beyond redundant boundary Ditch B.

One of the most interesting aspects of the tombstone is that the carving in the pediment has been deliberately defaced: a chisel had been used to score across the face, crab claws and tendril ends of the representation of Oceanus. Otherwise the tombstone was untouched. The care with which the defacement was effected surely indicates that this was a deliberate act, and Henig (Section 4.1) identifies this as an act of 4th-century Christian iconoclasm. While this is a highly plausible interpretation, we must be aware that motivations behind the defacement or dismemberment of sculpture were complex, and not always necessarily to have been a product of religious hatred (Croxford 2003). Evidence for iconoclasm in Britain is very limited (with the exception of Mithraism), and stands in marked contrast to some other parts of the Empire such as Gaul and Germany (Sauer 2003, 60). At the rural sanctuary of Mercury at Uley, Gloucestershire, the cult statue had been dismembered, but with care and the severed head purposefully placed within a pit (Woodward and Leach 1993, 71–4). The motivations here seem not to have been a Christian fanaticism to destroy pagan idols per se, but something more subtle and not necessarily associated with Christianity. At Chester the human faces on a number of tombstones had been deliberately disfigured and were reused in a reconstruction of the fortress wall, which may date either to the late Roman or medieval period (LeQuesne 1999, 120–1). These images are not of course religious, and Clay (2004) suggests that their mutilation may have been a consequence of the disgrace of the Legio XX Valeria Victrix after its involvement in the usurpation of Carausius (although if the later dating for the rebuilding of the city wall is accepted, it is possible that the defacement in fact occurred in the medieval period). So there could be other motives for disfigurement. Sauer considers that the lack of evidence for religiously inspired iconoclasm in Britain shows that the transition from paganism to Christianity was much less of a cultural revolution here than in some other provinces. This is also shown by the continued prosperity of pagan rural cult centres such as Uley and Lydney well into the 4th century (Woodward and Leach 1993, 310–18; Wheeler and Wheeler 1932; Casey and Hoffmann 1999). He only identified a single likely case of (non-Mithraic) iconoclasm from Britain, although for what it is worth that was from the Cotswolds. Lower Slaughter was an extensive rural settlement 24km north-east of Cirencester (Timby 1998, 384–9) which presumably contained a shrine, although the precise site of this is not known. A 4th-century well yielded a collection of uninscribed altars, votive slabs dedicated to Mars, a Celtic triad and the *genii cuculatti*, and small sculptures of two seated deities (probably Minerva) which had been deliberately beheaded prior to deposition (O'Neil and Toynbee 1958; Henig 1993, nos 76, 86–7, 95, 98,

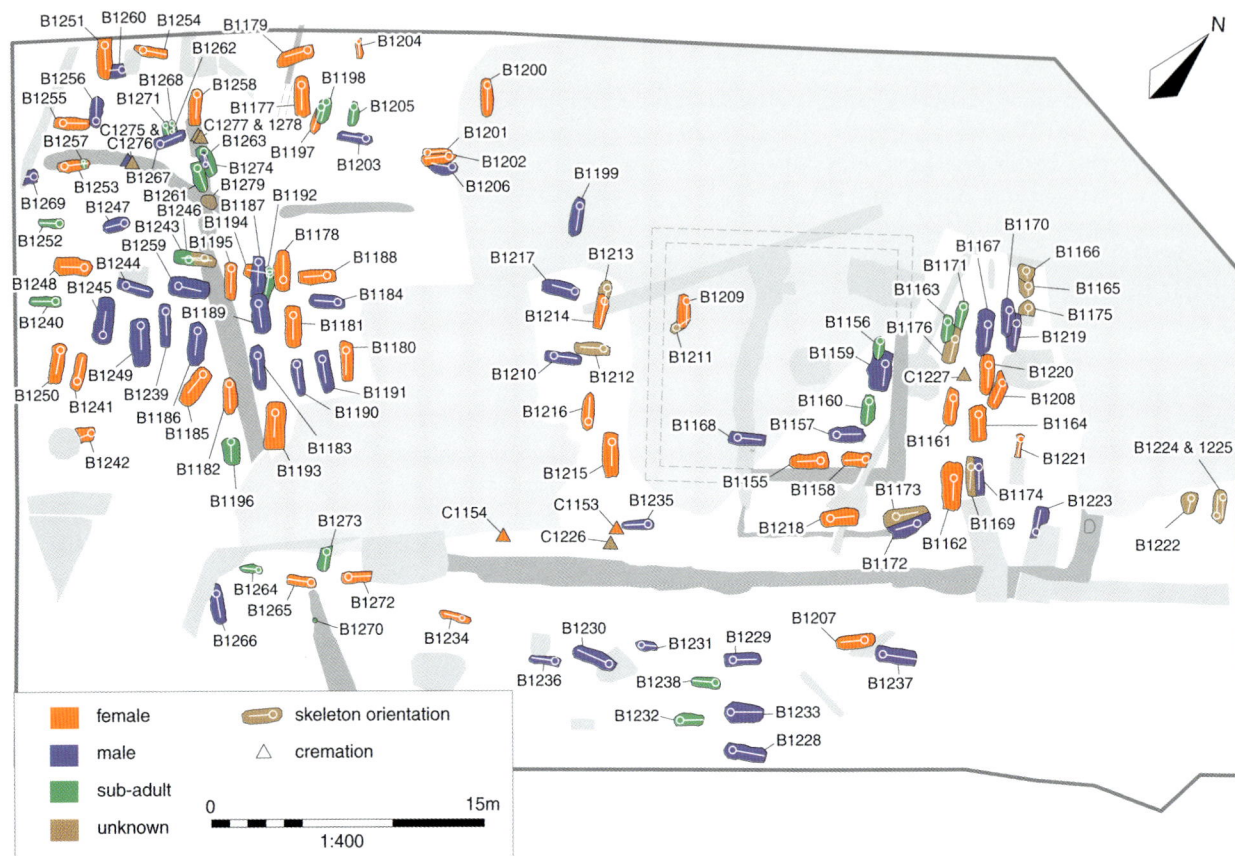

Fig. 7.1   Distribution of burials by sex

131). Sauer (2003, 60) considers that the 4th-century context for the deposition of the headless sculptures points 'with a high degree of probability to a Christian image raid in this particular instance'.

Elsewhere it is hard to be prescriptive that decapitated images were the product of deliberate rather than accidental damage. For instance there is a representation of a *mater* and three *genii* recovered from Stratton, just outside Cirencester (Henig 1998). The stone is broken, with the heads missing, but whether this was the consequence of a deliberate act is nigh on impossible to determine.

Unequivocal evidence for Christianity in the Cotswolds, like much of Roman Britain, is in short supply (Petts 2016; Boon 1992 provides a summary of the evidence for the West Country). If Cirencester was the capital of *Britannia Prima*, and that is by no means assured, then it would likely have been the seat of a bishop, and it was perhaps he who was absent from a church council at Arles in AD 314 and was instead represented by a priest and a deacon (Mann 1961; Birley 2005, 397–8). But this is supposition. More tangibly there is the famous inscription from Cirencester that records the restoration of a statue and column dedicated to Jupiter by the *rector* (presumably governor)

of the province of *Britannia Prima* (RIB 103). The interpretation and dating of this inscription has been much debated (Birley 2005, 426–7), but the reference 'erected under the ancient religion' presumably means that the 'new religion' (i.e. Christianity) had some traction in the area, at least for certain periods of the 4th century. At Chedworth villa, 10km from Cirencester, three slabs surrounding a nymphaeum were adorned with Christian chi-rho monograms, but these slabs were themselves reused in a later construction, so presumably their Christian connotations were not subsequently considered significant (Esmonde Cleary 2013, 97–101).

What significance should we attach to the burial of a purposely defaced epitaph in a 4th-century grave? The grave itself is unremarkable, although it was dug somewhat off alignment compared to the prevailing orientation of the cemetery and the man had been placed in the grave with his arms behind his back and pelvis, an unusual arrangement. The grave also cut through three sequential young child, infant and neonate burials (B1271 was cut by B1268 which was in turn cut by B1262), an unusual concentration of child burials. Might the locality have had a significance that influenced the decision to bury this individual here, and place the defaced tombstone on top of his wooden coffin? The

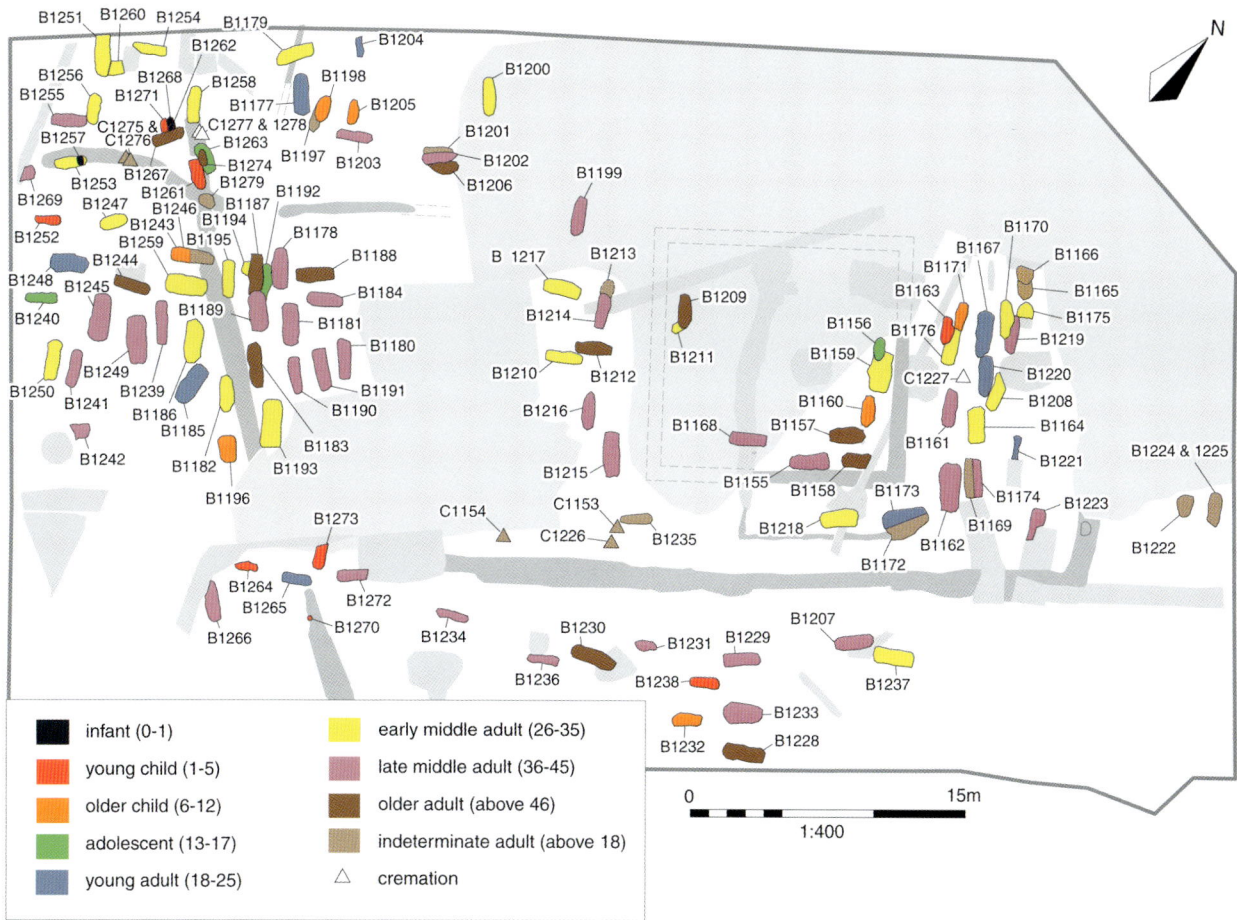

Fig. 7.2   Distribution of burials by age

reuse of earlier tombstones in later burials is reasonably well attested in the western provinces of the Roman empire, including examples of pagan tombstones reused as sarcophagus lids or parts of cist graves in 5th-century Christian graves at Sion, Switzerland (Carroll 2006, 84–5). In Britain the three cist graves from Brougham and a grave from London which incorporated broken-up tombstones have already been mentioned, but the covering of a body with a monolithic slab, whether inscribed or not, cannot be readily paralleled. Adcock (2015, 5) suggested that it might have a Christian significance, intended to recall the great stone which sealed the tomb of Christ which was miraculously rolled away at the Resurrection to reveal the missing body. The use of a monolithic stone is unusual, although it could be associated with the better attested practice where a body or coffin was covered with a number of flat slabs or a pile of stones (Philpott's 1991, 63–4, Type 5 cist graves). Perhaps it was thought that these stones would prevent the body or spirit leaving the grave, and it may be significant that in the Eastern Cemetery at London the trait was associated with two deviant burials: a prone burial had two large rubble blocks placed on its back (B459) and a decapitated chalk burial had

ragstone boulders piled up on top of the coffin (B733; Barber and Bowsher 2000, 87, 99). At the most prosaic level, the slab covering could be regarded as merely an extension of the tradition of stone-packing which is well represented on this site, and capped stone cist graves that have been found on a number of sites in the Cotswold region, most recently at Bourton-on-the-Water (Hart *et al.* 2016). In conclusion, if the defaced tombstone of Bodicacia is an example of Christian iconoclasm, and it is plausible that it was, it is a remarkably rare occurrence in Roman Britain. Certainly the highly unusual burial rite adopted for B1267 most likely requires an equally rare motivation amongst his survivors. While this could be an example of a Christian grave, it would be unwise to rule out other potential causes for the defacement and deposition of the tombstone.

7.4 Grave Goods

Nine burials contained grave goods which included bracelets/armlets (Fig. 7.3), six had strings of beads of jet or glass, six contained bronze coinage, three were accompanied by glass vessels and three by pottery vessels (or four if the fineware beaker found with Reece's (1962,

Fig. 7.3　Distribution of grave goods (other than footwear)

59) BK3 is included) (Tables 4.1–4.3). Only three of the early inhumation burials (B1160, B1163 and B1164) contained grave goods (two pottery vessels, an iron key and the figurine of the cockerel) while burials furnished with jewellery and glass vessels all date to the later Roman period, and in the case of B1177, B1185, B1218, B1263, B1265, B1266 and B1273 no earlier than the mid 4th century to judge from the stylistic attributes of the grave goods. Not all of the jewellery found in a grave was worn on the body, although post-depositional movement can complicate the picture. Some items were placed at the foot of the grave (B1171.1–2); near the legs (B1263.1–2; B1171.4); above the shoulder (B1173.1) and near the hand, perhaps contained within a bag (B1177.1–6). At Lankhills it was commoner for personal ornaments placed in graves not to be worn, and detailed analysis been undertaken to seek patterns determined by the age of the individual (Booth *et al.* 2010, 295–303, 496). The pottery vessel accompanying B1266 was placed at the foot of the grave cut, outside the coffin, a tradition also apparent at Lankhills, and as mentioned above in five instances nailed footwear had been placed in the grave but not worn.

The emphasis on the burial of grave goods with females is marked, although the number of furnished graves is too small for any detailed statistical analysis by age. At Lankhills (Clarke excavations) Gowland (2001) observed that over half of all grave goods buried with women were found with those in their late teens or early 20s, an observation that still holds good when applied to the more recent Oxford Archaeology excavations (Cool 2010, 301–3). While the level of disturbance and comparatively small burial population at the present site hinders the reliability of statistics analysing the prevalence of grave goods, some broad conclusions are possible. For these purposes the burial population is taken as 120 inhumations, 118 from this site plus the two examples from the former Cattle Market (the circumstances of discovery of the nine inhumations from Oakley Cottage were too ill-known for reliability to attach to the presence or absence of grave goods). At a basic level it is apparent that grave goods were more prevalent in the Western Cemetery than the Bath Gate Cemetery (Table 7.1). In the Western Cemetery 7.5% (9/120) of inhumation burials contained bracelets, compared to only 0.7% (3/450) at the Bath Gate. The corresponding statistics for glass vessels are 2.5% (3/120) in the Western Cemetery and 0.4% (2/450) at the Bath Gate. The greater level of wealth displayed by the burials in the Western Cemetery compared to those at the Bath Gate is therefore evident and the use of the cemetery alongside Tetbury Road by higher

Fig. 7.4   Distribution of graves containing iron hobnails from nailed footwear

status groups evidently persisted from the 2nd century through to the middle of the 4th century.

Animal remains from graves

No complete animals were placed in graves as part of the burial ritual, although animal bones were recovered from 50 inhumation graves (Table 6.2). When only a small number of animal bones are present it is difficult to differentiate between deliberate placements for food, and chance casual inclusions within the grave backfill. In no case during excavation was a joint of meat laid next to a body identified, and there is a good chance that the presence of most cattle, caprovine, pig and horse bones in graves is simply incidental. More confidence for deliberate deposition attaches to the bird bones recovered from ten graves, of which fowl could be identified in six cases. In two graves (B1165 and B1171) a minimum of two birds were represented; in all other cases there was a minimum of only one bird. Amongst the fowl the most common skeletal elements represented were limb bones which derive from the meat-rich portion of the carcass, and so this is conceivably an example of deliberate selection (Table 6.3). Support for the deliberate deposition of these fowl joints is provided by an examination of their spatial distribution, which demonstrates that the graves cluster around the walled cemetery (Fig. 7.5). One burial within the walled cemetery (B1160) produced a single fowl bone, while the two burials that produced the most bones lay to the north-east of the walled cemetery. The bone from B1160 dates to the 2nd century on the basis of a grave good associated with that burial, although the practice evidently continued until at least the late 3rd century given the date of the artefacts accompanying B1171. No obvious correlation between the presence of fowl bones and the age or sex of the burial is apparent, with both children and adults represented. As discussed above (Section 6.1) the presence of fowl bones in Roman graves is a well attested occurrence and occasions no surprise (Lauwerier 1993). At the Bath Gate Cemetery it was also the case that no deliberate placements of meat joints were detected, with the exception of a pot containing a carcass of a chicken placed within a stone coffin (CE II, 129, burial 719). At Lankills seven graves contained the remains of fowl, but the birds were mostly complete so a somewhat different tradition is represented there (Booth *et al.* 2010, 430–1).

7.5 Demography

The demographic profile of the Western Cemetery shows an even sex ratio amongst the adults, with children

Fig. 7.5   Distribution of graves containing fowl bones and of prone and decapitated burials

poorly represented (Table 5.11). This occasions little surprise, and is the pattern found in many Romano-British cemeteries (Pearce 2001; 2015, fig. 12). The special character of a couple of the sub-adult burials has already been remarked upon and the majority of individuals who died during childhood must have been disposed of in a way which leaves little archaeological trace. The spatial distribution of burials by age and sex shows the normal mixed distribution, with no evidence for obvious segregation (Figs 7.1–7.2). Geber has identified some notable pathologies from his osteological analyses, such as an adult of unknown sex (B1166) who is likely to have suffered from psoriatic arthritis which would have considerably reduced the quality of life for this individual. Another four individuals displayed skeletal lesions which suggest scurvy. The pattern of dental health visible in the burial population is comparable with that found in other Romano-British urban cemeteries. Fractured bones were identified in 19 individuals, which include 13 adult males, 1 adolescent male and 5 adult females (Table 5.18). One late middle adult male (B1157) had multiple healed fractures and one late middle aged female (B1214) a so-called 'clay-shoveler's fracture' of the fourth thoracic vertebra which likely indicates that this woman had been involved in

heavy and straining labour. Her body was accompanied in the grave by a copper-alloy bracelet. B1244, an older adult male, displayed a possible fracture across the right nasal bone, which might indicate interpersonal violence, but poor bone preservation precludes a confident diagnosis. One late middle aged adult female (B1155) had a well-healed fracture of the right ulna, a so-called 'parry fracture'. While this type of fracture can result from interpersonal violence, where the arm attempts to shield the face against an aggressor, other causes are possible.

7.6 Status, Social Identity and Community

As is apparent from the preceding sections the Western Cemetery was used as an area for wealthy burial from early in its life, if indeed not from the outset. We can say relatively little about the cremation cemetery adjacent to Tetbury Road given the high degree of disturbance here, other than to note the lack of obvious signs of status amongst the surviving interments. The burials were placed in utilitarian vessels and were not otherwise accompanied by grave goods. No richly furnished cremation burials of the kind found in the south-eastern parts of Britain in the 1st century AD have been found, although status is evidenced elsewhere in the Western

Cemetery by the furnished cremation burial B1060 and the use of hollowed-out stone block receptacles.

It is suggested that Ditches A and D may have served to separate the dense zone of cremation burials from the walled cemetery and its environs which was probably reserved for burial by a special group, perhaps a leading family of the early town, or else the members of a corporate sect or guild? This group adopted inhumation rather than cremation as their dominant burial ritual and the presence of grave goods with some burials marks their status, as does the use of a lead cremation vessel. This group also indulged in distinct burial rituals involving wine, most likely the pouring of it into a grave as a libation, and the burning of substances in tazze. It is reasonable to associate the tombstone dedicated to Bodicacia, and the fragmentary one found by Reece (RIB III, 3065) to this wealthy social group, and conceivably both stones came from a monument within the walled cemetery.

Burial is presumed to have occurred more or less continuously in the Western Cemetery into the late Roman period, although status display only becomes apparent again in the 4th century when a tradition of placing personal ornaments in certain graves once again allows us greater insights, and in particular permits comparison with the Bath Gate Cemetery. In the preceding sections various aspects of the Western Cemetery have been compared and contrasted with that outside the Bath Gate. In some aspects the two cemeteries show considerable differences. Traits which are more prevalent in the Western Cemetery include the much greater proportion of burials in wooden coffins; use of stone packing in graves; presence of nailed footwear with bodies, and the deposition of vessels, coins and jewellery as grave goods. Conversely there are some traits in which the two cemeteries show general similarities, most notably the position that bodies were placed in the grave; the proportion of prone and decapitated burials, and a similar level of bone fractures. The demographic composition of the burial populations also seems to have differed, for Wells reported that males were more than twice as common at the Bath Gate compared to women (245 males, 100 females, 62 juveniles), whereas there was a much greater equivalence between the sexes in the Western Cemetery (Table 5.11). Caution is required here, however, as Wells was working over 40 years ago and methodological advances since then have in some cases served to at least partly ameliorate formerly reported male skewing in cemetery populations (Pearce 2015, 155). Nevertheless a male imbalance in certain cemetery populations does appear to be a real phenomenon, and the sex balance at the Western Cemetery might be another marker of the higher status of this population. In a number of different respects, therefore, the people buried in the Western Cemetery look to have been wealthier and of higher status compared to those interred at the Bath Gate. This

differentiation is not absolute, however, if stone coffins are considered a mark of status. Four or five stone coffins are recorded from the Western Cemetery, including one discovered in 1933 which was retrieved from within the bounds of the present site. This compares with six stone coffins from the Bath Gate Cemetery, which suggests that the cemetery was not solely reserved for the urban poor. Variation in the proportion of burials furnished with grave goods of different types in different cemeteries around a single town need not surprise us (it is also the case at Winchester, for example), although Pearce warns against studies that focus solely on grave goods to the exclusion of other types of evidence for burial ritual and the lived experience of the burial population. That said, Lankhills stands out at Winchester as a cemetery that demonstrates greater evidence for burial display and the assertion of status than the other sites investigated (Pearce 2013, 75–7).

Looking beyond Cirencester the Western Cemetery is comparable with a number of other Romano-British urban cemeteries where markers of wealth are apparent (Table 7.1), although within this overall picture individual cemeteries display different trends which must relate to local traditions. As has already been mentioned, the prevalence of nailed footwear at the Western Cemetery and Lankhills stands in contrast to the other major urban cemeteries. Jewellery is comparatively well represented in the Western Cemetery and in broadly similar proportions at Butt Road, Colchester (Period 1), East London and Lankhills. The incidence of glass and pottery vessels is scarce at the present site in comparison to some other cemeteries, although this scarcity also seems to have been the case in Gloucester and so might be a western tradition. The absence of brooches and belt sets seems to be broadly the norm across all the cemeteries with the exception of Lankhills which has an exceptional showing of these two finds categories, an observation that has fuelled the argument that the burial population there contained an element of late Roman officialdom (although the issue is complex; cf. the discussion in Booth *et al.* 2010, 509–16). Overall therefore the Western Cemetery is broadly comparable in terms of its grave goods and other traditions with a number of other 'wealthy' Romano-British urban cemeteries.

That there was private wealth in late Roman Cirencester is of course well known, best exemplified by the high representation of 4th-century mosaics from both the town and surrounding villas. It is therefore no surprise that the population also sought to assert their status through burial rituals which would have been recognisable to comparable groups in a number of other major towns in southern Britain. Interestingly the late Roman population chose to do this in a cemetery where wealthy townspeople had been buried for two centuries. There was therefore a strong continuity in status here, something not represented at the Bath Gate Cemetery where burial did not commence until the early 4th century on an area formerly used for the disposal of rubbish. For a person of substance, the Western Cemetery was always a good place to end up.

7.7 Public Archaeology Outcomes

Unusual discoveries made during commercial archaeological investigations in advance of developments have an enduring public fascination, due no doubt to the perception that such finds might have been destroyed without record if prior investigation had not occurred. When an exciting find of this type turns up on site it can pose issues to the investigating organisation and their clients concerning how best to present the findings to the public and the media, and how to handle the flurry of interest that can ensue. For entirely understandable reasons many clients prefer a low-key approach, but this does mean that the unique moment of discovery, which has such powerful popular resonance, is lost. At this excavation circumstances combined to allow the

discovery of an inscribed tombstone to be captured by the media and this generated massive interest in a way that simply would not have been possible if the find was just 'reported' weeks or months later.

When the tombstone first became visible in the excavation, only its rough, unworked, rear face was exposed (Fig. 2.5). Interpretations considered at the time were that this was merely a stone block in the backfill of a ditch, or conceivably the monolithic lid of a stone coffin. Investigation around the stone revealed that there was no coffin beneath it, and also began to expose the triangular shape of the pediment, with curious tooth-like indentations (these were in fact the rear side of the cresting along the pediment; Fig. 3.123). When a human skull was also revealed the excavation team realised that this was potentially a gabled tombstone collapsed face down over a burial. Only 15 inscribed tombstones are recorded from Cirencester, the last one found in 1973. Cotswold Archaeology thought that the potential discovery of the first inscribed tombstone in the town for 40 years could be newsworthy and so agreed

Fig. 7.6   Live coverage by BBC reporters of the discovery of the Bodicacia tombstone

with its clients St James's Place Wealth Management that the media should be invited to be present when the stone was turned over. Of course there was a risk that the stone would prove to have no inscription at all, but the media were happy to take a chance on that. We therefore decided to leave the investigation of this grave to almost the very end of the excavation, and pre-planned the moment when the stone would be turned over with the BBC and the Corinium Museum. We agreed with BBC Radio Gloucestershire to reveal the stone live on air during their breakfast programme at 8.15 in the morning on 25 February 2015, while BBC Points West were on hand to film the event for the regional early evening news (Fig. 7.6). We invited Richard Reece, the original investigator of the cemetery, to be present, both as a nice touch and also hopefully to assist in reading the inscription. Our expectations were surpassed. The inscription was remarkably clear and could be read, and the sculpted pediment depicting Oceanus had a highly visual appeal (Fig. 7.7). After a few moments of sponging down the whole stone was revealed (Fig. 7.8).

The live radio broadcast created genuine excitement thanks to the enthralling commentary from reporter David Smith; it was one of the most popular news stories on BBC Radio Gloucestershire in 2015. We also did live reporting via Facebook and Twitter which captured the real time excitement of what it is like to uncover a great archaeological find. The social media presentation was remarkably successful: the overall reach of the story on Facebook and Twitter was 29,462 with 6,724 individuals actively engaging with it via click throughs, likes and shares. We had an astonishing 38,000 visits to our website from all over the world in the two days following its discovery, with communications received from as far away as Australia and the USA.

The presentation had a number of positive outcomes. Public service broadcasting by regional BBC outlets brought home how the heritage of a local place can have international appeal. The message was also conveyed in an accessible, enjoyable fashion, but with strong academic underpinning, and neat interplay with professional broadcasters allowed archaeologists to express their evolving thoughts and ideas in the hours and days after the discovery. The immediate interest generated then resulted in the story being picked up by magazines such as *National Geographic* and *Current Archaeology*, and it was on the cover of the 2015 edition of *Britannia*, the leading academic journal of Romano-British studies. While the Bodicacia tombstone is undoubtedly a remarkable discovery, the strong lesson from the events of 25 February 2015 is that it is often not so much what you find, but how you present it.

Fig. 7.7   The first glimpse of the face of the Bodicacia tombstone as the slab was turned over

Fig. 7.8   Initial cleaning of the Bodicacia tombstone moments after the slab was turned over. The inscription was remarkably clear and could be easily read

The enamelled bronze figurine of the cockerel discovered in the grave of a 2 to 3-year-old child (B1163) also proved to have a continuing newsworthiness. In 2015 the figurine featured in a temporary exhibition at the Corinium Museum entitled *Food for Thought* and the Museum commissioned Dan Simpson to compose a poem inspired by the find, which can be found at the start of this volume. Dan can also be heard reading his poem, *Corinium Cockerel*, on the museum website at https://coriniummuseum.org/corinium-poetry/.

References

Adams, A.E. and MacKenzie, W.E. 1998 *A Colour Atlas of Carbonate Sediments and Rocks under the Microscope* London, Manson

Adcock, K. 2015 'From the Isles of the Blessed to the Empty Tomb – the newly discovered Roman tombstone from Cirencester', *ARA News* **33** (March 2015), 4–8

Allason-Jones, L. 1996 *Roman Jet in the Yorkshire Museum* York, Yorkshire Museum

Allason-Jones, L. 2011 'Jet, shale and other allied materials', *Roman Finds Group Datasheet* **2**

Allason-Jones, L. and Miket, R. 1984 *Catalogue of Small Finds from South Shields Roman Fort* Soc. Antiq. Newcastle upon Tyne Monogr. Ser. **2**, Newcastle upon Tyne

Amherd-Hoekstra, A., Näher, H., Lorenz, H.-M. and Enk, A.H. 2010 'Psoriatic arthritis: A review', *J. Dtsch. Dermatol. Ges.* **8**, 332–9

Anderson, S. 1997 *Human Skeletal Remains from Long Melford (LMD 115)* Unpublished report for Suffolk County Council Archaeology Service, http://www.spoilheap.co.uk/pdfs/LMD115SK.pdf

Anekar, J. 2011 'Diet and oral health', *J. Dent. Sci. Res.* **2**(1), 175–82

Arcini, C. 1999 *Health and Disease in Early Lund: Osteopathologic Studies of 3,305 Individuals Buried in the Cemetery Area of Lund 990–1536* Lund, Lund University

Arcini, C., Ahlström, T. and Tagesson, G. 2012 'Variations in diet and stature: Are they linked? Bioarchaeology and paleodietary Bayesian mixing models from Linköping, Sweden', *Int. J. Osteoarchaeol.* **24**, 543–6

Arkell, W.J. 1970 *The Jurassic System in Great Britain* 2nd edition Oxford, Clarendon Press

Aufderheide, A.C. and Rodríguez-Martín, C. 1998 *The Cambridge Encyclopedia of Human Paleopathology* Cam-bridge, Cambridge University Press

Baratte, F., Painter, K. and Leyge, K. 1989 *Trésors d'orfèvrerie Gallo-Romains* Paris

Barber, B. and Bowsher, D. 2000 *The Eastern Cemetery of Roman London: Excavations 1993–90* MoLAS Monograph **4**, London, Museum of London Archaeology Service

Barrett, A.A. 1991 'Claudius' British victory arch in Rome', *Britannia* **22**, 1–19

Bauchhenss, G. 1979 *Corpus Signorum Imperii Romani. Deutschland III.2 Germania Inferior. Bonn und Umgebung. Zivile Grabdenkmäler* Bonn, Habelt

Bayley, J. 1998 'Spoon and vessel moulds from Castleford, Yorkshire', in S.T.A.M Mols (ed.) 'Ancient Bronzes. Acta of the 12th international congress on ancient bronzes, Nijmegen 1992', *Nederlandse Archaeologische Rapporten* **18**, 105–11

BGS (British Geological Survey) 2011 Geology of Britain Viewer http://maps.bgs.ac.uk/geologyviewer_google/googleviewer.html

Biddulph, E. 2006 'The Roman pottery from Pepper Hill, Southfleet, Kent', CTRL Specialist Report series, Channel Tunnel Rail Link Section 1 [data set]. York: Archaeology Data Service [distributor] (doi: 10.5284/1000230)

Biddulph, E. and Walsh, K. 2011 *Cirencester before Corinium. Excavations at Kingshill North, Cirencester, Gloucestershire* Thames Valley Landscapes **34**, Oxford, Oxford Archaeology

Binford, L.R. 1963 'An analysis of cremations from three Michigan sites', *Wisconsin Archeologist* **44**, 98–110

Birley, A.R. 2005 *The Roman Government of Britain* Oxford, Oxford University Press

Bishop, M.C. 1983 'The Camomile Street solider reconsidered', *Trans. London Middlesex Archaeol. Soc.* **34**, 31–48

Black, E.W. 1986 'Romano-British burial customs and religious beliefs in south-east England', *Archaeol. J.* **143**, 201–39

Blagg, T.F.C. 1983 'The reuse of monumental masonry in late Roman defensive walls', in J. Maloney and B. Hobley (eds) *Roman Urban Defences in the West. A Review of Current Research on Urban Defences in the Roman Empire with Special Reference to the Northern Provinces* Council British Archaeology Research Report **51**, London, 130–5

Blagg, T.F.C. 1993 'Architectural carvings', in Henig 1993, 63–77

Blagg, T.F.C. 2002 *Roman Architectural Ornament in Britain* Brit. Archaeol. Rep. Brit. Ser. **329**, Oxford

Bloemers, J.H.F. 1977 'Archeologische kroniek van Limburg over de jaren 1975–1976', *Pub. Societé Historique Archéologique Limbourg* **113**, 7–33

Boon, G.C. 1992 'Traces of Romano-British christianity in the west country', *Trans. Bristol Gloucestershire Archaeol. Soc.* **110**, 37–52

Booth, P. 2009 'Roman Britain in 2008. 8. South-Western counties', *Britannia* **40**, 266–71

Booth, P., Simmons, A., Boyle, A., Clough, S., Cool, H.E.M. and Poore, D. 2010 *The late Roman cemetery at Lankhills: Excavations 2000–2005* Oxford, Oxford Archaeology

Brailsford, J.W. 1958 *Guide to the Antiquities of Roman Britain* London, Trustees of the British Museum

Bräuer, G. 1988 'Osteometrie', in Knußman 1988, 160–232

Breeze, D.J. (ed.) 2012 *The First Souvenirs: Enamelled Vessels from Hadrian's Wall* Cumberland and Westmorland Antiquarian and Archaeological Society

Brickley, M. and Ives, R. 2008 *The Bioarchaeology of Metabolic Disease* Amsterdam, Academic Press

Brickley, M. and McKinley, J.I. 2004 *Guidelines to the Standards for Recording Human Remains* Institute Field Archaeologists Paper **7**, Reading

Brinch, O. and Møller-Christensen, V. 1949 'On comparative investigations into the occurrence of dental caries in archaeological skulls, with a preliminary report on investigations of caries frequency in medieval times in Denmark (Aebelholt Abbey)', *Odontologisk Tidskrift* **57**, 357–80

Briney, W.G. 2001 'Neck pain and selected cervical syndromes', in H.H. Friedman (ed.) *Problem-orientated medical diagnosis* Philadelphia, Lippingcott, Williams and Wilkins, 318–20

Broadbent, B.H., Broadbent, B.M. and Golden, W.H. 1975 *Bolton Standards of Dentofacial Developmental growth* St Louis, C.V. Mosby

Bron, J.L., von Royen, B. and Wuisman, P.I.J.M. 2007 'The clinical significance of lumbosacral transitional anomalies', *Acta Orthop. Belg.* **73**(6), 687–95

Brooks, S.T. and Suchey, J.M. 1990 'Skeletal age determination based on the os pubis: A comparison of the Ascádi-Nemeskéri and Suchey-Brooks methods', *Hum. Evol.* **5**, 227–38

Brothwell, D.R. 1981 *Digging up Bones: The Excavation, Treatment and Study of Human Skeletal Remains* Ithaca, Cornell University Press

Brothwell, D.R., Powers, R., Hirst, S.M., Wright, S.M. and Gauthier, S. 2000 'The human biology' in Rahtz *et al.* 2000, 131–56

Brown, D. 1976 'Archaeological evidence for the Anglo-Saxon period', in A. McWhirr (ed.) *Archaeology and History of Cirencester* Brit. Archaeol. Rep. Brit. Ser. **30**, Oxford, 19–45

Buikstra, J.E. and Swegle, M. 1989 'Bone modification due to burning: Experimental evidence', in R. Bonnichsen and M. Sorg (eds) *Bone modification* Orono, University of Maine, 247–58

Buikstra, J.E. and Ubelaker, D.H. (eds) 1994 *Standards for Data Collection from Human Skeletal Remains*, Arkansas Archeological Survey Research Series **44**, Fayetteville, Arkansas Archeological Survey

Buxton, L.H.D. 1938 'Platymeria and platycnemia', *J. Anat.* **73**(1), 31–6

CA 2012 *Former Bridges Garage, Old Tetbury Road, Cirencester, Gloucestershire. Post-excavation Assessment and Updated Project Design*, Cotswold Archaeology Rep. **12240**

CA 2014 *The Western Cemetery of Roman Cirencester: Excavations at the former Bridges Garage, Old Tetbury Road, Cirencester, 2011. Draft Publication Report*, Cotswold Archaeology Rep. **14388**

CA 2017 *A 1st-century Funerary Enclosure at Barnwood, Gloucestershire: Excavations in 2013–14*, Cotswold Archaeology Rep. **17263**

Cahn, H.A. 1997 'Oceanus', in *Lexicon Iconographicum Mythologiae Classicae Vol. VIII*, Zurich and Düsseldorf, 907–15, plate vol. 599–607

Cameron, J. 1934 *The Skeleton of British Neolithic Man* London, Williams and Norgate

Campbell, G. 2004 'Charcoal and other charred plant remains', in Cool 2004, 267–71

Carroll, M. 2006 *Spirits of the Dead. Roman Funerary Commemoration in Western Europe* Oxford, Oxford University Press

Casey, P.J. and Hoffmann, B., 1999 'Excavations at the Roman temple in Lydney Park, Gloucestershire in 1980 and 1981', *Antiq. J.* **79**, 81–143

CE II: McWhirr, A., Viner, L. and Wells, C. 1982: *Romano-British Cemeteries at Cirencester* Cirencester Excavations **2**, Cirencester, Cirencester Excavation Committee

CE V: Holbrook, N. (ed.) 1998 *Cirencester: The Roman Town Defences, Public Buildings and Shops*, Cirencester Excavations **5**, Cirencester, Cotswold Archaeological Trust

CE VI: Holbrook, N. (ed.) 2008 *Excavations and Observations in Roman Cirencester 1998–2007 with a Review of Archaeology in Cirencester 1958–2008*, Cirencester Excavations **6**, Cirencester, Cotswold Archaeology

Challinor, D. 2009 'Wood charcoal', in K. Powell, G. Laws and L. Brown, 'A late Neolithic/early Bronze Age enclosure and Iron Age and Romano-British settlement at Latton Lands, Wiltshire', *Wiltshire Archaeol. Natur. Hist. Mag.* **102**, 97–8

Challinor, D. 2010 'Chapter 14: Charcoal', in A. Smith, K. Powell and P. Booth (eds) *Evolution of a Farming Community in the Upper Thames Valley. Excavation of a Prehistoric, Roman and Post-Roman Landscape at Cotswold Community, Gloucestershire and Wiltshire. Volume 2: The Finds and Environmental Reports* Oxford, Oxford Archaeology, 195–202

Church, A.H. 1922 *A Guide to the Museum of Roman Remains at Cirencester* 11th edition, Cirencester

Clarke, G. 1979 *Pre-Roman and Roman Winchester Part II: The Roman Cemetery at Lankhills* Winchester Studies **3**, Oxford

Clarke, N. 1993 'Periodontitis in dry skulls', *Dent. Anthropol. Newsl.* **7**(2), 1–4

Clay, C. 2004 'Iconoclasm in Roman Chester: the significance of the mutilated tombstones from the North Wall', *J. British Archaeol. Assoc.* **157.1**, 1–16

Clough, S. and Boyle, A. 2010 'Human remains' in Booth *et al.* 2010, 339–428

Cobain S. 2016 'Plant macrofossils and charcoal', in J. Hart, A. Mudd, E.R. McSloy and M. Brett, *Living Near the Edge. Archaeological Investigations in the Western Cotswolds along the Route of the Wormington to Sapperton Gas Pipeline, 2006–2010* Cotswold Archaeology Monograph **9**, Cirencester, 144–55

Cohen, A. and Serjeantson, D. 1996 *A Manual for the Identification of Bird Bones from Archaeological Sites* London, Archetype Press

Cool, H.E.M. 2004 *The Roman Cemetery at Brougham, Cumbria. Excavations 1966–67* London, English Heritage and Society for the Promotion of Roman Studies

Cool, H.E.M. 2006 *Eating and Drinking in Roman Britain* Cambridge, Cambridge University Press

Cool, H.E.M. 2010 'Objects of glass, shale, bone and metal', in Booth *et al.* 2010, 267–309

Cool, H.E.M. and Price, J. 1995 *Roman Vessel Glass from Excavations in Colchester, 1971–85* Colchester Archaeological Report **8**, Colchester, Colchester Archaeological Trust

Coombe, P.C., Grew, F., Hayward, K.M.J. and Henig, M. 2015 *Corpus Signorum Imperii Romani. Great Britain 1.10 Roman Sculpture from London and the South-East* Oxford, Oxford University Press

Cosh, S.R. and Neal, D.S. 2010 *Roman Mosaics of Britain IV Western Britain* London, Society of Antiquaries of London

Coulston, J.C. and Phillips. E.J. 1988 *Corpus Signorum Imperii Romani. Great Britain 1.6 Hadrian's Wall West of the North Tyne and Carlisle* London, British Academy

Croxford, B. 2003 'Iconoclasm in Roman Britain', *Britannia* **34**, 81–95

Crummy, N., 1983 *The Roman Small Finds from Excavations in Colchester 1971–9* Colchester Archaeological Report **2**, Colchester, Colchester Archaeological Trust Ltd

Crummy, N. 2006 'Worshipping Mercury on Balkerne Hill, Colchester', in P. Ottaway (ed.) *A Victory Celebration: Papers on the Archaeology of Colchester and Late Iron Age-Roman Britain Presented to Philip Crummy* Colchester, Colchester Archaeological Trust, 55–68

Crummy, N. 2007 'Brooches and the cult of Mercury', *Britannia* **38**, 225–30

Crummy, P. 1993 'The cemeteries of Roman Colchester', in N. Crummy, P. Crummy and C. Crossan, *Excavations of Roman and Later Cemeteries, Churches and Monastic Buildings in Colchester, 1971–88* Colchester Archaeological Report **9** Colchester, Colchester Archaeological Trust, 257–75

Cunliffe, B. 1969 *Roman Bath* Rep. Res. Comm. Soc. Antiqs. London **24**, London

Cunliffe, B. and Davenport, P. 1985 *The Temple of Sulis Minerva at Bath (Vol. 1 the Site)* Oxford University Comm. Archaeol. Mon. **7**, Oxford

Davies, B., Richardson, B. and Tomber, R. 1994 *A Dated Corpus of Early Roman Pottery from the City of London* Council British Archaeol. Res. Rep. **98** York, Council for British Archaeology

Davies, G., Gardner, A. and Lockyear, K. (eds) 2001 *Proceedings of the 10th Theoretical Roman Archaeology Conference* Oxford, Oxbow

Darvill, T. 2014 'Grismond's tower, Cirencester, and the rise of springhead super-mounds in the Cotswolds and beyond', *Trans. Bristol Gloucestershire Archaeol. Soc.* **132**, 11–27

Derks, T. 2015 'Inscripties en graffiti', in Derks and de Fraiture 2015, 148–55

Derks, T. and de Fraiture, B. (eds) 2015 *Ein Romeins heiligdom en een vroegmiddeleeuws grafveld bij Buchten* Amersfoort, Rapportage Archeologische Monumentenzorg **226**

De Schaetzen, P. and Vanderhoeven, M. 1956 'De Romeinse lampen in Tongeren', *Het Oude Land van Loon* **9**, 5–31

Dias, G.J. and Tayles, N. 1997 '"Abscess cavity" – a misnomer', *Int. J. Osteoarchaeol.* **7**(5), 548–54

Dobney, K. 2001 'A place at the table: The role of vertebrate zooarchaeology within a Roman research agenda for Britain', in S. James and M. Millett (eds) *Britons and Romans: Advancing an Archaeological Agenda* Council British Archaeol. Res. Rep. **125**, York, Council for British Archaeology, 36–45

Dunham, R.J. 1962 'Classification of carbonate rocks according to depositional texture', in Ham 1962, 108–21

Ellis, P., Henig, M. and Hayward, K. forthcoming 'The Well's Bridge ash-chest and cremation cylinder', *Trans. Bristol Gloucestershire Archaeol. Soc.*

Ellis, P. and King, R. 2016 'A Romano-British rural cemetery at Well's Bridge, Barnwood: excavations 1998–9', *Trans. Bristol Gloucestershire Archaeol. Soc.* **134**, 113–26

Ertas, Ü. and Tozoglu, S. 2003 'Uncommon peripheral osteoma of the mandible: Report on two cases', *J. Contemp. Dent. Pract.* **4**(3), 98–104

Esmonde Cleary, S. 2013 *Chedworth. Life in a Roman Villa*, Stroud, History Press/National Trust

Esperandieu, E. 1910 *Recueil General des Bas-Reliefs, Statues et Bustes de la Gaule Romaine III* Paris, Imprimerie Nationale

Faccia, K.J. and Williams, R.C. 2008 'Schmorl's nodes: Clinical significance and implications for the bio-archaeological record', *Int. J. Osteoarchaeol.* **18**(1), 28–44

Farwell, D.E. and Molleson, T.I. 1993 *Excavations at Poundbury 1966–80 Volume II: The Cemeteries* Dorset Natur. Hist. Archaeol. Soc. Monogr. **11**, Dorchester, Dorset Natural History and Archaeological Society

Featherstone, J.D.B. 2000 'The science and practice of caries prevention', *J. Am. Dent. Assoc.* **131**(7), 887–99

Feldman, V.B. and Astri, F. 2001 'An atypical clay shoveler's fracture: A case report', *J. Can. Chiropr. Assoc.* **45**(4), 213–20

Ferembach, D., Schwidetzky, I. and Stloukal, M. 1980 'Recommendations for age and sex diagnoses of skeletons', *J. Hum. Evol.* **9**(1), 517–49

Folk, R.L. 1959 'Practical petrographic classification of limestones', *American Association of Petroleum Geologists Bulletin* **43**, 1–38

Folk, R.L. 1962 'Spectral subdivision of limestone types', in Ham 1962, 62–84

Frere, S.S. 1991 'Roman Britain in 1990 I: sites explored', *Britannia* **22**, 222–92

Frere, S.S., Stow, S. and Bennett, P. 1982 *Excavations on the Roman and Medieval Defences of Canterbury* Archaeology of Canterbury **2**, Canterbury, Canterbury Archaeological Trust

Gale, R. 1997 'Charcoal', in A.P. Fitzpatrick, *Archaeological Excavations on the Route of the A27 Westhampnett Bypass, West Sussex, 1992. Volume 2: the Late Iron Age, Romano-British and Anglo-Saxon Cemeteries* Wessex Archaeology Report **12**, Salisbury, Wessex Archaeology, 253

Gale, R. and Cutler, D.F. 2000 *Plants in Archaeology: Identification Manual of Artefacts of Plant Origin from Europe and the Mediterranean* Otley, Westbury and the Royal Botanic Gardens Kew

Gallucci, M., Puglielli, E., Splendiani, A., Pistoia, F. and Spacca, G. 2005 'Degenerative disorders of the spine', *Eur. Radiol.* **15**(3), 591–8

Geber, J. 2007 'Human remains', in J. Timby, R. Brown, A. Hardy, S. Leech, C. Poole and L. Webley, *Settlement on the Bedfordshire Claylands: Archaeology along the A421 Great Barford Bypass* Bedfordshire Archaeology Monograph **8**, Oxford, Oxford Archaeology, 303–27

Geber, J. 2009 'The human remains', in M. McQuade, B. Molloy and C. Moriarty, *In the Shadow of the Galtees: Archaeological Excavations along the N8 Cashel to Mitchelstown Road Scheme* NRA Scheme Monograph **4**, Dublin, National Roads Authority, 209–40

Geber, J. 2016 'Human bone', in Hart *et al.* 2016, 87–9

Geber, J. and Murphy, E. 2012 'Scurvy in the Great Irish Famine: Evidence of vitamin C deficiency from a mid-19th century skeletal population', *Am. J. Phys. Anthropol.* **148**(4), 512–24

Gejvall, N.-G. 1948 'Bestämning av de brända benen från gravarna i Horn', in K.E. Sahlström and N.-G. Gejvall (eds) *Gravfältet på kyrkbacken i Horns socken, Västergötland* Stockholm, Wahlström and Wikstrand, 153–99

Goodman, A. H. and Song, R.-J. 1999 'Sources of variation in estimated ages at formation of linear enamel hypoplasias', in R. Hoppa and C.M. Fitzgerald (eds) *Human Growth in the Past: Studies from Bones and Teeth* Cambridge, Cambridge University Press, 210–40

Gowland, R. 2001 'Playing dead: implications of mortuary evidence for the social construction of childhood in Roman Britain', in Davies *et al.* 2001, 152–68

Greep, S. 1993 'The bone objects', in Farwell and Molleson 1993, 105–10

Guido, M. 1978 *The Glass Beads of the Prehistoric and Roman Periods in Britain and Ireland* Res. Rep. Comm. Soc. Antiqs. London **35**, London

Guido, M. and Mills. J.M. 1993 'Beads', in Farwell and Molleson 1993, 100–2

Hall, J. 1996 'The cemeteries of Roman London', in J. Bird, M. Hassall and H. Sheldon (eds) *Interpreting Roman London: Papers in Memory of Hugh Chapman* London, Oxbow, 57–84

Ham, W.E. (ed.) 1962 *Classification of Carbonate Rocks* American Association of Petroleum Geologists Memoir **1**, Tulsa, American Association of Petroleum Geologists

Hamerow, H., Hollevot, Y. and Vince, A. 1994 'Migration period settlements and 'Anglo-Saxon' pottery from Flanders', *Medieval Archaeol.* **38**, 1–18

Harden, D.B. 1979 'Glass vessels', in Clarke 1979, 209–20

Hart, G.O. 2005 'Fracture pattern interpretation in the skull: Differentiating blunt force from ballistics trauma using concentric fractures', *J. Forensic Sci.* **50**(6), 1276–81

Hart, J., Geber, J. and Holbrook, N. 2016 'Iron Age settlement and a Romano-British cemetery at the Cotswold School, Bourton-on-the-Water. Excavations in 2011', *Trans. Bristol Gloucestershire Archaeol. Soc.* **134**, 77–112

Hayward, K.M.J. 2006 'A geological link between the Facilis monument at Colchester and first-century army tombstones from the Rhineland frontier', *Britannia* **37**, 359–63

Hayward, K.M.J. 2009 *Roman Quarrying and Stone Supply on the Periphery – Southern England. A Geological Study of First-Century Funerary Monuments and Monumental Architecture* Brit. Archaeol. Rep. Brit. Ser. **500**, Oxford

Hayward, K.M.J. in prep 'The worked stone' in Esmonde Cleary, S (ed.) *Chedworth Roman Villa* Britannia Monogr. Ser., London, Society for the Promotion of Roman Studies

Heighway, C.M., 1980 'Roman cemeteries in Gloucester district', *Trans. Bristol Gloucestershire Archaeol. Soc.* **98**, 57–72

Henig, M. 1993 *Corpus Signorum Imperii Romani. Great Britain 1.7 Roman Sculpture from the Cotswold Region, with Devon and Cornwall* Oxford, Oxford University Press

Henig, M. 1998 'A relief of a *mater* and three *genii* from Stratton, Gloucestershire', *Trans. Bristol Gloucestershire Archaeol. Soc.* **116**, 186–9

Henig, M. 2004 *Corpus Signorum Imperii Romani. Great Britain.1.9 Roman Sculpture from the North West Midlands* Oxford, British Academy

Henig, M. 2015 'Oceanus and the British Fleet', *ARA News* **34** (September 2015), 6–7

Herrmann, B. 1980 'Kleine Geschichte der Leichenbrand-untersuchung', *Fornvännen* **75**, 20–9

Herrmann, B. 1988 'Behandlung von Leichenbrand', in Knußman 1988, 576–85

Hiller, J.C., Thompson, T.J.U., Evison, M.P., Chamberlain, A.T. and Wess, T.J. 2003 'Bone mineral change during experimental heating: An X-ray scattering investigation', *Biomaterials* **24**(28), 5091–7

Hillson, S. 1996 *Dental Anthropology* Cambridge, Cambridge University Press

Hillson, S. 2005 *Teeth* Cambridge, Cambridge University Press

Holbrook, N. 2006 'The Roman period', in N. Holbrook and J. Juřica (eds) *Twenty-Five Years of Archaeology in Gloucestershire. A Review of New Discoveries and New Thinking 1979–2004*, Bristol Gloucestershire Archaeol. Rep. **3**, Cirencester, Cotswold Archaeology, 97–131

Holbrook, N. 2008 'The evolution of early Roman Cirencester and the Cotswolds', *J. Roman Archaeol.* **21**, 304–23

Holbrook, N. 2013 'Ambiguous evidence and obscured stratigraphy: Interpreting the archaeology of late and early post-Roman Cirencester, in H. Eckardt and S. Rippon (eds) *Living and Working in the Roman World. Essays in Honour of Michael Fulford*, J. Roman Archaeol. Supp. Ser. **95**, Rhode Island, 31–46

Holbrook, N. and Bidwell, P.T. 1991 *Roman Finds from Exeter* Exeter Archaeol. Rep. **4**, Exeter, Exeter County Council and University of Exeter

Holck, P. 1997 *Cremated bones: A Medical-Anthropological Study of an Archaeological Material on Cremation Burials,* Antropologiske Skrifter **1c** Oslo, University of Oslo

Holland, T.D. 1995 'Brief communication: Estimation of adult stature from the calcaneus and talus', *Am. J. Phys. Anthropol.* **96**(3), 315–20

Holst, M. 2007 *Osteological Analysis: Land North of 25 & 27 Welton Road, Brough, East Yorkshire* Unpublished report for MAP Archaeological Consultancy Ltd. York, York Osteoarchaeology Ltd, http://www.yorkosteoarch.co.uk/pdf/1807.pdf

Hoss, S., Kempkens, J. and Lupak, T. 2015 'Bronzen beeldje van een haan met voetstuk', in Derks and de Fraiture 2015, 159–71

Hummel, S. and Schutkowski, H. 1986 'Neue Ansätze in der Leichenbranduntersuchung', in B. Herrmann (ed.) *Innovative Trends in der prähistorischen Anthropologie* Mitteilung der Gesellschaft für Anthropologie, Ethnologie und Urgeschichte **7**, Rahden, Verlag Marie Leidorf, 141–6

ILS: Dessau, H. (ed.) 1892–1916 *Inscriptiones Latinae Selectae* Berlin, Weidmann

Iregren, E. 2002 *Bildkompendium: Historisk osteologi* Department of Archaeology and Ancient History Report Series **85** Lund, University of Lund

Iregren, E. and Jonsson, R. 1973 'Hur ben krymper vid kremering', *Fornvännen* **68**, 97–100

İşcan, M.Y., Loth, S.R. and Wright, R.K. 1984 'Metamorphosis at the sternal rib end: A new method to estimate age at death in white males', *Am. J. Phys. Anthropol.* **65**(2), 147–56

İşcan, M.Y., Loth, S.R. and Wright, R.K. 1985 'Age estimation from the rib by phase analysis: White females', *J. Forensic Sci.* **30**(3), 853–63

Isidro, A., Castellana, C. and Malgosa, A. 2000 'Massive tarsal ankylosis in a prehistoric skeleton', *Foot Ankle Surg.* **6**(4), 239–47

Isings, C. 1957 *Roman Glass from Dated Finds* Archaeologica Traiectina **2**, Groningen/Djakarta

Jacobsen, R., Møller, H. and Mouritsen, A. 1999 'Natural variation in the human sex ratio', *Hum. Reprod.* **14**(12), 3120–5

Jeffreys, E. 1993 'Congenital malformations and deformities of the cervical spine', in E. Jeffreys (ed.) *Disorders of the Cervical Spine* Oxford, Butterworth-Heinemann, 41–53

Jessup, R.F.J. 1959 'Barrows and walled cemeteries in Roman Britain', *J. Brit. Archaeol. Assoc.* **22**, 1–32

Jope, E.M. 1964 'The Saxon building-stone industry in Southern and Midland England', *Medieval Archaeol.* **8**, 91–118

Judd, M.A. 2008 'The parry problem', *J. Archaeol. Sci.* **35**(6), 1658–66

Kelley, M.A. 1982 'Intervertebral osteochondrosis in ancient and modern populations', *Am. J. Phys. Anthropol.* **59**(3), 271–9

Knußman, R. (ed.) 1988 *Wesen und Methoden der Anthropologie: Wissenschaftstheorie, Geschichte, morphologische Methoden* Stuttgart, Fischer Verlag

Koval, K.J. and Zuckerman, J.D. 2002 *Handbook of Fractures* London, Lippincott Williams and Wilkins

Künzl, E. 2012 'Enamelled vessels of Roman Britain', in Breeze 2012, 9–22

Lantzsch, J. and Schuster, K. 2009 'Socioeconomic status and physical stature in 19th-century Bavaria', *Econ. Hum. Biol.* **7**(1), 46–54

Lauwerier, R.C.G.M. 1983 'A meal for the dead: Animal bone finds in Roman graves', *Paleohistoria* **25**, 184–92

Lauwerier, R.C.G.M. 1993 'Bird remains in Roman graves', *Archaeofauna* **2**, 75–82

Lawson, A.J. 1976 'Shale and jet objects from Silchester', *Archaeologia* **105**, 241–75

Leary, E. 1989 *The Building Limestones of the British Isles* Building Research Establishment Report, London, HMSO

Leech, R. 1981 'The excavation of a Romano-British farmstead and cemetery on Bradley Hill, Somerton, Somerset', *Britannia* **12**, 177–252

LeQuesne, C. 1999 *Excavations at Chester. The Roman and Later Defences, Part 1* Chester Archaeology Excavation and Survey Report **11**, Chester

Lerz, A., Henig, M. and Hayward, K.M.J. 2017 'The Minories eagle: A new sculpture from London's eastern Roman cemetery', *Britannia* **48**

Lewis, J.E. 2008 'Identifying sword marks on bone: Criteria for distinguishing between cut marks made by different classes of bladed weapons', *J. Archaeol. Sci.* **35**(7), 2001–8

Lewis, M.E. and Roberts, C. 1997 'Growing pains: The interpretation of stress indicators', *Int. J. Osteoarchaeol.* **7**(6), 581–6

Liversidge, H.M., Herdeg, B. and Rösing, F.W. 1998 'Dental age estimation of non-adult: A review of methods and principles', in K.W. Alt, F.W. Rösing and M. Teschler-Nicola (eds) *Dental Anthropology, Fundamentals, Limits and Prospects* Vienna, Springer Verlag, 419–42

Lovejoy, C.O., Burstein, A.H. and Heiple, K.G. 1976 'The biomechanical analysis of bone strength: A method and its application to platycnemia', *Am. J. Phys. Anthropol.* **44**(3), 489–505

Lovejoy, C.O., Meindl, R.S., Mensforth, R.P. and Barton, T.J. 1985a 'Multifactorial determination of skeletal age at death: A method and blind test of its accuracy', *Am. J. Phys. Anthropol.* **68**(1), 1–14

Lovejoy, C.O., Meindl, R.S., Pryzbeck, T.R. and Mensforth, R.P. 1985b 'Chronological metamorphosis of the auricular surface of the ilium: A new method for the determination of age at death', *Am. J. Phys. Anthropol.* **68**(1), 15–28

Lovell, N.C. 1997 'Trauma analysis in paleopathology', *Yearb. Phys. Anthropol.* **40**, 139–70

LRBC: Carson, R.A.G., Hill, P.V. and Kent, J.P.C. 1960 *Late Roman Bronze Coinage Part 1*; Carson, R.A.G. and Kent, J.P.C. 1960 *Late Roman Bronze Coinage Part 2* London, Spink and Son

Luff, R.M. 1982 *A Zooarchaeological Study of the Roman North-West Provinces* Brit. Archaeol. Rep. Int. Ser. **S137**, Oxford, Tempus Reparatum

Lukacs, J.R. 2017 'Bioarchaeology of oral health: Sex and gender differences in dental disease', in S.C. Agarwal and J.K. Wesp (eds) *Exploring Sex and Gender in Bioarchaeology* Albuquerque, University of New Mexico Press, 263–90

Lyman, R.L. 1994 *Vertebrate Taphonomy* Cambridge, Cambridge University Press

Lynch, L.G. and O'Donnell, L. 2007 'Cremation in the Bronze Age: practice, process and belief', in E. Grogan, L. O'Donnell and P. Johnston, *The Bronze Age Landscape of the Pipeline to the West: An Integrated Archaeological and Environmental Assessment* Bray, Wordwell, 105–29

Maat, G.J.R. 1990 'Growth changes in bones: A means of assessing health status and the relative position of secular growth shifts in stature', in E. Iregren and R. Liljekvist, *Population of the Nordic Countries: Human Population Biology from the Present to the Mesolithic* Lund, University of Lund, 88–93

Mackinder, A. 2000 *A Romano-British Cemetery on Watling Street*, MoLAS Archaeol. Stud. Ser. **4**, London, Museum of London Archaeology Service

Mackintosh, M. 1986 'The sources of the horseman and fallen enemy motif on tombstones of the Western Roman Empire', *J. Brit. Archaeol. Assoc.* **139**, 1–21

Mairat, J. 2015 'Allectus coin', *Ashmolean Magazine* **69** (Spring 2015)

Mann, J.C. 1961 'The administration of Roman Britain', *Antiquity* **35**, 316–20

Manning, W.H. 1985 *Catalogue of Romano-British Iron Tools, Fittings and Weapons in the British Museum* London, British Museum

Márquez-Grant, N. and Loe, L. 2008 'Unburnt human bone', in A. Simmonds, N. Márquez-Grant and L. Loe, *Life and Death in a Roman City: Excavation of a Roman Cemetery with a Mass Grave at 120–122 London Road, Gloucester* Oxford Archaeology Monograph **6**, Oxford, Oxford Archaeology, 29–72

Matthews, C.L. 1981 'A Romano-British cemetery at Dunstable', *Bedfordshire Archaeol. J.* **15**, 1–73

McKinley, J.I. 1989 'Cremations: Expectations, methodologies and realities', in P. Roberts, F. Lee and J. Bintliff (eds) *Burial Archaeology: Current Research, Methods and Developments* Brit. Archaeol. Rep. Brit. Ser. **211**, Oxford, Archaeopress, 65–76

McKinley, J.I. 1993 'Bone fragment size and weight of bone from modern British cremations and the implications for the interpretation of archaeological cremations', *Int. J. Osteoarchaeol.* **3**(4), 283–7

McKinley, J.I. 1997 'Bronze Age "barrows" and funerary rites and rituals of cremations', *Proc. Prehist. Soc.* **63**, 129–45

McKinley, J.I. 2000 'Funerary practice' in Barber and Bowsher 2000, 60–81

McKinley, J.I. 2004 'Compiling a skeletal inventory: Disarticulated and co-mingled human remains', in M. Brickley and J.I. McKinley (eds) *Guidelines to the Standards for Recording Human Remains*, IfA Papers **7**, Reading, Institute of Field Archaeologists / British Association for Biological Anthropology and Osteoarchaeology, 14–17

McSloy, E.R. forthcoming 'Anglo-Saxon pottery', in A. Hardy, S. Sheldon and J. Schuster, 'Iron Age burial and Anglo-Saxon occupation at All Saints Academy, Cheltenham. Excavations in 2010' *Trans. Bristol Gloucestershire Archaeol. Soc.* **135**

McSloy, E.R. and Watts, M. 2013 'Excavations at Bridges Garage, Tetbury Road, Cirencester', *Glevensis* **46**, 32–6

Meadow, L. and Jantz, R.L. 1992 'Estimation of stature from metacarpal lengths', *J. Forensic Sci.* **37**(1), 147–54

Meindl, R.S. and Lovejoy, C.O. 1985 'Ectocranial suture closure: A revised method for the determination of skeletal age at death based on the lateral-anterior sutures', *Am. J. Phys. Anthropol.* **68**(1), 57–66

Menzel, H. 1986 *Die römischen Bronzen aus Deutschland III* Mainz, Philipp von Zabern

Mills, J.M. 1993a 'Hobnails', in Farwell and Molleson 1993, 99

Mills, J.M. 1993b 'Iron coffin nails and fittings', in Farwell and Molleson 1993, 114–34

Molleson, T.I. 1993 'The human remains', in Farwell and Molleson 1993, 141–214

Moorrees, C.F.A., Fanning, E.A. and Hunt, E.E. 1963 'Age variation of formation stages for ten permanent teeth', *J. Dent. Res.* **42**(6), 1490–502

Munsell Color Group 1980 *Munsell Soil Color Charts* Baltimore, Munsell Color Group

Neal, D.S. and Cosh, S.R. 2009, *Roman Mosaics of Britain III South-East Britain* London, Society of Antiquaries of London

O'Neil, H. and Grinsell, L. 1960 'Gloucestershire barrows', *Trans. Bristol Gloucestershire Archaeol. Soc.* **79**, 5–149

O'Neil, H.E. and Toynbee, J.M.C. 1958 'Sculptures from a Romano-British well in Gloucestershire', *J. Roman Studs.* **48**, 49–55

Orofino, C., Sherman, M.S. and Schechter, D. 1960 'Luschka's joint: A degenerative phenomenon', *J. Bone Joint Surg.* **42**(5), 853–8

Ortner, D.J. 2003 *Identification of Pathological Conditions in Human Skeletal Remains* London, Academic Press

Ortner, D.J. and Ericksen, M.F. 1997 'Bone changes in the human skull probably resulting from scurvy in infancy and childhood', *Int. J. Osteoarchaeol.* **7**(3), 212–20

Østigård, T. 2000 *The Deceased's Life Cycle Rituals in Nepal: Present Cremation Burials for the Interpretation of the Past* Brit. Archaeol. Rep. Int. Ser. **S853**, Oxford, Archaeopress

Oxenham, M.F. and Cavill, I. 2010 'Porotic hyperostosis and cribra orbitalia: The erythropoietic response to iron-deficiency anaemia', *Anthropol. Sci.* **118**(3), 199–200

Parsons, F.G. 1914 'The characters of the English thigh-bone', *J. Anat.* **48**(3), 238–67

Pearce, J. 2001 'Constructions of infancy–mortuary rituals for infants in the Roman provinces', in Davies *et al.* 2001, 125–42

Pearce, J. 2013 *Contextual Archaeology of Burial Practice: Case Studies from Roman Britain* Brit. Archaeol. Rep. Brit. Ser. **588**, Oxford, Archaeopress

Pearce, J. 2015 'Urban exits: the contribution of commercial archaeology to the study of death rituals and the dead in the towns of Roman Britain', in M. Fulford and N. Holbrook (eds) *The Towns of Roman Britain: the Contribution of Commercial Archaeology since 1990* Britannia Monogr. Ser. **27**, London, Society for the Promotion of Roman Studies, 138–66

Petts, D. 2016 'Christianity in Roman Britain', in M. Millett, L. Revell and A. Moore (eds) *The Oxford Handbook of Roman Britain* Oxford, Oxford University Press, 660–80

Philpott, R.A. 1991 *Burial Practices in Roman Britain: A Survey of Grave Treatment and Furnishing, A.D. 43–410* Brit. Archaeol. Rep. Brit. Ser. **219**, Oxford, Tempus Reparatum

Piontek, J. 1976 'Proces kremacji i jego wpływ na morfologię kości w świetle wyników badań eksperymentalnych', *Archeologia Polski* **21**(2), 247–80

Porter, D.A. 2009 'Evaluation and treatment of ankle syndesmosis injuries', *AAOS Instructional Course Lectures* **58**, 575–81

Powell, K. 2010a 'Footwear: Hobnails and boot plates', in Booth *et al.* 2010, 311–20

Powell, K. 2010b 'Structural nails and coffin fittings', in Booth *et al.* 2010, 320–33

Price, J.E. 1880 *On a Bastion of London Wall, or, Excavations in Camomile Street, Bishopsgate* London, London Middlesex Archaeological Society

Price, J. 1982 'The glass', in Webster and Smith 1982, 174–85

Rahtz, P., Hirst, S. and Wright, S.M. 2000 *Cannington Cemetery: Excavations 1962–3 of Prehistoric, Roman, Post-Roman, and Later Features at Cannington Park Quarry, near Bridgwater, Somerset,* Britannia Monogr. Ser. **17**, London, Society for the Promotion of Roman Studies

RCHME 1976, *Ancient and Historical Monuments in the County of Gloucester. 1. Iron Age and Romano-British Monuments in the Gloucestershire Cotswolds* London, HMSO

Redfern, R. 2008. 'A bioarchaeological investigation of cultural change in Dorset, England (mid-to-late fourth century BC to the end of the fourth century AD)', *Britannia* **39**, 161–91

Reece, R. 1962 'The Oakley Cottage Romano-British cemetery, Cirencester', *Trans. Bristol Gloucestershire Archaeol. Soc.* **81**, 51–72

Reece, R. 2003 'The siting of Roman *Corinium*', *Britannia* **34**, 276–80

Reichart, P.A. and Philipsen, H.P. 2000 *Oral Pathology* Stuttgart, George Thieme Verlag

RIB: Collingwood, R.G. and Wright, R.P. 1965 *The Roman Inscriptions of Britain. 1. Inscriptions on Stone* Oxford, Clarendon Press

RIB III: Tomlin, R.S.O, Wright, R.P. and Hassall, M.W.C. 2009 *The Roman Inscriptions of Britain Vol. III. Inscriptions on Stone Found or Notified between 1 January 1955 and 31 December 2006* Oxford, Oxbow

Roberts, C.A. and Cox, M. 2003 *Health and Disease in Britain: From Prehistory to the Present Day* Stroud, Alan Sutton

Roberts, C.A. and Manchester, K. 2012 'Calvin Percival Bamfylde Wells (1908–1978)', in J.E. Buikstra and C.A. Roberts, *The Global History of Paleopathology: Pioneers and Prospects* Oxford, Oxford University Press, 141–5

Robertson, A.S. 1978 *Roman Imperial Coins in the Hunter Coin Cabinet, University of Glasgow IV. Valerian to Allectus* Oxford, Oxford University Press

Roe F. 2003 'Whetstones, querns and other non-structural worked stone', in A. Hardy, A. Dodd and G.D. Keevill, *Aelfric's Abbey: Excavations at Eynsham Abbey, Oxfordshire, 1989–1992* Thames Valley Landscapes Mon. **16**, Oxford, Oxford Archaeology/Oxford University School of Archaeology, 290–7

Rogers, J. 2000 'The palaeopathology of joint disease', in M. Cox and S. Mays (eds) *Human Osteology in Archaeology and Forensic Science* Cambridge, Cambridge University Press, 163–82

Rogers, J. and Waldron, T. 1995 *A Field Guide to Joint Disease in Archaeology* Chichester, John Wiley and Sons

Rogers, J., Waldron, T., Dieppe, P. and Watt, I. 1987 'Arthopathies in palaeopathology: The basis of classification according to most probable cause', *J. Archaeol. Sci.* **14**(2), 179–93

Rösing, F.W., Graw, M., Marré, B., Ritz-Timme, S., Rothschild, M.A., Rötzscher, K., Schmeling, A., Schröder, I. and Geserick, G. 2007 'Recommendations for the forensic diagnosis of sex and age from skeletons', *Homo* **58**(1), 75–89

Ross, A. 1975 'A wooden statuette from Venta Belgarum', *Antiq. J.* **55**, 335–6

Rouvier-Jeanlin, M. 1972 *Les Figurines Gallo-Romaines en Terre Cuite au Musée des Antiquités Nationales, XXIVe suppl. à Gallia* Paris, Éditions du Centre National de la Recherche Scientifique

Russell, P. 1988 'The suffix *ako* in Continental Celtic', *Études Celtiques* **25**, 131–73

Saluja, G., Fitzpatrick, K., Bruce, M. and Cross, J. 1986 'Schmorl's nodes (intravertebral herniations of intervertebral disc tissue) in two historic British populations', *J. Anat.* **145**, 87–96

Sauer, E. 2003 *The Archaeology of Religious Hatred* Stroud, Tempus

Scheuer, L. and Black, S. 2000 *Developmental Juvenile Osteology* London, Academic Press

Schmid, E. 1972 *Atlas of Animal Bones: For Prehistorians, Archaeologists and Quaternary Geologists* Amsterdam, Elsevier Publishing Company

Schoch, W., Heller, I., Schweingruber, F.H. and Kienast, F. 2004 *Wood Anatomy of Central European Species* Online version www.woodanatomy.ch

Schoppa, H. 1959 *Roemische Götterdenkmäler in Köln* Cologne

Schutkowski, H. 1991 'Experimentelle Befunde an Brandknochen und ihre Bedeutung für die Diagnose von Leichenbränden', *Archäologische Informationen* **14**, 206–18

Schwartz, J.H. 1995 *Skeleton Keys: An Introduction to Human Skeletal Morphology, Development, and Analysis* Oxford, Oxford University Press

Seager-Smith, R.H. 2001 'The coarse pottery', in A.S. Anderson, J.S. Wacher and A.P. Fitzpatrick, *The Romano-British 'Small Town' at Wanborough, Wiltshire* Britannia Monogr. Ser. **19**, London, Society for the Promotion of Roman Studies, 232–301

Selwitz, R.H., Ismail, A.I. and Pitts, N.B. 2007 'Dental caries', *Lancet* **369**(9555), 51–9

Sigvallius, B. 1994 *Funeral Pyres: Iron Age Cremations in North Spånga* Thesis and Papers in Osteology **1**, Stockholm, Stockholm University

Simpson, G. 1957 'Metallic black slip vases from Central Gaul, with applied and moulded decoration', *Antiq. J.* **37**, 29–42

Simpson, G. 1973 'More black slip vases from Central Gaul, with applied and moulded decoration in Britain', *Antiq. J.* **53**, 42–51

Sjøvold, T. 1988 'Geschlechtsdiagnose am Skelett', in Knußman 1988, 444–80

Sjøvold, T. 1990 'Estimation of stature from long bones utilizing the line of organic correlation', *Hum. Evol.* **5**(5), 431–47

Smith, B.H. 1991 'Standards of human tooth formation and dental age assessment', in M.A. Kelley and C.S. Larsen (eds) *Advances in Dental Anthropology* New York, Wiley-Liss, 143–68

Smith, R.A. 1922 *A Guide to the Antiquities of Roman Britain in the Department of British and Medieval Antiquities* London, Trustees of the British Museum

Stace, C. 1997 *A New British Flora* Cambridge, Cambridge University Press

Stuart-Macadam, P.L. 1989 'Nutritional deficiency diseases: A survey of scurvy, rickets, and iron-deficiency anemia', in M.Y. İşcan and K.A.R. Kennedy (eds) *Reconstruction of Life from the Skeleton* New York, Alan R. Liss Inc, 201–22

Stuart-Macadam, P. 1991 'Anaemia in Roman Britain: Poundbury Camp', in H. Bush and M. Zvelebil (eds) *Health in Past Societies – Biocultural Interpretations of Human Skeletal Remains in Archaeological Contexts* Brit. Archaeol. Rep. Int. Ser. **S567**, Oxford, 101–14

Sumbler, M.G., Barron, A.J.M. and Morigi, A.N. 2000 *Geology of the Cirencester District*. Memoir of the British Geological Survey Sheet 235 (England and Wales) London, HMSO

Swift, E. 2000 *Regionality in Dress Accessories in the Late Roman West* Monographies Instrumentum **11**, Montagnac, Editions Monique Mergoil

Szilvázzy, J. 1988 Altersdiagnose am Skelett, in Knußman 1988, 421–43

Taylor, A. 2008 'Aspects of deviant burial in Roman Britain', in E. Murphy (ed.) *Deviant Burial in the Archaeological Record* Oxford, Oxbow, 91–114

Taylor, J. and Flitcroft, M. 2004 'The Roman period', in M. Tingle (ed.) *The Archaeology of Northamptonshire* Northampton, Northamptonshire Archaeological Society, 63–77

Tilley, L. 2015 *Theory and Practice in the Bioarchaeology of Care* Cham, Springer International Publishing

Timby, J.R. 1998 *Excavations at Kingscote and Wycomb, Gloucestershire* Cirencester, Cotswold Archaeological Trust

Timby, J.R. 2003 'Anglo-Saxon pottery', in C. Bateman, D. Enright and N. Oakey, 'Prehistoric and Anglo-Saxon settlements to the rear of Sherborne House, Lechlade: excavations in 1997', *Trans. Bristol Gloucestershire Archaeol. Soc.* **121**, 58–63

Timby, J.R. 2006 'The pottery', in D. Kenyon and M. Watts, 'An Anglo-Saxon enclosure at Copsehill Road, Lower Slaughter: excavations in 1999', *Trans. Bristol Gloucestershire Archaeol. Soc.* **124**, 95–100

Timby. J. 2011 *Assessment of Roman and Saxon Pottery from Bourton Business Park, Bourton-on-the-Water, Glos.* Unpublished report for Gloucestershire County Council Archaeological Service

Todd, T.W. 1921a 'Age changes in the pubic bone. I: the male white pubis', *Am. J. Phys. Anthropol.* **3**(3), 285–335

Todd, T.W. 1921b 'Age changes in the pubic bone. III: the pubis of the white female', *Am. J. Phys. Anthropol.* **4**(1), 1–70

Toller, H. 1977 *Roman Lead Coffins and Ossuaria in Britain* Brit. Archaeol. Rep. Brit. Ser. **38**, Oxford

Tomber, R. and Dore, J. 1998 *The National Roman Fabric Reference Collection: A Handbook* London, Museum of London Archaeology Service

Tomlin, R.S.O. 2015 'Roman Britain in 2014. III. Inscriptions', *Britannia* **46**, 283–420

Toynbee, J.M.C. 1971 *Death and Burial in the Roman World* London, Thames and Hudson

Trotter, M. and Gleser, G.C. 1952 'Estimation of stature from long bones of American whites and negroes', *Am. J. Phys. Anthropol.* **10**(4), 463–514

Trotter, M. and Gleser, G.C. 1958 'A re-evaluation of estimation of stature based on measurements of stature taken during life and of long bones after death', *Am. J. Phys. Anthropol.* **16**(1), 79–123

Tucker, K. 2014 'The osteology of decapitation burials from Roman Britain: A post-mortem burial rite?', in C. Knüsel and M. Smith (eds) *The Routledge Handbook of the Bioarchaeology of Human Conflict* London, Routledge, 213–36

Turner, W. 1887 'On variability in human structure, as displayed in different races of men, with especial reference to the skeleton', *J. Anat. Physiol.* **21**(3), 473–95

Waldron, T. 2003 'The human remains', in A. Thomas, N. Holbrook and C. Bateman, *Later Prehistoric and Romano-British Burial and Settlement at Hucclecote, Gloucestershire* Bristol Gloucestershire Archaeol. Rep. **2**, Cirencester, Cotswold Archaeological Trust, 56–7

Waldron, T. 2014 'Crooked timber: The life of Calvin Wells (1908–1978)', *J. Med. Biogr.* **22**, 82–9

Walker, P L., Bathurst, R.R., Richman, R., Gjerdrum, T. and Andrushko, V.A. 2009 'The causes of porotic hyperostosis and cribra orbitalia: A reappraisal of the iron-deficiency-anemia hypothesis', *Am. J. Phys. Anthropol.* **139**(2), 109–25

Webster, G. and Smith, L. 1982 'The Excavation of a Romano-British rural establishment at Barnsley Park, Gloucestershire, 1961–1979: Part II, c. AD 360–400+', *Trans. Bristol Gloucestershire Archaeol. Soc.* **100**, 65–189

Webster, P. 1976 'Severn Valley Ware: a preliminary study', *Trans. Bristol Gloucestershire Archaeol. Soc.* **94**, 18–46

Weekes, J. 2011 'A review of Canterbury's Romano-British cemeteries', *Archaeologia Cantiana* **131**, 23–42

Wells, J., McSloy, E. and Duncan, H. 2004 'Functional categories of registered artefacts', in M. Dawson, *Archaeology in the Bedford Region* Bedfordshire Archaeol. Mon. **4**, Brit. Archaeol. Rep. Brit. Ser. **373**, Oxford, 371–433

Wheeler, E.A., Baas, P. and Gasson, P.E. 1989 'IAWA list of microscopic features for hardwood identification', *Int. Ass. Wood Anatomists Bulletin ns* **10**, 219–332

Wheeler, H. 1985 'The Racecourse cemetery', *Derbyshire Archaeol. J.* **105**, 222–80

Wheeler, R.E.M. 1929 'A Roman pipe-burial from Caerleon, Monmouthshire', *Antiq. J.* **9.1**, 1–7

Wheeler, R.E.M. and Wheeler, T.V. 1932 *Report on the Excavation of the Prehistoric, Roman and Post-Roman site in Lydney Park, Gloucestershire* Reps. Res. Comm. Soc. Antiq. London **9**, Oxford

White, D.J. 1997 'Dental calculus: Recent insights into occurrence, formation, prevention, removal and oral health effects of supragingival and subgingival deposits', *Eur. J. Oral. Sci.* **105**(5), 508–22

Woodward, A. and Leach, P. 1993 *The Uley Shrines. Excavation of a Ritual Complex on West Hill, Uley, Gloucestershire 1977–79* English Heritage Archaeol. Rep. **17**, London

Worrell, S. 2012 'Enamelled vessels and related-objects reported to the Portable Antiquities Scheme 1997–2010', in Breeze 2012, 71–84

Wright, N. 2008 'A lead-lined stone coffin cremation burial from Harnhill, Gloucestershire', *Trans. Bristol Gloucestershire Archaeol. Soc.* **126**, 83–90

Yeroulanou A. 1999, *Diatrita. Gold Pierced-Work Jewellery from the 3rd to the 7th century* Athens, Benaki Museum

Yoshida, M. 2006 'Pathology of ossification of the ligamentum flavum', in K. Yonenobu, K. Nakamura and Y. Toyama (eds) *OPLL: Ossification of the Posterior Longitudinal Ligament* Tokyo, Springer, 49–57

Young, C.J. 1977 *The Roman Pottery Industry of the Oxford Region* Brit. Archaeol. Rep. Brit. Ser. **43**, Oxford

Zadoks-Josephus Jitta, A.N., Peters, W.J.T. and Van Es, W.A. 1967 *Roman Bronze Statuettes from the Netherlands, Vols I and II* Scripta Archaeologica Groningana **1** and **2**, Groningen, Wolters-Noordhoff

Index

Illustrations are denoted by page numbers in *italics* or by *illus* where figures are scattered throughout the text. Places are in Cirencester unless indicated otherwise.